WINDY DRYDEN COLLECTED!

WINDY DRYDEN
COLLECTED!

Windy Dryden

Rationality Publications

Rationality Publications
136 Montagu Mansions, London W1U 6LQ

www.rationalitypublications.com
info@rationalitypublications.com

First edition published by Rationality Publications
Copyright (c) 2022 Windy Dryden

A catalogue record of this book is
available from the British Library.

First edition 2022

ISBN: 978-1-914938-01-6

Publishing history

*Are You Sitting Uncomfortably? Windy Dryden
Live and Uncut* (PCCS Books, 1998)

Up Close and Personal (PCCS Books, 2002)

Strange, But Rational (PCCS Books, 2010)

Acknowledgements

Chapter 13 was previously published in E. Spinelli & S. Marshall (eds), *Embodied Theories*. London: Continuum, 2001.

Chapter 14 was previously published in J.D. Geller, J.C. Norcross & D.E. Orlinsky (eds), *The Psychotherapist's Own Psychotherapy*. New York: Oxford University Press.

Chapter 15 was previously published in the *Romanian Journal of Cognitive and Behavioral Psychotherapies*, 2001, 1(1), 17-30.

Chapter 16 was previously published in W. Dryden (ed.), *Hard-Earned Lessons from Counselling in Action*. London: Sage, 1992.

Chapter 17 was previously published in *Counselling Psychology Review*, 1998, 13(4), 15–22.

Chapter 18 appears in Weinrach, S.G., Dryden, W., DiMattia, D.J., Doyle, K.A., MacLaren, C., O'Kelly, M., & Malkinson, R. Post-September 11th perspectives on religion, spirituality, and philosophy in the personal and professional lives of selected REBT cognoscenti. *Journal of Counseling and Development,* 2004, 82(4), 426–28.

Chapter 19 was previously published in S. Greenberg (ed.), *Therapy on the Couch: A Shrinking Future?* London: Camden Press, 1999.

Chapter 20 was previously published in the *Journal of Rational-Emotive & Cognitive-Behavior Therapy*, 1996, 14(2), 81–4.

Chapter 21 was previously published in the *Journal of Rational-Emotive and Cognitive-Behavior Therapy,* 2002, 20(2), 159–62.

The author appreciates the courtesy of republication.

Gratitude

The following people (in alphabetical order) have made an important contribution to my career and I am grateful for their help:

Aaron Beck	Kristene Doyle
Michael Bernard	Albert Ellis*
David Burns	Arnold Lazarus*
Sheila Chown*	Walter Matweychuk
Martin Cole*	Richard Nelson-Jones
John Davis	Janet Stockdale
Marcia Davis	Brian Thorne
Ray DiGuiseppe	Richard Wessler
Dom DiMattia	Ruth Wessler

* Deceased

Contents

Introduction

This Collection brings together three books that I prepared for publication that reflected my views about Rational Emotive Behaviour Therapy (REBT), in particular, and about counselling and psychotherapy, in general. The individual books are now out of print, but I think that they are still worthy of being read and therefore I decided to bring them together and call the book, *Windy Dryden Collected!*[1] In addition to the three books, I have added a postscript that reviews my personal contributions to REBT.

This book is my 250th book publication and, as such, I thought I would mark the occasion by including in the Appendix, a year-by-year list of all 250 books.

Introduction to Part I

As many writers have noted before me, one of the best ways of discovering what you think about a topic is to write about it. I've also found that one of the best ways of knowing what I think about a subject is to speak on it. In the first part of this Collection, therefore, I present 12 invited talks that I gave in the 1990s on a number of themes. In general, these talks were given in response to invitations to address a variety of audiences. Most of these audiences were professional, but several of the lectures were broadly advertised and open to members of the public as well as counselling professionals and students of counselling.

In the dim and distant past, whenever I was invited to give a lecture I regarded it as something of a chore and talked off the cuff without much preparation. Then I realised that I was short-changing both myself and particularly my audience. So, in the 1990s, I subjected myself to the discipline of preparing and reading

---

[1] In a Collection such as this, some repetition is unavoidable. While I considered omitting repeated passages, I decided against this since doing so would have adversely affected the integrity of the chapters that contained the repeated material. I hope you will understand my decision and bear with me.

a formally presented paper whether I was giving a keynote address and at an international conference or a talk to a local audience at a bookshop. The discipline of preparing a timed lecture both sharpened and clarified my thinking in a number of key areas of counselling and psychotherapy I hope you, the reader, benefit as much from reading these lectures as I gained from preparing and delivering them

Introduction to Part II

Counselling is a personal endeavour and in the second part of this Collection I present the personal side of Windy Dryden. In Chapters 13 and 14, I outline my experiences of personal therapy and explore the extent to which I use Rational Emotive Behaviour Therapy in my personal life. In Chapter 15, I outline the distinctive features of my work as a practitioner of REBT, an approach to counselling and psychotherapy that I have practised now for 45 years. Chapters 16 and 17 are reflections on what I have learned and struggled to learn over the years while in Chapter 18, I reflect on what spirituality and religion mean to me. Chapter 19 is a personal view on why seeking help from a therapist is different from seeking help from a friend.

So far, the chapters that I have listed have been serious in content. But humour plays a large part in my life and this volume would not be personal without this important ingredient. So Chapters 20 and 21 are humorous pieces that have gone down well in the REBT community, but are worthy of a wider audience. Finally, controversy and Windy Dryden are rarely apart for too long and I bring the book to a close by publishing an interview that I did with Professor Dave Mearns that was supposed to be published in a leading counselling journal. However, it did not appear and in my view the editor chickened out of publishing it. I don't know this for sure since neither Dave Mearns nor I received an adequate explanation for its non-publication. I am pleased to have it published here since it does deal with one or two controversial issues.

Introduction to Part III

In the third part of this Collection, my intention is to discuss some ideas that are central to the theory that underpins Rational Emotive Behaviour Therapy (REBT).

REBT has spawned some ideas that may seem at first sight to be strange but when fully understood they are, as the name of the therapy suggests, rational. This is why I have called this part of the Collection 'Strange, but Rational'. It is my hope that you will be provoked by the chapters in this part of the Collection and stimulated to learn more about this approach to therapy.

In preparing this book, I have kept the ideas intact, but have modified my language in two main ways. First, I have used the generic they/their rather than he/his and she/her. Second, I have used the terms, 'rigid/extreme attitudes' and 'flexible/non-extreme attitudes rather than 'irrational beliefs' and 'rational beliefs' for reasons that I explain in the postscript and more extensively in Dryden (2016).

I hope you enjoy this book and if you want to give me any feedback, please write to me at windy@windydryden.com

Windy Dryden
London, Eastbourne
July 2021

PART I

ARE YOU SITTING UNCOMFORTABLY?

WINDY DRYDEN LIVE AND UNCUT

1

Thirty Ways to Improve Counselling

This paper was delivered as the tenth Hartop Lecture and took place at Grey College. University of Durham, on 5 May 1993. The Hartop Lectures are given annually in memory of Ben Hartop, Senior Lecturer in Education at Durham, who helped to pioneer Guidance and Counselling in Initial Teacher Training. It was planned to terminate the Hartop Lectures after ten years, but the organising committee, encouraged by the packed audience at my lecture, decided to continue to arrange them.

The subject of the lecture was based on a book I wrote with Colin Feltham entitled Developing the Practice of Counselling *(Sage, 1994) and I wish to acknowledge Colin's influence on the lecture. I also wish to thank the organising committee for giving permission to include the paper in this collection.*

There are many different approaches to counselling, and consequently it is difficult to gain a consensual view concerning how counsellors can improve their practice. None the less, in this lecture I intend to outline thirty ways in which counsellors from most orientations can improve the effectiveness of their work. I have divided these thirty points into five sections.

I

Improvements in Forming an Ethical Alliance with Clients

1. Develop the use of contracts

One of the easiest ways for counsellors to improve their work is by developing the use of contracts with their clients. By this I do not mean that legally binding contracts should be established where one or other of the people concerned can be sued if the contract is broken. Rather, I am suggesting that counsellors develop a shared understanding with their clients and come to an explicit agreement concerning the nature of the work that they are going to undertake together.

To this end, some counsellors have prepared written handouts which they give to prospective clients. These handouts contain information about the counsellor, their training, a statement about their approach to the work of counselling, the ethical code to which they adhere and other pertinent information. Such information helps prospective clients to make informed judgements about whether or not they wish to consult this particular counsellor.

In the field of counselling a distinction can be made between a business contract and a therapeutic contract. A business contract contains agreements that the counsellor makes with their client about issues such as the frequency of consultations, where the consultations will occur, the fee to be paid and the terms of the counsellor's cancellation policy.

A therapeutic contract, on the other hand, includes such points as the goals that the counsellor and client are working towards, a shared conceptualisation of the client's concerns and which therapeutic tasks or techniques the counsellor and client are going to use in the service of the client's goals. It is important to realise that the therapeutic contract does not include promises to achieve specific outcomes.

Most contracts that counsellors seek to negotiate with their clients include the issue of confidentiality and its limits. In my view, this issue straddles the business and therapeutic contract in that it does not easily fit into either single category. In this respect, some interesting American research has shown that clients desire more information about confidentiality and its limits than counsellors tend to provide (Miller & Thelen, 1986). Indeed, this research showed that clients expect more exceptions to complete confidentiality than they encounter. The BAC[2] *Code of Ethics and Practice* stresses that accepted limits to confidentiality occur when clients are either at risk to themselves or constitute a risk to the welfare of other people. My own experience is that, when this is explained to clients clearly and professionally, they understand the reasons for these limits and are happy to agree to them.

---

[2] Now BACP.

It is important to stress that the contracts that I have described are subject to negotiation between counsellor and client. As such, therefore they can be renegotiated during the counselling process. They are not set in stone. The explicit nature of the discussions that occur during the development of these contracts helps move counselling away from being a mysterious process towards being a comprehensible, collaborative process which empowers the client.

2. Develop and maintain the reflection process

The reflection process in counselling occurs when counsellor and client step back from the work that they are undertaking together and reflect on and discuss this work. It is, if you like, a process of talking about the process of counselling. I wish to stress that I am not suggesting that counsellors do this in an obsessive way, but that they take sincere steps to involve their clients in a process of mutual feedback.

Various psychoanalytic theorists have distinguished between the observing ego and the experiencing ego. Such a distinction is particularly relevant here. In the reflection process, the observing ego of the client and the observing ego of the counsellor step back and talk about what the experiencing egos of both of them have encountered. In some approaches to counselling, namely cognitive therapy, this is done routinely at the end of every counselling session. Thus, a cognitive therapist will ask the client at the end of a session 'Can you tell me what about today's session was helpful to you and what was unhelpful for you?' While counsellor and client are more likely to refer to the reflection process at the end of a session and formally, in structured review sessions, they can refer to this process at any time during counselling.

I have learnt a great deal from inviting a client to reflect on the process of counselling, and as a result of feedback I have received from my clients I have made important modifications to my counselling approach. I doubt whether I would have made such changes if I had not initiated and nurtured the reflection process. Herbert Strean (1959), a psychoanalytic author, has originated a term that is particularly relevant to what I am talking about. He calls the client 'a consultant' – a term I particularly like in that it empowers the client and stresses that they can actively and productively contribute to the counselling process.

Counsellors can use the reflection process to clarify a number of issues. They can use it, for example, to determine whether or not the client is in the most useful therapeutic arena. It may transpire, when discussing the client's experience of counselling, that seeing the client in individual counselling may not be as helpful to the client as seeing them with their partner in couple counselling. Knowing this can lead to useful and substantive alterations in counselling strategy.

Another issue that can be referred to the reflection process concerns changes in the therapeutic goals that clients have negotiated with their counsellors. Without a forum where the changing nature of these goals can be discussed, it may well be that counsellors assume that the goals that they negotiate with their clients at the outset of counselling are still relevant in the middle phase of counselling. Other issues that can be discussed in the reflection process concern whether or not the counsellor in the best person to help the client, the accuracy of the counsellor's conceptualisation of the client's problems, and the pacing of the work that is being done (a subject of which I have more to say later).

3. Identify and use the most helpful arena for clients

I alluded to this issue briefly in the previous section and will now elaborate on it here. It is important to stress that not every client who seeks counselling will be most helped by working in the arena of individual counselling. What I am suggesting is that counsellors need to be aware of the advantages and disadvantages of different therapeutic arenas so that a productive match between client and therapeutic arena can be made.

Let me give some examples of how different clients may be suited to different arenas. In my experience, individual counselling is the most suitable arena for clients who are particularly concerned about confidentiality and for vulnerable clients who need to develop a one-to-one trusting relationship with the counsellor. In addition, individual counselling is the arena of choice when clients need an ongoing and extended in-depth exploration of intrapsychic issues.

However, if a client has a relationship problem with a named individual such as a spouse, then the counsellor should carefully consider using the arena of couple counselling, particularly if the client's partner is willing to be involved in counselling. Family counselling is particularly indicated when more than one significant other is involved in the 'identified' client's problem, whereas group counselling is frequently the arena of choice for clients who have difficulties forming and developing interpersonal relationships in general, who experience themselves as alienated or who consider that they are the only individual in the world with a particular type of problem.

Most counselling takes place in the arena of individual counselling. However tempting it may be, therefore, to suggest to all clients that they be seen in this arena, to do so will limit the usefulness of counselling for a significant number of clients.

4. Make suitable referrals in clients' best interests

It is tempting for counsellors to believe that they can help everyone who seeks their services. This is especially true for keen and enthusiastic trainees. However, experience teaches us that it is important to be humble in this field and to ask two questions of oneself: (i) 'Am I the best person to help this particular individual?' and (ii) 'Is there another counsellor who may be more helpful to this client?'

I have become sensitive to this issue because over the years I have received numerous telephone calls from potential female clients who think that I am a female counsellor and become quite confused when it becomes apparent that I am male. In such circumstances I refer these enquirers to a female counsellor.

There are a number of client concerns which, in my opinion, require a specialist referral. For example, it is really helpful for Holocaust survivors or their children to be seen by counsellors who have either survived the Holocaust themselves or have experienced growing up in a family where at least one member has been a Holocaust survivor. Indeed, clients who have the Holocaust in their background seem to want and, in some cases, expect to see a counsellor who has had some direct or indirect experience of this tragedy.

I am less impressed, however, by the argument that is strongly advanced in some areas of alcohol counselling that it is necessary to be a recovering alcoholic to work effectively with alcoholics. This seems to me dogmatic, and, while I can appreciate that in certain circumstances with certain clients a counsellor who is themself a recovering alcoholic would be the helper of choice, to make a sweeping statement that all alcohol counsellors need to be recovering alcoholics seems to go too far.

While I am advocating making specialist referrals in certain circumstances, this does not obviate the need for counsellors to be knowledgeable in these areas, since they will be consulted by clients' who do not want such a specialist referral.

5. Form, maintain and vary different therapeutic bonds with different clients

While it is commonly agreed that the bond formed and developed between client and counsellor is a primary healing agent in the process of counselling, it is less well accepted that different clients may require different bonds with their counsellors. As such, it is important for counsellors to become flexible in the way they relate with their clients – to become what Arnold Lazarus (1981) has called 'an authentic chameleon', i.e. being able to 'change one's interpersonal style to meet the needs of clients but in a way that is congruent and authentic'. There are a number of important dimensions to consider here and I will mention just a few of them.

Some clients seem to value a self-disclosing counsellor who at poignant times in the counselling process shares their own experiences which are similar to those of their clients. While this can be a liberating and growth-promoting experience for such clients, other clients consider counsellor self-disclosure to be quite inappropriate. Earlier in my career I was working with an older woman and ventured to disclose a personal experience which I thought might be helpful to her. However, this was not the case and the client said to me: 'Young man, I am not paying this centre a lot of money to hear about your problems. Please focus on me.'

Some clients seem to do much better with an active-directive counsellor than with someone who is passive and less directive, and of course the reverse is also true. Some clients seem to respond well to judiciously timed, humorous interventions, while others do not.

Some clients are more influenced by the expertise of the counsellor, while others are more influenced by the counsellor's likeability. Some clients prefer to work with a counsellor who is warm and nurturing, while others prefer a more formal businesslike relationship, and, strange as it may seem, some clients respond very well to a sergeant major type of counsellor who is going to knock them into shape.

While I advocate interpersonal flexibility in forming and developing bonds with clients, it is important that counsellors do not strive to work beyond the limits of their flexibility. I do not want counsellors to put on an act.

6. Make use of formal review sessions

Earlier I discussed the importance of counsellors developing and maintaining the reflection process, by which I meant a process where counsellor and client stand back from the work and reflect on their experiences of this work. Holding formal, structured review sessions is a formal extension of the use of this process. The main purpose of holding such review sessions is for counsellor and client to gain a greater understanding of the progress that the client has made, either since counselling started or since the last formal structured review. In contemporary language, this is an important part of evaluation and audit.

Many counsellors do this particularly at the beginning of the counselling process, when they offer clients a period of time to experience counselling in order to judge whether or not it will be a valuable source of help. These counsellors may say: 'Let's meet for six sessions and then review where we have reached.' In doing so they are offering counselling on a trial basis. The important thing to convey to clients here is that it is a review of counselling that is to be conducted, rather than an assessment of the client. In this review, counsellor and client will focus on what the client has found helpful and unhelpful about the process so that they can develop a more productive relationship as a result. My own experience is that carrying out such periodic reviews gives both counsellor and client an opportunity to identify the client's doubts, reservations and objections about the counselling process in a time-allocated manner. If this is sensitively handled, and if the counsellor can offer the client unconditional acceptance, the working alliance between them can be strengthened. If this is achieved, subsequent obstacles to client change can be identified and constructively dealt with.

II

Improvements in Understanding and Working with Effective Tasks and Goals

7. Monitor and improve the goal directedness of counselling

That perennial analysand, Woody Allen, was once asked how his analysis of twenty years was going; he replied, 'slowly' – and presumably aimlessly. There is a danger that counselling can become an end in itself where there is a timeless and directionless quality about the work. By contrast, effective counselling is more likely to occur when both counsellor and client have agreed explicitly or implicitly about the client's goals. I am not suggesting that counsellors become goal-directed with clients before the latter have had the opportunity to disclose their concerns. What I do want to stress is the important purposive aspects of counselling. I want counsellors to become sensitive and orientated towards client goals rather than to become obsessed with them.

Effective goals are those that are mutually agreed between counsellor and client and which stem logically from a shared understanding of the client's concerns and the issues that relate to these concerns. Goals are best phrased in a positive manner rather than indicating the absence of a negative state. For example, instead of a client's goal being 'not to feel anxious in social situations', the objective may be phrased thus: 'initially to feel concerned in social situations and later to feel relaxed in these situations'. In general, clients' goals need to be stated in their own language, to be as specific as possible and to be achievable. Thus, if a client states 'I want my partner to change', this is not a feasible goal since it is not within the client's control. In this situation, the counsellor might encourage the client to set as their goal changes in their own behaviour which may lead to changes in their partner's behaviour. It should be made clear, however, that the work the person does with their counsellor may not directly lead to changes in their partner.

It goes without saying that productive goals need to be consistent with the client's value system and should not be based on the counsellor's value system. In addition, clients need to be helped to distinguish between goals that have been introjected, that is accepted uncritically from a significant other, and goals that have been explored, and owned. It is the latter to which the client is likely to show commitment. Counsellors need to recognise that client goals change over time, and it is important to monitor these goals and to identify what may lead to their shifting nature.

Some client goals reflect the level of their own disturbance and are not in their healthy self-interest. Thus, counsellors need to be sceptical while discussing goals with clients and should not take an overly consumeristic approach to goal setting. A typical example of a goal that is based on the client's level of disturbance and is not in the long-term interest of the client is the anorexic's goal of losing more weight.

My final point with respect to client goals concerns how explicit to make the discussion of such goals. I mentioned earlier that it is possible for client and counsellor to agree implicitly on the client's goals. However, in such circumstances there is the danger that the more implicit the agreement, the greater the scope for misunderstanding and error.

8. Vary the use of structuring

Structure in counselling varies from the very unstructured, where the counsellor does not attempt to influence the course of sessions at all, to the very structured, where the counsellor has every minute accounted for and has their own agenda which excludes any items the client might wish to discuss. In my opinion, both extremes need to be avoided. Different clients benefit from different degrees of structuring. For example, some clients, who are histrionically organised in their personality and are disorganised in their attempts to make sense of their experiences, benefit from a structured approach to counselling, while others who are obsessionally organised in their personality, require less structure in counselling sessions. In the latter case decreasing structure needs to be introduced gradually, since these clients are quite intolerant of experiences that are loosely organised.

Convention in counselling has it that sessions are 50 minutes long, enabling the counsellor to have a 10-minute break between clients. However, there is nothing sacred about the 50-minute hour and, under some circumstances, variations in this convention is essential. Sometimes, for example in dealing with certain post-traumatic stress disorders, the 50-minute hour is insufficient if the client is repeatedly to process their traumatic experience in a way that enables them to integrate it into their meaning structure. In these circumstances, counsellors need to set aside a longer period in order to deal with the situation.

For other clients, and here I am thinking of those whose attention span and ability to comprehend is limited, 50 minutes is far too long and sessions lasting for 15 or 20 minutes are much more productive. Here, as elsewhere, it is important for counsellors to avoid rigidity and to be flexible.

While I advocate flexibility within counselling sessions, I do not advocate that counsellors violate the healthy boundaries that need to surround the counselling process. For example, if at the end of a session a client says: 'I think we need to continue this. Why don't we meet over dinner', warning bells should ring loudly for the counsellor. However, in the literature there are a number of accounts which demonstrate that important turning points in the counselling relationship occurred when the counsellor responded to a client's invitation to meet outside the counselling session – perhaps to go home and meet the client's family. I realise that I am now entering a veritable minefield. My own position is that healthy boundaries are those that are rigorously, rather than rigidly, upheld. Any changes in the counsellor's usual practice need to be explored carefully with their supervisor.

9. Work with one problematic theme at a time

It is usual for clients to seek counselling for several problems which may be based on a small number of underlying themes. While it is important to respect the complexity of a client's problems, it is also important to work with these problems in a way in which they can be solved.

Normally this means dealing with one client problem or theme at a time. It is important for counsellors to avoid trying to solve all the client's problems at once. If they try to do this they are in the same situation as the person in the circus who attempts to keep a large number of spinning plates going all at once; eventually they get tired and the plates come crashing to the ground. Thus, it is important for counsellors to work with one focus at a time, by which I mean a client issue that has a discernible theme. Sometimes this cannot be done since changes in the client's life circumstances preclude this thematic focus. Once again, counsellors need to be flexible; they should stay with a particular theme, when this is indicated, and work on a problem with which the client is currently preoccupied when it is more productive to do so.

10. Vary counselling from a narrow focus to a comprehensive focus from client to client

Psychodynamic counsellors are very much concerned with in-depth counselling and criticise their non-psychodynamic colleagues for not working deeply enough with client material. In this point, I am concerned with the question of breadth; namely, are counsellors working broadly enough (rather than deeply enough) with their clients?

There are some clients who seek help for a particular problem and do not wish to discuss any other issue in their lives. For such clients, narrow-focused counselling is called for. Although many counsellors may wish to broaden the counselling, this should be resisted because these clients are just not interested in doing so. Other clients, however, have problems in large areas of their personal functioning. They may have problems in the areas of behaviour, affect, sensation, imagery, cognition and are also experiencing problems in their interpersonal relationships and their biological functioning. I am referring here to the seven modalities of human experience that Arnold Lazarus (1981) argues a counsellor needs to be sensitive to when working with clients.

Counsellors need to be aware, then, that their work is going to vary from a narrow focus to a broad, comprehensive focus from client to client. With some clients, counsellors may start out with a narrow focus and the client may later become aware of other problems in their life. The work then will become more comprehensive. However, this shift from the narrow to the comprehensive does not inevitably occur as counselling proceeds, and counsellors should resist the temptation to broaden the work with clients when this is not indicated.

11. Be flexible using within-session and between-session foci

Some counsellors, particularly those who adhere to the Kleinian school of psychodynamic psychotherapy, believe that almost every word uttered by the client refers to some unconscious aspect of their relationship with the counsellor. I call this process 'hothousing', in that the exploration between client and counsellor becomes focused on the suffocating aspects of their relationship. Other counsellors believe that they have very little stimulus value for their clients. The entire thrust of their work with their clients is focused on the clients' outside life and contains little if any reference to the developing relationship between them. I call this 'coldhousing', in that the relationship between counsellor and client is, as it were, put into cold storage.

It is often stated by counsellors that seeing a client weekly involves one hour's contact out of a possible 168. The argument continues that, in order for counselling to make a difference for clients, counsellors need to encourage them to apply what they have learnt in the counselling room to their outside lives. However, one of the ways of ensuring that counselling makes a difference is for counsellors to deal with issues that emerge in the therapeutic relationship and which seem to parallel the problems that clients experience in their everyday lives. It is therefore important for counsellors to realise that clients differ concerning how much the focus of counselling needs to be placed on the here-and-now relationship, with all its historical ramifications for the client, and how much it needs to be placed on the there-and-now aspects of the client's life outside counselling. To assume that all clients need a there-and-now approach or a here-and-now approach is demonstrating again the type of black and white thinking that the field needs to avoid.

12. Ensure that counsellors and clients have a mutual understanding of relevant change-enhancing tasks and can use them suitably

A task in counselling is something that the counsellor or the client engages in. A task can refer to a specific activity such as a homework assignment; for example, the client agrees to spend 10 minutes a day keeping a 'feelings' diary. Alternatively, a task can refer to a more general activity such as self-exploration. Counselling tasks can occur within the session or between sessions. Needless to say, different counselling orientations advocate different tasks for both counsellor and client.

When considering tasks, it is important that clients (i) understand what they may have been asked to do; (ii) have sufficient competence to do it; and (iii) see the sense and relevance of doing it, i.e. understand that engaging in relevant task activity can help them to achieve their goals.

Three or four years ago an article appeared in the *Guardian* entitled 'Probationer did not understand Apple Therapy'. The client, who was on probation, went to a day centre where he attended a group in which role playing was used. In one of the exercises the group leader encouraged him to play the role of a fruit, more specifically an apple. He absconded from the centre because, he claimed, this activity did not really get to the 'core' of his issues. By running away, we could say that he 'blew a raspberry' at the leader for asking him to engage in a meaningless task. This example rather neatly and humorously illustrates the importance of clients' understanding the relationship between what they are being asked to do and their counselling goals. Counsellors need to discuss their tasks openly and explicitly with their clients if they are to prevent their clients from being mystified as was the probationer.

When planning effective therapeutic tasks, counsellors need to take into account a number of important variables. They need to consider, among others, a client's personality, gender, race, world view, learning style and speed of learning. In addition, the possible therapeutic potency of the tasks needs to be appraised. For example, there are some therapeutic tasks that do not have sufficient potency to enable clients to achieve certain goals. Thus, a client can be asked to stand on their head and chant a mantra several times a day for many months, but doing so, in all probability, will not help them to get over their panic attacks.

Thus, counsellors need to become knowledgeable about the research literature in counselling in order to identify those tasks that are potent enough to help clients solve their problems. Too often, counselling is guided not by the client's problems but by the counsellor's predilections. This is reflected in an old joke: that if you go to a Freudian therapist you begin to dream in Freudian symbols; if you go to a Jungian you dream in Jungian symbols, and if you go to a behaviour therapist you don't dream at all!

13. Tailor the use of therapeutic interventions to the client's unique set of circumstances, interests, characteristics, learning style and other salient variables

By now it should be clear that I am a strong advocate of flexibility in counselling. The idea that all clients benefit from a single approach to counselling is one that goes against not only clinical sense, but also common sense. Individual differences between clients need to be respected and counsellors need to tailor their interventions accordingly.

There is some evidence that in certain British sub-cultures making links between past and present, disclosing one's problems to a stranger and exploring these problems are alien activities. Consequently, if a counsellor expects a client who comes from such a sub-culture to adjust to the counsellor's approach rather than vice-versa, it is likely that the counselling will stall quite quickly.

For example, if I were to go into therapy now, I would not work well with a counsellor who advocated the use of imagery interventions because I really do not have a vivid pictorial imagination and find working with symbols quite alien. In addition, I would not work well with a counsellor who has a decided spiritual orientation, since I am a dyed-in-the-wool atheist, and I would quickly become frustrated with a counsellor who is silent and quite passive in their interactive style. This personal example demonstrates, I hope, that different counsellors need to use different interventions with different clients.

Being aware of a client's understanding of language is particularly pertinent here, since effective counselling depends upon counsellor and client developing a shared language framework. I once encouraged one of my female clients to accept herself as a fallible human being and was taken aback when this produced a hostile response from her. 'What do you mean?' she said. 'I'm not that fat!' To her, 'fallible' meant obese!

When tailoring interventions, it is helpful for counsellors to know what interests their clients have so that they can use analogies that make sense to these clients. For example, I am quite interested in boxing and would resonate to a knowledgeable analogy involving pugilism as its content; however, if a counsellor started using an opera analogy or one from the world of ballet, I would quickly turn off. Arnold Lazarus (1981) has said that counselling/psychotherapy is both an art and a science. Thus, scientific research might indicate that a particular counselling technique needs to be used with a particular client. However, how the counsellor employs the technique with due regard to voice tone, voice cadence, imagery and language can make a crucial difference to the success or failure of the intervention. Knowing the kind of language and the type of imagery that a client is likely to respond favourably to is part of mastering the art of counselling.

14. Adjust the pace of making interventions to the client's pace and style of processing information

It is important to adjust the pace of making counselling interventions to take into account the client's pace and style of processing information, among other learning variables.

One of the most influential figures on my career as a counsellor has been Albert Ellis,[3] who is the founder of Rational Emotive Behaviour Therapy, an approach for which I am quite well known in this country. Every year I go over to America to find out the latest developments in REBT and to talk to Ellis about matters of theoretical and practical interest. Occasionally in the context of these discussions I talk to him about a personal concern. When I do this he intervenes quite quickly with me because he assumes that, as I understand REBT very well and can think as quickly as he can, I

---

[3] Ellis died in 2007.

can process information as quickly as he comes up with it. I frequently have to tell him to slow down as I cannot process the information that quickly.

It is important, therefore, that counsellors adjust their pace of making interventions to enable their clients to process information fully. This will enable clients to get the most out of what the counsellor is saying. Some counsellors work well with quick thinking clients, but become impatient with clients who process information more slowly. Other counsellors prefer to work with the latter group and would struggle with clients who think very quickly on their feet.

Some clients tend to act first and process information later, while others prefer to chew matters over before they act. Given this, when counsellors work with these two different types of individual, they need to adjust their interventions accordingly. For example, encouraging the latter group to act before thinking things through thoroughly is likely to prove unproductive. It follows from this analysis that counsellors need to become aware of salient aspects of their clients' styles of learning and to pace their interventions accordingly.

15. Use the 'challenging, but not overwhelming' principle

It is my view that, when clients engage in tasks that are challenging for them, but not overwhelming, their progress in counselling is enhanced. As such, counselling needs to be neither too threatening and overwhelming on the one hand, nor too cosy and unchallenging on the other. It is the task of counsellors to encourage their clients to engage in tasks that pose a challenge, while at the same time to protect them from engaging in tasks that may be overwhelming for them at a given point in the counselling process. Many clients deprive themselves of making gains in counselling by waiting until they feel comfortable before doing something constructive, when in fact a sense of comfort comes from acting uncomfortably and does not predate such action. Thus, I frequently encourage my clients to do things unconfidently, uncomfortably and uncourageously if they want to become comfortable, confident and courageous. This of course involves their taking a risk and undertaking a challenging activity. There is, regrettably, no substitute for this, if clients are to make progress.

III

Improvements in Identifying and Addressing Clients' Obstacles to Change

16. Be mindful of and guided by the client's stage of change

Prochaska and DiClemente (1984) have identified five stages of personal change. The first stage is called 'Pre-contemplative' and describes a situation where a client has yet to decide that they have a problem that they wish to change. Such clients are referred by outside agencies such as the courts or feel compelled to attend counselling, for example by a partner; however, they do not consider that they have a problem. The second stage is called 'Contemplative'. At this point the client has begun to recognise that they do have a problem that they may wish to change and is exploring the nature of their concerns. The third stage involves 'Decision-making'; the client does now recognise that they have a problem and decides to do something about it. The fourth stage is the 'Action' stage of change, where the client is ready to act to overcome their problem and to work towards achieving their goals. The final stage of change is called 'Maintenance'. The client has made progress and needs to maintain these gains; if they do not do so, relapse is likely to occur.

The important implication of this model is that it is necessary for a counsellor to use interventions that are suitable for the stage of change that the client is in. For example, when a client is ready to act to overcome their problems, an intervention more suited to the contemplative stage of change is inappropriate. On the other hand, a counsellor who encourages action when a client is in either the pre-contemplative or contemplative stapes of change is likely to engender resistance. Thus, it is crucial to tailor counselling interventions according to the stage of change that clients are at.

17. Discover the client's past attempts at solving problems and create distance between these strategies and what the counsellor will be offering

It is frequently helpful to ask clients questions about their previous attempts to cope with their problems. It is also useful to find out what informal and formal sources of help they have sought prior to seeking counselling and what the outcomes of these endeavours were. In exploring this issue, it is important that counsellors discover not only what clients have done that has not proven helpful to them, but also strategies that have been helpful to them, so that the counsellor can avoid the former and build on the latter.

When the counsellor has identified previously ineffective strategies, it is important to create a distance between these strategies and the interventions that the counsellor intends to use. Since individuals find it easy to keep using ineffective strategies, part of the work of the counsellor is to help the client to realise the ineffective nature of such strategies and to encourage him to try something different.

18. Discover and deal with client's obstacles to change at each point in the counselling process

Obstacles to client change can occur throughout the counselling process. Thus, at the outset clients may come into counselling harbouring certain fears about the counselling process. For example, some clients fear that the counsellor is going to take away their autonomy or encourage them to become dependent on the counselling process. In such situations, it is important for counsellors to identify such fears and help to dispel them.

In the middle phase of counselling, the full implications of personal change have often become apparent and clients will have become aware of what they may have to give up in order to overcome their problems. Thus, clients may realise, albeit implicitly, that if they are to change they will lose any secondary gains that they have derived from their problems. Thus, they may lose a sense of familiarity that is experienced because they have lived with their problems for a long period of time. They may also lose a related sense of identity if they overcome their problems. Here, it is important for counsellors to help their clients recognise that there are both gains and losses that occur when striving towards personal change, and also to encourage them to accept that this is a natural aspect of such change.

At the end phase of counselling, obstacles to leaving counselling tend to surface. Questions such as 'Can I cope on my own?' need to be addressed. Clients need to be helped to realise that, not only have they benefited from the work they have done in counselling, but they have also internalised a way of helping themselves which they can utilise without the presence of the counsellor.

In addition, at the end phase of counselling, clients' ambivalences about ending relationships in general tend to surface. Bringing the counselling process to a suitable end not only serves to encourage clients to cope on their own, but also serves as a healthy model for ending relationships and moving on.

19. Monitor and learn from things left unsaid

Regan and Hill (1992) discovered that both clients and counsellors are able to identify a range of experiences which they have during counselling sessions, but which they do not articulate in these sessions. I am not suggesting here that counsellors compulsively encourage their clients to articulate all of their experiences, nor that they disclose all of their own experiences. I do suggest, however, that counsellors are aware that clients do not disclose certain aspects of their experience during counselling (both about the nature of their problems and about the counselling process itself) and that they need to help clients to talk about those aspects that are useful to explore. There are two ways of doing this: first, to refer the issue to the reflection process mentioned earlier, and second, to deal with it in a structured formal review session.

Counsellors may need to make sense of their own unexpressed experiences during the counselling process. One good way do this is to audio-record counselling sessions and to play them back periodically in order to identify their unexpressed experiences. These can be discussed with supervisors and decisions can be made concerning how they need to be dealt with in the counselling relationship.

20. Attend to and learn from one's own feeling reactions to clients and use this learning accordingly

This issue is emphasised by psychodynamic counsellors and points to the fact that one fruitful source of learning about one's clients is from one's own emotional responses to them. These are called counter-transference reactions in the literature. The value of using one's own feeling reactions to clients as a guide for learning about the possible interpersonal impact that clients have upon others rests on the extent to which counsellors can rely on their feeling responses as accurate, undistorted sources of evidence. It is for this reason that counsellors are frequently encouraged to have personal therapy, so that they can explore their own emotional sensitivities and become aware of possible distortions in their counter-transference reactions.

While there is much research which shows that counsellors value their personal therapy (e.g. Norcross, Dryden & DeMichele, 1992), it remains to be shown that having personal therapy leads counsellors to become more effective practitioners, and little is known of its effect on the way counter-transference reactions are used in the counselling process. Nevertheless, counsellors from all orientations need to attend to their own reactions as a valuable source of learning about their clients, and they need to be trained explicitly how best to do this.

IV

Making Improvements in Helping Clients to Consolidate Their Gains in Counselling

21. Understand and capitalise on client change; attribute change to clients and empower them

I want to emphasise here how important it is for counsellors to understand client change as it occurs. In particular, this involves discovering from clients which psychological processes they have modified. By so doing, counsellors can encourage their clients to learn from their own change processes and to capitalise on this learning.

As such, it is important to explore with clients whether the gains they have made can be explained by modifications in their own psychological processes or by the occurrence of fortuitous changes in their physical or interpersonal environment which are outside of their control.

When counsellors discover that change has been effected by clients themselves, it is important to help clients to attribute such changes explicitly to their own efforts. Counsellors should not take the major credit for client change. Thus, when a client says to a counsellor, 'You have helped me enormously. Without you I could not have achieved so much', it is important for the counsellor to remind the client that, while the counsellor's input may have been important, it is the client themself who has derived benefit from the counselling process by putting into practice in their everyday life what they have learnt from the counselling process.

When it is apparent that a client has improved without effecting any changes in their psychological processes, it is important for the counsellor to encourage them to acknowledge this. Then, it is important to explore with them how they could have effected change in themself even if the adverse circumstances which have now changed for the better still existed.

22. Encourage clients to generalise their learning

This point follows naturally on from the previous one. Once clients have attributed change to their own efforts and understood how they brought about such change, it is important for counsellors to help them to consolidate this learning and to generalise it. It is important to recognise, then, that, if counsellors want clients to generalise their learning, they need to plan for it to happen. In short, generalisation should not be taken for granted. For example, if a client is dealing productively with a conflict that they have been having with a co-worker and understands how they are changing, it should not be expected that they will, as a matter of course, generalise this learning to dealing more constructively with similar people in other settings. Indeed, it frequently happens in counselling that clients express surprise that they can generalise their learning from one situation to another. Therefore, counsellors who place this issue firmly on the counselling agenda at an appropriate time will help their clients more effectively than counsellors who wait for clients to bring up the issue of generalisation.

23. Anticipate and address relapse

Counsellors who work in the addiction field know only too well that relapse frequently occurs. Consequently, there has been a great deal of interest in this field in what is called 'relapse prevention'. Anybody who has tried to give up smoking or remain on a calorie-controlled diet will know what I mean when I say that relapses frequently occur in behaviour change. As Mark Twain said about smoking, 'Giving up smoking is easy. I have done it thousands of times!' However, it is important to recognise that so-called relapses occur in all areas of life, not only in the addictions. When anticipating any kind of relapse, it is important for counsellors to convey to clients that this is a natural process in human change and yet one where they can exercise some control.

Relapse prevention involves clients' (i) identifying vulnerable situations in which relapses may occur; (ii) identifying relevant psychological processes (such as black and white thinking) that may promote relapse; and (iii) constructing, practising, maintaining and generalising a variety of coping strategies to ensure that relapses do not occur or if they do that their onset may serve as a cue for productive problem-solving rather than as a cue for reinstatement and continuation of the previously entrenched self-defeating behaviour.

24. Encourage clients to become their own counsellors

In my view, it is insufficient for counsellors to help clients to identify and deal with their problems. Additionally, it is important for counsellors to help clients to internalise a way of helping themselves in the future so that they do not become dependent on counselling. In the world of psychology much is made of the importance of 'giving psychology away'. Along with other counselling authorities such as Robert Carkhuff and Richard Nelson-Jones, I advocate 'giving counselling away' in that we should deliberately train clients in self-helping skills. This will most frequently take place during the late phase of the counselling process, and it is likely to occur at a time when clients are seeking to leave counselling because they have derived benefit from the process. However, if counsellors give their clients an adequate rationale for a period of deliberate self-help skills training, clients will often see the sense of this and will opt for it. This will ensure that clients get the most from counselling.

25. Prepare for ending and use follow-up sessions

Many counsellors believe that implicit in many client problems is a difficulty in ending relationships. If this is correct, then it follows that counsellors need to help clients deal explicitly with the end of the counselling relationship.

As a client, my own experience of therapists helping me deal with the end of therapy has been mixed. One carefully helped me to prepare for its end, while another abruptly announced that the current session was to be our last. So, I know how difficult it is to deal with poorly managed endings. Some proponents of brief psychodynamic counselling argue that it is important to prepare for the ending of the counselling process right at its beginning.

Having said this, in my experience, clients differ quite markedly concerning their attitudes towards the ending of counselling. Some are prepared to stop quite abruptly – at their own behest, I might add – while others require quite a long period of preparation for, and grieving over the loss of, what has been for them an important relationship.

The two main ways of ending that seem to be favoured by most counsellors concern (i) the setting of an ending date with no change in the frequency of sessions and (ii) a gradual increase in time between sessions with the final session decided upon during this winding down process. Here counselling sessions may move from being held weekly to being held fortnightly, then monthly and so on. In my own experience, when I have outlined these two ways of ending to clients (i.e. when we have begun to talk about endings), I am quite happy for them to choose whichever method of ending seems to be most helpful to them.

In addition, the issue of follow-up sessions needs to be considered by counsellors. If counsellors are to evaluate their work properly, they need to measure not only the immediate outcome of their work with particular clients, but also the durability of such outcomes. This can be done by holding periodic follow-up sessions which might take place face-to-face or, if a client lives a long distance from the counsellor, over the telephone. The purposes of follow-up sessions are (i) to determine the extent to which the client has maintained the gains that they have derived from counselling and (ii) to deal with any issues that may be preventing them from maintaining their gains. If serious obstacles to maintenance of client gain are discovered, or, indeed, if the client has deteriorated, then counsellor and client need to discuss the possible resumption of counselling for an agreed (perhaps brief) period.

V

Improvements in Professional Knowledge and Self-Reflection

26. Use questionnaires and inventories for a variety of purposes

There is a myriad of useful questionnaires and inventories in the counselling literature that can be used for the purposes of helping counsellors and clients to (i) clarify clients' issues, (ii) stimulate the work of counselling, and (iii) evaluate that work. It is my view that counsellors tend to see the use of such questionnaires and inventories as mechanistic and somewhat dehumanising. I believe this is an unfortunate view. Such questionnaires can be introduced into the counselling process in a way that is in keeping with the basic philosophy of counselling, i.e. of demonstrating respect for clients. If a rationale for their use is carefully explained and clients are given the option not to complete them, I cannot honestly see any realistic objection to their employment. I use questionnaires that assess (i) clients' opinions about the cause of their problems and what may constitute the most effective approach to these problems, (ii) the stage of change that clients are in, and (iii) clients' underlying belief systems. I also make regular use of Lazarus's (1991) Life History Inventory, which gives a broad picture of the clients' past and present functioning.

I would, thus, urge counsellors to reconsider their views on the use of such questionnaires, since in my experience they can enhance rather than impede the counselling process and can be used in a way that respects clients and protects their autonomy.

27. Utilise research findings

In 1980 I published an article encouraging counsellors to make use of the counselling research literature (Dryden, 1980). I wrote this paper when a survey of the membership of BAC (now BACP) that was conducted in the late 1970s indicated that counselling research was the least important priority with which the organisation should be concerned (Nelson-Jones & Coxhead, 1978). The current picture is slightly more favourable to research, but not that much. While BAC has a sub-committee on research, it still seems to me that most counsellors do not see the relevance of research findings or are frightened of counselling research since research papers are often written in a complex manner. It is the case that counsellors frequently encourage their clients to enter into zones of discomfort to confront what they find frightening. Thus, I urge counsellors to do the same with respect to counselling research. When they do so, it is important for them to read research literature critically. For example, when reading up on research on college students, it is important to question the relevance of the findings for other client populations.

Indeed, having a sceptical, research-orientated perspective on counselling would lead counsellors to be wary of the extravagant claims made in some quarters for the quickness of 'cures'. Doing so would mean that research evidence would be requested to support such claims before one parted with not inconsiderable amounts of money to be trained in such 'magical techniques'.

However, if counsellors do not keep up to date with the research literature on counselling, then they are going to be ignorant of modern developments in the treatment of, for example, panic disorder and post-traumatic stress disorder.

28. Develop an informed and disciplined eclectic and integrative approach (including when not to be eclectic)

This point is particularly salient after counsellors have been trained professionally and have obtained a lot of counselling experience. Eclecticism in counselling means having a particular theoretical approach to the work and using diverse sources, systems and styles borrowed from other approaches, but in a way that is consistent with one's theoretical approach. Integration, on the other hand, involves not only drawing from a diverse range of therapeutic approaches but also integrating these at a theoretical level. Eclecticism and integration in counselling and psychotherapy are becoming more popular as people come to see the limitations of specific orientations. While I applaud and advocate this development, I am beginning to be concerned that it is not being appreciated that moving towards an eclectic or an integrative mode of practice is an activity that depends upon a thorough grounding in training and experience. Whenever I increasingly encounter counselling trainees who claim to be eclectic or integrative without having such solid foundations on which to draw, I sigh inwardly and express doubt about their claims.

Having said this, the movement towards eclecticism and integration involves the breakdown of rigid barriers between practitioners of differing approaches and promotes a healthy dialogue among workers from diverse schools. As such it is to be welcomed.

However, a note of caution is in order here. We need to ask whether integrative or eclectic approaches to counselling are in fact more effective than specific approaches. Indeed, it is likely that under specific circumstances such specific approaches may well be more effective than eclectic or integrative approaches. In this vein, there is research that indicates that a standard approach to simple phobias is more effective than a more eclectic (tailor-made) approach to this particular problem (Schulte et al., 1992). The sceptical but informed counsellor needs to ask under what circumstances are specific non-eclectic, non-tailor-made approaches more useful than bespoke approaches to the same problem.

29. Develop a counselling profile

As counsellors gain more experience and develop their skills, it is important for them to monitor their strengths and weaknesses. Thus, I suggest that, no matter how experienced or well trained a counsellor is, they would be wise to develop what I call a counselling profile to keep an ongoing record of these strengths and weaknesses. So many counsellors, in my experience, do not do this. Thus, they attend supervision and further training sessions but tend to forget what they have learnt in such sessions, with the result that they repeatedly make the same mistakes. Even though I applaud the emerging trend in counselling towards continuing professional development (CPD), without an ongoing record of one's strengths and weaknesses to act as a spur for further development, this trend may be an empty exercise of collecting continuing CPD hours rather than furthering expertise.

30. Supervise yourself and also seek supervision from others

It is commendable that in Britain ongoing supervision of one's work as a counsellor is deemed to be a required activity no matter how experienced one is. Supervision can occur in many different modes, from individual and group supervision to peer supervision. However, it is also important for counsellors to supervise themselves and not to rely solely on help from others.

I encourage counsellors to continue to digitally record their counselling sessions and listen periodically to randomly selected sessions. Using one of a number of self-supervision inventories, counsellors can gain a lot from listening to themselves and from supervising themselves on their work. I wish to stress that I do not regard self-supervision as a replacement for supervision from others. Rather, I argue that the two activities complement each other.

Conclusion

Counselling is a dynamic professional activity in which improvements in theory and practice continue to be made as the profession develops. Consequently, the thirty improvements suggested here should be regarded as interim suggestions and should themselves be subject to improvement.

2

Keeping the Door Open

The Need for Counselling in a Complex, Ever-Changing World

I gave this paper in Eastbourne Town Hall on 11 June 1997. I had previously read in the Eastbourne Herald that Open Door in Eastbourne would have to cease offering a counselling service due to a significant reduction in its funding. Since Eastbourne is now my second home, I wanted to make a tangible contribution to helping with Open Door's plight. This paper was the result and it raised £1,500 which, I am very pleased to report, helped to save Open Door's counselling service, at least for another year. I was not sure who would attend this lecture so I decided to deliver a paper for the general public.

When I read in the *Eastbourne Herald* that the existence of the counselling service offered by Open Door was threatened due to lack of funding, I experienced a strong desire to do something to help. This lecture is the product of this strong desire.

The field of counselling has experienced tremendous growth in the last fifteen years. Agony aunts and uncles regularly advise their correspondents and readers to seek counselling for a whole range of problems. Soap opera characters are increasingly seen going to consult a counsellor, and counselling training courses from introductory to Masters level are proliferating like rabbits on heat. But perhaps the most telling sign that counselling is no longer a fringe activity is that it is increasingly being attacked and criticised both from within the field and from without. When counselling and therapy was for the few it could be safely ignored. Now it is a form of help to which people are increasingly turning, it can no longer be ignored and is therefore a target for criticism. I don't think that the field should be at all threatened by the critiques of counselling that now appear even if some of the critics are sadly misinformed and show a shockingly prejudiced view of those who seek counselling. Clients are portrayed either as self-indulgent people with too much time on their hands and too much money in their pockets or as weak, spineless, dependent individuals who flock to the inner sanctum of the counselling confessional at the drop of an emotional hat.

Since I passionately believe in free speech, I welcome these critics of counselling. We in the field have the freedom to respond as we see fit and even if the criticisms receive more space or airtime than the responses, this is the way of the world. The field of counselling has no right to receive special treatment. As a tender-minded profession we have to live in what is increasingly a tough-minded world. Counsellors face the challenge of marrying our traditional tender-minded attitudes with the tough-minded attitudes of a sceptical, cost-effective society if we are to work effectively within this society. This does not mean that we should stop trying to make the world a more tender-minded place in which to live. Far from it. However, if we ignore that world and its developing attitudes we will eventually return to being a fringe activity.

What does this mean for voluntary-aided counselling agencies? It means that they will have to make the case for funding of counselling services and to compete aggressively with other equally deserving agencies for a share of dwindling resources. In short, such services will have to dig in and fight. I am particularly pleased to help Open Door in its particular fight and to have the opportunity to talk about how the field of counselling can survive and indeed thrive well into the next millennium, by marrying its traditional tender-minded strengths with tough-minded qualities. Doing so will make counselling, in my view, a more well-rounded profession.

Traditional Tender-Minded Counselling Qualities

Let me begin my discussion by reviewing counselling's tender-minded core. Although there are many different counselling approaches (see Dryden, 1996), most counsellors share some common ideas. The first of these ideas concerns the therapeutic value of talking. When people are confused, they tend to toss these confused ideas around in their heads in a way that often results in increased confusion and stress. Being able to externalise their confusion in words often leads to a decrease in tension and an emerging clarity, particularly if the person listening allows this process to occur and does not cut the person off with well-meaning phrases which serve only to curb self-exploration.

Critics of counselling claim with some truth that friends and relatives can offer this listening ear and thus make counsellors redundant. The bit that is true in this critique is that if we are lucky we may have friends and relatives who can offer a non-intrusive listening ear. However, more often than not our friends and relatives find it difficult to tolerate our distress. They try to help us to feel better by saying things such as: 'Don't cry, it will all turn out for the best', 'We all feel like that at one time or another.' If we are less fortunate we may hear the following: 'Pull yourself together', 'Don't be silly', or even 'What's wrong with you?' It is an indictment of present society that while we are making stupendous advances in the field of technology, we still find it enormously difficult to listen to one another with compassion and empathy.

One of the central skills that trained counsellors bring to the process of counselling is the ability to provide a climate where clients can put into words their inner distress and confusion. As I said earlier being able to do this is therapeutic in itself and many clients require nothing more than to be allowed to explore themselves in their own way. Exactly forty years ago in a seminal article on counselling, Carl Rogers (1957) argued that if counsellors genuinely show their clients an attitude of respect and if they communicate to their clients an accurate understanding of what their clients are expressing, then they will help their clients to deepen their ability to explore their concerns in a way which results in greater clarity about their inner experiences. When a person tries to communicate their inner experiences to another person and this person either cuts off this process or responds in a way that deepens the other's shame, three things may happen.

First, the person in distress may retreat within themselves. They may keep their feelings to themself and sometimes from themself with the result that their distress is intensified and a sense of hopelessness about themself and about their ability to resolve their problems is engendered. Second, the person may externalise their distress and act in ways which society labels as anti-social. Such is the nature of this 'anti-social' behaviour that people only see the overt behaviour and not the inner concealed distress which has occasioned it. Third, the person may attempt to deal with their distress by abusing substances of one sort or another. This inevitably creates a second problem – that stemming from a dependent reliance on the substance which even if resolved will leave the person with their original problem unresolved. The irony is that society pays more in financial terms to clear up this mess caused, in part, by its failure to provide such people with early effective counselling than it will ever pay in providing such counselling in the first place.

I have emphasised that all many clients require is a safe place where they can explore themselves in the presence of a well-intentioned person who can offer empathy and a non-intrusive therapeutic space where the person can explore their confused feelings and experiences. Sadly, numerous clients require more than this and this is where friends and family get completely out of their depth. The second idea that I want to discuss within counselling's tender-minded core, then, concerns the importance of offering clients a framework within which they can develop a coherent and personally meaningful way of understanding themselves and their experiences. Different counselling approaches have different frameworks that they offer clients and perhaps the most important ingredient here is this: that the counsellor offers the client a framework for understanding themself which makes sense to them and which they can use as a springboard for personal change. If this is not the case, then the client may not be helped to go beyond the benefits of exploring themself and having their explorations understood and accepted. Depending on their therapeutic approach, the counsellor may formally introduce this framework to the client or it may be more implicitly introduced and become apparent in the counsellor's interventions.

In my own approach to counselling, known as Rational Emotive Behaviour Therapy, I introduce this framework in an explicit manner since I believe that doing so helps the client to decide whether or not they want to go beyond what they have achieved from being allowed to explore themself in an open-ended manner. However, my psychodynamic colleagues, for example, do not do this since they believe that a formal exposition of the psychodynamic framework is neither necessary nor helpful to the client. Their framework is therefore implicit in the way they respond to their clients.

I want to stress here that this second idea usually becomes salient after the client has experienced a relationship with their counsellor based on the principles that I outlined when discussing the first idea i.e. the importance of being heard and being allowed to explore oneself in one's own way. Indeed, if the client has not been allowed this period of unfettered self-exploration, they are likely to experience this framework for understanding themself either as a set of interesting ideas which they cannot directly relate to their own experience or as something imposed on them at a time when they are unable to digest it.

The third idea that is part of the tender-minded core of counselling concerns the importance of the client using this new understanding to promote change. If this is not done then the client will not integrate it into their life in a way that makes a difference. When this is not done the client experiences their new understanding as intellectual rather than emotional. They will say things like 'I understand it in my head but not in my gut.' For new understanding to make a difference to the client's life it has to be acted on and acted on repeatedly. This is the stage of counselling that is called working through. Counsellors differ in how much they leave this to chance. My own approach is to encourage clients to act on their new understanding in a structured way in the form of homework assignments, but this practice is by no means common practice in counselling.

The title of this talk contains the phrase '...in a complex ever-changing world'. While humans vary in how we respond to change, it is a feature of our species that we do not readily embrace it. We value familiarity and tend to resist attempts to bring about change, often seeing it as change for the worse rather than change for the better. I mention in passing that there was more passionate reaction against plans to build a refreshment kiosk on the promenade beneath Meads than there was when the threat to the Open Door counselling service was announced! But we face much more threatening changes than tea kiosks, even though they are less discernible.

Here is a brief resume of old certainties that we can no longer take for granted. We can no longer take for granted that we can be secure in our chosen job or occupation. Here, we face the breakdown of employment security due to increasing technological advances. We can no longer take for granted that our children and grandchildren and even ourselves will live together in the sanctity of marriage. Divorce rates are rising and marriage is no longer generally accepted as an inevitable consummation of a committed relationships. We can no longer accept without question that men will do 'men's' work and women will do 'women's' work. Here we face the breakdown of gender-specific occupations and roles and we enter an area where boys can no longer be expected to be boys and sugar and the Spice girls are not invariably nice!

I mentioned technology in the above statement. One of my clients mentioned the other day that a few years ago when they went to work they began the day by opening their mail. Now, they have to open their mail, listen to their messages on their answer machine, deal with their email and check their voice mail. They may be fortunate to have a job, but they, like tens of thousands of others, are being bombarded from all sides by the products of our technological ingenuity. This figure will soon run into the millions.

My purpose here is not to argue for or against these developments, but to note the impact that these changes will have on the human mind. This impact is not direct, but mediated by the attitudes that we hold towards ourselves, others and the world around us. My view is that the more these attitudes are rigid, the more we will disturb ourselves in the face of the breakdown of old certainties. The more we base our self-esteem on things like having a job or marriage, for example, the more we will be vulnerable to emotional disturbance if these once accepted givens are threatened. Counselling cannot reverse this trend towards increasing complexity and change nor should it try to do so. But it can help us develop a set of flexible attitudes to cope with an increasingly flexible world. Black and white thinking may have been sufficient when things were black and white, but it won't help us to adapt productively and thrive in a postmodern world dominated by shades of grey.

If counselling cannot and should not hold up the force of change, what can it do? Counselling can help people to explore their feelings about threats to the expected order; it can then help them to use a framework which will enable them to re-evaluate themselves and their experiences in the light of increasing complexity and change; and it can help them to use this understanding in their everyday lives.

To achieve this, counselling itself will first have to survive and then thrive in this same complex and ever-changing world. How can the field of counselling do this? First, it will have to engage in a period of self-exploration. It will then have to develop a new understanding of itself in the context of this world and it will finally have to act on this understanding. In short, counselling will have to seek counselling! Unfortunately, I do not have the time tonight to counsel counselling. I will, however, outline my views of what counselling has to learn to survive and thrive in the new millennium. In brief, it will have to develop some tough-minded practices and marry these with its tender-minded philosophy.

Counselling and Tough-Minded Practices

Evaluation

We live in a climate when people demand that services give good value for money. Thus, rail services have to provide evidence that a large majority of trains run on time and health trusts have to provide evidence that they are cutting waiting lists. It doesn't seem to matter that the trains are filthy and the toilets don't work and it doesn't seem to matter that once you get into hospital the food is unpalatable and the nurses are too busy to be concerned that you are in pain. In this evaluation and audit culture, what matters is what you can count rather than what you can feel. The irony here is that the buzzword of this culture is quality and that is perhaps the one thing that does not seem to count when you strip away the fancy language and listen to the accounts of people's painful experiences of these services.

What this means for counselling is that we will increasingly be asked to prove that our services work and we will have to prove this in ways that the field is not generally comfortable with. For the field of counselling is concerned with such elusive things as the quality of the counselling relationship and what the client 'feels' that they have derived from counselling. Frankly, this won't wash with people who have control over the purse-strings. They want to know that counselling results in a measurable reduction in suffering, that our clients are being helped to get back to 'normal' in ways that can be quantified. This means that we will have to give our clients before and after counselling valid and reliable questionnaires that measure symptoms of depression, anxiety and other psychological problems. This is going to cause a lot of soul-searching amongst counsellors many of whom have a basic distrust of such questionnaires thinking that they objectify the client and introduce an unwarranted mechanistic attitude into the counselling process. However much counsellors find this approach to their work distasteful, my view is that they are going have to bite the bullet and prove to the satisfaction of other more tough-minded people that counselling works.

Managed care

There is another spectre on the horizon which will cause even more consternation amongst counsellors. Remember the name of this spectre for you will hear a lot more of it in the future. The name of the spectre is 'managed care'. The concept of managed care originated in North America where much health care is private and costs are largely borne by insurance companies. Now insurance companies are not known for their generosity or for their caring despite what their glossy brochures say. They are primarily interested in making money and they do this in two ways; first, by encouraging people to take out private insurance policies and second by restricting the amount of money that they pay out. By and large they do this legally.

In the world of private psychiatric health care in North America, someone hit on the brilliant idea that this care had to be managed.

Previously, care was in the hands of the practitioners and insurance companies paid out according to what the practitioners thought their clients needed. You might think that this is a sensible way of going about things. However, this was a recipe for disaster for the insurance companies since they were footing the spiralling bill and they realised that they would soon lose their huge profits if this situation was allowed to continue. So, they decided to take over the business of managing care. Practitioners in North America now have to specify a psychiatric diagnosis for their clients and are told by the insurance company how many therapy sessions they will be paid for. If they think that their clients need more sessions they have to wrangle with the insurance company. The effect that managed care has had is to restrict long-term therapy and to lead to a burgeoning interest in brief therapy amongst therapists as they realise that will only be reimbursed for brief work.

Now you may think that this situation will not happen here, but you would be wrong. It is already here at least in the private sphere. Increasingly in Britain, insurance companies are asking therapists to submit treatment plans and they will only pay for acute conditions. For acute read brief. Clients who have chronic psychiatric conditions will have to pay for longer-term therapy themselves. My guess is that it will not be long before managed care becomes the norm in NHS psychiatric and psychological clinics up and down the country. The mechanisms are already in place. NHS Trusts already invite tenders for their services and so do GP Fundholders. If you are a GP Fundholder who are you going to employ: a consortium submitting a package based on managed care lines which will offer your patients a service at a reasonable price or a consortium submitting a package where patients receive therapy managed by the therapists themselves which is costed at a far higher price?

What implication does all this have for Open Door? Let's suppose that it receives the money that it needs to run a proper counselling service. What is to stop another agency claiming that it can offer a service at a competitive price? It could happen and if it does and Open Door wishes to compete in such a climate then it will have to undercut other tenders. This will inevitably lead to clients receiving less counselling than they probably need. But if Open Door does not seek funding for its counselling service as I am helping them to do now then it may close and where will its clients go then? So in the near future I predict that agencies like Open Door will have to compete aggressively for resources. Let me repeat that phrase: 'compete aggressively for resources'. This is hardly the language of the tender-minded.

Marketing and lobbying

Over recent years we have seen numerous charitable groups employ marketing experts and lobbyists. The primary tasks of such people are basically to bring in money and to facilitate a change in the law so that the charities can offer their services to more and more people. This is an area where counsellors and psychotherapists have tended to lag behind although there have been recent attempts by the United Kingdom Council for Psychotherapy to lobby MPs in their attempt to set up a statutory register for psychotherapists. While counselling agencies like Open Door do not have the money to hire marketing and lobbying experts, they should, I believe try to persuade such people to give their services free of charge. Certain marketing companies, for example, like to demonstrate that they have a social conscience by offering their services gratis. It is their way of saying: 'We care'. A word of warning though. Beneath their soft exterior these companies are hard-headed and will not give away their services to agencies who portray themselves in an overly tender-minded way. So even here you will have to come across in a tough-minded manner.

Let me end with a story that I heard when I worked as a Marriage Guidance Counsellor about fifteen years ago that captures the essence of marrying tough-minded and tender-minded attitudes. This was before the National Marriage Guidance Council changed its name to Relate. One of the counsellors who had worked in the service from the outset told us of a client whom they saw many years before. At the beginning of every counselling session, the client put half a crown down on the table. For those of you unfamiliar with the term 'half a crown' it is currently worth twelve and a half pence. If the client thought that the session was of value to them they would leave the money on the table; however, if they thought that the session hadn't been of use to them they would pick up the money and take it away with them. Perhaps this is the best way that counsellors can marry tender-minded and tough-minded attitudes – by offering the best possible service and encouraging the client to have the final say.

3

Why I No Longer Practise Person Centred Therapy and Psychodynamic Therapy
Some Personal Reflections

At the time of writing this paper, I was Honorary Visiting Professor in the Psychology Department at the University of East London and giving occasional lectures to its students was a major part of this post. I delivered this paper on 25 April 1997 to second year students on the MSc Counselling Psychology course.

In the lecture I wanted to show the students that one's initial training is but the first step in one's career as a counsellor and to invite them to reflect on the relationship between counselling orientation and the personality of the counsellor.

I first became interested in counselling and psychotherapy when I was doing a doctorate in social psychology at Bedford College, University of London in 1972. My thesis was on 'Self-disclosure' and many of the references in this area related to counselling. During my reading, I decided that I wanted to pursue a career in counselling and this decision prompted me to apply to be a volunteer for both the Samaritans and Nightline, the student telephone service. In the last year of my PhD, I took an introductory course in counselling at South West London College run by Brigid Proctor and her staff which reinforced my decision to train professionally as a counsellor.

Early Days: Trainee Counsellor at Aston University, 1974–5

In 1974, I applied for a place on the one year, full-time Diploma in Counselling in Educational Settings course at Aston University in Birmingham. This was a person-centred course run by Richard Nelson-Jones and Donald Biggs, an American counselling psychologist who was seconded for a year to the course as a Fulbright fellow.

Initially I was very attracted to person centred therapy because of its optimistic view of human beings. As is well known, Carl Rogers (1957), the founder of the approach, held that the person would inevitably move toward healthy personal development if they experienced the presence of certain core facilitative conditions when these conditions were offered by a significant person or persons in that individual's life. People sought counselling because they had not experienced the enduring presence of these conditions in their lives and had developed problems as a result. Many of these problems stemmed from a failure of clients to accept themselves and were reflected in disturbed emotions and self-defeating behaviour which themselves were often manifest in their relationships with others.

The role of the counsellor, from a person-centred perspective, was to develop psychological contact with the client and to offer a safe environment in which the client could explore themself. The features of this safe interpersonal environment were the core facilitative conditions mentioned earlier. Specifically, these conditions are i) empathy (the ability to sense and communicate an accurate understanding of the person's experiences from that person's point of view); ii) unconditional positive regard (the genuine communication of an unconditional prizing of the client as that person is, not conditional of what the person may become); and genuineness (the therapeutic communication of one's real feelings and reactions to the client and a congruence between one's feelings and one's behaviour in the counselling relationship). Genuineness involves the counsellor not hiding behind the facade of the role of counsellor, but involving the client in an honest, I–Thou encounter. This latter condition resonated strongly with the research subject of my PhD thesis, self-disclosure. Sidney Jourard (1971), the father of self-disclosure research, had written that honest self-disclosure was a key feature of psychological health. This resonance led me to believe that I was on the right lines in my counsellor training and provided an important continuity between my academic interests and my emerging professional interests.

This view of the role of the counsellor put forward by Rogers emphasised how important the counsellor was in the therapeutic process. For if the counsellor succeeded in communicating these core facilitative conditions to the client and if the client experienced these counsellor-offered conditions, the client's movement toward psychological health would be inevitable. Rogers's view then offered two important things to me as a trainee counsellor: a sense of importance and a sense of being socially useful.

Looking back, it seems to me that I was desperately looking for these two qualities in my life. Although gaining a PhD was immensely important to me, it did not give me a sense of importance. I had only succeeded in achieving yet another academic degree and I was aware even at that time that my research findings were far from earth shattering, of interest perhaps to only a handful of self-disclosure researchers. Indeed, such was my disappointment about the likely impact of my research that I didn't even bother to write up my findings for publication. The idea that I could make such a powerful difference to the lives of my clients was a real attraction and I couldn't wait to start seeing clients.

In retrospect, it also seems that the promise of doing something socially useful was also very appealing. I had been very much aware of the pain of having psychological problems from first-hand experience (to which I will return later) and the idea of assisting people to live more fulfilled lives fulfilled in me an important strong desire. So I could help myself as well as helping others. What bliss!

The first term at Aston involved trainees in intensive skills-based empathy training where we counselled one another, had our interviews video-recorded and analysed these interviews response by response so that we could learn how to make more empathic responses. We also participated in a personal development group run by one of the university chaplains who was a trained TA therapist. And, of course, we made an intensive study of person-centred theory. Looking back it was an adequate preparation for seeing clients, but the course was not entirely internally consistent. The personal development group experience was inconsistent with the person-centred focus of the course and there were signs that neither trainer was thoroughly committed to the person-centred model. Indeed, 1974-5 marked the beginning of Richard Nelson-Jones' own journey towards a more integrative approach to counselling. Nevertheless, I 'felt' and was deemed ready to see clients at the beginning of the second term. Full of idealism, I looked forward to beginning clinical work with much enthusiasm.

I had two placements, one at the University Counselling Service and the other at the Psychology Department of the Uffculme Clinic, a local psychiatric clinic. I was fortunate in that my clients were assessed as being able to benefit from person centred counselling and thus, I began the practical part of counsellor training under ideal conditions, something that today does not happen as frequently as it ideally should. In my zeal, I did not think about the clients who were not deemed suitable to be counselled by me. I was far too enthusiastic for such questions and doubts. The clients whom I did see were indeed good candidates for person centred therapy as practised by a trainee in that they were all reasonably functioning individuals with mild to moderate self-esteem problems. Initially, I formed good relationships with them and they all stated that counselling helped them to feel better. However, as counselling proceeded, most of my clients became stuck. They could not get beyond their original gains and began to ask me for advice about how to deal with their problems. I was fleetingly aware that many of them were expressing rigid and extreme attitudes, which according to REBT (which we had a lecture on in the second term of the Diploma course) helped to explain their problems. But I was convinced that if I only persisted in offering empathy, respect and genuineness, my clients would all get over their stuckness as person-centred theory hypothesised they would. They didn't and I became convinced that the fault lay with me. Of course, I didn't give them any of the advice that they sought – to do so would be to commit one of the cardinal sins of counselling, certainly of the person-centred variety.

Looking back, I think I was partly right in my assessment. My training was strong on helping us to develop the skills of empathy, but I'm not too sure that it helped us to truly develop a deep sense of empathy as a way of being which Rogers (1975) emphasised in an important later paper. In retrospect, I don't think I really engaged any of my clients in a meaningful I–Thou encounter. I think that it was hoped that our participation in the personal development group would help us to do this, but since this was not a person-centred group, it was unlikely to help us in this way. Supervision on the course also focused more on the skills of empathic responding than on the other two conditions.

I realise now that in addition to the above factors, my increasing frustration was really symptomatic of a lack of congruence between me as a person and the practice of person centred counselling. I still resonated with its theory, but increasingly not with its practice. I should stress that I did not conclude this at the time. No, at the time, I alternated between thinking that I was at fault for not being able to offer the requisite core conditions and that the approach was at fault for not offering clients the something extra that many of them explicitly asked for.

Post Diploma Training at the Uffculme Clinic, 1975–7

It was while I was in the latter frame of mind i.e. thinking that the fault lay with person centred therapy and not with me that I applied for and was offered a place on the two year psychodynamic course at the Uffculme Clinic. By this time, I had not only qualified as a counsellor from Aston, they had appointed me to the staff! The arrangement that enabled visiting Americans to spend a year at the university as a Fulbright fellow had ceased and a full-time position as a counsellor trainer had become available. I was encouraged to apply for it (after all I did hold a Diploma in Counselling *and* a PhD in psychology) and I was appointed. To give the university its due, I had a very gentle introduction to life as an academic. I was mentored by Richard Nelson-Jones and had a very light initial teaching, training and supervision load. This would not happen today when if appointed under similar conditions, I would have been thrown into the deep end of a full teaching and training timetable.

For the first year at Aston, I led a very split existence. Publicly, I was upholding the virtues of person centred counselling to the incoming trainees; privately, I was leaving this approach behind as I settled into my psychodynamic course. I should state quite clearly at this point that this course was not a proper training in psychodynamic therapy as would be understood today. But, it was the first training endeavour to be introduced in the Midlands and beggars can't be choosers. The course, which was held every Tuesday afternoon for two years, was divided into two parts. The first part of the afternoon was devoted to theory and (later in the course) practice and the second part to participation in a group, the exact nature of which was not specified. There was no skills training and no supervision.

In my naivete, I thought that I could begin to practise psycho-dynamically fairly soon after the course started, but I quickly concluded that I had neither the knowledge nor the temperament for this kind of work. I found the neutral stance of the therapist quite difficult and was unsure about how to make interpretations. Also during my year at Aston and during the year under discussion, I had been a client (or more accurately a patient) with three psycho-dynamically oriented therapists and just didn't get on with the therapy. It is in the nature of this kind of therapy that you are not supposed to come to such conclusions quickly so I persisted with it until the coming together of my experiences as a trainee and as a client/patient led me to admit finally that this therapy was not for me either as a practitioner or as a client. I physically gave up being a patient and mentally gave up hopes of becoming a psychodynamic therapist. I left the course in the second year to pursue training in what is now REBT.

The Man with the Pink and White Check Suit

When I first learned about what is now known as Rational Emotive Behaviour Therapy, I was both attracted to it and repelled by it. I was attracted by its ideas, but repelled by an interview that I saw where Ellis counselled Gloria, a woman who had volunteered to be filmed being interviewed in the mid 1960s by Carl Rogers, Fritz Perls and Albert Ellis. You must remember that when I saw the Gloria interviews I was steeped in and embraced the idea that counsellors had to be non-intrusive, gentle and kind. And here was this brash American talking ten to the dozen and recommending to Gloria that it was perfectly in order for her to ask her physician out for a date. And yet, something must have taken hold because after I had abandoned my final attempt as a client in psychodynamic therapy I read *A New Guide to Rational Living* (Ellis and Harper, 1975) was attracted to the ideas, applied its techniques to myself and got over, in fairly short order, the mild feelings of anxiety and depression that had prompted me to go into therapy in the first place.

Soon after, in early 1977, I attended a one-day workshop in Rational-Emotive Therapy that was held at an American airbase in Suffolk and run by an American psychiatrist named Maxie C. Maultsby Jr. What was remarkable (to me at any rate) was that he was wearing a very loud pink and white check suit. What left a more enduring impression on me was that I suddenly realised that I had found what I had been looking for. Maultsby spoke a lot of sense and showed several videotapes demonstrating that REBT could be practised in a way that involved the client in a slower paced dialogue than that shown in the Ellis–Gloria film. To be fair to Ellis, the interview with Gloria was carried out under difficult conditions and as Ellis now freely admits it was not a good example of the therapy even as it was practised then. Indeed, it only lasted 18 minutes and Ellis experienced self-imposed pressure to cram too much into this short interview.

At the end of the Maultsby workshop, I joined with several people who resolved to bring over an REBT therapist for a more extended training with the result that I attended later that year a five-day workshop in REBT given by Virginia Anne Church from San Francisco. This experience clinched things for me and the following year I embarked on a full training in REBT in New York at the then Institute for Rational-Emotive Therapy. The rest is history and I have been an REBT practitioner ever since.

On reflection, I experienced a congruence between my ideas, temperament and natural problem-solving tendencies and the theory and practice of REBT. With respect to ideas, I agreed with Ellis that cognitive factors are at the core of our psychological problems. Rogers's view is not too dissimilar, but the language that he uses is less precise than that used by Ellis and I have always valued precision. With respect to temperament, I tend to favour an active-directive approach to life and realise now that I felt constrained by the active, but relatively non-directive approach advocated by person centred therapy and by the relatively inactive and neutral style advocated by psychodynamic therapy. REBT also resonated closely with my own natural problem-solving tendencies. Let me dwell on this particular issue at some length.

In my youth, I had a stammer and made myself quite anxious about speaking in public. I tried quite a number of speech therapists who neither helped me with my anxiety about my stammer nor with the stammer itself. It was only when I heard Michael Bentine on the radio explain how he conquered his stammer-related anxiety that I was given the help that I needed. He helped himself by convincing himself that if he stammered, he stammered; too bad. I embellished this somewhat and showed myself that if I stammered, I stammered; *fuck it!* Using this philosophy, I resolved to speak in public at every possibility as opposed to my usual pattern of avoidance where I would duck out of speaking in public whenever I could. After a while, I found to my great satisfaction that I lost my anxiety about speaking in public. I still stammered from time to time, but far less so than hitherto, but anxious I was not. Since that time, I have spoken and stammered on radio, television and in large public lectures that I have delivered, but undeterred I press on. Disfluency rules OK!

As I examine it now, what I did then was very much in keeping with REBT theory and practice. I practised a healthy philosophy both cognitively and behaviourally. I really convinced myself of my new philosophy by using a forceful self-statement and I persisted with this form of self-help until I had dealt with my anxiety. Also, I avoided my tendency to avoid and thus prevented myself from relapsing. I hadn't heard about counselling at that time let alone REBT yet here I was practising REBT on myself. Remember too that years later I helped myself to get over my mild anxiety and depression by reading an REBT self-help book and applying what I had read.

Conclusion

I no longer practise person centred therapy or psychodynamic therapy because I disagree with person-centred practice and with both the theory and practice of psychodynamic therapy. My ideas about how humans disturb themselves and what can be done to help them and to help them help themselves resonate very closely with the theory and practice of REBT. I like and agree with its emphasis on psychological education and experience a sense of congruence between my penchant for being active-directive in my personal life and the emphasis that REBT places on the therapist being active and directive in his professional life. I experience a sense of genuineness when I practise REBT that I never experienced when practising PCT and fleetingly psychodynamic therapy because I have used its ideas to help myself and continue to do so.

Do I then conclude that REBT is necessarily a better therapy or more effective than the two other approaches that I used to practise, but later gave up? Not at all. Do I say that all clients will benefit from REBT? No. Clients have their own ideas about what will be helpful to them and what not. Some do and others do not resonate with the active-directive and psycho-educational nature of REBT, for instance. However, since REBT therapists believe in being explicit about the therapy, clients are likely to discover this sooner rather than later and save themselves valuable time and money. Finally, am I urging you to abandon your studies and come to train in REBT with me? You can if you like, but this is not my intention.

My intention has been to help you to reflect, through listening to my own personal and professional journey, on the degree of congruence between yourself as a person and in particular your ideas, temperament and natural problem-solving tendencies and the therapy that you practice. If you experience such congruence, fine, but if not, maybe it is time to embark on a similar journey that I took 20 years ago.

Of course, there are other important factors to being a counsellor than the congruence between yourself and the approach you practice. But without such congruence will you truly embrace the tenets of this approach and thus be an effective practitioner? Here I can only answer for myself. I could never become an effective person centred or psychodynamic practitioner because I could not personally resonate with its central tenets. This realisation was painful, but ultimately fruitful.

4

Rational Emotive Behaviour Therapy

Why I Practise an Approach to Counselling that is Unpopular

This lecture develops the theme that I first took up in the previous chapter and was delivered to the Wessex affiliated branch of the British Association for Counselling at Bournemouth on 18 June 1997. At the end of the lecture I went to dinner with a small group, which included my friend and colleague Albert Kushlik, who had driven over from Southampton to hear my lecture. He was on top form and enjoyed the dinner tremendously. Sadly, it was the last time I saw Albert for he died later that year. I dedicate this chapter to his memory.

Which approach do most counsellors in Britain practise? My guess is that it is either psychodynamic counselling or person centred counselling. One thing is clear; it is not Rational Emotive Behaviour Therapy. In this lecture, I will make clear why I practise an approach to counselling that is not only manifestly not popular, but is also in all probability unpopular. Let me state at the outset that I am not unduly troubled about this state of affairs. Indeed, it probably suits me psychologically, for I have never been very comfortable being involved with anything that is popular. I am something of a loner and practising an approach to counselling that has many practitioners would not appeal to me. However, this does not fully explain why I practise REBT since if I really wanted to be on my own in Britain I would practise Reality Therapy or Morita Therapy, both of which have very few advocates in this country. No, aside from this psychological fit, I practise REBT for reasons that have much more to do with its theoretical principles and its stance on practice. In this lecture, I will discuss these factors and point to ways in which they contrast with more popular thinking about counselling theory and practice.

First, let me discuss why I think REBT is unpopular rather than merely not popular. The roots of this unpopularity can be traced back to the 'Gloria' film where a client known as Gloria, now sadly deceased, was counselled by three famous therapists: Carl Rogers, Fritz Perls and Albert Ellis. This film was made in the mid 1960s and for many years it was routinely shown to trainees on counselling courses up and down the country and for all I know it is still shown in some quarters. Ellis's interview with Gloria is the third of the screened interviews and lasts approximately 18 minutes. Ellis has admitted that it was not a good example of REBT even as it was practised then. He tried to cram too much into the interview with the result that Gloria seems confused at various points in the session. With Ellis, Gloria spoke mainly about her difficulties in meeting eligible men and Ellis seemed to suggest to her that it was perfectly acceptable for her to ask her physician out for a date, a practice that at the very least is frowned on today and more likely viewed as the therapist encouraging the client to invite her GP to act unethically. The point that I would like to make to you is this: Would you be happy to be judged on your current work by work that you did for 18 minutes over thirty years ago and in difficult circumstances?

Another reason why REBT is unpopular in Britain is due to what people have learned about Ellis's personality and behaviour. Stories have circulated that he is rude, unsociable, bad-tempered, freely uses profanity in his workshops and with clients and is openly contemptuous of other approaches to counselling and psychotherapy. Like many rumours, there is a grain of truth to these criticisms, but they have been blown out of proportion. Indeed, people have experienced Ellis as exceptionally kind and encouraging and in a small-scale survey of some of his clients, my colleague, Joseph Yankura and I found that these clients remarked that Ellis was remarkably accepting of them and they considered that they could tell him anything and he would not be shocked by it (Yankura & Dryden, 1990). This side of Ellis rarely sees the light of day. In any case, it is unfair to criticise a therapy system such as REBT because of the behaviour of one its practitioners even if that practitioner is the founder of the therapy. While I am on the subject let me state unequivocally that you do not have to model yourself after Albert Ellis to be an effective Rational Emotive Behaviour Therapist. But let me also state that Ellis's behaviour as a therapist is not nearly as outrageous as some people have made out.

REBT is also unpopular for reasons unconnected with the behaviour or personality of Albert Ellis. Thus, it is unpopular because it is a directive and structured approach to counselling. This is the antithesis of the psychodynamic and person centred approaches. While there is no such thing as a non-directive approach to therapy in that even if you remain totally silent during a counselling session, doing so represents taking a direction in the interview, it is true to say that counselling approaches vary from being highly directive to being less directive. I practise REBT because it is directive. As I will presently discuss REBT – like other approaches to counselling – has a perspective on psychological disturbance and REBT counsellors direct their clients to this perspective in an explicit way so that the latter can decide whether or not this perspective will be of benefit to them. In other words, REBT counsellors elicit their clients' informed consent about participating in this therapy approach. Once this consent is given, REBT therapists direct their clients to the REBT model of psychological disturbance so that they can begin to help themselves in a time efficient manner. I should add that effective REBT therapists are sensitive to their clients' readiness for such a directive approach and will be less directive when the situation calls for it. Believe it or not good REBT therapists are sensitive and flexible practitioners.

I mentioned that REBT is, by and large, a structured approach to counselling. As such, it is often criticised for not giving clients an opportunity to explore themselves in an unstructured manner. This criticism is understandable, but incorrect. It is understandable because whenever REBT therapists give demonstrations of REBT we are keen to show its distinctive features and thus we tend to emphasise REBT's structured and directive approach. However, in actual practice there is nothing in REBT theory and practice that forbids its practitioners from giving clients an unfettered opportunity to explore themselves in their own way at various times in the counselling process. But structure informed by REBT principles will be brought to REBT counselling sooner or later otherwise the work will become unfocused and unproductive. In my experience as a counselling trainer and supervisor and as an external examiner, I have heard many audio-recordings where it was clear that the client was becoming thoroughly confused precisely because the counsellor failed to provide sufficient structure to the interview, structure which would have helped the client to use counselling much more productively.

I have discussed elsewhere the personal underpinnings of my choice of REBT as a counselling orientation (Dryden, 1997c; see Chapter 3). Briefly, it suits my temperament and there is a close relationship between my natural problem-solving tendencies and the approach to emotional problem-solving advocated by REBT. What I will emphasise here concerns selected elements of the theory and practice of REBT that I consider particularly therapeutic.

The Empowering Aspects of the ABC Framework

REBT has, from its inception, advocated an ABC theory of psychological disturbance. Here A stands for an adversity, B for the basic attitudes towards this adversity, and C for the emotional, behavioural and cognitive consequences of holding these attitudes. This model is very empowering for clients in that it shows them that they are not passive reactors to life events and that while they will be inevitably influenced by these events, they have the power not to disturb themselves about them.

While other counselling approaches take a similar phenomenological line, REBT is unique in being very precise about the basic attitudes that are at the core of psychological disturbance and those that are at the core of psychological health. It is this precision that I find particularly useful in that it helps clients to identify their own rigid and extreme attitudes when they feel emotionally disturbed. For those of you who are unfamiliar with REBT's theory it posits four major rigid/extreme attitudes (rigid attitudes, awfulising attitudes, unbearability attitudes and devaluation attitudes held towards self, others and/or life conditions) and four flexible/non-extreme attitudes (flexible attitudes, non-awfulising attitudes, bearability attitudes and unconditional attitudes of self, others and/or life conditions). It follows that a major goal for REBT counsellors is to encourage clients to surrender their rigid/extreme attitudes and to develop their flexible/non-extreme attitudes.

REBT counsellors have been heavily criticised for forcing the ABC model onto their clients and for preventing the development of their clients' inherent tendencies to actualise themselves. Both of these criticisms are unwarranted in my view. REBT counsellors do offer their clients a particular perspective on psychological problems and their remediation. But, as I said earlier, in keeping with good ethical practice, we spell out this framework and its implications for client participation early in the counselling process to enable clients to make an informed decision about whether or not they wish to commit themselves to this form of counselling. As such, effective REBT therapists abide by the principle of informed consent and certainly do not impose the ABC framework on their clients.

In response to the criticism that by offering a particular framework for understanding personal problems and their remediation, REBT counsellors interfere with their clients' self-actualising tendencies, REBT would argue as follows. REBT recognises that humans have a drive towards self-actualisation, but it also states that we have a strong tendency to disturb ourselves and to easily prevent ourselves from remaining on this arduous, life-long path. REBT counsellors view the ABC framework for understanding personal problems as a tool to help clients stay on this path. REBT therapists would differ from their humanistic colleagues in their view that in taking the road towards self-actualisation, clients often need a map to understand the obstacles that they will encounter along the way and a variety of tools or techniques to help them surmount these obstacles. In this way REBT promotes rather than inhibits the process of self-actualisation.

The Distinction between Healthy and Unhealthy Negative Emotions

As far as I am aware, REBT is the only therapeutic approach which keenly differentiates between healthy and unhealthy negative emotions. Yes, I did say healthy negative emotions. When a client is confronted by an adversity, it is healthy for them to feel badly about this event. We don't want the client to have good feelings about a negative event, nor do we want them to feel indifferent about it. However, in stating that it is healthy for clients to feel bad about bad events, REBT recognises that it is easy for clients to have disturbed negative feelings rather than healthy negative feelings about adversities. How are we to differentiate between the two? REBT theory argues that healthy and unhealthy negative emotions can be distinguished as follows:

1. Unhealthy negative emotions (such as anxiety; depression; guilt; hurt; shame; demanding, condemnatory anger; unhealthy envy and jealousy) stem from rigid and extreme attitudes, while healthy negative emotions (such as concern; sadness; remorse; sorrow; disappointment; non-demanding, non-blaming anger; healthy envy and concern for one's relationship) stem from flexible and non-extreme attitudes.

2. Unhealthy negative emotions are associated with actions and action tendencies that are self-defeating, relationship-defeating and impede the pursuit of one's personally meaningful goals, whereas healthy negative emotions are associated with actions and action tendencies that are self-enhancing, relationship-enhancing and facilitate the pursuit of one's personally meaningful goals.

3. Unhealthy negative emotions (and the rigid and extreme attitudes that underpin them) lead to distorted, negative inferences (Bond & Dryden, 1996a) and blinkered attention while healthy negative emotions lead to reality-based inferences (Bond & Dryden, 1996a) and non-blinkered attention.

A major goal of REBT is to help clients experience healthy negative emotions about negative activating adversities rather than unhealthy negative emotions. It is important to realise that healthy negative emotions can be of equal intensity to their unhealthy counterparts. Thus, REBT counsellors do not endeavour to help clients to reduce the intensity of unhealthy negative emotions since less unhealthy negative emotions are still regarded as unhealthy. Experiencing healthy negative emotions of whatever intensity enables clients to adjust constructively to negative activating adversities and move on while unhealthy negative emotions lead to clients becoming bogged down and stuck, unable to adjust constructively to these negative adversities and unable to move on. Healthy negative emotions thus promote coping and learning from experience while unhealthy negative emotions interfere with coping and discourage learning from experience.

REBT's Position on Unconditional Self-Acceptance

REBT has a unique position on self-esteem which avoids many of the difficulties associated with this concept. Basically, REBT theory considers the concept of self-esteem to be pernicious and discourages clients from improving their self-esteem. Instead, REBT counsellors encourage their clients to work towards unconditional self-acceptance.

Let's have a close look at the concept of self-esteem and then consider why REBT is against this concept. In REBT, the 'self' is defined as 'every conceivable thing about you that can be rated' (Hauck, 1991) and 'esteem' is derived from the verb to estimate which means to rate or to judge something. REBT's position is that it is impossible to legitimately give the 'self' a single global rating because the self is far too complex to merit such a rating, It is also constantly in flux so that even if it could be legitimately rated, it would have changed as soon as the rating was made. In addition, as soon as you ask people to tell you what would improve their self-esteem, it soon becomes clear that even if they were to achieve high self-esteem, this is a tenuous state. Thus, if someone says that being loved would improve their self-esteem, that person would also acknowledge that their self-esteem would plummet if the other person would cease to love them.

Unconditional self-acceptance is a better alternative to self-esteem for several reasons. First, it involves the person acknowledging that they are a unique, fallible human being who is constantly changing and is too complex to merit a single global rating.

Second, unconditional self-acceptance does not preclude the person from taking responsibility for aspects of themself. When a person takes responsibility for that which is within their purview without rating themself, they are more likely to work constructively towards changing aspects of themself that they do not like than would be the case if such responsibility was underpinned by self-rating. If you rate your 'self' negatively for aspects of yourself that you do not like, you tend to focus on your negative self-rating rather than work towards changing those negatively rated aspects.

Third, if the person accepts themself unconditionally, they are not anxious about losing love, for example, because they do not base their worth on being loved. This does not mean that the person will be indifferent towards losing love. Unconditional self-acceptance encourages the person to be concerned (but not anxious) about the loss of love and this is regarded to be a healthy response to the prospect of losing something important to the person.

Finally, unconditional self-acceptance helps the person to accept other people unconditionally as unique, fallible human beings with good, bad and neutral aspects and thus facilitates good egalitarian relationships with others. In contrast, self-esteem leads to problematic relationships with others. Thus, when a person rates themself negatively, they will either tend to rate others negatively, a situation which leads to increased conflict in relationships or to rate others too positively, a situation which leads to dependency and naivete.

REBT's Focus on Discomfort Disturbance

REBT distinguishes clearly between ego disturbance and discomfort disturbance. In ego disturbance, a person holds an attitude towards themself which is self-devaluing in nature (e.g. I am a failure), whereas in discomfort disturbance the person holds an attitude that they cannot bear something that is in their interests to bear. While ego disturbance and discomfort disturbance frequently co-exist in people's problems (e.g. in the addictions) and frequently interact with each other, it is important to work on them separately if as a counsellor you are to avoid becoming hopelessly lost when dealing with complex client problems. REBT theory helps me to understand these two different types of psychological disturbance and to respond with different interventions suited to each.

REBT's Focus on Meta-Emotional Problems

REBT theory hypothesises that clients often (although not always) have meta-emotional problems. A meta-emotional problem can be defined as an emotional problem about an emotional problem. Thus, if a client is depressed about the loss of their job and is ashamed about being depressed, their depression can be seen as their original emotional problem and their shame about their depression as their meta-emotional problem.

The REBT view of counselling practice specifies when it may be particularly important to help clients deal with their meta-emotional problems before their original emotional problems. Thus, I recommend working on a meta-emotional problem first (i) when this problem is clinically the most important of the two (as in generalised anxiety disorder, for example); (ii) when the existence of this problem will interfere with the work you will do with your client's original problem in the counselling session (e.g. the client becomes preoccupied with feelings of shame as you focus on their depression); and (iii) when the existence of the meta-emotional problem interferes with the work that the client needs to do on their original problem between counselling sessions (e.g. when the client makes themself anxious (meta-emotional problem) about their anxiety about speaking in public (original emotional problem).

Thus, I find that the concept of meta-emotional problems is particularly useful when understanding a person in the context of their problems and when planning counselling strategies over time.

REBT's View of Therapeutic Change

REBT has a definite view of therapeutic change which, while unattractive to many clients, is realistic and can help sustain clients when the going gets tough for them. This view stresses that changing rigid and extreme attitudes is at the heart of long-term therapeutic change. While clients can benefit in the shorter-term by changing their inferences (or interpretations) about adversities, by modifying their behaviour when faced with these events or by removing themselves from the events, such strategies tend not to help them deal effectively with these and similar adversities in the future. Thus, facilitating attitude change is the objective of REBT therapists.

Clients begin the process of changing rigid and extreme attitudes to their flexible and non-extreme alternatives by first understanding why their rigid and extreme attitudes are false, illogical and self- and relationship-defeating and why their flexible and non-extreme attitudes are true, logical and self- and relationship enhancing. This is so-called intellectual insight and is an important first step in the attitude change process. However, on its own, such intellectual insight will not promote long-term therapeutic change because the person has not integrated their flexible/non-extreme attitudes into their system of attitudes. Such integration means that the new flexible/non-extreme attitudes have a significant impact on how the client feels, acts and thinks. This integration is brought about by the client repeatedly acting in ways that are consistent with the new flexible and non-extreme attitudes and by refusing to act in ways that are consistent with the older rigid and extreme attitudes.

In order to sustain this process of weakening conviction in one's rigid/extreme attitudes and strengthening conviction in one's flexible/non-extreme attitudes, the client needs to keep in mind four points. First, the client needs to have a clear idea that changing their attitudes in this way will lead them to achieve their desired therapeutic goals. Second, they need to realise that the process of change is difficult and uncomfortable and it would be easy to gain immediate comfort by going back to familiar patterns of behaviour which although self-defeating are comfortable to the person because of their familiarity. Third, the person needs to embrace the idea that therapeutic change is rarely linear and that they will, in all probability, experience setbacks along the way. If they refuse to disturb themself about these setbacks, they can learn from them and get back on the path towards personal change. The fourth and final point that the client would be wise to acknowledge is that even when they have made a great deal of progress and have consistently acted in a way that is in keeping with their increasingly believed flexible and non-extreme attitudes, it is still very easy for them to slip back into old unhealthy patterns of thinking and behaving. Consequently, some form of life-long commitment to personal development work and associated vigilance is necessary.

As you can probably imagine, many clients are not exactly thrilled by this 'Protestant Ethic' perspective on therapeutic change, but it is valuable to them in the long-term because in my view it is realistic and reflects the difficulties that we all have as human beings in sustaining meaningful personal change. Here as elsewhere, REBT therapists do not take an overly consumeristic line and tell the punters what they want to hear (Ellis, 1989). Rather, we tell it like we believe it is even if it is somewhat unpalatable. In some respects, REBT is the cod liver oil of the counselling world!

REBT's Position on the Value of the Working Alliance

Like virtually all approaches to counselling and psychotherapy, REBT regards the development and maintenance of a good working alliance between the counsellor and client as a very important therapeutic ingredient (Bordin, 1979). Thus, it holds that it is important that the counsellor and client agree on the goals of counselling and it stresses that each participant needs to understand and agree to the tasks that both are called upon to carry out in the pursuit of these goals. Finally, it holds that a good bond between counsellor and client facilitates the counselling process.

However, REBT does not hold that the therapeutic relationship is the sine qua non of counselling. Its position on the 'core conditions' issue is virtually unchanged from Ellis's (1959) original view which he outlined in a response to Rogers's (1957) seminal article on this topic. This position holds that while it is important for the client to experience the counsellor as empathic, respectful and genuine in the therapeutic encounter, these conditions are neither necessary nor sufficient for therapeutic change to occur. This makes it unpopular with person centred counsellors who do hold that these conditions are necessary and sufficient for change to occur.

Furthermore, REBT counsellors strive to develop and maintain an adult–adult relationship with clients. Clients are treated as adults who have views about what will benefit them and who need to understand the nature of REBT before they can be expected to give their informed consent for receiving this form of counselling. This means that at the outset and throughout the counselling process, REBT counsellors will be explicit about their therapeutic intentions and activities and elicit agreement from clients to play their part in the process as adult consumers who need to be informed throughout counselling if they are to participate fully in the process.

REBT counsellors do not think that it is important to look for and interpret clients' transferential reactions. This not to say that we do not recognise that such reactions exist. It is just that we do not go out of our way to encourage them. When they do emerge, we tend to help clients to look for, examine and change the rigid and extreme attitudes that underpin these transferential reactions. As you can tell, this puts REBT therapists at variance with our psychodynamic colleagues who tend to view transference and its resolution as a more central part of the therapeutic process than we do. Also our psychodynamic colleagues tend not to be as explicit about therapy as we are.

REBT's Psycho-Educational Approach

I have practised REBT for twenty years and now see it as a psycho-educational approach to counselling. I see effective REBT therapists as practitioners who:

1. Are explicit about the way REBT theory conceptualises clients' difficulties.
2. Explain both their role as REBT counsellors and their clients' role as REBT clients.
3. Elicit their clients' informed consent to proceed in counselling.
4. Teach clients the REBT skills of assessment and intervention so that they can learn to become their own therapists, and
5. Outline the REBT view of therapeutic change so that clients can have a realistic view of what they have to do to initiate and sustain personal change. In particular, this involves clients making a commitment to undertake a range of homework assignments which are designed to help them to change their rigid and extreme attitudes and to deepen their conviction in their new flexible and non-extreme attitudes.

In performing these tasks, effective REBT therapists adopt wherever possible an active-directive style, particularly at the beginning of the counselling process after they have given their clients an opportunity to explore themselves in their own way. As I mentioned earlier, this is perhaps one of the aspects of REBT that make it so unpopular with the majority of counsellors in Britain. However, as counselling proceeds,

REBT therapists become less active and less directive particularly as clients begin to take increasing responsibility for facilitating their own change.

In conclusion, it has never bothered me too much that REBT is unpopular in Britain. Although I have an interest in seeing REBT develop, I do not think that it is right for me to present REBT in ways which make it attractive to counsellors, but which disguise its intrinsic nature. In true REBT fashion, it would be nice if you all wanted to become REBT therapists on the basis of my presentation, but if none of you do so, that would be sad, but hardly the end of the world.

5

The Counsellor as Educator

This paper was originally given as a Keynote address in Dublin at the European Association for Counselling conference in November 1995. While I did not regard the subject matter as controversial, it was viewed as such by the audience and one person loudly walked out during question time. In retrospect, it did challenge more traditional views of counselling. I later delivered the paper as the 1996 Frank Lake Memorial Lecture at Bourneville College, Birmingham on 11 July 1996 for the Clinical Theology Association where it was received more favourably.

One can think of a counsellor as an educator, and a client as a learner. This educator–learner simile for the counsellor-client relationship is, of course, only one of a number that exist in the counselling and psychotherapy literature. Don Bannister discussed five such similes: doctor–patient, trainer–trainee, friend–friend, priest–penitent and supervisor–researcher (1). Perhaps facilitator–developer – one of the most popular similes for this relationship – is at the heart of humanistic approaches to counselling, which together with psychodynamic approaches dominate the counselling scene in Britain.

In considering the counsellor as an educator I shall refer to my experiences both as a counsellor and as a client. Although these experiences should not be considered prescriptions for how all counselling should be practised, some of my experiences as a client may well be shared by others.

Psychological Education

One of the most profound statements I have come across in the counselling and psychotherapy literature was made by an American psychiatrist, Maxie C. Maultsby Jr.: 'No method of counselling works unless the person being counselled decides to use it' (Maultsby, 1975). If this is true and I prejudicially think it is, then it implies that effective counselling is ultimately effective self-counselling. There are two ways to approach the issue of self-counselling: one can approach it systematically or one can leave it to chance. Most counselling leaves to chance what clients learn and take away from the process.

73

If the counsellor is an educator, they are a specific kind of educator. They educate in the area that spans human thought and imagery, emotions, behaviour, sensations and relationships. Broadly speaking, this area is known as psychology. So, more specifically, the counsellor can be seen as a psycho-educator, and I will refer to the terms educator and psycho-educator synonymously.

The idea that a counsellor is a psychological educator has not gained much support from the field, although several people have written about it. Richard Nelson-Jones, previously a colleague of mine at the University of Aston in Birmingham, noted that there are six broad uses of the term psychological education. It encompasses:

1. training people in life skills;
2. combined academic and experiential approaches to the teaching of psychology;
3   humanistic education;
4   training paraprofessionals in counselling skills;
5   running a range of counselling outreach activities;
6   educating the general public in psychological matters.

(Nelson-Jones, 1982)

I shall touch on several of these issues, but will focus on the application of one particular counselling approach – Rational Emotive Behaviour Therapy (REBT) (Dryden, 1995a) – in a way that attempts to 'give it away ' to clients so that they can learn to use its framework and skills to help themselves. Although I practise REBT, what I have to say is, I believe, applicable to other approaches too.

In this context, I define psycho-education as the systematic approach to helping clients use the method of counselling advocated by the counsellor. Many would object to this view because it directly challenges their own view of the nature of the counsellor–client relationship. Am I advocating that counsellors explicitly teach their clients counselling methods? That we should in effect 'give counselling away' to our clients? Well, yes and no. I do not wish to persuade counsellors to practise as I do – only to consider the merits of another way of construing counselling and one that may benefit some of their clients.

I have been in this profession too long to ignore a basic fact that counselling trainees are taught on their first day: that clients are different from one another. Not all of them will benefit from one particular kind of therapy. If there are counsellors who claim otherwise, my advice is to avoid them, at least professionally. What follows from this is that we need to match client to therapy, and if what I have to offer does not suit the client in front of me, I should 'refer on'. (I do this routinely, although the issues that this viewpoint raises are outside the scope of this lecture.)

However, even when a client is matched with an approach to counselling that is best suited to their problems and the way that they conceptualise them, Maultsby's basic point still holds: that counselling will work to the extent that the client uses the methods that they learn explicitly or implicitly from the counselling endeavour.

Educating Clients in Their Tasks

I defined psycho-education as 'the systematic approach to helping clients use the method of counselling advocated by the counsellor'. People may object to this statement for another reason. It may seem that the counsellor has in mind what clients need to do in counselling sessions and in their everyday lives, and that this is far too prescriptive. But do not all counselling approaches have explicit or, more frequently, implicit tasks with which clients have to engage? I believe they do. Are not clients of psychodynamic therapists called upon to engage in 'free associative processes' and clients of humanistic counsellors to engage in the tasks of self-exploration? I agree that these tasks are broad in nature, but they are tasks none the less. In REBT they are as given in Box 5.1 (see next page).

The psycho-educational approach to counselling states that it is important for REBT counsellors to deliberately train clients to engage effectively in these tasks, rather than to leave this to chance. My hypothesis is that counsellors from other orientations will also help their clients more if they explicitly train them to engage in the tasks that the orientation asks them to carry out. There is research to confirm this hypothesis. One of the most robust findings to emerge from psychotherapy research shows that when clients are educated in their role and the tasks that are associated with this role before they see their therapists, then they achieve more positive outcomes than clients who do not receive such pre-therapy training (Garfield, 1994).

Box 5.1   The client's tasks

1   Specify problems.
2   Be open to the therapist's REBT framework.
3   Apply the specific principle of emotional responsibility, that people disturb themselves by holding sets of rigid and extreme attitudes towards actual or inferred adversities.
4   Apply the principle of therapeutic responsibility, that in order to achieve therapeutic change the client needs to put into practice in their everyday life the change tactics that they learn in therapy sessions.
5   Disclose doubts, reservations or objections about REBT concepts, difficulties in applying these concepts and other obstacles to personal change.

Gaining Informed Consent from Clients

The psycho-educational approach to counselling is based on the idea that counsellors need to be explicit about their role in the counselling process and that of their clients. As such it is very much in accord with the principle of informed consent. Many professional codes of ethics and practice in counselling and psychotherapy advocate that clients need to give their informed consent before therapeutic techniques can be ethically used with them. This consent can only be given when clients understand both their counsellors' tasks and their own.

I have just outlined what the client's five tasks are in REBT. I make these tasks explicit at the outset of counselling precisely because it helps my client to make an informed decision about whether or not REBT is likely to be of use to them. In doing so, I explain these tasks in a way that the client is likely to understand, omitting any REBT jargon. Thus, I may say something like this:

All approaches to counselling require something from clients if counselling is to be effective. In the approach that I practise, I'll ask you to specify your problems as clearly as you can. Then I'll offer you a framework which I hope will help you to understand what has led to the development and maintenance of your problems. Your task here is to listen to my explanation with an open mind. If this framework makes sense to you, I'll help you to apply it to your problems and suggest how you can tackle these problems in your everyday life. If you agree to act on these suggestions, then it's your responsibility to put these into practice in your daily life. Your last task is to be as honest as possible about any doubts, reservations or objections you have about the framework I put to you, about any difficulties you have putting into practice what you learn from me and about any other obstacles that may interfere with counselling. During the counselling I'll help you to perform these tasks so that you'll get the most from it.

If I present the above material without a break, as I have just done, I then invite my client to give their reaction to what I have said and answer any questions they may have about their tasks. Usually, however, I would pause at various points, discuss salient issues and respond to queries before proceeding to the next point. If what I have said makes sense to the person, I ask them to give their informed consent to proceed. If, as a result, they indicate that they are looking for a different kind of therapy, I will gladly offer to refer them to a therapist who practises an approach consistent with their expectations.

If the client wishes to proceed, this is not the end of the education process. Far from it. At every stage, I outline explicitly what is required of the client and negotiate with them any modification to their tasks. As counselling proceeds and they become more familiar with REBT concepts, my explanations will reflect their increasing knowledge and probably include more REBT jargon.

Explaining a Counsellor's Role and Associated Tasks to Clients

I outline my tasks to clients at the outset of therapy, so that they may decide in an informed way whether or not to proceed with REBT; Box 5.2 shows how they change during the therapeutic process.

Box 5.2 The counsellor's tasks

The beginning stage
1   Establish a working alliance by encouraging the client to outline their problems, responding empathically and helping them to set therapeutic goals.
2   Socialise the client into REBT.
3   Begin to assess and intervene in the client's target problem.
4   Teach the ABCDE of REBT, where A stands for an actual or inferred adversity, B for the client's basic rigid/extreme attitudes towards this adversity, C for the emotional and behavioural consequences of these attitudes, D for dialectically examining the client's rigid and extreme attitudes and E for the effects of these latter strategies.
5   Identify and deal with the client's doubts, reservations or objections (and do so throughout the REBT process).

The middle stage
6   Persevere with the client's target problem.
7   Encourage the client to engage in relevant change-related tasks both inside therapy sessions and in their everyday life.
8   Work on the client's other problems.
9   Identify and encourage the client to change their underlying rigid and extreme attitudes.
10 Identify and deal with their obstacles to change.
11 Encourage them to maintain and enhance their gains.
12 Help them to prevent any relapse, and deal with vulnerability factors.
13 Encourage them to become their own counsellor.

The end stage
14 Decide with the client how and when to end the counselling.
15 Encourage them to summarise what they have learned.
16 Show them what their efforts have achieved.
17 Deal with obstacles to ending the counselling.
18 Agree with them about criteria for follow-ups and resuming therapy.

Thus I might say something like:

> *I see my role in counselling in the following terms. First I'll listen to and try to understand your problems and help you to work out what you want to achieve from counselling. Then I'll explain to you something about the therapy that I practise. Since I believe that the best way forward is to deal with your problems one at a time, we'll begin to work on the problem you want to start with. In doing so I'll outline a framework for understanding this problem and particularly help you to identify the attitudes that are at its core. Here and elsewhere I'll encourage you to ask questions about my view of your problem and to voice any doubts, reservations or objections you may have about my approach.*
>
> *Then I'll suggest various techniques that you can use inside and outside the therapy sessions to confront the attitudes that I think are at the core of your first problem. After we have made some progress with your first problem, we'll begin to deal with others. As we do so, I'll be looking to identify a few fundamental rigid and extreme attitudes that might account for all your problems. When we find them, I'll suggest how you might change them. As you begin to make progress with your problems, I'll suggest how you might maintain and continue with this progress and how you might prevent any relapse. Then I'll show you how you might become your own counsellor, so that you can deal on your own with any future problems that might develop. At this point, we'll discuss how we might end the therapy and we'll review what you have learned. Finally, we'll make arrangements for any follow-up sessions and discuss the conditions under which you might resume therapy if you need to in the future.*

Although I have presented the tasks as a fairly lengthy monologue, in practice I would regularly pause to gauge my client's reaction to what I have said, to discuss any issues that they wish to raise and to answer any questions they might have. Then, just as I would have done after outlining their own tasks, I would ask the client if they wish to proceed. Whether they do or whether they require a different way of tackling their problems, their decision will be an informed one. If the latter is the case, I would again be happy to effect a suitable referral.

Training Clients to Carry Out Their Tasks

It is important to spell out for clients the task that they and their counsellors will be called upon to carry out in REBT, but perhaps the heart of the psycho-educational approach to counselling lies in training clients to *execute* their tasks effectively. Although pre-therapy training is important, I shall focus here on the training that clients are given once therapy has begun. In dealing with this issue I shall again draw upon my work as an REBT therapist. Some clients are able to put REBT assessment methods and therapeutic techniques into practice without being specifically taught how to do so. However, such clients are few, and my hypothesis is that for REBT to have its greatest impact clients need to be deliberately trained to use its assessment methods and therapeutic techniques.

Box 5.3 (pp. 81–2) shows one example of how I train my clients to assess and deal with their own problems, using the framework that I described earlier. It is a version of a form I ask them to fill in, together with some explanatory notes to help them complete the form.

A Brief Reprise

Having given one example of how I train my clients to use a basic REBT skill let me summarise what a psycho-educational approach to counselling involves. First, the counsellor makes clear at the outset what the approach to counselling that they use involves, both for them as a counsellor and for their client. This enables the client to decide in an informed way whether or not the approach to counselling practised by their counsellor is likely to be helpful. This is the heart of eliciting the client's informed consent to begin therapy. This approach is in accord with recent thinking in social work (Garvin & Seabury, 1984), which distinguishes between an applicant and a client. When a person first seeks help from a counsellor, they are in the position of an applicant. They become a client when they give their informed consent that they understand what help is to be provided and wish to take advantage of this help.

Second, it is important for the counsellor to be explicit about the approach to counselling that they practise, emphasising how it views psychological problems and psychological well-being and how it conceives of the process of therapeutic change. They should judge what their client can understand and provide explanations to the client based on that judgement. This spans the entire therapeutic process.

Third, the counsellor is advised to be explicit about the tasks that the counsellor and the client will carry out during counselling. The more the client learns about the therapeutic approach the fuller the therapist's explanation will have been.

Box 5.3   An REBT client self-help form

Situation =

Adversity ('A') =

Basic Attitudes ('B') (Rigid and Extreme) *Rigid =* *Extreme =*	Basic Attitudes ('B') (Flexible and Non-Extreme) *Flexible =* *Non-Extreme =*
Consequences ('C') (Unhealthy and Unconstructive) *Emotional =* *Behavioural =* *Thinking =*	Goals ('G') (Healthy and Constructive) *Emotional =* *Behavioural =* *Thinking =*

1. Write down a brief, objective description of the *situation* you were in.
2. Identify your *'C'* - your major disturbed emotion, your unconstructive behaviour and, if relevant, your distorted and/or ruminative subsequent thinking.
3. Identify your *'A'* - this is what you were most disturbed about in the situation (Steps 2 and 3 are interchangeable).
4. Set emotional, behavioural and thinking goals at *'G'*.
5. Identify your rigid/extreme basic attitude i.e. rigid attitude + awfulising attitude, unbearability attitude or devaluation attitude.
6. Identify the alternative flexible/non-extreme basic attitudes that will enable you to achieve your goals i.e. flexible attitude + non-awfulising attitude, bearability attitude or unconditional acceptance attitude.

OVERLEAF

7.   Examine (at '*D*') both your rigid/extreme attitudes and flexible/non-extreme attitudes and choose one set to operate on. Give reasons for your choice. Which set would you teach a group of children, for example and why? Remember that you are choosing attitudes that will help you to achieve your emotional, behavioural and thinking goals. The effects of dialectical examination (or '*E*' should be your goals at '*G*').

8   List the actions you are going to take to achieve your goals.

9.   Examine '*A*' and consider how realistic it was. Given all the facts, would there have been a more realistic way of looking at '*A*'? - if so, write it down.

'D' (Dialectical Examination) =

Taking Action =

Examine 'A' =

Fourth, the counsellor teaches the client how to assess their problems and how to use the therapeutic techniques or processes advocated by the approach at hand.

Finally, once the fourth step has been successfully accomplished, the counsellor serves as a consultant to the client for their self-change efforts. In this way they helps the client to become their own counsellor.

Personal Experiences of Being a Client

At this point, let me refer to my experience of being a client, as it is relevant. In my mid-twenties, I experienced a low-level depression which I could not shift. As I was undertaking training as a counsellor at that time it seemed sensible to deal with this issue. So, I sought therapy and was referred to a therapist with good credentials. When I first saw him I asked what therapeutic approach he practised. This was met by silence. I then asked him to explain his role, an enquiry that was again met by silence. When I repeated my request (since I naively thought that my therapist may have been hard of hearing), it was met first with an implied question – 'I wonder why this is so important to you' – and when I pushed the issue I was met with an interpretation – 'You seem to want me to feed you'; it was a response I found most puzzling. It will come as no surprise that my first therapist was a Kleinian. This episode reveals that I received no education from my first therapist concerning his role, about which I did enquire, and concerning my own role, about which I did not. How could I then give my informed consent to participate in this therapy? The answer is that I could not. Although I do not have any data to confirm my hunch, I believe that my experience is the norm.

Because I was new to being a client and thought that my experienced therapist knew best (an assumption that most clients make and one which leaves them susceptible to all kinds of abuse), I persisted with this therapy for a number of months, all the time puzzled by his lack of responsiveness.

I quit at this point, not because I was getting anywhere – I was not and still had my low-grade depression – but because I moved.

Then I saw a kindly man who practised a hybrid of psychodynamic therapy and psychodrama. Again, I received no proper introduction based on the principle of informed consent. I enjoyed the psychodrama more than the psychodynamic therapy, but got no better.

Then my therapist announced, with proper warning, that he was giving up his practice. I do not think I was responsible for this, but I cannot be sure!

He referred me to a man who taught me a very valuable lesson: how *not* to practise therapy. He neither educated me into my role nor explained about his own; moreover, he pathologised my attempts to find out. At the beginning of my eighth session with him, he announced that this was to be my last session with him on the NHS, but that he would continue to see me if I could pay as a private patient. I left in disgust.

Soon after, I read a self-help book entitled *A New Guide to Rational Living*, written by Albert Ellis (the founder of REBT) and Robert Harper (Ellis & Harper, 1975). This book clearly explained to my satisfaction why I was depressed and showed me what I needed to do to stop feeling depressed. I followed this advice – and stopped feeling depressed. I responded to the REBT approach and was able to use it on my own without any outside assistance. It turned out that I became a therapist who has not been helped by being in therapy, but who has helped himself a great deal by practising self-therapy.

Now some might conclude from this that I wish to eradicate therapy and recommend that people should buy a book instead. Nothing is farther from the truth. What I conclude from my experiences is that I was poorly served by my three well-qualified therapists, none of whom took any trouble to educate me about our roles. Had they done so, each would quickly have determined that his approach was not right for me and would, I hope, have effected a judicial referral.

Advantages and Criticisms of the Psycho-Educational Approach to Counselling

The advantages of the psycho-educational approach seem to be the following:

1. It empowers clients by encouraging them to focus as early as possible on self-change.

2. Clients can be educated in individual counselling or in small or large groups, and some by the use of self-help material. It is thus an efficient approach to counselling and can reach more people than a non-educational approach.

3. It can guide the construction and implementation of personal and social education programmes in school. It can therefore help to prevent the development of problems rather than just approach their remediation.

4 It promotes peer counselling communities and self-help groups to which the counsellor can serve as a consultant.

Finally, here is a list of some of the criticisms of the psycho-educational approach to counselling, together with my responses:

1. Clients may resist the psycho-educational approach for a number of reasons. For some it may remind them of being back at school. For others it may seem that their counsellors are trying to make them fit into a pre-existing system.

   Response In using an educational approach to counselling, a counsellor will quickly recognise this and should suggest an appropriate referral. The counsellor should not think that they have to be able to help all those who apply for their help.

2. A client may not think of the counsellor as an educator and may want a different kind of relationship with a helper.

   Response Using the educational approach the counsellor will identify this at a very early stage and refer on.

3. Some clients may be too distressed or too disturbed to make informed decisions at the beginning of their therapy.

   Response If the counsellor is flexible, they will not burden a distressed client with inappropriate information that the client will not be able to process; rather they will respond to the client's distress. However, once the distress has receded, the counsellor should adopt an educational stance. With a very disturbed client, the educational approach can be used, but first the counsellor has to encourage the client to stand back and engage with their observational self.

4. The educational approach to counselling will appeal to administrators, who will see its value in offering intervention for a brief period to large numbers of clients. Counsellors will come under increasing pressure 'cram in' clients.

   Response Both statements may well be true. However, using an educational approach to counselling does not mean that the counsellor has to bow to such pressure. Rather, they need to educate such administrators in the legitimate and illegitimate uses of the educational approach.

5. Not all counselling approaches lend themselves to psycho-education.

   Response True, but all counsellors need to be able to explain their approaches so that applicants for their help can give their informed consent to become clients. All counsellors have something to learn from the psycho-educational approach to counselling.

6. Therapists who take an integrative approach to their work cannot educate their clients at the outset since they have no way of knowing what blend of approaches they will be taking.

   Response Integrative therapists can explain the integrative nature of their work at the outset although this will have to be in broad terms. However, once they have decided on the particular blend of methods they will use with particular clients there is nothing to prevent them from explaining this blend to their clients. They can then train them to use these methods for themselves.

6

Feel Better, Get Worse; Feel Worse, Get Better

I delivered this lecture to Obsessive Action, a self-help organisation for those who suffer from obsessive-compulsive disorder (OCD) and their families at their day of lectures and discussion groups on 4 October 1997. While I do not specialise in working with those with OCD, I have seen a number of such clients over the years largely due to my professional association with Dr David Veale, a Consultant Psychiatrist working at what is now called Priory Hospital North London. In this paper, I outline my views on OCD and how it can be addressed therapeutically from an REBT perspective. The language and tone of the lecture reflect the fact that I was speaking to a lay audience.

I am very pleased to talk to you today, although I do so with some trepidation. Sharing the platform with me today is Dr. Salkovskis who is one of the world's leading theorists and researchers in the field of OCD and Dr. Toates who is not only a leading psychologist, but knows from first-hand experience what it is like to suffer from OCD and will be drawing on this experience in his talk which follows mine.

When I found out that I would be sharing a platform with such distinguished colleagues, I wondered what tack I should take. I am not a specialist in OCD although I keep up to date with the research in the area and I have seen a good many clients with OCD in my time. Nor do I suffer, if that is the right word, from OCD, although there are those who know me who claim that OCD really stands for 'Obsessive-Compulsive Dryden'. Despite this and although I do own up to some obsessive-compulsive features in my personality, I do not, by any criteria that I know of, suffer from OCD. I should know since I have checked all the books that have ever been published on the subject fifty-five times!!

So, what can I offer you today? I offer you some thoughts and insights from the approach to therapy that I practise known as Rational Emotive Behaviour Therapy. This approach to therapy can be located in the cognitive-behavioural tradition which states that psychological problems can be understood by examining carefully how people think and behave. Now, I do not for one moment wish to imply that OCD can be understood just with reference to the cognitive-behavioural model. I believe that OCD is more complex than that, that it is not just one disorder, but a range of disorders that can be placed under a broad obsessive-compulsive umbrella and that there are complex psychological and neurological interactions to consider if we are to understand this family of disorders properly.

Today, then, I will attempt to show the contribution that REBT has to make to the psychological understanding and treatment of obsessive-compulsive disorders.

Responsibility and Risk Appraisal

Currently, there is much debate in the field concerning the roles that responsibility and risk appraisal play in the genesis and maintenance of certain obsessive-compulsive disorders. In particular, cognitive distortions of risk appraisal and responsibility for harm have been claimed to be at the heart of many obsessions and some compulsions. An example from the field of obsessions is that a person has a thought such as 'I may harm my child' and considers that as a result there is a very good chance of doing so. Here the appraisal of risk is exaggerated. In addition, the person attempts to avoid all potentially dangerous situations that the child may be exposed to and also attempts either to neutralise the thought (e.g. by saying 'I am a loving mother') or to suppress the thought. These manoeuvres are deemed to stem from an exaggerated sense of responsibility as shown in the thought, 'If something bad happens to my child then it will be all my fault.'

Why do people develop an exaggerated appraisal of risk and an excessive sense of responsibility? Rational Emotive Behaviour Therapy's view is that these cognitive distortions stem from the person's attitude to safety and to responsibility. REBT argues that this attitude is dogmatic or absolutistic in nature.

Let me give an example from my clinical practice. I have a client, who I will call Janet, whose problem concerns preventing harm to others who do or may come into contact with her. She has a range of symptoms; thus, she is terrified of contracting Aids; not, I should stress, because of concerns about her own welfare, but because she may infect other people. In addition, if she sees a child at the school where she teaches display an unexplained bruise, she experiences a compulsion to tell somebody in authority about this. Her current preoccupation concerns smoke. She is convinced that she can see and smell smoke in other people's houses and is compelled to bring this to their attention. Finally, she refuses to go on holiday lest she sees unattended luggage which, of course, contains a terrorist's bomb. You will see clearly here the twin distortions of risk appraisal and the responsibility of harm. What is this woman's underlying philosophy concerning risk and responsibility. It is this:

'When I am involved, I must *discharge my responsibility perfectly and it would be terrible if I don't. If something bad happens, which it is bound to if I do not make absolutely certain that I have done everything I can to prevent it, then this will be all my fault and will prove that I am a thoroughly rotten person'.*

When this attitude has been activated in the client's attitudinal system, how will she answer the following questions?

Question: How likely do you think it will be for something dreadful to happen if you do not act to prevent it?

Answer: It will definitely happen.

Question: How responsible are you for anything that happens if you do not act to prevent it?

Answer: Totally responsible.

Question: How certain do you have to be about preventing harm to others and about discharging your responsibility?

Answer: Totally certain.

Question: How safe do you have to make it for others who come into contact with you?

Answer: Totally safe

The REBT perspective, I believe, explains why people with OCD see things related to their problems in black and white terms. As can be seen from Janet's answers, she holds the following black and white ideas:

1. Either something tragic definitely won't happen or it definitely will. Here, there is no room for the concepts of possibility and probability.

2. Either I am totally free of responsibility or I am totally responsible. Here, there is no room for degree of responsibility or shared responsibility.

3. Either I am certain that harm won't happen or it definitely will. Here, the person has no concept that harm may not happen if she is not certain. Personal experience of doubt is associated in the person's mind with the certainty of harm.

4. Either things are totally safe or they are dangerous. Here, there is no room for slight danger. Because slight danger must be eradicated it becomes extreme danger in the person's mind if it cannot be gotten rid of.

If my client has a predisposition to OCD, which I believe to be the case, is it any wonder that this absolutistic attitude renders them vulnerable to one of the obsessive-compulsive disorders? I would argue that it is not.

This attitude, then, leads the client to act in a way that is consistent with it and these actions serve to perpetuate this attitude. This mutual strengthening of attitude and behaviour is what makes it so important to address both their behaviour and their attitudes in therapy. In the past, we thought that interventions targeted at behaviour would automatically lead to attitude change. We are now older and wiser. We also know from clinical experience that if we just target attitudes for change, then the client may undermine our efforts by continuing to behave in obsessive-compulsive ways. So, we target both. I argue that we first need to help the person to develop a healthy, flexible alternative to their rigid attitude, In the case of Janet, here is the attitude that we worked together to construct:

'When I am involved, I want to discharge my responsibility perfectly, but I do not have to do so, nor is it healthy for me to attempt to do so. If I don't do all I possibly can to discharge my responsibility as I don't have to do, this has advantages and disadvantages and does not mean that something bad will inevitably happen. I can take reasonable steps to prevent bad things from happening without guaranteeing that they won't. If something bad happens as a result that is very unfortunate, but not the end of the world. If it does happen, I will accept my share of the responsibility which is not total. If I do the wrong thing, I am not a bad person, but a fallible human being who has a

responsibility to my own psychological health and happiness as well as a responsibility to take a reasonable amount of care in preventing bad things from happening to others.'

When this attitude has been activated in the client's attitudinal system and she has conviction in it, how will she answer the same questions?

Question: How likely do you think it will for something dreadful to happen if you do not act to prevent it?

Answer: It could happen, but the greater likelihood is that it will not.

Question: How responsible are you for anything that happens if you do not act to prevent it?

Answer: I have responsibility, but others who are involved also have responsibility. There will be occasions when I will have total responsibility, but there will be many more situations when responsibility will be shared.

Question: How certain do you have to be that you have prevented harm to others and discharged your responsibility?

Answer: Reasonably certain, but not totally so.

Question: How safe do you have to make it for others who come into contact with you?

Answer: Reasonably safe, but not totally so.

Janet's flexible and non-extreme attitude will lead her to be more flexible in her thinking which contrasts with the black and white thinking that stems from her rigid and extreme attitude. This can be seen in the following:

1. Tragic events do happen, but they are rare and they are not inevitably related to what I do or fail to do. The events that I am concerned with exist along a continuum of probability rather than in two categories labelled 'definitely won't happen' and 'definitely will happen'.

2. In most cases responsibility can be divided and assigned differentially.

3. If I am not completely certain that harm won't happen, it does not follow that it definitely will. Events in life are not controlled by my experience of being certain or uncertain. I just don't have that degree of control over events.

4. Threat and danger can be placed on a continuum where there is room for slight as well as great danger. Danger can rarely, if ever, be eradicated and certainly not by me.

In order for Janet to really be convinced of her flexible and non-extreme attitude and the flexible forms of thinking that stem from it, she will have to act in ways that are consistent with it. This is a crucial point. It is possible for someone like Janet to understand intellectually that her flexible and non-extreme attitude is true, logical and self- and relationship enhancing, but to continue to act in ways that are consistent with her rigid/extreme, obsessive-compulsive disposing attitude, in which case her self-defeating behaviour will nullify her flexible/non-extreme attitude. Given this, it is crucial that her behaviour is in line with her flexible/non-extreme attitude.

If she follows this latter principle, Janet will have to act against her habitual way of behaving. In doing so she will experience discomfort which unfortunately is unavoidable. Consequently, in order to maintain this behavioural-cognitive consistency, Janet will have to bear this sense of discomfort. In other words, she will have to bear feeling worse in order to get better. If she opts to feel better in the short term by going back to her behaviour, the purpose of which is to eradicate doubt and risk, she will get worse in the longer term.

In order to sustain and enhance the gains she made through refraining from acting in accord with her flexible and non-extreme attitude and through choosing to act in a way that is consistent with this attitude, I encouraged Janet to expose herself in a planned way to situations which previously would have triggered her obsessive-compulsive related dogmatic and extreme attitude. Thus, among other activities, Janet agreed to stand in dog shit, wipe it off thoroughly as any person not suffering from OCD would, and wear the shoes to work while rehearsing her flexible/non-extreme attitude. She also agreed to go to Heathrow Airport, look for unattended luggage and go home without ascertaining who owned it and without reporting the incident to a member of the airport security staff. She resolved to do such assignments once a week and although she reported feeling very uncomfortable while undertaking such tasks, she made substantial improvements in her OCD symptomatology.

Gaining Control by Giving up Control

Let me turn my attention to obsessions which are kept alive by the person's attempts to not think certain thoughts. It is a fact of human life, which is not fully appreciated by those suffering from intrusive thoughts, that as humans (i) we may think various thoughts which are alien to us and (ii) we are limited in our ability to control our thoughts. Indeed, the more we try to banish unwanted thoughts from our mind, the more we are likely to think them.

In this respect, let me tell you about Fiona who has again given me permission to tell you her story. Fiona is an orthodox Jewess who in early twenties had a lesbian dream which she found very disturbing because she thought that this meant that she was a lesbian. Consequently, she tried not to look at women in case she looked at their breasts and private parts. The more she tried not to look at women sexually, the more she did so. Fiona consulted me precisely because I was a man, since by that time she tried to solve her problem by avoiding women as much as possible. Thus, she had stopped travelling by tube because things had escalated to such a degree that she started having intrusive thoughts and images that she would wrestle a woman to the ground and carry out oral sex on her in front of other passengers. Later on in therapy, we would humorously refer to this as the 'assault on the Licktoria Line' incident! Parenthetically, I think that a therapist who works with people with OCD needs to have a good sense of humour.

Fiona's obsessions stemmed and were kept alive by the following rigid and extreme attitudes:

1. I must be thoroughly heterosexual and not have any thoughts about women of a lesbian nature.

2. I must be able to control my thoughts perfectly, even in my sleep.

3. If it turns out that I am a lesbian, which I absolutely must not be, then I am a disgusting person.

4. If others in my religious community discover that I have been having lesbian thoughts, then they will ostracise me and I could not bear that.

These attitudes led Fiona to try desperately not to have such thoughts which, as many of you know, is the best way to increase the intrusiveness and aversiveness of unwanted thoughts. This also led her to attempt to avoid contact with people and situations which triggered these thoughts. Again, this is a good way of making it more likely rather than less likely that obsessive thoughts will intrude into the person's mind in the long term.

I first helped Fiona by showing her the crucial role that her rigid and extreme attitudes played in the genesis and maintenance of her obsessive-compulsive symptoms. Second, I helped her to construct the following set of alternative flexible/non-extreme attitudes:

1. I'd prefer to be thoroughly heterosexual and not have any thoughts about women of a lesbian nature, but there is no law of the universe which states that I must achieve either of these things. Indeed, a person's sexuality is best placed along a continuum rather than in two non-overlapping categories and if I calm down about my thoughts about women, I will be able to be clearer about my sexuality.

2. I'd like to be able to control my thoughts perfectly even in my sleep, but I don't have to do so. In fact, I now see that desperately trying to control my thoughts will only lead to an increase in such thoughts rather their elimination.

3. If it turns out that I am a lesbian, which I would prefer not to be, then this certainly does not prove that I am a disgusting person. Rather, it proves that I am a fallible human being who would prefer to be heterosexual.

4. If others in my religious community discover that I have been having lesbian thoughts and ostracise me, then I would really find it difficult to bear this, but I could bear it. If this happens, then I can make a life for myself in a more liberal Jewish community.

Fiona came to see that these flexible/non-extreme attitudes were consistent with reality, logical and healthy and that her rigid and extreme attitudes were false, illogical and unhealthy, but fully recognised that she needed to work towards really believing them. This work involved Fiona allowing herself to think lesbian thoughts and to have lesbian images while practising her flexible/non-extreme attitudes. She was to do nothing to eliminate or reduce the frequency of these thoughts and images. She was to wait until they passed through her mind no matter how long this took.

After doing this, Fiona began to confront situations which she had previously avoided and to practise her new set of flexible/non-extreme attitudes while doing so. For example, she spent a day going up and down the Victoria Line sitting next to and directly opposite women and standing close to them in the rush hour.

All this work left Fiona feeling worse in the short term, but helped her to get better in the longer term. She made great strides in therapy and a year after we had finished therapy, she rang to tell me that she had lost her virginity to a man she had been dating for about six months who, believe it or not, happened to be a trainee rabbi!!

REBT's Contribution to the Understanding and Treatment of OCD in a Nutshell

Let me now make a few general remarks about REBT's contribution to the understanding and treatment of OCD.

1. REBT holds that at the psychological core of most forms of OCD lie a set of rigid and extreme attitudes towards certain key themes such as responsibility, threat and control. These attitudes are false, illogical and unhealthy. There are four such attitudes.

    (i) Rigid attitudes (which takes the form of musts, absolute shoulds, etc.).

    (ii) Awfulising attitudes (e.g. 'It's awful, terrible or the end of the world that...').

    (iii) Unbearability attitudes (e.g. 'I can't bear it').

    (iv) Self-devaluation attitudes (e.g. I am bad, defective or worthless).

2. These rigid and extreme attitudes lead to the cognitive distortions often found in OCD. Thus, they help to explain why people with OCD greatly overestimate risk to themselves and to others and why they take complete responsibility in situations where objectively responsibility is shared.

3. These rigid and extreme attitudes and the cognitive distortions that they help create also explain the overt and subtle cognitive and

behavioural manoeuvres that people with OCD undertake to try to deal with their problems, but which serve only to perpetuate them. In short, these manoeuvres are designed to help you feel better but which in fact help you to get worse.

4. You can through understanding and a dedication to hard work learn to change these rigid and extreme attitudes and learn a much healthier set of flexible/non-extreme attitudes (which take the form of flexible attitudes, non-awfulising attitudes, bearability attitudes and unconditional self-acceptance attitudes). This work involves non-OCD rehearsal of these flexible and non-extreme attitudes, confronting previously avoided situations and a willingness to let yourself think whatever you think without neutralisation and other attempts to control your thinking. This work will lead you to feel worse in the short term, but will help you to get better in the longer term.

If I were to sum up REBT's perspective on OCD in a nutshell it would be this. OCD is maintained by your attempts to feel better, but which only lead you to get worse. Therapy involves you doing things which will lead you to feel worse, but will help you to get better. So, if you all feel worse at the end of this talk, I will be very pleased!!

7

REBT and Relate

I delivered this lecture (originally titled 'Rationality and Relate') at the AGM of the Wimbledon and Merton office of Relate on 3 July 1997. As I note in my lecture, I used to be a Marriage Guidance Counsellor and took the invitation to talk as an opportunity to reflect upon my current thinking on couples counselling.

My Experiences with Relate

I used to work for Relate or more accurately I used to work for your organisation when it was known as the National Marriage Guidance Council. This was back in the early 1980s when I was looking to work more extensively with couples. I was at that point fully trained as a Rational Emotive Behaviour Therapist, but in order for me to offer my services to the local centre, which incidentally was Birmingham, I had to go to Rugby for training. So off to Rugby I went for Marriage Guidance counsellor training which at that time comprised a mixture of theoretical sessions and discussion groups which focused on our personal reactions to the material and to each other. What it didn't do was to teach us about how to work with couples in a practical way. I understand that matters have since changed, but not being au fait with current training at Rugby, I couldn't possibly comment.

Apart from insisting that I attend training at Rugby, which they were obliged to do, Birmingham Marriage Guidance allowed me to practise couple counselling in my own way – i.e. as a Rational Emotive Behaviour Therapist – and while they supervised me in a general manner, they had no objection to me seeking specialised REBT supervision elsewhere. This involved making audiotapes of counselling sessions which I was allowed to do as long as my clients gave their informed consent.

This state of affairs continued happily until I moved to London in 1985. My wife, who also was a Marriage Guidance Counsellor (doesn't it feel good to hear that phrase again!), and I decided that we wanted to continue to work for MGC and applied to London. We met with Renate Olins, but were not accepted by London because we were not prepared to offer three evenings per week to the organisation. We could only offer two and this brought to an end my career as a

Marriage Guidance Counsellor. Sadly, I never did become a Relate Counsellor.

Actually, I wrote a formal letter of complaint to Rugby about London's inflexibility, but received a reply which in essence said 'London do their own thing, we have no control over them'. That was in the days before London declared UDI.

I recently had an experience which reminded me of London's inflexibility and would like to share this with you. One of my REBT trainees is a trained Relate Counsellor and wanted to receive supervision from me on his REBT work with couples. His supervisor at Relate was adamant that he could not audio-record his sessions and that was the end of that. This contrasted with Birmingham's more flexible, encouraging attitude fifteen years earlier.

I mention these incidents to you first, to show you that I have been part of the organisation in which you work and second, to highlight what I see as the ambivalent attitude that Relate has towards diversity of counselling approach. For while I have heard representatives of the organisation say that they would welcome outside practitioners from a variety of different approaches, when it comes to it they back away from creating opportunities to allow this to happen. I was fortunate to encounter a local centre which encouraged me to bring my REBT skills to couple work. My trainee and others that I have met have been less fortunate.

You may be thinking at this point that you would be against the practice of allowing Relate counsellors to audio-record their counselling sessions. However, if the reasons for the use of audio-recordings are explained to clients and they are given an opportunity to decline their use, then in my opinion there is no valid argument against this practice. After all it was Carl Rogers who pioneered the use of such recordings in counselling and if it was good enough for Rogers, it's good enough for Relate.

Couple Dissatisfaction and Couple Disturbance

Having got that off my chest, let me turn my attention to the contribution that Rational Emotive Behaviour Therapy has to make to work with couples. REBT theory argues that each partner in a couple brings to the relationship a number of preferences about (i) aspects of the relationship, (ii) their partner and/or (iii) themself in the relationship. Problems begin both when these preferences aren't met and when the two people have incompatible desires. In REBT theory, these problems come under the heading of couple dissatisfaction in that one or both people in the relationship are dissatisfied when their preferences are not met. This is why it is so important for people to be as honest as possible with themselves and with their potential partners about their true preferences with respect to relationships so that both people can make informed choices about making a commitment to a long-term relationship. This is also why it is important that the focus of premarital counselling should be on helping engaged couples to discover and share their true desires with one another about married life.

In general, the more important the desire the greater the dissatisfaction when that desire is not met. However, dissatisfaction on its own does not usually lead to destructive couple discord. What tends to lead to such discord, or what REBT theory calls couple disturbance, is when one or both partners transform their *desires* into absolute demands about (i) aspects of their relationship, (ii) their partner and/or (iii) themselves in the relationship.

These demands, which are often couched in the form of musts, have to's, got to's and absolute shoulds, lead to a whole range of unhealthy negative emotions which partners experience when they don't get their demands met. When your clients tell you that they experience anxiety, depression, unhealthy anger, shame, guilt, hurt, jealousy and unhealthy envy, this is a clue that they have one or more relationship-oriented demands which are not being met.

While this is the core of the REBT view of couple disturbance, the situation is far more complex than this. Thus, people often act in self-, partner- and/or relationship-defeating ways either to stop themselves from experiencing unhealthy negative emotions, in the first place or to get rid of these emotions once they have started to experience them, in the second place. In addition, people can act in ways that are consistent with their unhealthy negative emotions and the attitudes that underpin them and these actions are more often than not also self-, partner- and/or relationship defeating. Add to this the tendency of partners to locate their emotions in the behaviour of the other rather than in the attitudes that they hold towards the behaviour of the other and what do you get? You get the fact that dealing with couples' problems is frequently a very complex business.

The Desire for Active Counselling and Practical Learning

Over the years I have seen many couples who have come to me in my private practice after seeking help from Relate counsellors. Since I routinely ask all my clients about their previous experiences of counselling, I have discovered two sources of dissatisfaction about Relate counselling. First, many of my ex-Relate couples have said that their counsellors were too passive to be helpful. These counsellors either kept quiet while the partners rowed or encouraged the couples to talk to one another which in many cases was an invitation to row even more. Second, these couples complained that they did not learn anything that was of *practical* use to them at Relate. This latter theme crops up time and time again. Now I am enough of a scientist to be sceptical of these impressions. They are taken from an unrepresentative sample and a fairly small one at that. But, it does echo what Pat Hunt (1985) found just over a decade ago in her study of client experiences of Relate counselling.

My personal view is that counsellors cannot afford to be passive when they work with couples. If they are they will fail to model one crucial quality that many partners in disturbed couple relationships lack: the skill of focusing on disturbed interactions and on the issues that underpin them. This focusing skill is a prelude to understanding the factors involved and to learning how to deal with them in more productive ways. By and large you just cannot wait and hope that couples will do this for themselves. No, as counsellors you have to intervene actively and help your couples to create a space where they can focus on their problems long enough to understand and deal with them. My view is that the more successful Relate counsellors do this. It will come as no surprise to you to learn that REBT therapists are active in this way as a matter of course.

However, creating a focus is not therapeutic on its own. What is therapeutic is what the partners learn about themselves within that focused space: not just any old learning, but learning that can make a real difference in their lives. I am speaking of learning that can help both partners deal productively with their disturbed emotions and the dysfunctional interactions that are closely associated with these emotions. This is not to say that my couple clients claimed that they learned nothing from their Relate counsellors. Far from it. Many of them stated that they learned how their current problems had roots in their past. But, and I want to emphasise this, they claimed that this learning was neither practical enough to help them to change how they felt, nor to help them to change how they acted towards one another. Again, I do not want to overplay this. I am referring to an unrepresentative, small sample, but nevertheless these people have something important to say. They are saying that they value insights that they can use in their everyday life. May I modestly point out at this juncture that this is the kind of learning that REBT couple counselling endeavours to facilitate.

The Counsellor's Tasks in REBT Couple Counselling

So how do I as an REBT couple counsellor work? The best way that I can explain this is to outline eight tasks that I perform in working with couples. While I will outline these tasks in the most logical order, I wish to state at the outset that in practice the order of these tasks is quite flexible and fluid.

Task 1: Understanding the problems

First, like any other couple counsellor, I ask the partners to tell me about their reasons for seeking help and what they would like to achieve from counselling. In doing so, I steer quite carefully between giving the couple an unfettered opportunity to express themselves and helping them to keep to the point. While listening to them I formulate hypotheses which I test out by asking the couple questions, the answers to which help me to reject any hypotheses that are disconfirmed.

During this opening period I also make notes, mainly of the problems that the partners are expressing. I do this because I find it helpful to encourage the couple to develop a problem list. This is effectively a list of problems the partners wish to address in counselling. Since it is important, in my view, for counselling to be goal-directed as well as problem-focused, I also help them to develop a goal for each expressed problem.

I agree with those couple counsellors who say that it is also helpful to encourage couples, as early as possible, to focus on their strengths as a couple as well as on the areas of conflict between them. I also like to do this in the early phase of couple counselling, but if it seems that a particular couple is a long way from considering this issue, I do not press the point.

Task 2: Giving a thumbnail sketch of Rational Emotive Behavioural Couple Counselling and eliciting informed consent to proceed

One of the principles that I hold dear in the field of counselling is that which is known as informed consent. With respect to counselling, the principle of informed consent states that it is important for counsellors to explain to clients the nature of the approach to counselling that they practise in ways that are likely to be understood by the clients. The purpose of this explanation is to help clients make up their minds whether or not to proceed with this particular approach to counselling.

At this stage, the explanation that I give is likely to be brief, but it does need to inform. Typically, I explain to my couple clients that the approach to couples counselling that I practise involves helping them to understand why they have problems and what they can do to address these problems. In doing so, I explain that I will help them to focus on the attitudes they hold towards their relationship, their partner and themselves in the relationship. I explain that unhealthy rigid and extreme attitudes are at the core of many couples' problems. I continue by saying that holding healthy flexible/non-extreme attitudes helps partners to communicate and solve problems more effectively, while holding unhealthy rigid and extreme attitudes leads to communication breakdown and an increase in couple conflict rather than its effective resolution. I then mention that I am also willing to teach them a range of skills as appropriate and at the right time.

I then ask the couple whether or not what I have said makes sense to them. If so, I ask them whether or not they wish to proceed. If not, I answer any questions the couple may have and elaborate on any points that may be unclear and then I ask them whether or not they wish to proceed. I stress to the couple that my goal at this point is to give them a thumbnail sketch of my approach and that I will explain more about my approach as we proceed. If it transpires that a couple prefers a different counselling approach, I endeavour to effect a suitable referral.

Task 3: Teaching the distinction between couple dissatisfaction and couple disturbance

If a couple gives their informed consent to proceed, my next task as an REBT couple counsellor is basically an educational one. It is to teach the couple the REBT model of couple dissatisfaction and couple disturbance. I do so by following a number of steps in sequence.

First, I ask both partners independently what they want from the relationship, what they want from the other person and what preferences they have of themselves in the relationship.

Second, I ask both partners to indicate to what extent their desires are being met in each of the three aforementioned areas.

Third, I ask them to indicate how they feel and respond in each of the areas where their desires are not being met. At this point I introduce the concept of healthy and unhealthy negative emotions. I show them that, in general, the following emotions are both negative and unhealthy: anxiety, depression, unhealthy anger, shame, guilt, hurt, jealousy and unhealthy envy, and that the following emotions are both negative and healthy: concern, sadness, healthy anger, disappointment, remorse, sorrow, healthy jealousy (or concern for one's relationship) and healthy envy. I help the couple to see that the latter emotions are healthy alternatives to the former.

I also show the couple, in some detail, that unhealthy negative emotions tend to lead to self- and relationship-defeating behaviour and distorted negative thinking, while healthy negative emotions tend to lead to self- and relationship-enhancing behaviour and realistic thinking. I then ask them to return to their list of thwarted desires and ask them to indicate whether they are responding to each with a healthy negative emotion or an unhealthy negative emotion.

Fourth, I take the issues where one or both partners are experiencing an unhealthy negative emotion and ask whether or not this emotion helps the person to address constructively the issue where their desire is thwarted. Invariably, the couple can see that unhealthy negative emotions lead to couple conflict and discord and do not in any meaningful, long-term way help them deal with the issue of their thwarted desires.

Fifth, having established that unhealthy negative emotions lead to conflict and discord in the couple and that these emotions prevent effective problem solving of thwarted desires, the next step is to encourage the couple to deal with their unhealthy negative emotions. I explain that the initial focus of Rational Emotive Behavioural Couple Counselling will be on helping them to change these emotions to their healthy negative equivalents.

At this point, you may be thinking what some of my couples put into words: that I am helping partners in a couple to feel bad. This is, in fact, exactly what I am trying to do. My initial aim is to help partners to feel healthily bad about not getting their important desires met. I don't want them to feel good about this, nor do I want them to feel indifferent about it. I want them to experience healthy negative emotions because i) it is realistic and healthy for them to do so and ii) these emotions will motivate them to have meaningful, productive discussions about how they can address the issue of their thwarted desires. As one couple insightfully put it: 'You want us to feel bad about the state of our relationship, whereas we have been feeling miserable and disturbed about it.'

Put more technically, if I have been successful at this stage, I have helped the couple to see that we need to focus on issues of couple disturbance before we can productively deal with issues of couple dissatisfaction. I believe that much couple counselling goes awry either because counsellors attempt to help their couple clients deal with issues of couple dissatisfaction without helping them to address and overcome couple disturbance issues or because they try to deal with both at once.

Task 4: Teaching the ABCs of couple disturbance and couple dissatisfaction

My fourth task is also an educational one. Having explained the difference between couple disturbance and couple dissatisfaction and helped both partners to use this model to understand their problems, I proceed to help them to understand that underlying their healthy negative emotions is a set of flexible and non-extreme attitudes and underlying their unhealthy negative emotions is a set of rigid and extreme attitudes.

Using a particular episode where both partners (rather than one of them) experienced unhealthy negative emotions, I teach them the ABCs of couple disturbance. In doing so, I show them one at a time that their disturbed feelings are largely determined by one or more of the following rigid and extreme attitudes: rigid attitudes, awfulising attitudes, unbearability attitudes and attitudes where they devalued themselves, their partner and/or the relationship. By using the same episode, I show them that if they were to hold the flexible/non-extreme alternatives to these rigid and extreme attitudes, then they would experience healthy distress about the event and this would help them to deal with the event more productively. These flexible and non-extreme attitudes take the form of: flexible attitudes, non-awfulising attitudes, bearability attitudes and attitudes where they unconditionally accept themself, their partner and/or the relationship.

Task 5: Teaching partners how to examine their rigid and extreme attitudes

This fifth task involves me teaching the couple to examine their rigid and extreme attitudes. I generally do this by examining the empirical, logical and pragmatic basis of these attitudes. In doing so, I make sure that I examine each partner's unhealthy rigid and extreme attitudes in a given session. If I only examine one partner's unhealthy rigid and extreme attitudes in a session, that partner may experience me as siding with their partner against them or they may think that I view them as the sick one in the relationship and their partner as the healthy one. So, even if I only succeed in partially examining both partners' rigid/extreme attitudes in a given session, this is preferable to examining one partner's unhealthy rigid/extreme attitudes fully.

The goal of this examining process is twofold. First, I strive to help partners see that their rigid/extreme attitudes are inconsistent with reality, illogical and yield unhelpful results. Second, I strive to help them understand that their flexible and non-extreme attitudes are consistent with reality, sensible and yield helpful results that are realistic given the adversity that we are analysing. For more information about how to examine clients rigid and extreme attitudes consult Dryden (1995a).

Task 6: Helping partners to weaken their conviction in their rigid/extreme attitudes and to strengthen their conviction in their flexible and non-extreme attitudes

Helping partners to examine their rigid/extreme attitudes once is insufficient to promote meaningful attitude change. Such change involves partners repeatedly examining their own rigid/extreme attitudes and practising the rational alternatives to these attitudes. REBT has many different techniques to aid this process. Basically, we have a host of cognitive, imaginal, emotive and behavioural techniques that we can teach clients to help them to weaken their conviction in their rigid/extreme attitudes and strengthen their conviction in their flexible/non-extreme attitudes. I recommend that you consult one of the many texts on REBT for more information about such techniques (e.g. Dryden, 1995a; Ellis et al., 1989).

Task 7: Dealing with couple dissatisfaction

This penultimate task involves helping couples to address their dissatisfaction about their relationship. For reasons that I have already discussed, this task is best done once both partners have made progress at overcoming their disturbed unhealthy negative emotions about their thwarted desires. There are a number of ways of addressing issues of couple dissatisfaction and the ones chosen will depend on what form the dissatisfaction takes.

Common methods of dealing with issues of couple dissatisfaction include:

1. empathy training – where partners complain that they do not 'feel' understood by the other;

2. communication training – to encourage partners to take responsibility for and own their own feelings in their communications to one another;

3. assertiveness training – to encourage partners to express their negative feelings in constructive ways and to express their positive feelings whenever possible;

4. negotiation training – to encourage partners to get more of what they want from the relationship while helping their mate to get more of what they want also;

5. problem-solving – where partners have difficulty solving practical and emotional problems);

6. effective relationship management – to help couples spend more quality time with one another;

7. tolerance training – to help partners to agree to differ and to show tolerance for the other person's position;

8. attributional training – to help partners make healthy attributions about each other's behaviour;

9. training in good parenting skills; and

10. sex therapy training.

I wish to stress that the above is only a partial list, but it will give you a flavour of the work that REBT couple counsellors do in this phase of the work.

As you can tell the emphasis here is on good relationship skills and these skills are tailored to the individual styles of the partners concerned. However, as appropriate, the focus of the work returns to attitude change when it becomes apparent that one or both partners have unhealthy rigid/extreme attitudes that will otherwise interfere with the skills-based work that is characteristic of this phase of couple counselling.

Task 8: Promoting relationship actualisation

The final task that I wish to discuss here is one that counsellors either do not offer or couples do not avail themselves of. This task involves the counsellor helping a couple to strive towards maximising the potential in their relationship. When couple counselling is effective, couples often leave happy with the gains that they have made, particularly when they look back and recall the conflictual state of their relationship before they came to counselling. However, they either do not realise or their counsellors do not bring to their attention the fact that they can have an even better relationship.

Relationship actualisation work focuses on helping couples to identify what they ideally want from their relationship and to encourage them to work towards realising these lofty goals. Love has been defined as an emotional and psychological state which occurs when one partner meets the deepest desires of the other. Couples who sustain love at this deep level are fully committed to meeting the deepest desires of the other and are prepared to take active steps to do this. While I believe that it is inhuman to expect couples to do this consistently for one another, the happiest couples do reach these peaks reasonably often. If, as counsellors, we do not offer such work to our clients, we are short-changing them at the last hurdle.

I hope I have given you at least an idea of what REBT couple counselling is like. Perhaps it is a pipe dream, but I would like to see REBT training offered on the Relate curriculum, not as the dominant counselling method, but as an option for those counsellors who want an alternative to the current training fayre. If tonight I have planted a seed, maybe Wimbledon and Merton MG can provide the soil and the water for the seed to flower. Thank you.

8

Why I Do Not Help My Clients to Raise Their Self-Esteem

This lecture was given on 9 October 1997 to the Department of Psychology at the University of East London as part of their Invited Speakers Programme. As most of the audience were likely to be interested in counselling psychology, I decided to speak on Rational Emotive Behaviour Therapy's unusual stance on self-esteem.

It doesn't take trainee counsellors long to discover that many of their clients suffer from low self-esteem, for low self-esteem lies at the bottom of many psychological problems. It would seem logical, therefore, if one of the primary goals of counselling were to help clients raise their self-esteem. While this may seem a sensible and non-controversial objective for counsellors, I will argue in this paper that pursuing this seemingly laudable objective is fraught with problems and dangers and if I am right, counsellors would do well to re-think this whole issue before unthinkingly going along with the crowd on this point.

What I will do in this paper is first, consider to what extent low self-esteem underpins clients' psychological problems. Second, I will take a close look at the concept of self-esteem and outline some of its difficulties. Finally, I will outline an alternative to helping clients raise their self-esteem which renders them less vulnerable to relapse. It will come as no surprise to those who are acquainted with some of my writings that my thesis is informed by the theory and practice of Rational Emotive Behaviour Therapy, an approach to counselling that falls squarely in the cognitive-behavioural therapeutic tradition and that I have been practising now for twenty years.

The Role of Low Self-Esteem in Clients' Problems

As I mentioned above, problems to do with low self-esteem can be found across the range of problems for which clients seek help. Whichever way you wish to categorise these problems, self-esteem is there lurking in the background. Sometimes it is very much in the foreground and may in fact be the first thing that your client may mention to you. How many times has a client said to you at the very beginning of therapy: 'My problem is that I suffer from low self-esteem' or 'I guess it all boils down to the fact that I don't like myself very much.'

If we take the major disturbed emotions that clients keep referring to in counselling, we again find the omnipresence of low self-esteem. For example, many anxiety problems can be attributed to a person's perception of threat to their self-esteem; in depression, a person may be preoccupied with their unworthiness and the fact that they are a failure; in guilt, a person considers themself bad for breaking or not living up to their moral code and in shame, a person considers themself to be defective, for example, when they fall very short of their ideal, particularly when this occurs in public.

I do not mean to imply that we can completely account for clients' problems by referring to the concept of low self-esteem, for this would be a gross oversimplification. Indeed, quite a few client problems have more to do with non-ego issues than ego issues. Nevertheless, such is the frequency with which low self-esteem, in all its different forms, crops up in counselling that it deserves close critical scrutiny.

The Concept of Self-Esteem

If we are to help clients to raise their level of self-esteem, it would be useful if we first understood what it is that we are attempting to help raise. In other words, what exactly is self-esteem. The REBT answer to this question involves defining the terms 'self' and 'esteem'. Paul Hauck (1991), a noted REBT therapist and writer defines the 'self' as 'every conceivable thing about you that can be rated'. Now what can be rated about a person? Let me answer this question with reference to Arnold Lazarus's (1989) modality view of humans. Lazarus argues that you can assess people and their problems in the following seven modalities: behaviour, affect, sensation, imagery, cognition, interpersonal relationships and physiological and bodily functioning. Using this framework, we can say that the self must include the following:

1. All the behaviours that a person has performed in their lifetime.

2. All the emotions that the person has felt in their lifetime.

3. All the sensations that the person has experienced in their lifetime.

4. All the images, dreams and fantasies that the person has had in their lifetime.

5. All the thoughts, beliefs and attitudes that the person has had in their lifetime.

6. All the interactions with other people that the person has had in their lifetime and

7. All aspects of the person's physiological and bodily functioning.

To which can be added the person's characteristics and traits and their various talents, skills and abilities.

The term 'esteem' comes from the verb 'to estimate' which means to rate, evaluate or judge. The question then is: can we legitimately rate the 'self'? Clearly, the REBT answer to this question is a resounding 'no', because as we can see from Hauck's definition and what follows from it, the self is far too complex to be rated. In addition, even if we could rate the person after discovering and rating the billion pieces of data gathered under the above headings, then as soon as we have done this, the rating would be out of date because the person would have changed and produced more data in each category.

Thus, the self is not only too complex to be rated, it is constantly in flux and you cannot legitimately give a static rating to a constantly changing phenomenon.

Why Raising Self-Esteem is Problematic

Whenever I have asked a person who suffers from low self-esteem what would raise their self-esteem, on most occasions the person says something like: 'a better body, more friends, being more interesting to people, being more successful at work, a better career, more money etc.' Indeed, the list is endless. However, if the person was magically given the missing ingredient, this would emphatically NOT solve that person's self-esteem problem. REBT argues that this is the case for the following reasons.

1. Self-esteem is conditional

Let's suppose that Janet holds the attitude that she is less worthy without a partner than she would be with a partner. Now clearly if she does not have a partner, she will think badly of herself. And if she meets a partner she will think better about herself. However, even if Janet has a partner, her attitude would lead her to experience a lot of anxiety because she has the idea that she would be less worthy again if she lost her partner. This is an example of conditional self-esteem where a person's self-esteem fluctuates according to whether she has or whether she has not something that she values.

2. Conditional high self-esteem is fleeting

Let's suppose that Janet meets someone special. Operating on her attitude – that she is more worthy if she has a partner than if she is without one – she begins to think and feel better about herself. However, she is still vulnerable to emotional disturbance because it is very likely that she places additional conditions on her self-esteem. Thus, she may think that she would be a failure if she does poorly at work. Her self-esteem has been raised because she has met a new partner and she considers that she is now worthwhile as a person. But, how would she feel if she gets a very poor appraisal at work? Because of her work-related attitude she would think that she were a failure for doing poorly at work. Her increased worth that has come about through meeting a new partner is not sufficient to sustain her self-esteem.

Human beings are frequently more preoccupied with what they do not have than with what they have. Thus, if we are in good health we take this for granted and hardly give it a thought. But, if we become ill we suddenly become preoccupied with the state of our health. When, we return to full health, we may for a while give thanks that our health has been restored, but this awareness of our good health will not last long. Similarly, when Janet does not have a partner and holds that she is less worthy as a result, she will be preoccupied with her lack of a partner and with her lack of self-esteem. When she has a partner in her life, Janet will temporarily focus on the fact that she has what she values in her life and that her self-esteem has been raised, but she will soon adjust to this new state of affairs and when she experiences a lack in some other area of her life to which she attaches her self-esteem, she will become preoccupied with this lack and with the accompanying decrease in her self-esteem. This is why conditional high self-esteem is fleeting.

3. Self-esteem involves two ratings when one will suffice

When Janet does not have a partner in her life and she holds that this makes her less worthy than when she does have a soulmate, she is in fact making two ratings or evaluations.

First, she is rating the lack of a partner in her life negatively, but then, second, she goes on to evaluate her 'self' negatively. Janet's lack of a partner is discrete enough to merit a rating and indeed, it is healthy for Janet to rate this lack negatively. For if she did not do so then she would not be motivated to do something about it. However, her rating of her entire 'self' is needless for three reasons. First, as we have seen it is empirically inconsistent with reality, since Janet is far too complex to be given a global rating. Second, it is very poor logic for Janet to conclude that not having a partner in her life means that her worth as a person is diminished. Third, Janet's conclusion that her worth as a person is diminished if she does not have a partner does not help her at all. In fact, this conclusion may well lead to greater misery in the long term for Janet. For her attitude that her worth is diminished if she does not have a partner may well lead her to try desperately to find someone to be her partner. And we all know how successful being desperate is in helping us to find a suitable long-term mate. So, when Janet does have not have a partner, she benefits from rating number one i.e. rating the lack of a partner negatively. However, she largely suffers from rating number two i.e. rating her 'self' negatively as a result.

What happens when Janet finds a soulmate and is still operating on the idea that her worth is dependent upon having a partner? Once again, she makes two evaluations. First, she wisely and healthily evaluates positively the presence of a partner in her life. This makes sense because it reflects Janet's values and preferences and it leads her to experience pleasure and satisfaction. But then, unwisely and we would argue in REBT unhealthily, she evaluates herself positively. This second evaluation is problematic even though it is positive. It is problematic for the same reasons that Janet's negative self-evaluation when she did not have a partner is problematic. First, it is inconsistent with reality. We can prove that it is good for Janet to have a partner in her life, but we cannot prove that this makes her a worthier person. Indeed, she has not changed, the only thing that has changed is her partnered status. Second, it is illogical. For Janet to conclude that the worth of her 'self' has increased because she now has a partner is as illogical as her conclusion that the worth of her 'self' is diminished when she is without a partner. Third, it does not help Janet to maintain that her worth has increased when she has a partner, precisely because this situation may change in the future. As we have already seen, her conditional attitude that she is more worthy with a partner than without one leaves her vulnerable to anxiety when she thinks that it is possible for her to lose him. It also leaves her vulnerable in other ways too. Thus, she may experience jealousy when her partner speaks to another woman because her underlying low self-esteem leads her to think that the other woman is more attractive and more interesting than her and that her partner will see this and prefer to be with the other woman. Additionally, given her underlying low self-esteem, Janet may be prepared to tolerate bad behaviour from her partner and be very reluctant to end her relationship with him. Low self-esteem is a major reason why people are prepared to tolerate abusive behaviour from partners since any relationship, however bad, is better than no relationship at all.

Unconditional Self-Acceptance: REBT's Preferred Alternative to Self-esteem

If REBT therapists do not encourage their clients to raise their self-esteem, what do they do instead? In a phrase, they encourage their clients to work towards unconditional self-acceptance. What does this involve? Let me answer this question from my own practice by outlining six steps.

First, having helped my client to see the drawbacks of self-rating, I explain what self-acceptance is. I help the client to understand that the 'self' is unrateable, complex, in flux, fallible, and unique. Accepting oneself unconditionally means acknowledging this fact. While all humans are unrateable, complex, in flux and fallible, I stress that it is the quality of uniqueness that distinguishes one human from another. This uniqueness is based on the idiosyncratic combination of many different aspects and means that an individual cannot be replicated. Even if we could clone a person, their clone will differ from the original in a variety of respects.

Second, I underline that unconditional self-acceptance encourages the person to rate different aspects of themselves and to rate their experiences, but it discourages the person from assigning a global negative rating to themselves as a whole. I stress that refraining from rating oneself is not something that one can do easily and certainly not perfectly, since self-rating comes relatively easily to human beings (Ellis, 1972). As Neenan (1997) has said, it is more realistic to help clients to achieve greater unconditional self-acceptance rather than to achieve full unconditional self-acceptance.

I go on to say to the person that rating aspects of themself is helpful because it alerts them to what they need to change in themself. In contrast, self-rating discourages the person from changing negative aspects of themself because it focuses their attention on their global negativity rather than on their specific negative aspect.

Third, I stress that unconditional self-acceptance allows the person to see themself in a very broad context. It helps the person to take a realistic view of their strengths and weaknesses. If the person adopts a self-esteem perspective, they are automatically biased when viewing these strengths and weaknesses. Thus, when they are judging their 'self' negatively (i.e. when they have low self-esteem), they are likely to see many more weaknesses than strengths. The weaknesses that they list will be very negative while any strengths that they list will be moderate or mild. Thus, the person is likely to overestimate their weaknesses and underestimate their strengths.

On the other hand, when the person is judging themself positively (i.e. when they have high self-esteem), the opposite effect is likely to occur. In other words, they are likely to list more strengths than weaknesses and the strengths that they list will be very positive while their weaknesses will this time be moderate or mild. Thus, the person is likely to overestimate their strengths and underestimate their weaknesses.

However, when the person accepts themself unconditionally they will tend to list strengths and weaknesses in equal measure and the valence of these strengths and weaknesses will be evenly distributed. This, I would venture, is the most realistic of the three outlined.

Fourth, I explain that adopting an attitude of unconditional self-acceptance increases the chances that the person will make accurate, realistic inferences about the adversities that they focus on, while, an attitude of self-esteem will lead to the formation of biased inferences.

When the person has low self-esteem (i.e. when they evaluate themself in a global negative way), they are likely to make inferences about reality that are distorted and exaggerated in a negative direction, These inferences are likely to be examples of what cognitive therapists have called cognitive distortions. For instance, the person may magnify the negative aspects of a situation and minimise its positive aspects. On the other hand, when the person has high self-esteem (i.e. when they evaluate themself in a global and positive way), their inferences are likely to be characterised by positive illusions. For instance, the person may minimise the negative aspects of a situation and maximise its positive aspects.

By contrast, when the person accepts themself, their inferences are likely to be realistic and non-distorted. They are likely to be balanced and incorporate both the positive and negative aspects of a situation. This is one reason why healthy thinking is more conducive to good mental health than positive thinking.

Fifth, I demonstrate that unconditional self-acceptance and self-esteem are likely to differentially affect the person's behaviour. Thus, when the person has low self-esteem this attitude will inhibit healthy risk-taking and promote avoidant behaviour, whereas high self-esteem will promote ill-considered risk-taking and grandiose behaviour. On the other hand, unconditional self-acceptance encourages healthy risk-taking and constructive behaviour.

Finally, I explain to my client that conditional self-esteem tends to stem from a rigid philosophy of demandingness where the person absolutistically insists that they must get what they want or that they must not get what they do not want. REBT theory posits that this philosophy is at the core of much psychological disturbance. Unconditional self-acceptance, by contrast, is deemed to stem from a flexible, preferential philosophy where the person has a clear idea of what they want and what they don't want, but where they recognise both that they do not have to get what they want and that they are not immune from getting what they don't want and neither do they have to have such immunity. REBT theory holds that this flexible, preferential philosophy lies at the core of psychological health.

Thus, if a person believes that they must succeed in business, then they are likely to think poorly of themself if they don't do well (which is the low self-esteem position) and they are likely to think well of themself if they do do well. Consequently, they will tend to live a kind of yo-yo existence where their worth and their emotions will go up and down depending on the conditions that currently exist in their life.

However, if the person wants to do well in business but does not believe that they must do so, then they will tend to accept themself unconditionally whether they do well or they do poorly in this area of their life. This flexible, preferential philosophy will enable them to feel good about their success on the one hand, and bad about their failure on the other, but it will stop their worth as a person from rising or falling accordingly.

At this point, you may be wondering what is wrong with high self-esteem since it has positive benefits. While this is the case, it is important to distinguish between positive benefits and healthy benefits, on the one hand and short-term benefits and long-term benefits, on the other.

First, the positive benefits of high self-esteem may not be healthy. I stressed that high self-esteem leads a person to overestimate their strengths and underestimate their weaknesses. While this may help to generate positive feelings, it gives the person a false picture of themself and they may think that they may be doing better in life than they actually are. Thus, they may be unprepared when they confront grim reality on this point. Also, high self-esteem doesn't help them to focus on their weaknesses and to improve those aspects of themself that need improving.

The above benefits are also short term in nature and tend not to endure. Thus, you cannot have high self-esteem without being vulnerable to low self-esteem since they are opposite sides of the same attitude coin. Thus, if you think that you are worthy because you have a partner (the high self-esteem position), you will also think that you are less worthy if you are without a partner (the low self-esteem position). So, if your client wants the benefits of high self-esteem, they will also have to accept the costs of low self-esteem. There is, however, one way in which a person can have high self-esteem and not suffer and it is to this point that I now turn.

Unconditional Positive Self-Esteem: The Other Alternative

Unconditional self-acceptance is the preferred REBT alternative to conditional self-esteem because it discourages the person from rating himself and because it advocates that when the person accepts themself they do so unconditionally, i.e. the person is advised to accept themself no matter what. However, some clients want to rate themselves. If I am not able to dissuade them from doing so, I will implement REBT's other alternative to conditional self-esteem. This is known as unconditional positive self-esteem and involves the person considering themself to be worthwhile and to base their worth on conditions that do not change. These conditions are that they are a fallible human being, that they are unique and that they are alive. As can be seen the person will always be fallible, always be unique and will remain alive until they die. So, a person who believes: 'I am worthwhile because I am human, unique and alive', will not get into trouble emotionally. This shows that the real problem with conditional self-esteem is its conditionality as when a person believes, for example, that they are worthwhile *as long as* they are successful.

However, as Ellis (1972) has said in his seminal article on self-acceptance, unconditional positive self-esteem is problematic because it cannot be proven. Thus, a person could hold the attitude: 'I am worthless because I am human, unique and alive' and this attitude is equally unprovable. Whereas unconditional self-acceptance, with its emphasis on the acknowledgment of who we are rather than on the evaluation of who we are is amenable to proof. It is for this reason that most REBT therapists prefer the unconditional self-acceptance solution to the unconditional positive self-esteem solution, but will accept the latter when for one reason or another the client is not prepared to implement unconditional self-acceptance.

The Importance of *Teaching* Unconditional Self-Acceptance

REBT therapists adopt an educational approach to helping clients to develop unconditional self-acceptance. We believe that we can teach clients both the principles that form the philosophy of unconditional self-acceptance and a variety of techniques that can be used by them to deepen their conviction in this philosophy between sessions. This educational emphasis is in direct contrast to the approach adopted by person centred therapists, for example, who hold that the client can develop an attitude of unconditional positive regard if they experience the therapist's unconditional positive regard for them.

The main difference between the REBT position and the person centred position here concerns the importance of the educational phase. This phase plays little or no role in person centred practice where the focus is predominantly on the quality of the relationship between client and therapist. Here, during the therapeutic process the client learns that their therapist respects them unconditionally and begins to learn as a result that they are a person worthy of regard. As Patterson (1974) has shown, once the client learns to regard themself unconditionally, they can learn to regard others in the same way and more importantly demonstrate this attitude to others. Once these others have experienced the client's regard for them, they can reciprocate in kind and the whole tone of the client's relationships with others begins to be characterised by mutual regard and this helps to sustain the client's regard for themself.

I have several reservations with this position. First, the client's regard for themself tends to be conditional upon their experiencing the therapist's regard for them. They do not learn that they can accept themself even if the therapist does not have regard for them.

Second, I question whether the developing attitude of mutual regard between the client and their significant others, facilitated as it were by the client's own self-regard, occurs as frequently as Patterson claims. Thus, it is more than possible that in some cases, the client's attempts to show others respect will be exploited by other people for their own selfish ends. How many times have you heard clients complain that their good treatment of others has not been reciprocated or has been used against them?

This leads me to my third criticism of the person centred position: namely, that it does not help clients specifically enough to accept themselves unconditionally in the face of rejection and betrayal from others. Finally, even if the scenario put forward by Patterson does occur, can this effect be attributed to the client's experience of the therapist's regard for them? This has not been demonstrated.

REBT does not deny the importance of the therapist's acceptance of the client in the therapeutic process, but it argues that the long-term therapeutic potency of REBT unconditional self-acceptance therapy lies in the client understanding the principles of unconditional self-acceptance and putting this philosophy into practice many times in their own life. Unless the therapist teaches the client these principles and the fact that repeated practice of them is crucial, then the client may neither learn the principles of unconditional self-acceptance nor put them into practice on their own accord.

In REBT, we also argue that when the client experiences the therapist's acceptance this leads them to feel better, but on its own it does not lead them to get better, by which I mean developing a solid unconditionally self-accepting attitude that the person can sustain when the going gets tough. On the other hand, when the client commits themself to practising the principles of unconditional self-acceptance in their life and does so repeatedly over time, this practice helps them both to feel better and to get better. This proposition does, however, await empirical enquiry which in turn depends on the development of an adequate measure of unconditional self-acceptance.

In this talk, I have explained why REBT therapists do not try to help clients raise their self-esteem. Instead, we try to encourage them to develop and practise an attitude of unconditional self-acceptance. I appreciate that this is a contentious issue and that many of you may disagree with me. If you do agree with me, then that would be bad, but I will continue to accept myself unconditionally as a unique, unrateable, complex, fluid, fallible human being.

9

Influence Your Clients
for Their Health's Sake

A Rational Emotive Behavioural Perspective

I delivered this lecture at a conference entitled 'Power and Influence in Psychotherapy' on 15 November 1997. The conference, which was held at the University of London School for Oriental and African Studies (SOAS), was organised by the Universities Psychotherapy Association (UPA). This lecture marks the first occasion that I ever asked to speak at a conference having seen the original panel of speakers and lecture titles. I took this unusual step because I thought that it was important that the views of a cognitive behaviour therapist were represented at such an important conference.

There are many ways of viewing the role that psychotherapists adopt in the endeavour known as psychotherapy. Thus, therapists have been seen as facilitators of their clients' personal development (Mearns & Thorne, 1988), as friends from whom their clients purchase friendship (Schofield, 1964), as co-voyagers on a spiritual journey, as confessors who receive their clients 'shameful' revelations or as blank screens on whom patients (this time) project their unresolved transferences and with whom they act out their unresolved conflicts. While some of you may object to each of these roles, it is likely that these ways of conceptualising the role of the psychotherapist are likely to be viewed far more favourably than the roles that I will discuss in this paper. The roles that I will be discussing here today are that of the psychotherapist as an influencer and a teacher.

The idea that the major role of the therapist is to influence the client is unpopular for two major reasons. First, influence conjures up notions of brainwashing and cults where unscrupulous therapists influence clients for their own benefit rather than for the clients' benefit and do so in a way that encourages and, in some notable examples, forces clients to suspend their critical faculties so that they go along with the therapist's views just because they are the therapists' views. Therapists who influence their clients in this way, and fortunately such unscrupulous practitioners are in the minority, often suffer from a sense of inadequacy and need to have devoted disciples to feel powerful and gain a sense of importance. They are often dogmatists and believe that they have *the* truth and others have to go along with them to sustain their fragile egos. When such practitioners come to light they give influence a very bad press and other more ethical therapists tend to view all attempts to influence clients as malevolent. I will argue in this paper that this view is misguided and will put forward the view that influence, far from being a dirty word, is therapeutic when it is done ethically with due regard for a client's autonomy.

The second reason why influence is viewed negatively by therapists is that it threatens the self-image of therapists who would prefer to see themselves as benign facilitators whose major task is to provide a certain set of therapeutic conditions whose presence allows the healthy part of the client to flower and blossom. You will, of course, recognise the views of Carl Rogers (1957) and person centred therapists from this description. The idea that therapists should deliberately influence their clients rather than establish and maintain a therapeutic climate does not 'feel right' to many therapists who prefer to see themselves as companions on their clients' journey towards self-actualisation. An interesting paper published in the mid-1960s showed, however, that even Rogers was subtly influencing his clients by the differential use of minimal encouragers to talk. Rogers was shown to say 'mm-hmm' when his clients engaged in a certain type of talk and withheld the same when they engaged in another type of talk. The effect was that his clients more often engaged in the reinforced type of talk than in the non-reinforced type (Truax, 1966). I am sure that Rogers was unaware of this form of influence and therein lies the danger. It is my view that unaware attempts to influence clients are more abusive than explicit attempts. In the latter, therapists are open about what they are trying to do and elicit their clients' informed consent to be so influenced. If such consent is not obtained ethical therapists abandon their attempts to influence their clients and talk openly with them about alternative ways forward.

What I will do in the remainder of this paper is to discuss how I explicitly and openly attempt to influence my clients to adopt a perspective on emotional problem-solving and how I do this in a way which safeguards their autonomy. Before I do so, I wish to point out that there is an impressive body of literature that demonstrates that when therapy is effective, clients adopt their therapists' values and when it is not effective, clients fail to adopt these values. This effect has been termed 'value conversion' by Tjeltveit (1986) in an important review paper which repays careful reading.

In short, whether we like it or not, and whether we admit to it or not, as therapists we do influence our clients. Given this fact, my point is let us do so as explicitly and ethically as possible. If we adopt the safeguards that I will discuss in this paper we will be using our power is a non-abusive way.

Pre-Influence Considerations: Teaching the REBT Framework and Outlining Client and Therapist Tasks

One of the reasons why therapists influencing clients is a matter of concern is because of the ethical issues that such influence raises. My view is that the influence that I strive to exert over my client is ethical for two main reasons. First, this influence is in my client's interests and not in mine. If I succeed in influencing my client to apply in their life the principles and techniques of Rational Emotive Behaviour Therapy – which is the approach to therapy that I practise – then, I hypothesise, *they* will benefit. The only way *I* will benefit (apart from receiving a professional fee) is in the satisfaction of helping the client live a more fulfilled life.

Second, my influence is ethical because I explain to the client exactly in which ways I will be trying to influence them and I will only attempt to influence them in these ways when they give their informed consent for me to do so. As the 'Code of Conduct, Ethical Principles and Guidelines' of the British Psychological Society states: 'Psychologists shall normally carry out.... interventions only with the valid consent of participants, having taken all steps to ensure that they have adequately understood the nature of the intervention and its anticipated consequences' (BPS, 1997, p.2).

In this section, I will discuss how I explain to prospective clients how REBT conceptualises client problems and, broadly speaking, what tasks REBT expects the client and the therapist to carry out over the course of therapy. I want to stress at the outset that when the therapist gives such explanations, they do so while keeping very much in mind the ability of the client to understand these explanations and with due respect to the appropriate timing of these explanations. It is not then the case that a person comes in for the first time and I bombard them with a lot of explanatory information. Rather, I ask what the person is seeking help for and respond therapeutically to what they have to say. In doing so, I look for suitable opportunities to explain about REBT and associated client/therapist tasks, but I want to reiterate that this is done within the context of this therapeutic response.

Teaching the REBT Framework

As I have just mentioned, I am a practitioner of Rational Emotive Behaviour Therapy. As such, my initial task is to explain to people who seek my help how I am likely to conceptualise their problems. There are various ways that I do this. Thus, I may ask the person to give me a specific example of one of their problems and explain to them what factors I think are important to consider in understanding their problem. In particular, I will show the person the role that rigid and non-extreme attitudes play in their problem. Second, I may take a general example of the client's psychological problems and again explain to the person my view that at the core of this problem lie one or more rigid and non-extreme attitudes that account for the existence of this general problem. Finally, I may choose to teach the person a general model of psychological disturbance in which rigid and non-extreme attitudes are deemed to play a central, determining role. Whichever teaching method I use, I am careful to point out to the person that my way of conceptualising problems is but one of many that exist in the psychotherapeutic domain and if my approach does not make sense to them then I am happy to refer the person to a therapist whose view is congruent with the person's views.

To take a stark example, many years ago I was consulted by a man who rang me and asked me if I practised RT. Now REBT was known at its inception as Rational Therapy or RT and although I found it a little odd that the person was referring to REBT by its previous initials I thought no more about it. When I met the person I outlined the REBT model of psychological disturbance to which my client reacted with incredulity and remarked that he thought I practised Reichian Therapy or RT. I did not attempt to persuade this client to my way of thinking, even though I am personally highly sceptical of Reichian Therapy. Rather, I referred him to a local practitioner of this approach to psychotherapy.

This episode raises the following important and interesting

question: When does a person who seeks your help become your client? For me, the answer is when the person understands my therapeutic approach, understands what this approach will, in broad terms, require of us both and, based on this understanding gives their informed consent to proceed. Until the person has given such consent, they are best regarded as an applicant rather than as a client. After the person has given such consent they become a client.

Like other approaches to psychotherapy, REBT has a decided perspective on psychological disturbance and health. REBT's view of psychological disturbance is that at its core lie the following set of rigid and extreme attitudes:

1. Rigid attitudes (holding that one must get what one wants or must not get what one doesn't want);

2. Awfulising attitudes (holding that it is the end of the world if certain adversities occur and that nothing could be worse);

3. Unbearability attitudes (holding that one cannot bear adversities which are difficult to bear); and

4. Devaluation attitudes towards self, others and the world (holding that oneself, others and the world can be legitimately given a single negative evaluation and rating oneself, others and the world negatively when one's demands on self, others and the world are not met).

On the other hand, REBT argues that at the core of psychological health lie the following alternative flexible and non-extreme attitudes:

1. Flexible attitudes (holding that while it is desirable to get what one wants and not to get what one does not want, neither of these states is essential);

2. Non-awfulising attitudes (holding that it is bad if certain adversities occur, but it is not the end of the world if they do. Things could always be worse;

3. Bearability attitudes (holding that while it is a struggle to bear certain adversities, one can bear them, they are worth bearing (if they are), one is willing to bear them and one is going to bear them);

4. Unconditional attitudes towards self, others and the world (holding that oneself, others and the world cannot be legitimately given a single negative rating and acknowledging that when one's desires are not met, oneself and others are unique, complex ever-changing individuals with a mixture of positive, negative and neutral aspects and that the world is a complex place in which one sometimes has one's desires met, but not inevitably so).

After I have outlined this perspective and check with my client that they have understood the differences between these two sets of attitudes, I ask them the following question:

> *'Which of these two sets of attitudes would you teach your children and why?'*

Almost invariably, clients respond that they would teach their children the set of flexible and non-extreme attitudes because these attitudes are much healthier than the set of rigid and extreme attitudes. I then ask my client another important question:

> *'Which set of attitudes would you like me to help you acquire and why?'*

Once the person indicates that they wants me to help them acquire the set of flexible and non-extreme attitudes because these attitudes would help them to overcome their psychological problems and be healthier for them, then I have gained their informed consent on this issue to proceed to influence them to acquire these attitudes.

Outlining Client and Therapist Tasks

I then give the person an outline of the tasks that both they and I are likely to carry out in REBT. In his tri-partite reformulation of the psychoanalytic concept of the working alliance, Bordin (1979) argued that 'tasks' was one of the three components of the alliance and that effective therapy is characterised by therapist and client understanding their own and the other's tasks and agreeing to carry out their respective tasks. In addition, engaging in these tasks should lead the client to achieve their goals and they should clearly see the link between carrying out these tasks and achieving their goals. I explain to the person that as an REBT therapist I have the following tasks:

1. I will initially focus on the client's problems one at a time and help them to identify the rigid and extreme attitudes that lie at the core of their problems.

2. I will then help the client do two things: (a) examine their rigid and extreme attitudes and understand why they are false, illogical and unhelpful and (b) examine their flexible and non-extreme attitudes and understand why they are true, sensible and helpful.

3. I will follow this up by suggesting various tasks that the client can undertake to strengthen their conviction in their flexible and non-extreme attitudes and weaken their conviction in their rigid and extreme attitudes.

4. I will help the client to identify, examine and change their core rigid and extreme attitudes (defined as rigid and extreme attitudes that the client holds in a large number of problematic situations) and acquire and strengthen a set of alternative core flexible and non-extreme attitudes.

5. Throughout this process I will help my client to voice ther doubts, reservations and objections about the process of REBT and disclose obstacles to carrying out their tasks and I will deal with these as appropriate.

6. Finally, I will teach my client a number of other cognitive-behavioural techniques relevant to their situation which they can use to prevent relapse and to maintain, broaden and enhance their therapy-derived gains.

I also explain that if the person becomes a client of mine then it is likely that they will be asked to do the following:

1. At the beginning, discuss specific examples of their problems and help me to assess them using the ABC framework of REBT.

2. Learn to assess their problems using this ABC framework.

3. Join me in examining their rigid and extreme attitudes and their flexible and non-extreme attitude alternatives.

4. Learn how to examine these attitudes for themself.

5. Learn and practise a variety of techniques designed to help them to weaken their conviction in their rigid and extreme attitudes and strengthen their conviction in their flexible and non-extreme attitudes.

6. Generalise their gains by acting in a way that is consistent with their core flexible and non-extreme attitudes.

7. Voice their doubts, reservations and convictions concerning the process of REBT and discuss their obstacles to carrying out their tasks.

In conclusion, a person becomes my client when three conditions, related to the content of REBT are met. These conditions are:

1. The person understands REBT's perspective on psychological disturbance and agrees that they wish to acquire flexible and non-extreme attitudes.

2. The person understands, in broad terms, the tasks that REBT expects of them and agrees to carry out these tasks.

3. The person understands, in broad terms, the tasks that REBT expects of their therapist and agrees to proceed in therapy in the knowledge that the therapist will carry out these tasks.

Influence Compromises in the Process of REBT

My experience is that if I have explained to the client at the outset how REBT is likely to conceptualise their problems and what our respective tasks are, then REBT proceeds more smoothly than if I have not given my client such explanations.

As therapy proceeds, my influence attempts are as outlined in the tasks that I have as an REBT therapist. To reiterate, I attempt to influence my client by having them use REBT's ABC assessment framework, by challenging their rigid and extreme attitudes and encouraging them to adopt and act in ways that are consistent with their flexible and non-extreme attitudes. In short, all my influence attempts are to get my client to adopt and apply REBT to their own life.

Throughout this process and at every opportunity, I make explicit the basis for my interventions and elicit my client's cooperation. When this is not forthcoming, I am willing to make a number of compromises in my attempts to influence the client. Thus, negotiation between client and therapist in REBT occurs not only at its outset, but throughout the entire process. Let me now consider one important area of compromise (see also Chapters 8 and 30).

REBT theory argues that self-rating is problematic and is at the root of self-esteem problems, particularly when it is conditional (e.g. 'I am worthwhile if I do well'. According to REBT theory, the healthiest alternative to conditional self-rating is unconditional self-acceptance because this position does not involve self-rating at all. Another 'less elegant', but still acceptable alternative to conditional self-rating is unconditional positive self-rating where the person rates themself as worthwhile, for example, but does so unconditionally. In effect, they are saying, 'I am worthwhile because I am human, alive and unique'.

My practice is to outline the principles of unconditional self-acceptance and unconditional positive self-esteem to my client, stressing as I do so the advantages and possible disadvantages of each concept. But what if the client, having listened to and understood my explanations, still wants to operate according to the position of conditional self-esteem and consider their worth to vary according to their achievement, for example. How would I respond? My own practice is to reiterate the disadvantages of this position and the advantages of the other two positions, but I would respect my client's decision to adopt a solution that according to REBT theory still leaves them vulnerable. I would work within the client's paradigm and help them to be as healthy as I could within a potentially unhealthy paradigm.

I would compromise the REBT position here for three reasons, (i) to do otherwise would threaten the working alliance; (ii) while I might check from time to time whether the client would be willing to change their mind on this issue and adopt one of the other two healthier positions, to disregard the client's view and continue to persuade the client to adopt a position that they clearly does not wish to adopt is an abuse of power and of one's position as a benevolent influencer and (iii) the compromise does not pose a serious mental health risk for the client. If the compromise did pose a serious risk for the client and the client would not shift their position, I would stop working with the client and effect a suitable referral (normally psychiatric). I should add that this is a rare occurrence and is a last resort.

Other compromises are less controversial and usually concern how ambitious the client is prepared to be in carrying out homework assignments. I may suggest, for example, that a client carry out a particular assignment three times a day, but they may initially agree to do so once a day. Rather than immediately accede to the client's wishes, I would explain why I was asking more from them and suggest a compromise where they would carry out the task twice a day. As my mother used to say, 'If you don't ask, you don't get.' However, if you ask for a compromise and you don't get it, don't threaten the working alliance: go along with your client.

Let me review my position at this point. As an REBT therapist, I have a clear idea of what would be helpful to the client. I will explain this position and review its advantages and possible disadvantages. I will not impose the REBT preferred position on the client and will frequently make compromises with this position with clients who do not wish to adopt the REBT view. In making such compromises, I will still check from time to time to see if the client is prepared to change their mind on this issue, but again I wish to stress that I would not unilaterally impose my position on the client. If the client wishes to adhere to an attitude that is harmful for them, then I will be quite clear why I consider this to be the case and will reserve my right to discharge the client if the worst comes to the worst. I should add that this latter scenario has not yet happened to me in twenty-two years practice, but if it did, I would endeavour to place the client in an alternative treatment facility.

Some Dangers of Using Influence in REBT

If therapist influence in REBT has the potential for helping clients it also has the potential for harming them. In this section I will consider briefly the potential hazards of such influence. Unfortunately, unscrupulous therapists exist in all orientations and in the hands of an unscrupulous REBT practitioner, therapist influence can cause a lot of damage. Thus, an REBT therapist who seeks to be the powerful head of a cult may encourage their clients and disciples to use REBT mindlessly and dogmatically for the ego aggrandising effects that having a devoted, but suggestible following may bring. Although REBT discourages clients from uncritically and mindlessly accepting the word of an authority, just because that person is an authority even an authority on REBT, some of its practitioners who seek an adoring following may flout this important principle and create an oppressive environment where questioning or challenging the views of the therapist is not allowed.

Aside from this scenario, therapist influence in REBT may be harmful when the therapist holds a number of rigid and extreme attitudes that may lead to the dogmatic practice of REBT. Thus, a therapist who holds an attitude that they must be right may influence the client to adopt a view which is incorrect, but one which the therapist thinks is correct. Thus, the therapist may opine that the client holds a rigid and extreme attitude about achievement which the client may not, in fact, have. Holding that they must be right, the therapist may foist this view onto the client and brook no opposition. The client is in fact persuaded to accept an invalid position and learns that they have to accept the therapist's view just because it is the therapist's view. This state of affairs is not only potentially harmful, it can also be said to be abusive. What is lacking here is therapist humility where the therapist considers their views to be hypotheses about reality which need to be tested against reality and confirmed or disconfirmed by the client instead of pearls of truthful wisdom handed down by the infallible oracle.

A second harmful example of therapist influence occurs when the therapist believes that their self-worth depends on the client making progress in therapy. This may result in the therapist persuading the client to admit that they are making more progress than they actually are. Thus, the therapist may induce the client to claim that they hold flexible and non-extreme attitudes which they do not actually hold. The therapist may also influence the client to withhold their doubts, reservations and objections about REBT and to conceal their problems from the therapist because they intuit that the therapist is threatened by the reality of their continuing problems. To ensure that the client is not influenced by what may be called pernicious REBT, the therapist needs to challenge and change the idea they MUST help the client make progress and that they are an inadequate person if they don't.

Finally, I want to discuss the issue where a client is harmed because the therapist fails to influence them when it is healthy and in the client's long-term interests to be influenced. When an REBT therapist fails to appropriately influence the client, it is frequently due to the therapist's attitude that they need the client's approval. Thus, rather than run the risk of examining the client's rigid and extreme attitudes because doing so may temporarily discomfort the client, the approval-needing REBT therapist backs off from examining the client's attitudes. The result is that the client may feel better and think that the therapist is kind and caring, but may get worse (or at least will make no real progress) because they have not examined and changed their rigid and extreme attitudes which remain firmly in place.

An REBT therapist who, conversely, does not believe that they must have her client's approval does not back off from examining the client's rigid and extreme attitudes and does not shy away from debating with the client whether such ideas are true or false, logical or illogical and healthy or unhealthy even though the client may be discomfited during this debate and may consider the therapist temporarily harsh and uncaring. Effective REBT therapists do not see therapy as a popularity contest; rather we recognise that it is, at times, an uncomfortable experience for the client, but gain often does not come without pain and we continue to influence the client even when the going gets rough. Needless to say, effective REBT therapists carefully monitor the strength of the working alliance and may back off from influencing the client if doing so will threaten this alliance to the point of rupture. In short, effective REBT therapists are more concerned with how effective they are being than how positively they are thought of by their clients.

Conclusion

In conclusion, let me state that I regard the effective practice of REBT as ethical persuasion. It is persuasive in that I am attempting to persuade the client to adopt a healthy philosophy towards themselves, other people and the world. It is ethical in that I am completely open about what I am trying to do and why I am trying to do it and in that I elicit my client's informed consent to be persuaded before initiating the persuasive process. It is also ethical because I am prepared to compromise on my preferred REBT strategy and will work, with very few exceptions, to help my client become as healthy as they possibly can be within their paradigm when this is different from my preferred paradigm.

Let me close on a personal note. I sought individual therapy in my mid-twenties for a low-grade depression. For various practical reasons I saw three different therapists over an eighteen-month period, but derived little help from these therapists, all of whom were very experienced practitioners of their art. Not one of them explained to me how they practised therapy nor invited me to give my informed consent to proceed. If they had, I would have probably decided not to work with them because, as I figured out later, their ideas about what was effective in therapy were very different from mine and there was little scope for a useful rapprochement. I am not sure whether they thought that explaining how they worked would deleteriously affect the work that they did with me or whether it was a case that they thought that they knew best and my place was to go along with them because they saw themselves as experts. The point is that I didn't know what and how they practised and that is the problem.

Some of the people who consult me may think that REBT is nonsense or worse, dangerous. But the point is that they know what its basics are before they commit themselves to becoming clients. The fact that my therapists told me nothing about their practice meant in effect that they were attempting to influence me with their interpretations and other procedures in the absence of my informed agreement to be influenced. This, I put it to you, is the real danger of influence in psychotherapy.

10

Why Self-Help Books Don't Work

*I gave this talk on 18 November 1997 at the Eastbourne branch of Waterstone's bookshop to commemorate the publication of my latest self-help book (*Overcoming Shame, *Sheldon Press, 1997). It represents another mark of my affection for Eastbourne. As you will see when you read the chapter, the seeming contradiction between the title of the lecture and the public relations nature of the occasion is not as stark as the title of the talk suggests.*

You may think it peculiar that I am addressing you tonight on the subject of why self-help books don't work when I am celebrating the publication of my latest self-help book. Is this a cheap publicity stunt? Have I just made the terrible realisation that I have wasted my time writing about a dozen self-help books and am about to atone for my errors. Or have I just gone mad?

I can assure you that that this is not a cheap publicity stunt and I am, as far as I can judge, in the pink psychologically. And yes, I *do* still think that self-help books are valuable aids to mental health. So why do I say that self-help books don't work? Indeed, precisely what do I mean when I say that they don't work?

Recently, I suggested to one of my clients that they read my self-help book entitled *Ten Steps to Positive Living* (Dryden, 1994b). This book is a general text, based on the approach to counselling that I practise known as Rational Emotive Behaviour Therapy, and outlines the REBT view that people have psychological problems because of the rigid and extreme attitudes that they hold towards events. It also explains how people can identify, examine and change these attitudes so that they can live more fulfilled lives.

At their next counselling session, my client said to me: 'I've read your self-help book, but it doesn't work'. The way that this person phrased their remark gave me food for thought and the following dialogue ensued.

Windy: What do you mean by it didn't work?

Client: Well, I read what you had to say and it made perfect sense, but I didn't feel differently after I finished it.

Windy: But did you do any of the exercises that I suggested in the book?

Client: Well, I had a go at one or two, but they didn't help much.

Windy: How much time did you devote to the exercises?

Client: Oh, about a couple of minutes.

Windy: So, let me get this straight. You read my book and it made sense to you and you spent a couple of minutes doing the exercises that I suggested in the book, but that at the end of all this you didn't feel any better. Is that right?

Client: That's exactly so.

Effectively, what this client was expecting was to read my book and to feel better immediately with the very minimum of effort. They were demonstrating elements of two major ideas which almost guarantee that the person who holds these ideas will derive little lasting benefit from self-help books and the exercises that they recommend. These ideas are:

1.   All I need to do to benefit from a self-help book is to read it.

2.   I can derive benefit from any self-help exercise that the author suggests with a minimum of effort.

While many people when confronted with these ideas will deny that they hold them, nevertheless they act on these ideas. So effectively, they actually hold these ideas. Let me take a closer look at these ideas.

Reading Self-Help Books Is Sufficient to Effect Change

Occasionally, I come across people who have a large number of self-help books in their library. This is particularly the case with books that purport to help you lose weight. The idea such people seem to have and act on is that all you have to do to effect personal change is to read what an expert has to say about change. This is rarely, if ever, the case. Passively reading a self-help book will only give you cognitive insight into the nature of the problem being written about and the way the author suggests that you need to approach this problem in order to overcome it.

Now, I am not knocking passive reading or the insight it generates. You need to read a self-help book to judge whether or not what the author has to say about the problem and how to tackle it makes sense to you. If it does not, then by all means cast the book aside. However, if it does make sense to you, then it is important for you to fully appreciate that the insight you have gained is necessary for you to take the next step, but is insufficient for you to effect the desired change.

Half-Hearted Action Is Sufficient to Effect Change

Not everyone believes that all you need to do to effect change is to passively read a self-help book. Indeed, most people when asked, will say that change involves putting a set of procedures into practice. However, people who try a set of procedures that they have read about in a self-help book and quickly conclude that these procedures do not work are usually acting on the idea that half-hearted action is sufficient to effect change. Again, I want to stress that these people will often deny that they hold such an idea. Indeed, they may claim that they know that half-hearted action will not produce lasting change. Nevertheless, and this is the important point, they act as if they believe it.

Half-hearted action again rarely, if ever, produces a meaningful, lasting change. The reason for this is that change involves repeatedly going against ingrained habits and habitual ways of thinking and doing so means that the person will think and act in ways that are foreign to the person. In other words, change involves making a decision to commit yourself to taking repeated measures which are difficult and uncomfortable to take. Is it any wonder, then, that half-hearted attempts to change will bear no fruit?

Self-Help Books and the Search for Magic

When my client, who I discussed above, claimed that my self-help book didn't work, although they agreed with my approach and the measures that I suggested in it, they were operating as if they had conviction in magic. They did not realise this and would deny it if I put this to them, but nevertheless this is what their statement amounts to. For the idea that passively reading a book and taking half-hearted action on the principles outlined in that book will lead to long-lasting personal change is just this, a conviction in magic.

Let me put it this way. Let's suppose that you have a personal problem that you want to address and you attend a convention where several people are talking about their approach to personal change. At one stand, one of the speakers is advocating an approach to change which is quick, easy, comfortable and involves little or no effort on your part. All you have to do is to listen to a set of audio-recordings twice a day for two weeks and your problem will be solved. I am on another stand saying that change is a difficult, lengthy process and involves bearing discomfort and making a sustained effort. Which of these two approaches to personal change would you be drawn to? My guess is that in your head you would know that my approach was probably the right one, but in your heart of hearts you would hope that the other speaker was right. You might even buy a set of the recordings that the speaker was peddling – just in case.

It is this 'just in case' type of thinking, this clinging on to the slight hope that after all there just might be a quick, painless and easy way to change that is so seductive and so powerful here. It is magical in nature, of course, and thus in all probability untrue, but you never know... The 'just in case, you never know' idea is one of the reasons why people keep buying self-help books, in the hope that this latest book will lead them to the holy grail.

The trouble is that sometimes reading a self-help book can lead to a dramatic change. For example, on reading a self-help book you may clearly understand something that you have been puzzled about for a long time or you may try a technique that really seems to help. However, such dramatic change does not last without the sustained work necessary to maintain it.

The Nature of Personal Change

Let me now outline how I conceive of the process of personal change.

Step 1 Acknowledge that you are largely (but not completely) responsible for your emotional destiny

This is one of the hardest steps for people to grasp and fully implement. We are far more used to blaming our feelings on other people (e.g. 'You made me so angry') or on situations ('Not getting job the really depressed me') than we are to acknowledging that it is the way that we think about events that largely determines how we feel and act.

There are two other reasons why we are reluctant to accept responsibility for how we feel. First, we may think that doing so means that the way people treat us and the situations that we face are irrelevant to how we feel. This is certainly not true. Just because the way we think about events determines the way we feel more than the events themselves, it does not mean that these events are unimportant. My colleague Paul Hauck put this well when he said that how we are treated by others and the situations we encounter account for up to 49% of how we feel and act towards these events. We are thus responsible for the other 51% and above.

The second reason why we eschew responsibility for our feelings is that we may blame ourselves for the important part that we play in creating our own psychological problems. If taking responsibility means blaming ourselves, then faced with doing this or blaming others or situations it makes sense to do the latter. However, taking responsibility does not mean that we have to blame ourselves. Responsibility means saying: 'I did it and that was bad, but I'm not a bad person. I'm a fallible human being who did the wrong thing. What can I learn from this?' Blame, on the other hand, means saying: 'I did it and that was bad, and I am a bad person for acting in the way that I did'. This shows that accepting responsibility does not have to involve self-blame.

In summary, this first step in the change process is perhaps the most important step of all. It involves you acknowledging that you create, to a large degree, your own psychological disturbances and that while environmental conditions contribute to your emotional problems, they are in general of secondary consideration in the change process.

Step 2 Acknowledge that you have the ability to solve your emotional problems

This second step is important because if you do not think that you have the capability to solve your emotional problems, then you will not make the necessary effort to change. This lack of effort will, in turn, not produce the changes that you would ideally like to make, which is, of course, a self-fulfilling prophecy.

The main way to tackle obstacles to step 2 involves doing two things. First, you need to ferret out the precise reasons why you think that you are not capable of changing. For example, do you think you are too old to change or too set in your ways? Do you think that are too disturbed to change or come from too dysfunctional a background to be able to help yourself? The real change-blocker in all these views is the word '*too*'. Yes, you may be advanced in years and you may be set in your ways, but this doesn't have to pose an insuperable obstacle to solving your emotional problems given the right tools and the commitment to use them. But, add the word 'too' and you won't try to change and as a result you won't change. So, watch out for the word 'too' when it comes to step 2 and realise that it is just not true. The factors to which you attach the word 'too' may explain why you may find making a personal change difficult, but they do not, in general, explain why such change is impossible to achieve. Add the word 'too' and you make it impossible.

The second thing that you need to do is test out your idea that you are too old to change, for example. Set yourself a realistic target and work towards achieving it, but do so without constantly reminding yourself that you are too old to change. Keep an open mind about this point or even repeat to yourself that you are *not* too old to change. I know of cases where people in their nineties have made a significant personal change. If they can do this, you may be able to do so too.

Step 3 Understand that emotional and behavioural problems stem largely from rigid and extreme attitudes

All approaches to counselling and psychotherapy have their theories about what determines our emotional and behavioural problems. The approach to counselling that I practise holds that what largely determine these problems are the rigid and extreme attitudes that we hold towards important events in our lives. Thus, from my perspective the third step to personal change involves you acknowledging the important role that your attitudes play in determining and perpetuating your psychological problems.

Step 4 Analyse specific examples of your problems and identify the specific rigid and extreme attitudes that underpin these problems

The fourth step to personal change emphasises the importance of being as specific as possible at the beginning of the change process.

The reason for choosing specific examples of your problems to analyse is that these examples yield reliable information of what you actually felt in specific problem situations, what you did in these situations and most importantly what attitudes you held in these situations. There will be ample opportunity for you to generalise later, but at this point of the change process, the more specific you can be the better.

Step 5 Understand what are the healthy alternatives to your rigid and extreme attitudes

Before you examine the rigid and extreme attitudes you hold in problem situations, it is important to appreciate that there are viable healthy alternatives to these attitudes. In all my self-help books I argue that flexible and non-extreme attitudes are constructive alternatives to rigid and extreme attitudes.

Step 6 Examine your rigid and extreme attitudes and acknowledge that they are false, illogical and unhelpful

The best first step to take in undermining your rigid and extreme attitudes is to examine them. Ask yourself whether they are true, sensible in the circumstances and, most importantly, whether they help you or hinder you in your quest for mental health and happiness. In my self-help books I give precise instructions concerning how to do this and I show why such attitudes are in general false, illogical and largely unproductive.

Step 7 Acknowledge that your flexible and non-extreme attitudes are true, sensible and helpful

It is not sufficient to examine your rigid and extreme attitudes, you also have to examine the constructive alternatives to these attitudes in the same way. In the vast majority of cases you will acknowledge that your flexible and non-extreme attitudes are true, sensible and conducive to your mental well-being.

Step 8 Act on your new flexible and non-extreme attitudes

While challenging your rigid and extreme attitudes cognitively is an important first step to changing them, unless you act in ways that are inconsistent with such attitudes and in ways that are consistent with their constructive alternatives, you will not, in fact, change your rigid and extreme attitudes. Thus, action is a crucial ingredient in facilitating personal change.

Step 9 Keep examining your rigid and extreme attitudes and acting on your new flexible and non-extreme attitudes until you disbelieve the former and believe the latter

As I have stressed throughout this talk, the keys to personal change that is not fleeting are effort, repetition and persistence. Thus, it is important for you to examine your rigid and extreme attitudes in thought and in deed repeatedly, persistently and with force and energy, and unless you do so, any change in attitude will be short lived.

Step 10 Apply the above self-change sequence across the board

You can not only use the sequence of self-help steps that I have outlined so far in situations where you actually experience problems, you can use it as a general method of facilitating change. Thus, if you have worked on overcoming a specific fear of asserting yourself with your boss, you can then ask yourself who else you are scared of asserting yourself with and apply the same steps with them as you did with your boss. In this way you can broaden and extend the gains you have made in tackling specific examples of your problems and in doing so you begin to change more general core rigid and extreme attitudes.

Step 11 Recognise that lapses will occur and accept these when they occur and learn from them

Personal change is rarely linear and you will experience lapses along the path towards overcoming your problems. It is important that you understand this fact of psychological life and do not disturb yourself about these lapses. If you develop a realistic stance towards personal change and the hiccups you will experience along the way, you will prevent your lapses developing into a full-blown relapse. In addition, developing this realistic stance towards lapses will enable you to stand back and learn from them so that you get on with the difficult business of tackling your problems armed with increasing knowledge about what factors trigger a lapse and how to deal effectively with them.

Step 12 Identify, in advance, events that you are vulnerable to and use your newly learned self-change methods to confront and deal with them productively

Dealing effectively with lapses involves you learning from them after they have occurred. In addition, you can learn to tackle what I call your vulnerability factors before you encounter them unprepared. Doing so involves you identifying events which you would disturb yourself about should you face them, spotting the rigid and extreme attitudes that make these events vulnerability factors for you and examining and changing these attitudes in the same way that you examined and changed the rigid and extreme attitudes that lay at the core of your original problems. Then, armed with your new flexible and non-extreme attitudes, you should strive to practise them in situations that you find problematic and that you would normally go out of your way to avoid.

A word of caution here. I suggest that you follow a principle that I have called 'challenging, but not overwhelming' which means that you would choose to confront a difficult situation that would constitute a challenge for you, rather than one which would be overwhelming for you at any given point of time. If you follow this principle after a while you will find very few situations overwhelming, particularly if you strengthen your conviction in your flexible and non-extreme attitudes.

Step 13 Apply self-change methods for the rest of your life

Implementing this final step involves you acknowledging that if you wish to maintain personal change and extend it across the board then you will need to apply the self-change methods that you have learned for the rest of your life. This isn't as drastic as it may sound and will not usually involve much time and effort as long as you have consolidated your flexible and non-extreme attitudes. You will quite readily acknowledge that if you stop caring for yourself physically that your health will deteriorate. You would regard as preposterous the idea that you can achieve a level of physical well-being and maintain it no matter how much you subsequently neglect yourself. Thus, why should you be surprised that you need to take regular steps to maintain and extend your psychological well-being. Taking such steps when you feel fine psychologically may seem strange, but do so and you will increase the chances that you will live a mentally healthier and happier life.

The Main Limitation of Self-Help Books

All psychological methods have their limits and even if you take all the steps discussed above, you will still find that there are limits to self-help books. Let me discuss the main limitation of these books in the time that I have available.

The main limitation of self-help books is that they are not written especially for you. In order to help yourself from reading a book you will have to extrapolate from what the author has written and apply it to your own unique situation. Some people find doing this more easily than others and if you find such extrapolation and application difficult you may benefit from consulting a counsellor who practises an approach that is consistent with that put forward by the author of the book you are attempting to follow. I find that my self-help books very nicely complement my face-to-face counselling work with clients in that I can help them to apply my general points to their particular circumstances.

I have already mentioned that personal change is not linear and that you will experience obstacles to continued improvement. While good self-help books will alert you to some of the major obstacles to continued progress, they may not cover the very obstacle that may be holding you back. If you think that this may be the case for you, seeking guidance on this issue from a counsellor of the same school as the writer of the self-help book is probably the best way forward. A good self-help book, however, will alert you to this possibility and recommend face-to-face consultation in these circumstances.

Self-Help Books: For Better or Worse

I have just mentioned one characteristic of a good self-help book. Let me very briefly spell out some of the other characteristics of good examples of this genre and what distinguishes these from self-help books that are less useful.

1. Good self-help books tend to be written by those with professional credentials

While this point does not guarantee that a self-help book will be good, it does at least show you that the author knows what they are talking about and is qualified to write with professionally sanctioned authority.

2. Good self-help books tend to be written in clear, jargon-free language

Good self-help books tend to be written in clear everyday language and while they do not patronise their readership, they do not assume that this audience has specialised knowledge that they cannot be expected to have.

3. Good self-help books make realistic, not grandiose claims

Good self-help books, while offering hope that personal change is possible, do not make grandiose claims that you can change your life completely or change your personality. Be especially sceptical of promotional blurb that promises you the earth. However, be aware that authors do not always have control over the content of such material and unscrupulous publishers may not even show the author what some overly enthusiastic publicist has written.

4. Good self-help books provide concrete steps for you to follow

Many self-help books give very general guidelines about how you can implement a personal change programme and in my experience many people find it very difficult to follow these general principles on their own. The better self-help books provide very concrete steps that you can follow, but are not dogmatic in urging that you have to follow these steps slavishly in the order that they appear in the book.

5. Good self-help books make it clear that they are putting forward *a* perspective not *the* perspective

The field of counselling and psychotherapy is not a unified one. This means that there are a number of different perspectives on a given emotional problem. A good self-help book makes it clear which perspective is being taken and stresses that this is one perspective among many. Bad self-help books claim that the author's approach is the only approach to the problem that is worthy of consideration.

6. Good self-help books are based on an approach where there is research evidence

There is a growing body of research on the efficacy of psychological techniques and good self-help books draw upon this body of evidence. This is another reason why it is important that self-help books are written by people who are professionally trained, in that they are familiar with this research evidence, know how to evaluate its quality and are fully aware of its limitations. Authors without this professional background far too often take this research at face value if, indeed, they are aware of its existence at all.

Incidentally, some people in the field take the radical position that a self-help book should not be published if it has itself not been shown, by research, to be effective in controlled studies. I think that this is taking things too far and if applied rigorously, this restriction would mean that very few self-help books would be published at all and that you, the reading public, would be deprived of much valuable self-help material.

7. Good self-help books recognise the difficulty of personal change

Finally, good self-help books recognise the difficulty of making and sustaining personal change and repeat this message, as I have done here, throughout.

Conclusion

Let me end conclude by reiterating my main message. No matter how good a self-help book is, I want to remind you that *it won't work*. Rather, you will have to make it work by putting into practice repeatedly the clear, step-by-step guidelines to personal change that hopefully the author has provided. Remember that change is difficult, uncomfortable, time-consuming and involves sustained effort. If you follow this principle and still make no progress, it is useful to consult a counsellor to discuss what may be going wrong or it may be that the approach outlined in the self-help book that you are following is not the right one for you.

While I might have been expected to end my talk on an upbeat note of enthusiastic optimism – after all I would like you all to buy my new book, which by the way is called *Overcoming Shame* (Dryden, 1997a) – it is no bad thing to end on a note of realism. So, buy my book and realise that it won't work. However, if you are prepared to commit yourself to working hard to overcoming your life-inhibiting feelings of shame and recognise that doing so requires sustained effort, is time-consuming and involves discomfort, then the combination of your realistic view about personal change and my realistic views on how to tackle shame should bear fruit. Thank you for your attention.

11

Rationality, Outrageous Ideas and Sensitivity

In my opinion this is one of the most controversial lectures that I have ever delivered. It was given as a Keynote Address on 31 May 1997 at the 1st International Conference on Consulting Psychology organised by the Division of Counselling Psychology of the British Psychological Society, which took place at Stratford-upon-Avon. Nobody walked out of the talk and the discussion after the lecture was strangely muted. Either I overestimated the controversial nature of the lecture or the audience was dumbstruck!

In this talk, I am going to present some ideas that are derived from the theory of Rational Emotive Behaviour Therapy. If presented without explanation, these ideas will seem outrageous, but when embedded in the context of REBT theory they make perfect sense. I suppose at the outset, I should issue a health warning in that you may find some of what I say shocking and even offensive. You may even feel tempted to walk out. This is, of course, your prerogative. However, I would much prefer you to stay, express your displeasure and argue with me so that we can have a dialogue about what I have presented.

While much has been written about desirable counsellor qualities and attitudes, little has been written about the ability of counsellors to hear all manner of things from clients without being shocked by what they hear. My view is that the unshockability of counsellors is a much under-rated therapeutic condition. If the counsellor conveys that they will not be shocked by what the client says then they will create a space where the client will dare to speak the unspeakable and think the unthinkable. In this spirit, I will say things that you thought you would never hear in a keynote address at a distinguished gathering. Allow me, for a brief period to mention the unmentionable.

Beyond Belief: The Shocking ABCs of REBT

One of the core theoretical ideas of REBT is represented by the ABC model of human emotions. This can be summed up neatly by the statement: 'People are disturbed (at C) not by adversities (at A), but by the rigid and extreme basic attitudes that they hold towards these adversities (at B)'. For Albert Ellis, the founder of REBT, these rigid and extreme attitudes are at the very core of much psychological disturbance. As is now well known in the field of counselling and psychotherapy, dogmatic attitudes come in the form of musts, absolutistic shoulds, have-to's, etc., and are the breeding ground for three other attitudes which are extreme in nature. These are known as: awfulising attitudes, unbearability attitudes and attitudes where self, others and life conditions are devalued.

The constructive alternative to these four rigid and extreme attitudes are essentially flexible and non-extreme in nature. These attitudes are known as flexible attitudes, non-awfulising attitudes, bearability attitudes and attitudes where self, others and life conditions are accepted unconditionally.

Now the ABC model of REBT is not controversial until you begin to consider events at A which are highly aversive. Let's take rape, for example. The ABC model of REBT states as follows: Women (in this case) are disturbed not by being raped, but by the rigid and extreme attitudes that they take towards being raped. Now, I can well appreciate that for some of you this is a monstrous statement. A woman has been raped and now I (a man no less) am saying that this event did not cause her disturbed feelings, but that she made herself disturbed by holding a set of rigid and extreme attitudes toward being raped. How insensitive and how inaccurate. Furthermore, you may think that I am blaming the victim and minimising the responsibility of the man committing the rape. I can understand if this is your reaction, for stated in this stark manner the idea that a woman causes her own disturbed feelings about being raped is insensitive and I would never put this in such a stark way to clients.

Imagine this scene. A woman has been raped and seeks counselling. She is sobbing uncontrollably at which point the counsellor tries to show her that she is making herself disturbed about being raped. Is this insensitive? Of course it is and no good REBT therapist would intervene in this way. A sensitive and empathic response is called for and this is what the REBT therapist would offer. And yet, no matter how empathic and sensitive the counsellor is, this does not change the fact that the client is disturbing herself by the attitudes that she holds about the rape. But she is light years away from hearing this perspective. She is, however, closer to hearing that being raped can be said to cause her distress.

REBT makes a crucial distinction between healthy negative emotions (or distress) and unhealthy negative emotions (or disturbance). Distress stems from flexible and non-extreme attitudes and disturbance stems from rigid and extreme attitudes. Ruling out very unlikely reactions to rape such as pleasure and indifference, one can either feel distressed or disturbed about being raped. Now given that rigid and extreme attitudes are dogmatic and extreme versions of flexible and non-extreme attitudes, one can argue that it is highly likely that virtually everyone who is raped holds a set of flexible and non-extreme attitudes towards that severe adversity.

Thus, the woman in question is likely to have a very strong preference about not being raped, views it as something very, very bad and so on. These attitudes are so ubiquitous that we can say that being raped causes distress, whether this distress is overt or covert. But since rigid and extreme attitudes are rigid and extreme versions of these flexible and non-extreme attitudes they are not caused by the event (although I note in passing that the more aversive the rape, the more likely it is that the person will transform her flexible and non-extreme attitudes into rigid and extreme attitudes). No, these rigid and extreme transformations of flexible and non-extreme attitudes are the responsibility of the person who is raped. This, of course, does not mean that we should blame the woman for her disturbance. It means that we are empowering her. I'll say that again. Helping the woman at a therapeutically sensitive time to acknowledge that she is responsible for her disturbance is an act of empowerment. It is empowering because it enables the client to free herself from her disturbed feelings. She may not get over her healthy distress (although this will probably lessen over time), nor should we want her to, for it is healthy for her to be distressed about such a highly aversive event such as rape. But she does not have to be disturbed for an unduly long period about this event. She has the ability to transcend this experience in a healthy manner and it is this realisation that is empowering.

She can do this, according to REBT theory, by doing two things. First, she can rid herself of the rigid and extreme versions of her flexible and non-extreme attitudes. Examples of such extreme versions are 'Being raped makes me a dirty, repulsive person', and 'My life is completely ruined'. Second, she can actively stay with the flexible, non-extreme attitudes that are at the core of her healthy distress (e.g. 'Being raped is a disgusting thing to have happened to me, but it does not define me as a person. I am not a dirty person, I am a person to whom a dirty thing was done' and 'My life has been badly affected, but not completely ruined. Ruined means that I cannot recover, but I can recover even though I may never forget it and be somewhat influenced by it'.

Let me stress that it is probably normal for women (and men) who have been raped to be disturbed about it, but normal does not mean healthy. If we want to help people to overcome their disturbance, but not their distress, we can help them to remove what they themselves have added i.e. the rigid and extreme attitudes which are not an intrinsic part of the rape. This needs to be done with great sensitivity at a time when the client is ready to benefit from it and it should be emphasised that the client should not be blamed for needlessly, but understandably adding rigid and extreme attitudes to the experience.

Finally, this work can be done without minimising either the aversiveness of the rape or the responsibility of the person who perpetrated the rape. Let me be perfectly clear about this. Rape is an act of violence and the person perpetrating the rape is to be held fully responsible for it. The position that I have taken with respect to the source of disturbance does not detract one iota from this point.

Taking Offence at Shoulds

In REBT, as in life, the meaning of words is important. Unless, I am clear about the meaning of a word that I am using, you may easily take offence at what I say and even think that I am crazy for saying it. Let me take the word 'should', for example. As I have already mentioned, REBT theory posits that rigid attitudes are at the core of much psychological disturbance. Such attitudes take the form of musts, got to's and have to's. They also take the form of shoulds, but only when these shoulds are absolute. The word 'should' has several different meanings in the English language and this fact can lead to confusion, at best and to you taking offence and even my incarceration in a psychiatric hospital, at worst.

Listen carefully to my next statement and note your immediate reaction to it. 'The Holocaust should have happened'. Have you taken offence at that statement? Are you angry at me for saying it? Do you think that I have taken leave of my senses or think that I am a member of the British National Party? I am neither mad nor a Nazi. All I have done is to use the word 'should' in a manner to convey one meaning and you have reacted as if I have used the word 'should' in a way that conveys a very different meaning.

It follows therefore that when using language in REBT (or in any other approach to counselling) it is very important first, to be aware that a single word has different meanings and second, to take great care in differentiating and explaining these meanings when using these words with clients. This is precisely what I deliberately did not do when stating without any explanation that the Holocaust should have happened. I mentioned earlier that timing of one's interventions is a mark of therapeutic sensitivity. Here I am arguing that the explanation of terms that might be otherwise misinterpreted without further elaboration is another hallmark of such sensitivity.

Let me now consider the different meanings of the word 'should' before returning to my statement about the Holocaust. The first meaning of the word 'should' that I want to consider is the absolute should. This is the only 'should' that represents a rigid attitude. An example of an absolute should is as follows: 'You should not have treated me in this way'. What the person really means here is: 'You absolutely should not have treated me in this way'. In this example, the person is demanding or insisting that the other person not act in a certain way towards them. An absolute should also leads the person to hold one or more extreme attitudes which Ellis (1994) views as being derivatives from this absolute should (e.g. 'It's terrible that you treated me in this way', 'I can't bear the fact that you treated me in this way', and 'You are a swine for treating me in this way'). The absolute should also leads to an unhealthy negative emotion and in this example the person experienced demanding, condemnatory anger towards the other who treated him badly. As I mentioned earlier the absolute should is the only should that represents a rigid attitude and is thus the only should that is the target for change in REBT.

The second should that I wish to discuss is the preferential should. This is the healthy alternative to the absolute should and contains an implicit negation of it. If we make both the preferential nature of this should and this negation explicit in our example we get the following statement: You preferably should not have treated me in this way, but there is no law which states that you absolutely should not have done so'. As you can just hear this sounds very awkward so the person is more likely to say: 'You should not have treated me in this way'. This is, of course, confusing since it is exactly the same wording as was used to denote an absolute should. However, a preferential should leads to different effects than the absolute should. First, it leads to a one or more non-extreme attitudes (e.g. 'It's bad that you treated me in this way, but it is not terrible', 'It's difficult, but I can bear the fact that you treated me in this way', and 'You are not a swine for treating me in this way, but an unrateable, fallible human being who has acted badly'. The preferential should also leads to a healthy negative emotion and in this example the person experienced non-demanding, non-condemnatory anger about the other person's mistreatment of him. As the preferential should is healthy it is not targeted for change in REBT.

The third type of should that exists is the recommendatory should. Here, for example, you may recommend that a person take a particular course of action as in the statement: 'I recommend that you put your money into an ISA.' Assuming that the person is acting in good faith, what they are saying here is that they think that it would be good for you to take out an ISA and this is what they recommend you should do. While the content of the recommendation may be questioned an REBT therapist would not question the recommendatory should since it is, by itself, not dogmatic.

The fourth should that exists is the predictive should. When you use the term 'should' in this way, you are predicting what will happen based on past experience. An example of this type of should is found in the statement: 'The 6.05 from Waterloo should be five minutes late, since it usually is'. This type of should is again not usually targeted for change in REBT.

The fifth should that I wish to consider is the conditional should. Here the person specifies the conditions that have to be met for an outcome to be achieved (e.g. 'If I study hard, I should pass my exams'. There is, of course, an element of prediction about this should, but its defining characteristic is in the specification of the conditions that have to be met for something else to occur. Conditional shoulds frequently point to occurrences in the future, hence the overlap with predictive shoulds. However, neither this should nor the next are questioned in REBT since they are not implicated in psychological disturbance.

A sixth should that exists is the ideal should. This is really a special sub-type of the conditional should and is more formally known as the ideal conditional should in that it specifies a relationship between the meeting of ideal conditions and a particular outcome. 'The grey mare should win this race' is an example of the ideal should in that the person is saying that if ideal conditions exist, the grey mare should (or will) win the race.

A seventh should is one that may be called the deserving should. Here a person is specifying what 'should' occur on the basis of a sense of justice or fairness. 'He should be imprisoned for five years for what he did' is specifying a relationship between what the person did and what 'should' happen if justice were to prevail. It goes without saying that this sense of justice is subjective and will vary from person to person. 'He should get five years for what he did'. 'No, I think he should be hanged for it' is an exchange between two people indicating two different ideas of justice. Deserving shoulds are not targeted for change in REBT unless they are transformed into absolute shoulds.

The eighth and final form of should that I wish to consider is called the empirical should. When the empirical should is used, the person is indicating that they acknowledge that all the conditions were in place for what happened to have happened. Thus, when I use an empirical should in the statement 'The Labour Party should have lost the last election', all I am saying is that all the conditions were in place for them to lose the election, nothing more, nothing less. I am not indicating my personal preference in this statement, nor am I appealing to any sense of deservingness. I am outlining what happened and stating that it should have happened because it did i.e. all the conditions existed for it to happen. As such the empirical should is not the target for change in REBT.

Let me now return to my statement: 'The Holocaust should have happened'. In this statement, I am not saying that this is what I wanted to happen, nor am I saying that this was my recommendation. Furthermore, I am not saying that the Jews deserved their fate, nor am I saying that this is what ideally should have happened. All I am saying is that all the conditions were in place for it to happen, nothing more, nothing less. But because, my statement could have several different meanings, you can be forgiven if you thought that I was saying something very different. Because of this confusion over the meaning of the word 'should', I suggest that whenever possible we qualify the word when we use it and explain exactly what we mean. Thus, in my original statement what I meant was this: Tragically, catastrophically, unforgettably and shockingly, all the conditions were in place nearly sixty years ago for the Holocaust to have occurred and thus, the Holocaust should have happened because tragically, catastrophically, unforgettably and shockingly, it did.

On Thinking the Unthinkable

As I have stressed several times, rigid attitudes can be expressed as musts, absolute shoulds, got to's and have to's. However, they are expressed, they have many deleterious effects. REBT theory has focused a lot of attention on the impact of holding rigid attitudes on the way we feel and act. But, it has also more recently studied the effects of holding these attitudes on the way that we think. I have referred to these latter effects as cognitive consequences of holding dogmatic musts and absolute shoulds. Thus, with Frank Bond and others, I have discovered that if you hold a rigid attitude you are much more likely to subsequently make a range of negatively distorted inferences than if you hold a flexible attitude (Bond & Dryden, 1996a).

If you hold a rigid attitude, you are also more likely to develop a pattern of obsessive thinking if you are so prone, than if you hold a flexible attitude. Let me illustrate this with an actual case which I relate to you with the client's permission as there is hardly any chance that the person can be identified from what I will tell you now. The two therapeutic factors that I wish to highlight here are counsellor unshockability and the importance of explaining to clients how they unwittingly help to create and elaborate their own obsessions. Without the presence of the former, clients won't disclose the true nature of their obsessions. Without the latter, they will remain scared that they will completely lose control of themselves, a fear which will prevent them from healthily resolving this problem.

This client, who I will call Sally, was a regular churchgoer. She had little sexual education and was a virgin. One day when she was in church her mind wandered and she found herself looking at a statue of Christ and in particular, gazing at Christ's nipples. She was horrified about this, primarily because she held the attitude that while she was in church her thoughts had to be thoroughly pure. Given this demand, she tried not to look at the statue, but typically in such cases, she began to have involuntary unwanted thoughts about the naked Jesus and started to look at Christ's crotch. She redoubled her efforts not to think about and look at Christ in this way, forbidding herself to do so in an absolute fashion. She also went to different churches, hoping that she could leave behind her growing obsession. She could not. At her latest church she began to have fantasies about having sex with Christ and with every redoubled attempt to banish these thoughts and fantasies, they increased in both number and in vividness of sexual content. When I first saw her, it transpired, for it took her many weeks for her to tell me this, that she had begun to think about having oral sex with Christ while being taken from behind by the local vicar.

Using REBT theory I helped this woman to understand how her thoughts and images had developed from innocently gazing at Christ's nipples to a scene more at home in the steamy world of explicit adult videos. Her task was to go back to church and to allow herself to think and imagine anything that she thought and imagined. She was to banish nothing from her mind. Of course, I told her it was healthy for her to be strongly desirous of not thinking and imagining such distasteful things, but there was no earthly (or heavenly) reason why she must be free of such cognitive phenomena. I also helped her to see the difference between having so-called shameful thoughts and being a shameful person. In short, I helped her to accept herself unconditionally as a fallible human being who was not immune from thinking inappropriate and shocking things and neither did she have to have such immunity. It will come as no surprise to you that this woman held the rigid attitude that she always had to say and do the right thing as well as to think the right thoughts. She was a walking example of dogmatic moral correctness. Later in counselling I helped her to join the human race on this issue and surrender her wings.

Parenthetically, after the establishment of a working alliance, the judicious use of humour is particularly therapeutic in such cases. At the end of counselling she was back at her old church virtually free of her troubling thoughts. When she gets them she reminds herself of something that I want to leave you with. That sometimes it is therapeutic to go to church and think about giving Christ a blow job while being taken from behind by the local vicar (see also Chapter 32).

Oedipus Schmoedipus: Why You Don't Have to Gouge Your Eyes Out When You Have Discovered that You Have Killed Your Father and Married Your Mother

Most of you will be familiar with the story of Oedipus. For those of you who are not, let me briefly relate this tragic tale. The Chambers biography dictionary (Magnusson, 1990: 1098) states that Oedipus was the 'Greek legendary figure, who killed his father, Laius, and married his mother, Jocasta...An oracle had warned Laius, king of Thebes, that he would be killed by his son. Laius therefore exposed the infant Oedipus to die on the mountains after piercing his feet with a spike (hence the name Oedipus, which in Greek means 'with swollen feet'). The young Oedipus was rescued and adopted by Polybus, king of Corinth, and grew up with the idea that the rulers of Corinth were his parents. When told by an oracle that he was fated to kill his father and marry his mother, he left Corinth in an attempt to avoid fulfilling the prophecy. On his way through Boeotia, he was involved in a quarrel with his (to him unknown) father Laius, and killed him. He freed Thebes from the scourge of the Sphinx by solving her riddles, and in return married the now-widowed Jocasta, his mother, and became king of Thebes. At length, the terrible truth about his origins and parenthood was revealed to him. Jocasta took her life and Oedipus blinded himself'.

As you all know, this tale inspired Sigmund Freud who coined the term 'Oedipus complex' to describe a young boy's longing to oust his father and have his mother for himself. I want to focus on a different part of the story and argue that Oedipus's act of self-blinding stemmed from a rigid and extreme attitude. I am going to show you that there was no need for Oedipus to gouge his eyes out and no need for him to feel guilty about what he did. Let's assume that I was alive at the time practising REBT and Oedipus, in an obvious state of disturbance, consulted me. Here is how I would have endeavoured to help him.

Windy: OK, Oedipus, what's your problem?

Oedipus: I'm in a terrible state. I have committed two terrible sins.

Windy: What are they?

Oedipus: I've killed my father and married and slept with my mother?

Windy: Did you know that they were your mother and father before you killed the former and married the latter?

Oedipus: No, but that doesn't help me. People have tried to comfort me by reminding me that I didn't know this, but I still want to gouge my eyes out.

Windy: OK, which crime shall we discuss first?

Oedipus: Let's start with the murder of my father, Laius.

Windy: OK, how do you feel about killing your father?

Oedipus: Very guilty.

Windy: Right. Let me put this into REBT's ABC framework. A, which stands for the adversity, is murdering your father and C, which stands for your emotional consequence, is guilt.

Oedipus: What's B?

Windy: B stands for the basic attitudes that you hold towards murdering your father which account for your guilt. In REBT, A, (i.e. in this case you murdering your father), does not cause C, (i.e. your guilt), B does.

Oedipus: So what are my basic attitudes?

Windy: Well, let me put forward a couple of hunches and you correct me if I'm wrong. First, I think you are demanding that you absolutely should not have killed your father and second, I think that you hold that you are a thoroughly rotten person for killing him. Am I right?

Oedipus: That's exactly right, but aren't I a rotten person for killing my father?

Windy: Of course not. Let's leave aside for a moment that you didn't know that he was your father and accept that you did a rotten thing. How are you a rotten person for doing this rotten thing?

Oedipus: Well, I killed my father.

Windy: I'm not disputing that. Killing your father was wrong, it was a rotten deed, but how are you rotten through and through for doing this rotten thing?

Oedipus: I guess I'm not.

Windy: Why not?

Oedipus: Because as you say, one rotten deed does not make me rotten through and through.

Windy: That's right. If you were rotten through and through, you could never do anything good, but we know that you freed Thebes from the scourge of the Sphinx. Wasn't that a good deed?

Oedipus: Yes it was.

Windy: But if you were a rotten person how could you have done such a noble deed?

Oedipus: You're right, I couldn't.

Windy: So, if you aren't a rotten person, what are you?

Oedipus: I'm a fallible human being who can't be rated by my actions. Being fallible means that I can do good deeds and bad deeds.

Windy: That's exactly right. Now it's healthy to feel badly about your bad deeds and consequently, it would be healthy if you would feel very remorseful about killing your father, but guilt is an unhealthy emotion that would lead you to blind yourself. Is that clear?

Oedipus: So, remorse is healthy and guilt isn't.

Windy: That's right, remorse stems from your flexible and non-extreme attitude and guilt from your rigid and extreme attitude. Now let's look at the other part of your attitude: 'I absolutely shouldn't have killed my father'. Where is the law of the universe that states that you absolutely should not have done that?

Oedipus: Well it was very, very wrong.

Windy: You'll get no argument from me on that score, but being human are you immune from doing very, very, bad acts?

Oedipus: No, I don't have that immunity. But I was warned that I would kill my father. I absolutely should have known what I was doing and refrained from doing it.

Windy: Well, that would have been highly desirable, but does it follow that because it would have been highly desirable that you knew it was your father, therefore you absolutely should have known? Are you an oracle in your spare time?

Oedipus: Point taken.

Windy: And incidentally, if there was a law of the universe forbidding you from killing your father, there's no way that you could have killed him because you would have had to follow that law.

Oedipus: Right, reality should be reality however tragic it is.

Windy: Well put. Now I suggest that you go over these ideas for homework and next week I'll help you to get over your disturbed feelings about marrying your mother.

Oedipus: And also can we deal with my feelings of shame when others view me as an object of disgust?

Windy: We can indeed.

Oedipus: Great. How much do I owe you?

Windy: £200.

Oedipus: That's a small price to pay for saving my eyesight.

Windy: See you and be seen by you next week.

I wish to stress two points from this interchange. First, it is important that I agree with Oedipus that his 'crimes' were heinous. It is fundamental to REBT strategy that I did not try to show him what he already acknowledged, albeit intellectually, that he neither knew his father before he killed him nor his mother before he married her. Oedipus will be more open to this type of intervention once he has made strides in accepting himself unconditionally for his 'crimes'. Second, it is important to distinguish between normal, understandable responses, on the one hand and healthy responses, on the other. While it is very understandable and statistically normal for Oedipus to condemn himself for his actions, this does not mean that it is healthy for him to do so. If I do not target for change his guilt-producing, self-condemnatory attitude, he will remain vulnerable to deliberate self-harm (see also Chapter 31).

In summary, I have discussed why being raped does not disturb you, why the Holocaust should have happened, why it is sometimes therapeutic to think about giving Christ a blow job while being taken from behind by the local vicar and why it is not necessary to gouge your eyes out after killing your father and marrying your mother.

However, before I close, let me provide you with an alternative summary. I have discussed the empowering nature of the ABCs of REBT, but stressed that this framework has to be used with great sensitivity, particularly when clients' adversities are very aversive. I considered eight different meanings of the word 'should' and stressed the intended therapeutic benefits of differentiating these meanings to avoid the serious problems that can arise from misunderstanding the meaning of the word. I then argued that when working with clients with obsessive thinking, it is beneficial to explain how thoughts spiral out of our control in direct proportion to our dogmatic attempts to control them and stressed the therapeutic benefits of thinking the unthinkable. Finally, I discussed the unhealthiness of guilt and showed how to intervene to prevent its sometimes tragic consequences.

Rational Emotive Behaviour Therapy is based on a set of ideas that can be both enlightening and outrageous. I have reviewed some of these ideas and promise to review more in a future volume tentatively titled: *Strange, but Rational* (see Part III of this Collection).

12

Looking for the Good in Hitler and Acknowledging the Bad in Mother Teresa

This lecture was the 74th in the Public Lecture Series of the Associates of the University Counselling Service at the University of East Anglia on 12 December 1997. It was especially significant for me since it was the last in this long-running lecture series to be presided over by Professor Brian Thorne who was retiring from full-time service at the University that month. Brian continues to work part-time at UEA, running the University's Diploma in Counselling programme with Judy Moore. In effect, the change means that Brian has two full-time jobs rather than three!

Brian is perhaps the most reliable, conscientious and supportive person that I have encountered in the field of counselling. I value my professional relationship with Brian enormously and I was pleased to be a part of this occasion. Brian is no stranger to controversy himself, so I knew that I had at least one kindred spirit in the audience for another of my controversial lectures. As it transpired, the lecture was very well received and led to a lively but reflective discussion.

In this talk, I will argue that flexibility is central to our well-being and development as human beings and that this quality is germane to effective counselling. I will explore the implications of this view, some of which you may very well find shocking. If so, blame Brian Thorne since he invited me to speak this evening!

Twelve Men Attempt to Merge with or Break Through a Wall

Let me begin by taking you back to an all heterosexual male sexuality group that I attended almost twenty years ago. What was unique about this structured group experience was that it was facilitated by a woman. One of the exercises that she asked us to do was to imagine a line running between the left-hand and the right-hand walls of the room that we were in. We were asked to think of the left-hand wall as indicating 100% heterosexuality and the right-hand wall as indicating 100% homosexuality and to place ourselves along this line so as to represent our views of our own sexual orientation. The ensuing scene was a sight to behold as a group of grown men fought with one another to hug or, in some cases, to break through a brick wall! I don't think you need to ask which wall we all tried to merge with or smash down.

Once we had calmed down enough to process our reactions to this exercise, we began to understand our responses. We were terrified of admitting to ourselves and to others in the group that we had experienced any thoughts, feelings or reactions that could in any way be seen as homosexual. Now, it is not possible for any man to claim with any authority that he has never had such a thought, feeling or reaction, let alone a group of a dozen men. Once we began to accept ourselves unconditionally and the others in the group as complex human beings we could admit to having a sexuality that defied black or white categories.

The Creation and Maintenance of Obsessive, Unwanted Thoughts

This dogmatic attitude about sexuality can have decided disturbed effects. Thus, I once counselled a man who developed obsessions about being homosexual even though there was little in his history to indicate that he was gay. His obsession was rooted in a pornographic video that he once saw which had a scene depicting oral sex between men. A few days later he dreamt about this event, but without any accompanying feelings of desire. However, he was so horrified about the fact that he had had this dream that he became convinced that he was homosexual which, if true, meant that he would have to kill himself so devastating would this be for his view of himself. This man held a rigid attitude that he must not, under any circumstances, have a single thought that was homosexual in content. As you can imagine, this led to an increase of such thoughts and as they increased he redoubled his desperate attempts to exclude them from his consciousness. These redoubled desperate attempts only served to amplify the vividness and explicitness of his thoughts in this domain.

As most of you know, I am a practitioner of Rational Emotive Behaviour Therapy, an approach to counselling which places a high value on flexibility. The traditional REBT initial approach to this man would be to ask him to assume temporarily that he was homosexual and to encourage him to accept himself unconditionally for this. I suspected that this would not work with him and I was soon proved right. He became very agitated when I took this line because in his disturbed frame of mind he thought I was telling him that *I* thought he was homosexual.

Since I am not a dogmatic practitioner of REBT, I changed tack and was much more successful at showing him two things. First, I helped him to see that his desperate insistence that he only experience heterosexual thoughts and his rigid attitude that he must never think anything that could vaguely be construed as homosexual, in fact increased the likelihood that he would think such unwanted thoughts and that they would increase in number and become more explicit, the more desperate he tried *not* to have them. Second, I showed him that he was only seeing two options: either he was heterosexual (which meant to him having no homosexual thoughts) or he was homosexual. I helped him to see that people can be placed along a continuum and that it was entirely possible, and in his terminology 'normal', to be heterosexual and to have the occasional homosexual thought. I also related to him the wall incident in the male sexuality group that I told you about earlier. My client accepted this position and practised both of these ideas: that he was straight even though he had the occasional homosexual thought and the reason that he was flooded by these thoughts now was due to his misguided attempt to be absolutely free of them. With this more flexible philosophy he calmed down and stopped being obsessed with his thoughts and with his sexual orientation.

So, the message is this, if you try to exclude various unwanted thoughts from your awareness and in particular, if you do so in a dogmatic way, you will increase the number, frequency, explicit content and vividness of these thoughts and you will disturb yourself about their presence. However, if you recognise that as a person you are not immune from unwanted thoughts and neither do you have to have such immunity, and you allow yourself to have such thoughts, then these thoughts will decrease in number, frequency, explicit content and vividness and you will be healthily concerned and disappointed rather than unhealthily anxious and ashamed about their presence.

Attempting to Be Totally Different from Your Parents

This dogmatic attempt to exclude an experience can often relate to clients' views of their childhood. Thus, a man recently consulted me for an anxiety problem that he had about money. It transpired that money was a core conflictual area between his parents when he was growing up, both of whom were in the client's words 'hopeless about money'. Until recently, my client had always managed his finances well and it was when this management began to break down that his anxiety started, which by the time that I first saw him had increased to the level of panic. At the root of this man's anxiety was a rigid attitude that he must be nothing like his parents when it came to money and that his recent financial difficulties meant to him that he was just like them, an inference which was accompanied with much self-hate.

This man's distorted inference 'I am just like my parents when it comes to money' was created by his dogmatic insistence that he must not be anything like them on this issue. I helped my client by encouraging him to see that while it may be advantageous to be nothing like his parents when it came to money, it was very unlikely that he would achieve such immunity for two reasons. First, he was human and all humans have the potential to mismanage their finances at times. Second, he was biologically and socially influenced by his parents and it would be strange indeed if he was *nothing* like them on any issue. At the same time, I helped him to distinguish between his current, transitory difficulties with money which he could healthily dislike and his entire self which he could unconditionally and healthily accept. These two strategies helped him to see and fully acknowledge that while he was having difficulties with money, currently he was far more dissimilar to his parents on this issue than he was similar.

Once we insist that we are nothing like our parents, for example, we put ourselves in a different category to them. In our attempts to ban ourselves from having certain experiences, we become hypervigilant to their possible presence and are thus more likely to detect them as a result. Once we have detected even slight evidence of the experience we are desperately trying to exclude, we disturb ourselves about its presence and grossly exaggerate the threat posed by its presence. In such a frame of mind, we will be unable to stand back and understand what is going on and thus we will be unable to deal with it.

By contrast, if we accept ourselves unconditionally as human beings who have the potential to experience anything that human beings are capable of experiencing then we will not place ourselves in a different category to our parents. We will thus be far less likely to disturb ourselves about the presence of the unwanted experience and thus will not become hypervigilant to its possible presence. If we do detect slight evidence of the experience, we will be accurate in our judgment that it is slight and we will strive to understand what is going on so that we can deal with it.

Fear of Losing Self-Control

These dynamics are in operation when we consider other areas of disturbed and healthy human functioning. Let me consider, for example, cases where we are scared of losing control of ourselves. When this happens, typically we are demanding that we must always be in control of our feelings and other psychological processes. In these circumstances, when we become aware that our rigid control is beginning to break down we tend to think that this will have dire results. For example, we may think that we may go mad or run amok. Consequently, we try desperately to avoid situations where we think that we may lose self-control. As you may appreciate, this strategy is doomed to failure because there is no guarantee that there is any place which will provide us with the certainty that we will remain in total control of ourselves. You may recognise this dynamic as a core component of the agoraphobic experience.

What can we do in these circumstances? The main thing is to appreciate that dogmatic attempts to remain in control of ourselves are precisely the problem. Paradoxically, the best way to regain control of ourselves is to allow ourselves to experience feeling out of control and to recognise that as humans we are not built to be exempt from experiences which we label 'losing control'. It is ironic that the role model for people who demand perfect control is not a human being; rather, it is a programmable computer. While computers are not yet capable of experiencing anxiety and anger, two emotions that people with control problems are particularly scared of, this is not true of human beings. Again it is the rigid attitude that we must be in control which leads us to primitive all or nothing thinking: either I am in control or I am out of control. In reality, however, as humans we cannot realistically cram our experiences into an 'in control' box or an 'out of control' box. Our experiences are far too rich and fluid for such simple categorisation. Rather, control is best seen as lying along a continuum, the two ends of which are rarely experienced for long periods of time.

It is also a feature of people who have a rigid attitude towards self-control that they regard themselves as weak and defective if they do, in fact, experience some loss of control. These people also think that others will see them as weak and defective if they show publicly that they are losing control of themselves in any way. Interestingly, such people are quite ready to acknowledge that other people are allowed to experience lapses in self-control. But *they* are not allowed, or more accurately they do not allow themselves, to experience such lapses. They hold that *they* have to be in total control and if they are in any way out of control this proves that they are weak and defective and others will look down on them and scorn them. It is little wonder that shame is the constant emotional companion of people who have an inflexible attitude towards self-control; this emotion lurks in the shadows waiting to be experienced when the person reveals to himself and to others a breakdown in rigid self-control.

The key to helping people with control-related problems involves encouraging them to join the human race and to give up their self-imposed immunity from loss of self-control. Once they can give up the need to be godlike, they can come to earth and in embracing their uniqueness and their humanity, they can lose their fear of their own internal experiences. It is for this reason that their therapists also need to embrace their own uniqueness and humanity if they are to be truly helpful to such clients.

On Being Dogmatically Against Dogmatism

I want to dwell on this point for a moment for I have detected a worrying tendency in the field for counsellors to regard their clients as different from themselves. As an example, there is a real danger that Rational Emotive Behaviour Therapists will use REBT theory tyrannically against themselves. For example, this theory clearly distinguishes between healthy and unhealthy negative emotions and holds that flexible attitudes underpin the former and rigid attitudes the latter. Clients are encouraged to experience healthy negative emotions such as sadness, remorse and concern when they face adversities instead of experiencing unhealthy negative emotions such as depression, guilt and anxiety.

It is a real temptation for REBT therapists to deny to themselves and to other REBT therapists that they experience unhealthy negative emotions in their own lives. Such counsellors believe that as REBT therapists, they are not supposed to disturb themselves by holding rigid attitudes towards the adversities they encounter. In holding such a dogmatic attitude – which can comically and ironically be summed up in the phrase: 'I must not be dogmatic' – such REBT therapists are, in fact, placing themselves in a different category from their clients and from other people. This shows that human beings have the capacity to take any good idea or philosophy and turn this idea or philosophy into a rigid dogma. Thus, Christians can become dogmatic religionists, humanists can become rigid upholders of non-belief and REBT therapists can become dogmatically against their own and other people's dogmas.

Couple Conflict and Splitting

Dogmatism is the root of many ills in our society and is at the core of the 'I am right, you are wrong' idea that permeates our society. This is another instance of primitive black or white thinking which shows up in many forms of interpersonal conflict, of which marital conflict is but one vivid example.

It can be very difficult for some people to admit to themselves and to their partners that they may be largely wrong on a particular issue and that their partner may be largely right. There may be various reasons for this phenomenon. First, one or both partners may believe that they must not be wrong, a rigid view which leads them to locate wrongness in the other person and to defend their own position with rigid relish. Second, the person may think that if they admit that they may be wrong then this is an admission of a weakness and that this may be used against them by the other person. Third, one or both partners may lack a relative view of human endeavours and fail to recognise that in most forms of conflict there are likely to be rights *and* wrongs on both sides and that there are different perspectives to be taken of the same event. Imagine what it would be like if both partners held the following views:

1. In any disagreement with my partner I may be wrong in certain respects. This proves that I am a fallible human being who can be right and wrong and it is not terrible to admit my errors either to myself or to my partner.

2. Acknowledging to my partner that I may be wrong is not an admission of weakness. Quite the contrary, it is an admission of strength because I can admit without shame to my essential nature as a human being, which is fallibility.

3. I hold the same view of my partner as I do of myself on this point.

4. There is not one way of viewing a disagreement and it is unlikely that I am completely right and my partner completely wrong on any issue or vice versa. Rather, there are different ways of looking at a topic and I need to understand where my partner is coming from on any issue.

5. It would be nice if my partner held the above attitudes, but they don't have to.

It is my view that the five attitudes that I have just articulated encourage couple empathy and that partners need to be helped to develop these attitudes before they are taught any communication skills.

Another form of black and white thinking that is found in disturbed couple functioning is splitting. Here, one partner locates 100% of a given quality in himself and 0% in the other person or, of course, vice versa. For example, Jenny sought help from me for agoraphobia. Her husband, James, was very suspicious of therapy and denigrated it as a get-rich quick panacea for therapists. It transpired that James saw Jenny as a weak woman who needed to be looked after by him. His way of looking after her was to do everything for her outside of the home. He shopped for her and the family, took the children to school and picked them up at the end of the day. Everybody who knew James considered him to be a wonderful husband, as did Jenny herself. However, James put every obstacle imaginable in the way of Jenny's progress in therapy. For example, after agreeing to look after the children to enable Jenny to go out on her own for a short period, he would invariably contrive to cancel this arrangement for 'important work-related' reasons. Also, if he ever took Jenny out so that she could practise gradually acclimatising herself to an unfamiliar environment, he would always 'accidentally' take her too far beyond the agreed distance with the result that she became very frightened and tearful and consequently, had to be rescued by her 'strong, caring' husband.

Eventually, Jenny could see what was happening and informed James quite calmly that he would have to leave if he didn't play his part in her recovery. This resulted in James becoming quite depressed and desperate to save his relationship. In therapy, it transpired that James overvalued strength and abhorred weakness in himself. In order to maintain this rigid one-sided view of himself, he had to see himself as strong and his wife as weak. He projected, if you will, the idea and reality of his own weakness onto Jenny which enabled him to play the strong husband. It was only when James accepted himself as an unrateable, fallible human being who had strengths and weaknesses and acknowledged that he did not have to exclude the latter from either his functioning or his awareness that he began to make progress. Once he had began to make progress with himself he could not only tolerate strength in Jenny, he could also facilitate and benefit from her strengths.

Whenever I work with couples where one partner embodies a quality and the other embodies the opposite, I am alert to the possibility that one or both people are desperate to expel the quality that they claim not to have and recognise that projecting it onto their partner is a very commonly used defensive manoeuvre in the expulsion process. This desperate attempt to expel the unwanted quality is based on the rigid idea that the person concerned must not have this quality or anything resembling it and would be a thoroughly despicable person if they do have it.

The key to helping couples with this issue is to encourage them to accept themselves unconditionally if it transpires that they do have the unwanted quality. Unconditional self-acceptance helps to promote both ownership of the unwanted quality and understanding of the complex intrapersonal and interpersonal processes involved when one is intolerant of a part of oneself.

Tolerance and Respect among Psychotherapists

Many of you will recognise the influence of psychodynamic ideas and terms in my description and analysis of disturbed couple relationships. What am I, a Rational Emotive Behaviour Therapist, doing drawing on the ideas of psychodynamic therapists? Surely I should be slagging them off? If I did so, I would be acting at variance with the main thrust of my argument in this lecture. To argue that REBT is good and psychodynamic therapy is bad is to make the same all or nothing thinking error that I hold to be the root of many psychological ills. No, while I am happy to state publicly that I am an REBT therapist and argue in favour of its virtues, this does not mean that other approaches do not have their virtues. Thus, psychodynamic theory offers some surprising, but accurate accounts of human dysfunction. For example, a recent study has shown that there is evidence that homophobic men are aroused by homosexual imagery in a way that is consistent with Freud's views. Also, person centred therapy has its virtues. Its emphasis on the therapeutic relationship revolutionised the whole field and showed that it was not good for practitioners to hide behind the protective shield of professionalism.

I could go on, but I think I have made my point. One can practise on approach to therapy and still respect the contribution of other approaches. I would not like to see the future of our field being marked by a bland uniformity of theory and practice. Rather, I would like to see a diversity of ideas, but tolerance and respect for the work of colleagues from different therapeutic traditions.

The Importance of a 'Both/And' Approach to Human Life

This emphasis on recognising the strengths of counselling approaches other than one's own is an example of a both/and approach to life. This is in direct contrast to an either/or approach. Let me give a few examples of both approaches starting with one from our field.

There are those who emphasise the differences among approaches to counselling and psychotherapy. Such people know – or think they know – that their approach is the best approach and tend to denigrate what others have to offer. Other people in the field, on the other hand, focus on similarity among approaches and whose cri de coeur is that research evidence indicates that different approaches yield the same outcome. Both of these approaches are examples of the either/or approach.

By contrast, those who take a both/and approach have their therapeutic preferences, but recognise the value of other approaches. They see both the differences and the similarities among the available approaches and argue that the research evidence shows that there are therapies of choice for various client problems, yet for other problems different therapies will achieve comparable results.

Let me now change tack and consider one of the most important tasks that we have as humans. I refer to the ability of humans to be both separate from others and to be connected with others. Separateness is important to sustain our unique identity, while connectedness is important to sustain growth-enhancing intimacy with others. A both/and approach to separateness and connectedness can help people on the path to self-actualisation, while an either/or approach to these conditions can be seen in a variety of client problems.

Those who emphasise separateness to the exclusion of connectedness do not seek counselling as often as those who emphasise connectedness to the exclusion of separateness. However, they are often complained about by clients with whom they are in relationship. These are the people who clients see as closed off and unable to respond emotionally when this is appropriate. Such people tend to see all relationships in functional, highly stereotyped terms and do not view other people as a source of growth and development. The professional literature refers to those at the extreme of the separateness domain as schizoid. Such people erect rigid boundaries between themselves and others and often see relationships as a threat to their autonomy and identity. Their basic fear concerning relationships is engulfment.

Those who emphasise connectedness at the expense of separateness are overly focused on relationships as a source of identity. Some may even view relationship roles as synonymous with their identity (e.g. husband/wife; mother/father; son/daughter). Such people find it very difficult to bear being on their own and are often quite needy once they become related. Indeed, they tend to seek emotional sustenance from those with whom they are functionally related (e.g. their boss, teacher, doctor etc.). Such people have highly permeable boundaries between themselves and others and often see the absence of relationships as a threat to their identity. Their basic fear concerning relationships is abandonment and isolation.

People who have a both/and approach to separateness and connectedness are comfortable both in relationships and on their own. They can pursue non-relationship activities and can easily return to their relationships when it is appropriate to do so. They can express themselves both emotionally and functionally according to the nature of the relationship that they are involved in. They tend to be intimate in intimate relationships and functional in functional relationships.

People with a both/and approach to separateness and connectedness tend to have a flexible approach to boundaries. When necessary they can erect firm boundaries between themselves and others, while at other times their interpersonal boundaries can be healthily permeable as they let others into their personal space as an expression of their commitment to these significant others.

Another example of a both/and approach to life is illustrated by people who can admit to themselves and to others that they can both succeed and fail at important tasks. Such people tend to learn from their failures and take healthy risks as they strive for what is important to them. They neither regard themselves as successes or failures but as unique, unrateable, fallible human beings who incorporate both their successes and their failures into their construct system. On the other hand, people with an either/or approach to this issue tend to see failure as something to be avoided at all costs and as constituting their identity if they encounter it. Such people are fearful about taking sensible risks and are frequently indecisive as they wait fruitlessly for a course of action to appear which guarantees them success. As many student counsellors will testify even the most brilliant of individuals are not immune from this either/or approach to success and failure. Indeed, they are sometimes the very people who hold to this black and white ideology most rigidly.

One of my clients has spent most of her life in either/or territory. When she is in work mode, she rarely takes lunch or tea breaks and is often up half the night finishing some project or other. However, when she is at play nothing must interfere with her leisure. She has spent many years oscillating from stringent dieting to enormous bingeing and everything is either wonderful or terrible. Those of you who have worked with clients struggling with bulimia nervosa will not be surprised to learn that she this woman has suffered from this disorder. This client, who is currently struggling to experience life from a both/and perspective, recently came up with a vivid phrase which has remained with me ever since. She calls her problem 'bulimia lifeosa' and sees this as the antithesis to the balanced and flexible approach to life that she is striving to adopt. I think that this phrase says it all, don't you?

Some Shocking Implications

Let me now discuss some shocking implications of the ideas that I have presented so far. The first concerns what has been called political correctness, a term that I will use here to include its offshoots, 'emotional correctness' and 'therapeutic correctness'.

As a counsellor trainer I have seen the effects of internalised political correctness as trainees watch very carefully what they say in case they offend other trainees or their trainers. If trainees cannot take risks on counselling courses and express their real feelings even if these feelings may be examples of racism, sexism or any other -ism, where can they express themselves? My fear is that under the tyranny of political correctness, trainees will not only keep their true feelings from their fellow trainees and from their trainers, but will also learn to hide these feelings from themselves. Thus, for me, good counsellor trainers establish a climate where politically incorrect views can be tolerated and explored and where the trainees expressing them can be accepted before their views are challenged. Otherwise, we will be training a generation of counsellors who will be constantly monitoring what they say and feel to see if it is acceptable to the prevailing zeitgeist.

This is not to say that I want to unleash onto the world counsellors who hold racist and sexist views. It is just that I think that unless these views can be uttered they cannot be usefully explored and integrated into the totality of the person. Note that I said 'integrated' and not 'expunged'. That is the crucial point.

The second shocking implication of my views concerns an experience which a minority of women who have been sexually abused have had, but rarely talk about. Such women, to their horror, have found elements of the total experience enjoyable and some may have even have experienced an orgasm during the abuse. This is rare, but it does happen. By acknowledging the existence of this phenomenon, I am in no way minimising the aversiveness of the abuse, blaming the victim or reducing the culpability of the person responsible for the abuse.

It is in the unpredictable nature of human responsiveness that we can have an experience that we certainly don't want (like an orgasm in the course of an abusive attack) and we may not have an experience that we actively do want (like an orgasm with our partner during lovemaking). Helping women who have had an orgasm in the course of an abusive attack to understand this perverse fact of human life and to acknowledge that human sexual response, like other areas of human endeavour, is unpredictable, fluid and paradoxical can be enormously therapeutic for them and encourages them to view the situation in a much broader context than they have often done hitherto. Previously, they may have seen their orgasmic response as casting doubt on their motives, behaviour and even their identity (e.g. 'Maybe I wanted it to happen', 'Maybe I encouraged him in some way' and even 'What a sick person I am to feel this at that time'). And previously they have had a common sense, but incorrect either/or view of sexual response e.g. 'If you love someone you have an orgasm with him. You just don't have an orgasm during sexual abuse'. Here is a clear example where the either/or approach leads to disturbance and the both/and approach leads to a therapeutic resolution.

You may be wondering why I decided to entitle this talk 'Looking for the Good in Hitler and Acknowledging the Bad in Mother Teresa'? Well, your wait is over for the time has come for me to tackle this delicate subject. So far in this talk I have argued that a both/and way of approaching human experience yields better results than an either/or approach. Following from this, I will now argue that Hitler was not all bad, nor Mother Teresa all good. We may need to see them as all bad and all good respectively, but this says more about us than it does about them.

Let me briefly review some of Hitler's better qualities. He was a very good organiser and a very good public speaker. He showed great bravery in the First World Way capturing several enemy soldiers single-handedly. He was capable of love and was kind to animals. Please do not think that by saying these things that I am a neo-Nazi or an apologist for Hitler. He did, of course, do immense harm to Jews, of whom I am one, to gypsies and to homosexuals. I do not absolve him from the responsibility for any of this, but the fact of the matter is that he was not all bad. If he was, he would not be human.

You may have heard that Mother Teresa is on the fast-track to being made a Saint by Rome. Her name is synonymous with goodness and there is no doubt that her devoted efforts have brought succour to countless people over the years. But was she all good? Far from it. Her hospitals were poorly stocked with medical supplies and were often kept in a bare and freezing state. This despite the fact that her Mission received very generous financial support from many quarters.

Also, despite publicly stating that she would not accept money from the rich, she received donations amounting to $1.25m from Charles Keating who was sent to prison for ten years for fraud. Mother Teresa sent an unsolicited letter to the trial judge to ask for clemency. When the Deputy District attorney in Los Angeles County wrote to Mother Teresa explaining the facts of the case and requesting that she return the money donated to her by Keating, money which he stole from ordinary, working people, Mother Teresa did not respond.

In addition, perhaps because of her respected position, Mother Teresa's accounts were never audited and thus, large sums of money sent by her to 'her headquarters in Rome' have never been explained. I could go on and those of you who are interested in learning more should read a book entitled *The Missionary Position: Mother Teresa in Theory and Practice* by Christopher Hitchens (1995). Unfortunately, in his zeal to expose the 'sins' of Mother Teresa, Hitchens takes an either/or approach and fails to consider and evaluate her good works. My purpose in mentioning this lesser known side of Mother Teresa is not to discredit her, but to place her in full context, to acknowledge the bad in her as well as the good.

My point is that Hitler was not evil and Mother Teresa was not a saint. Hitler had his good side and Mother Teresa her bad. In taking this stance I do not for one minute wish to excuse Hitler for his crimes against humanity, nor do I wish to detract from Mother Teresa's good works. Rather, I wish to make the point that both were human and have features that we all share.

Conclusion

In conclusion, let me say that one of our tasks as human beings is to accept that we are capable of experiencing the entire range of human reactions and responses. We are all capable of the greatest of good and the vilest of evil. To use jargon for a moment, we all have a Hitler inside us as well as a Mother Teresa. If we fully accept ourselves as such we can learn to maximise the good in ourselves and to minimise the bad. However, if we try to expel our bad unwanted side and in particular, if we attempt to do so in a desperate manner, we create problems both for ourselves and for those with whom we come into contact. If we accept ourselves as fallible human beings capable of experiencing the entire range of human functioning and if we accept others as similar to ourselves in this respect, such acceptance will promote understanding and even compassion.

It is this understanding and compassion that is in desperate short supply as we approach the millennium. Is it naive and idealistic of me to hope that if we can accept ourselves and others unconditionally as fallible human beings then this will help us to live more peaceably with ourselves and with others? For our future, I trust it is not.

PART II

UP CLOSE AND PERSONAL

13

How Rational Am I?

Self-Help Using Rational Emotive Behaviour Therapy

I first received training in Rational Emotive Behaviour Therapy (REBT) in 1977 and have practised it ever since. Before that I was trained in person centred therapy and had some training in psychodynamic therapy, but neither of these therapeutic approaches resonated with me as much as REBT did, and still does. In this chapter I will consider:

1. why I resonate personally with REBT theory and practice;
2. how I implement REBT successfully in my personal and professional life;
3. in which areas I struggle implementing REBT in my life;
4. where REBT is not relevant in my life.

Let me stress at the outset that my account (and, if I may venture, that of my colleagues) is bound to be influenced by post-hoc rationalisations, and will therefore provide a more coherent narrative than is likely to be the case in reality. It will also be coloured by what I choose to disclose. On this latter point, my self-disclosure will not be as full as you, the reader, may wish. Since I do not know in advance how my revelations will be used in future, I will disclose as much as I feel comfortable about my professional life and particularly about my personal life.

While this chapter is decidedly not a chapter on the theory and practice of REBT, if you know very little about this approach then what I have to say will not mean that much to you. Consequently, let me first provide a thumbnail sketch of REBT so that you can understand to what extent REBT is for me an embodied theory.

The Essence of REBT

Rational Emotive Behaviour Therapy is an approach that is best placed within the cognitive-behavioural tradition of psychotherapy. It is based on a particular view of emotional disturbance which is summed up in a slightly altered version of a famous dictum, the original of which is attributed to Epictetus: people are disturbed not by things, but by their rigid and extreme views of things. In REBT theory, these views are known as rigid and extreme attitudes and take the form of demands (e.g. 'I must be loved by significant others'), awfulising attitudes (e.g. 'It would be the end of the world if I were not loved by significant others'), unbearability attitudes (e.g. 'I couldn't bear it if I were not loved by significant others') and devaluation attitudes where you devalue yourself (e.g. 'If I am not loved by significant others then this proves that I am unlovable'), devalue others (e.g. 'If significant others do not love me then they are no good') or devalue the world/life conditions (e.g. 'The world is no good for allowing me not to be loved by significant others').

The basic goal of REBT is to help clients to change these rigid and extreme attitudes to a more constructive set of flexible and non-extreme attitudes which are flexible and non-extreme in nature. These take the form of full preferences (e.g. 'I want to be loved by significant others, but I don't have to be'), non-awfulising attitudes (e.g. 'It would be bad if I was not loved by significant others, but it wouldn't be the end of the world'), bearability attitudes (e.g. 'It would be difficult for me to bear not being loved by significant others, but I would be able to bear it, it would be worth bearing, I am willing to bear it and I am going to bear it') and unconditional acceptance attitudes where you accept yourself unconditionally (e.g. 'If I am not loved by significant others then this would not prove that I am unlovable. It proves that I am a fallible human being who is deprived of the love that I want, but do not need'), accept others unconditionally (e.g. 'If significant others do not love me then they are fallible human beings who are depriving me of the love that I want, but do not need. They are not bad people') or accept the world/life conditions unconditionally (e.g. 'The world is a complex place where good things happen, bad things happen – like me being deprived of the love that I want, but do not need – and neutral things happen. It is not a bad place just because I am not loved by significant others').

REBT is a structured, educational, active-directive approach to therapy where, within the context of a good therapeutic relationship, clients are taught a range of cognitive, imaginal, behavioural and emotive techniques. The purpose of these techniques is to enable them to internalise and integrate flexible and non-extreme attitudes into their attitudinal system so that they make a real difference to the way that clients feel, think and act both intrapsychically and interpersonally. In this sense, REBT encourages clients to adopt a self-help philosophy. For more details on the principles and practice of REBT, consult Ellis (1994).

Why I Resonate Personally with REBT Theory and Practice

Although I was originally trained in person centred counselling and psychodynamic therapy, I did not resonate personally with either of these approaches. However, I did resonate with both the major theoretical principles of REBT and its practical ethos. For example, years before I became a counsellor I helped myself overcome my anxiety about the possibility of stammering in public by implementing what was in essence a typical REBT treatment approach. I heard Michael Bentine on the radio talk about how he coped with his stammer by convincing himself: 'If I stammer, I stammer, too bad.' I took this rational statement and made it more evocative by convincing myself: 'If I stammer, I stammer, fuck it!' Then I rehearsed this attitude while using every opportunity to speak up in public without modifying what I said so that I did not avoid words over which I was highly likely to stammer. In doing so, I lost much of the anxiety that I experienced about speaking in public and, as a consequence of this anxiety reduction, I stammered less. I believe this example shows that I naturally resonated with the following:

1   that one can help oneself by actively confronting one's fears (the principle of behavioural change);

2.   that one can influence the way one feels by changing one's attitudes (the principle of attitude change);

3. that one can help oneself without being in counselling or psychotherapy (the principle of self-help);

4. that one can help oneself by changing current factors that maintain one's psychological problems without necessarily exploring the past (the principle of present centredness).

The question is: why do I resonate with these and other REBT principles? The short and uninspiring answer to this question is that REBT suits my temperament and character. These are factors which are largely biologically based, which I am easily drawn to and find natural to actualise. These factors are both intrapsychic and interpersonal in nature. Let me then explore some of the elements of my temperamentally-based character and show how these lead me to be particularly suited to using REBT in my personal and professional life.

Activity Level

I have always had quite a high activity level. I am easily drawn to areas where I can actively do something to help myself and others and where I can be actively involved in personally meaningful projects like writing professional and self-help material. When I reflect in depth on my experiences of personal therapy which have been largely psychodynamic in nature (and which fall outside of the scope of this chapter), I conclude that one of the main reasons why I found these frustrating and largely unhelpful experiences was that they didn't help me to do something active to help myself. Also, when I am not actively involved in personally meaningful projects, I get restless and easily bored. Thus, I have made several decisions to stop writing which I have broken because I miss this activity. So, I have learned to go with my internal flow and give up making promises I really don't want, in my heart of hearts, to keep.

Self-Discipline

Without wanting to blow my own trumpet, I will admit that I have rarely had a problem with self-discipline. Again, this is largely due to my (in my view, largely innate) obsessive-compulsive traits. Thus, when I make up my mind to do something, I am very likely to persist until I have done it or until it becomes clear that I will not be able to do it. I almost always keep to deadlines and more often than not, I do things well before the deadline (like writing this chapter). Yes, I learned the value of self-discipline from my parents, but have very little difficulty putting it into practice. In short, it 'goes with' the grain of my temperament. In contrast, I learned the value of eating slowly from my parents, but have great difficulty doing so. This seems to 'go against' my temperamental grain. REBT stresses the need for humans to be self-disciplined and to view this as a lifelong project. I resonate with this view and have no problem with it (unlike the majority of my clients who initially view this with something akin to horror).

Self-Reliance

Whenever I have had an emotional problem, I have been drawn to help myself to overcome this problem. In the past I have failed to do so only because I lacked the knowledge of what to do to help myself, not because I have sought to be helped by others. I have, of course, sought help from others, but these help-seeking episodes have rarely borne substantial fruit largely because they failed to provide me with a sound and sensible course of psychological action to follow which would help me to overcome these problems (see Chapter 14). When I discovered REBT in 1977, it was as if I had 'come home' so to speak, so comfortable did I find it as a way of overcoming emotional problems. Yes, being an only child helped by providing me with an environmental context where I could easily express my tendency towards self-help, but I firmly hold that it did not originate this tendency. While many only children are natural self-helpers, many are not.

Cognitive and Philosophic Orientation

I mentioned above that I have a high activity level. I am also very much at home in the cognitive modality. Little wonder that I resonate with a cognitive-behavioural approach such as REBT. But why do I resonate more with REBT than with other cognitive-behavioural approaches? One of the reasons is that REBT has a decided philosophic emphasis. Far more than other CBT approaches, REBT outlines a philosophy of healthy living that is both realistic (e.g. it acknowledges that humans have a predisposition towards rigid and extreme thinking as well as towards flexible and non-extreme thinking) and optimistic (i.e. it argues that humans can transcend even tremendous tragedy with their spirit shaken, but not broken). It is the combination of the realistic and optimistic that appeals so much to me and helps explain why I never truly resonated with person centred philosophy (too idealistic for my realistic side) and psychodynamic philosophy (too pessimistic for my optimistic side). Other CBT approaches are either philosophically indifferent or philosophically poorly developed.

Humour

While others may disagree, I consider that I have always had a good sense of humour and fully agree with Albert Ellis (1987) who has said that psychological disturbance involves taking oneself, others and life *too* seriously. Not that I laugh inappropriately at myself, but I regard aspects of life that others cherish such as status, reputation and social standing as relatively unimportant. Thus, I am generally amused rather than angry when I hear of some rumour or other about myself that from time to time circulates in the counselling/therapy rumour mill. Even when I received a verbal warning at work for using profanity in the classroom (not, I hasten to add, for swearing *at* any of my students), I was amused as well as pissed off when contemplating the ease with which one or two of my students disturbed themselves about my language. Although this episode and its aftermath period had its trials, it also had its funny side as college wrestled with attempting to specify occasions when it is admissible to swear in class (apparently when you drop a heavy object on your foot and the expletive is involuntary). For me REBT is the Heineken of therapies, reaching humorous parts of myself that other therapies cannot reach.

Non-Religious, Anti-Mystical Orientation

I am also drawn to REBT because it resonates with my non-religious, anti-mystical side. While a number of REBT therapists have a religious faith, the theory does not encourage a 'faith unfounded on fact' view of the world and takes a decided stance against mystical, transpersonal ideas. The idea of a 'New Age' REBT is as likely as 'kosher bacon'. This suits me as I have never believed in God, reasoning quite early in my life that if there is a deity, why on earth (or heaven!) would he, she or it create Lot's wife a fallible human being and then turn her into a pillar of stone for showing her fallibility? No, I am an ethical humanist by persuasion and easily resonate with this aspect of REBT.

Lone Pioneer

Finally, I am drawn to REBT because it is not popular (certainly not in Britain anyway). I am, I believe, Britain's leading proponent of REBT and have been beavering away to make it more accessible on this island. There is a part of me that resonates to my role as a lone pioneer struggling to make REBT's voice heard in a crowded marketplace dominated by humanistic and psychodynamic practitioners. That part of me doesn't want REBT to be too successful. If it were, I would lose my lone pioneer role. While I don't make too much of this dynamic, it does exist in me.

Is there anything within REBT theory which resonates to this idea of the 'lone pioneer'? Yes, but in a way that is different from how this dynamic operates in me. I am referring here to the idea that it is important to pursue ideas which are personally meaningful even if it means incurring wrath and disapproval from others. REBT theory holds that it is self-defeating to hold the attitude that it is essential to be approved of by others; doing so will lead one to abandon one's pursuit of enduring meaning in favour of receiving approval which is transitory. I note that Albert Ellis himself pursued the promulgation of REBT in the face of severe criticism and personal abuse from the field in the mid-1950s and beyond. In those days he was a lone pioneer. But he did not waver from presenting his ideas whenever he could, because he did not need the approval of his peers.

Having speculated on why I am so drawn to REBT, let me go on to consider how I apply it in my life.

How I Have Implemented REBT Successfully in My Personal and Professional Life

The proof of the pudding of any therapeutic approach is in its eating. So how successful have I been in applying the principles of REBT to my personal and professional life? I think, in my biased view, that I have done so quite successfully and here are some examples of Dryden-centred REBT in action.

1. I practised the REBT principle of unconditional self-acceptance (Dryden, 1999a), after I left my lecturing job at Aston University in 1983 and I failed to get any of the 54 jobs I applied for over a two-year period. 'That must have been very depressing for you', people said when I told them about this period of my life.

    'Actually, it wasn't', I replied, 'because I had 54 job rejections and no self-rejections.'

2. I implemented a bearability philosophy once I learned that I had high cholesterol by adopting a low-fat, low-cholesterol diet and forgoing many of the high-fat foods that I love. Whenever I am tempted to break this diet, I acknowledge that I am tempted, I recognise that I would like the high-fat food, but show myself that I don't need what I want. Not that I deprive myself of all high-fat foods. I have four squares of chocolate every Friday! I have also exercised five times a week for years now and again implement a similar bearability philosophy in doing so. Most of the time I don't want to get up and exercise, preferring to remain in bed, but I push myself to get up while reminding myself that I can stand the discomfort of getting up and it is worth it to me to do so.

3. Whenever I am in writing mode (which is fairly often) I resolve to write 500 words a day and very often exceed this figure. What if I'm not in the mood? In such cases, I remind myself

that I don't need to be in the mood in order to write and push myself to get going. Most of the time I get in the mood after I have started, and even if I don't get myself in the mood I write anyway. In this way, I live a lifestyle which is rarely affected by procrastination (Dryden, 2000).

These three examples show that I am pretty adept at persisting through adversity as long as there is a point in doing so. As I said before, I believe that I have a temperament which facilitates this process, but I still have to push myself when the going gets tough.

Another good example of how I used REBT in action to cope with adversity concerns my reaction to the following episode. A number of years ago I wrote a self-help book entitled *Overcoming Shame*. As usual I finished this book ahead of schedule and effected a transfer of files from a memory card attached to my trusty Amstrad NC200 to a floppy disk. Unfortunately, I wiped the files from the memory card before checking that they had been successfully transferred to the floppy disk and, yes, you've guessed it, the floppy was blank. I had lost the whole book because, as I discovered later, I had used one full stop too many while naming each of the files. Initially I went berserk, started throwing things around and calling myself all the names under the sun. I was furious with the world for inventing f***ing stupid things called computers, and with myself for being such a f***ing stupid individual. Dear reader, please don't be offended by my language. If you are a counsellor or therapist, hopefully you should not be shocked by profanity, and I'm trying to give you an honest account of my inner dialogue at that time.

Well, you might argue this doesn't seem very rational; throwing things about and cursing the world and yourself for making a mistake – a mistake albeit with serious consequences – but a mistake nonetheless. But let me finish the story. This inner- and outer-directed tirade only lasted for about a minute, for I stopped myself in mid-rant, acknowledged to myself that I was unhealthily angry, accepted myself for adding self-inflicted insult to injury, and reminded myself forcefully that my anger wasn't helping me to solve my practical problem.

After I had calmed myself down, I went on to tackle my self-devaluation. Yes, I reasoned, I had acted stupidly, but no, I was not a stupid individual. I was and remain a fallible human being capable of creativity such as writing a book on overcoming shame, and of a stupid act such as failing to institute simple checks that I 'know' I should ideally have done. That's human beings for you, I reminded myself, fallible and capable of f***ing-up (I am using the actual words that I used with myself at the time because they did help me).

After accepting myself for my grave error, I then tackled my awfulising attitude. Yes, I acknowledged, the consequences of my stupidity were serious: six months of hard slog down the drain or into the ether, or wherever my damned data went. This was very bad, but awful, terrible or the end of the world? Hardly. I would always remember the incident, to be sure, but would I, I wondered, refer to this incident on my deathbed as the worst thing that happened to me, let alone the worst thing that *could* have happened to me? Definitely not, I exclaimed to myself. Yes, it's bad that I lost the book. I value my time, and the thought of devoting a good deal of it with nothing substantial to show at the end is difficult for me to tolerate. But losing the book is hardly awful and I can definitely bear it and, furthermore, doing so will help me to make the important decision concerning whether to rewrite the book or to give up on the project. Rehearsing these flexible and non-extreme attitudes helped me to feel the constructive emotions of annoyance and disappointment rather than the unconstructive emotions of unhealthy anger and depression that I would have experienced over time if I hadn't identified, examined and changed my rigid and extreme attitudes. These constructive emotions helped me to weigh up the pros and cons of rewriting the book, which I decided to do without complaint after I had concluded that this was what I wanted to do and that to do so was in my long-term interests. The result was the book *Overcoming Shame* (Dryden, 1997a) in which I discussed this entire challenging but growthful episode.

The final area in which I have used REBT successfully again concerns unconditional self-acceptance. The REBT concept of unconditional self-acceptance is a profound one (Dryden, 1999a). It encourages people to accept themselves for being fallible, unique organisms. I have already touched on how I used REBT to accept myself unconditionally as a fallible human being for my angry reaction to losing an entire manuscript. Here I briefly want to focus on unconditional self-acceptance for being unique. I have a number of idiosyncratic interests. Earlier in life I might not have pursued some of them because I would have believed that a person of my intelligence and professional standing shouldn't be pursuing such interests (e.g. watching boxing and the soaps on television). Now I see that I am a person of complex diversity; that there is no need for me to attempt to fool myself into thinking that I am other than multidimensional. So, these days, I am more in tune with my 'real' self and hardly inclined at all to pigeonhole myself.

Areas Where I Struggle to Implement REBT in My Life

Are there any areas where I struggle to implement REBT in my life? There most certainly are. Perhaps the area of personal difficulty that I struggle with the most is unhealthy anger. I very easily anger myself when others frustrate me in significant ways, when others get away with acting badly or when they receive advantages that (in my view) they do not deserve. I am well aware that when I make myself unhealthily angry I am holding strong demands about being significantly frustrated and about interpersonal unfairness, but I have great difficulty giving up these demands. I do so in the end, but it involves a great deal of forceful REBT-inspired effort on my part and often the effects only last until the next relevant episode.

Why do I struggle so much with unhealthy anger? Because in my view I have a strong genetic predisposition towards this unconstructive negative emotion. Virtually all the males on my father's side of the family have been quick to anger and this can be traced back over several generations. It's not that I fail to see clearly that unhealthy anger has far more costs than benefits, because I see this most clearly. It's just that on occasion (and sadly these occasions are becoming more frequent, the older I get), I experience a powerful push towards unhealthy anger. I am never violent and I do calm down fairly quickly, partly naturally and partly through using my REBT skills with myself very forcefully. But this doesn't stop me from making myself angry very easily the next time some

Windy Dryden Collected! Up Close and Personal

significant frustration or unfairness impinges upon my personal domain. I usually express my angry feelings verbally, but very occasionally have been known to throw the odd piece of furniture around (but not in the direction of another human)!

Another area in which I struggle to use REBT effectively may seem superficial, but it is important to me. As far back as I can remember, I have bolted down my food, often finishing a dish before the person I am lunching or dining with has half-eaten theirs. I find this habit frustrating because I would like to have a long, lingering meal and I am sure that eating more slowly would have a beneficial effect on my digestion. Again, my felt experience is that I am struggling with a habit with a genetic loading behind it, but whether or not this is the case, it takes a great deal of mindful REBT-inspired effort for me to slow down my eating. Even though I may have done this on one occasion, the very next time I eat, I may well mindlessly wolf down my food again if I am not vigilant.

As I said earlier, I like to be active and I find it fairly easy to be self-disciplined. This is just as well because I do struggle when I have too much work to do. When this happens – and typically it occurs when I come back from holiday and have a great deal of post to deal with both at home and at work – I am vulnerable to stress because I try to deal with the pile of letters *too* quickly. Here, my implicit attitude is that I have to be on top of things all the time and I can't stand it if I'm not. If I do not mindfully tell myself that I don't have to be on top of things at all times and that I can stand to work methodically rather than quickly, I will tend to try mindlessly to do several things at once and get myself quite stressed. This need to get things out of the way quickly has also led me on occasion to make impulsive decisions which I have later come to regret.

On thinking carefully about the issues that I struggle with, it seems to me that I find it much easier to bear the discomfort that is associated with making an effort and being disciplined than the more acute discomfort associated with not being on top of things and being frustrated.

Where REBT Is Not Relevant in My Life

REBT is a therapeutic approach which, like other therapies, has two basic goals: to help overcome disturbance and to promote psychological growth (Mahrer, 1967). In this chapter I have concentrated on showing how I have used REBT (or struggled to use it) to overcome psychological disturbance, although I have also alluded to how I have used it to promote growth in the areas of self-discipline and self-acceptance. However, there are numerous other areas where REBT is not relevant in my life. Thus, it has little or no impact on my political leanings and it has no bearing on what I find involving or interesting. For example, I enjoy football and am a season-ticket holder at Arsenal. Does REBT have an influence here? Decidedly not. It would be relevant if I disturbed myself about the grim fact that Manchester United beat us 2–1 at home in the 1999–2000 season. But I didn't, so it doesn't. Unlike psychoanalysis, REBT does not seek to take a position on a range of social, political and cultural issues. Rather, it sticks with what it is good at: offering a perspective on psychological disturbance and a set of procedures to help people overcome their disturbance and move toward psychological health.

In this chapter, I have outlined why I resonate with REBT, how I have used it successfully in helping me to overcome my own disturbance and to further my own development, and I have discussed areas where I struggle to use REBT effectively. In all other areas of my life, REBT has little or no relevance – and that, in my opinion, is as it should be.

14

The Personal Therapy Experiences of a Rational Emotive Behaviour Therapist

Introduction

In Britain today, most professional bodies require psychotherapists to have had personal therapy before being registered or accredited. While professional bodies representing different therapeutic approaches specify the length and frequency of such personal therapy, this is not the case with more general professional bodies. Both the British Association for Counselling and Psychotherapy and the Division of Counselling Psychology of the British Psychological Society now specify that accredited (in the first case) and chartered (in the second case) practitioners have to have a minimum of 40 hours personal therapy. What is so magical about 40 hours? Neither body has given a convincing argument for this figure and certainly not one that stems from the research literature.

When I began my training as a counsellor in Britain (in 1974), there were few general accrediting professional bodies and very little guidance (outside the analytic tradition) concerning whether to seek personal therapy, let alone what type one should seek and how long and how frequently one should seek it. What follows, then, is an account of my personal therapy experiences from my contemporary position strongly in the Rational Emotive Behaviour Therapy (REBT) tradition.

In recounting my history of personal therapy I will cover experiences of individual and group therapy that I had before my training as a counsellor and after I began training. I will also discuss the personal development groups that I attended which were a mandatory part of three periods of my professional training. Finally, I will discuss instances of self-help because they illuminate why I derived so little help from consulting my fellow practitioners. After relating each episode (or related episodes) of personal therapy, I will comment on my experiences.

Three Funerals and a Wedding

The first time that I entered personal therapy was at the end of 1974. I had just started my professional training as a counsellor and at the age of 24 years, I was suffering from general feelings of unhappiness, a sense that my life was something of an effort even though I had clear vocational goals and was pursuing them. Had I completed the Beck Depression Inventory at that time, I would have scored in the mild to moderate range of depression. So, I decided to seek personal therapy, partly to deal with this state of unhappiness, but also because I thought that I *should* be in personal therapy given that I was training to become a counsellor. Even though there was no edict at that time from any professional body that I was associated with, there was a 'feeling' that being in personal therapy was 'a good thing', a view that was expressed by the various psychoanalytic associations. In Britain, at that time (and to a lesser extent today), counselling in Britain was dominated by psychoanalytic and person centred practitioners. The person centred school recommended the inclusion of personal development groups in the therapeutic curriculum and the psychoanalytic school recommended personal therapy as a mandatory activity which had to take place away from the training institution where one was being trained.

I do not recall why I chose to seek a psychoanalytic personal therapist, but I do remember at that time uncritically accepting what I now consider to be a myth that psychoanalytic therapy is 'deeper' than other approaches.

Funeral 1

I am being somewhat unkind to therapists in this account by referring to my experience with them as *funerals*. What I mean to convey is that they were more or less ineffective from the point of view of helping me overcome my malaise. My first therapist was a middle aged, male Jewish therapist (as I am now) and, I think, a Kleinian. My uncertainty stems from the fact that the person who referred me to him only said he was psychoanalytic by persuasion. My therapist certainly didn't tell me anything directly about his therapeutic orientation and I didn't ask because at that time it never occurred to me to ask.

This therapist was not austere in his demeanour, but neutral and strictly interpretative. Whenever I was speaking he buried his head in his hands, and on the infrequent occasions when he was about to say something, he would rock forward, take his hands away from his mouth, make an interpretation – which I largely found puzzling – and then return to his normal pose. My attempts to seek clarification about his interpretations were met by silence or by a further interpretation along the lines that I wanted him to feed me (hence my guess that he was Kleinian). Indeed, as I recall, this was his favourite interpretation.

This therapy was unstructured and open-ended. I had the sense that I could talk about whatever I wanted and that I could see him for as long as I wanted. Actually, the therapy lasted for about six months of weekly sessions because I was moving away from London and was reluctant to make the weekly trips back to London to see him. While I was not sorry to end, I have always wondered how it would have (and indeed if it would have) progressed had I stayed. One thing was clear at the end of this episode of personal therapy: I still experienced the same sense of unhappiness.

Funeral 2

My second venture into personal therapy was with a psychiatrist who taught a module on 'Psychiatry' in the counselling programme that I had finished in July 1975 and in which I made the transition to lecturer in August 1975. I asked this man for a recommendation for someone who might take me on since I still wanted to get to the bottom of my unhappiness. He suggested that he could see me himself in his National Health Service clinic at the local psychiatric hospital. I should add in his defence that the issue of dual relationships was not as sharply drawn as is now the case. I was just pleased at his suggestion and gratefully accepted his offer.

I knew that this second therapist was also psychoanalytically oriented, but he was far more interactive than my previous therapist. He also practised psychodrama, and we used several psychodrama techniques over the time that I saw him. About five or six months after I had started to see him, he told me that he had to end the therapy because he was leaving his practice to work full-time as a Senior Lecturer in Psychiatry. I understood this and experienced a good sense of closure since he also arranged for me to see a colleague in the same clinic. My abiding memories of this second episode of personal therapy was that my therapist took voluminous notes at the beginning which I found off-putting. However, he was quite happy to stop doing so when I asked him to. I also remember the psychodrama techniques and found them quite useful in getting me out of my head and more into my experience. My most vivid memory, as I look back on this experience, was that we both smoked cigars during therapy sessions, but that his were longer than mine!

There was again no therapeutic contract at the beginning and, like my first experience, it had an open-ended quality about it. However, as you may have surmised, my feelings of unhappiness persisted.

Funeral 3

I was then referred to a man who was one of the few fully trained psychoanalysts working in the Midlands. However, he did briefer work in the clinic where I saw the second therapist and, as indicated above, he agreed to take me on at the request of that person. In all, I had eight sessions with this man, an experience which I found quite frustrating. Again, there was no therapeutic contract and no agreed time limit as part of this contract. In my innocence, I was operating on the assumption that again the therapy would be open-ended. My third therapist was neutral and cold with it. Looking back, I never experienced my first therapist as cold even though he was strictly neutral. Somehow, I sensed that he did have a concern for my well-being. However, this was not the case with my third therapist. I also remember, on one occasion, asking him whether what I was experiencing was transference and received quite a sarcastic reply. No, this man didn't show any concern for me as I look back and this was also how I felt at the time.

I am drawn to books on therapy which seek to explore key therapy moments, crucial sessions and turning points in the therapeutic process. For I can still remember quite vividly the eighth and final session that I had with this man. He began the session by announcing that this was to be our last session. I am very sure looking back that we had not agreed on an eight-session contract (or any other time-limited contract) and my sense of shock and bewilderment at the time strengthens me in my retrospective view on this point. He then said casually, and this is really clear in my mind, that if I wanted to continue to see him then I could do so in his private practice. I can't recall how I responded to this other than to decline the invitation and to get myself out of his office as soon as I could. The lasting impression that I have of this man is that he was arrogant. I recall him being late for one session and offering no apology or explanation for his behaviour. When I brought this up in the session he dismissed my legitimate complaint and proceeded to interpret my reaction.

I remember to this day feeling dazed as I made my way home after the final session. I just couldn't believe what had happened. Had I imagined it? Had I offended him in some way? I was given no explanation for this abrupt termination except that this was to be the last session.

. . . and a wedding

Having been dismissed by this third psychoanalytic therapist, I decided to fall back on my own resources. Earlier in my life I had overcome my public-speaking anxiety which I developed due to my attitude towards a speech impediment by implementing a technique that I heard described on the radio. In brief, I resolved to speak up at every opportunity – without recourse to the myriad of ways I had developed to prevent me from stammering – while telling myself: 'If I stammer, I stammer. F**k it!' Not only did I largely overcome my anxiety by this method, I stammered far less than hitherto.

Those of you who know anything about Rational Emotive Behaviour Therapy (REBT) will recognise this as an unschooled version of one of its major techniques: the rehearsal of a non-extreme attitude while simultaneously confronting one's fears. Consequently, it will not come as too much of a surprise to learn that in 1976 I turned for inspiration to *A New Guide to Rational Living*, an REBT self-help book written by Albert Ellis and Robert Harper (1975). We had briefly studied REBT during my counselling programme a year or so earlier, and I remembered resonating to Ellis's ideas about the theory and practice of psychotherapy, but didn't have time to study REBT in depth because we were mainly concerned with the work of Carl Rogers.

On reading about the REBT perspective on psychological problems and their remediation I quickly saw that my unhappiness was due to feelings of inferiority about various personal issues. I further realised that the reason I suffered from such feelings was because I held a number of rigid and extreme attitudes towards myself in relation to achievement and approval. At last, I had found what I was looking for: an approach which spelled out for me a perspective that I could make sense of and relate to (that I was unhappy because of the rigid and extreme attitudes that I held towards myself) and a way of overcoming these feelings (by identifying, examining and changing these attitudes using a variety of cognitive, imaginal, behavioural and emotive techniques).

So, my self-help therapy gave me what my therapist-delivered therapy failed to – clear information about a conceptualisation of my psychological problems that I accepted and specific guidelines of how to overcome these problems. Not one of my three individual therapists gave me any kind of account of how they conceptualised my problems, and none of them gave me any guidelines at all concerning how to remediate these problems. I am not saying that all clients require such clarity, but I certainly did. If they had given me specific directions about conceptualisation and treatment, I could have given my informed consent to proceed or decided that I did not want to continue.

You may be wondering whether I was not given this information because I was expected to know it being a trainee counsellor. I doubt this because (a) openness was not a feature of my therapists' behaviour in other areas and (b) they did not even inquire of me whether I wanted this information. Therefore, if any of my therapists decided not to give me information about conceptualisation and treatment because they thought I would know this already, then they were sadly mistaken.

Comments

None of my three therapists made any significant attempt to explain to me how they conceptualised psychological problems in general or my problems in particular. This is what Bordin (1979) considers a key therapist task and forms an important part of eliciting informed consent from the patient. Thus, none of my three therapists elicited my informed consent to proceed with therapy. While some would regard this as an ethical oversight, I will be charitable and say that my therapists were following the analytic tradition where such explicit explanations are generally eschewed. Clearly, this lack of explanation did not meet my psychological 'need' for explicitness. I am a person who likes to know clearly what help I am being offered so I can make my own mind up whether or not I wish to proceed. My attempts to elicit such clarity were either ignored, interpreted or, in the case of my third therapist, ridiculed. Why did I not decide earlier that psychoanalytic therapy was not for me? Simply because I did not have the confidence in my judgement to do so.

Looking back, I thought that if I stayed in psychoanalytic therapy long enough, I would be helped by the process, despite evidence to the contrary. This taught me that clients may place too much faith in their therapists who they think know what is best for them. As a therapist, I emphasise to my clients that what I have to offer them is one approach to understanding client problems and how to address them, and I stress that there are other approaches available. I tell them that if what I have to offer is not perceived as helpful to them then they are not to blame and that I will make every effort to refer them to a practitioner who may be able to help them more effectively. As my late friend and colleague, Arnold Lazarus (Dryden, 1991) said, making judicious referrals is a skill and a mark of therapist maturity. None of my individual therapists raised this as a possibility. Did they fail to do so because they knew I was a therapist-in-training and thought that I could be expected to know about their approach to that therapy they were practising? Did they assume that I had already made an informed decision that I wished to proceed with therapy in each case? As I said earlier, I doubt that they had made such assumptions and even if they had, then they were in error. What I have learned from this is not to assume that therapists in training or even trained therapists have given informed consent to proceed without explicitly eliciting such consent first, unless there is powerful evidence to the contrary.

None of these three therapists discussed in this section explained to me what my tasks were in therapy or for that matter explained what tasks they were going to engage in during the therapeutic process. My guess is that either I was expected to know as a counselling trainee, or more likely I was expected to just talk about whatever I was disturbed about at the time. It was all very unstructured and loose when I needed clarity and structure. The exception to this was the second therapist who asked me if I wanted to try out some psychodrama techniques on several issues that I was exploring. My recollection was that this therapist introduced the possibility of using these techniques in a relaxed, non-pressuring way and I was pleased with both the offer and how it was made.

Bordin (1979) has argued that it is important for therapist and client to agree on the latter's *goals* for change. This does not mean that the therapist uncritically accepts the client's goals. Rather, it means discussing openly the issue of goals so that agreed objectives emerge from such dialogue. It would have been helpful to me if my individual therapists had initiated such a discussion (for I do believe that it is the therapist's responsibility to do so). While I now understand the psychoanalytic position on goals, I did not realise this then and therefore I was looking towards my therapists for guidance on this issue – guidance which never came. Even if I couldn't realistically have expected my therapists to change their practice to accommodate to my preference, was it too much to expect them to elicit my position so that they could judge whether I was suitable for their mode of treatment? I think not. Again, in my practice, I attempt to elicit my clients' views on this point and I am clear with them concerning my position on eliciting goals for change.

It should be clear by now that none of my therapists understood what I thought might be most helpful to me from therapy. Such understanding forms one important part of what Bordin (1979) refers to as the *bond* component of the working alliance. Another aspect of the bond relevant to these personal therapies concerns the interpersonal connection between therapist and client. The relationship between the first therapist and myself was fairly neutral. Behind his steadfast interpretative stance, I sensed he was a fairly kindly man, but this was only a shadowy impression.

As I said earlier, I knew the second therapist in a different context in that he taught in my counsellor training programme when I was a student and continued to teach this module during the time that I consulted him when I was lecturing on the same course. So, I knew him in other contexts and experienced him as someone who was reasonably caring. This side of him came to the fore after I had requested that he stop taking notes and give me greater face-to-face contact. Before this I sensed that he was hiding behind his psychiatrist role. He responded well to my request and from that point I would characterise our therapeutic relationship as two colleagues, one senior and the other junior, working to help the latter towards some unspecified goal. Of all the individual therapists that I consulted, he was the one who best understood my need to be active in therapy and suggested on occasion that we use psychodrama techniques. I would say that of the three therapists discussed in this section, I had the smoothest relationship with him and the most difficult relationship with the third therapist.

I didn't have the sense that the third therapist was listening attentively to me. He may have been, but as Rogers (1957) wisely said, for the core conditions to have a therapeutic impact on the client, the client has to experience their presence. If the therapist is listening attentively and the client does not experience this then there will accrue no positive impact for the client. Indeed, I experienced him as detached, uncaring and somewhat arrogant. The way he abruptly and unilaterally terminated therapy accompanied by the offer that he could continue to see me as a patient in his private practice showed the somewhat exploitative nature of this man's work with me and perhaps his greed. In brief, I didn't much care for him and sensed also that he didn't much care for me. By today's standards, I suppose one could argue that there were abusive elements to this relationship. I am thinking here of his unilateral announcement, without any prior warning, that he was terminating the therapy.

To be charitable, one might argue that in 1976 the importance of planning for termination was not as much appreciated as it is now and the practice of moving patients from the National Health Service where therapy is free to the private (fee-paying) sector may not have been viewed as unethical as it would be now. However, this man was a fully trained psychoanalyst, for goodness sake, and a full member of the Institute of Psychoanalysis, one of the most prestigious psychoanalytic institutes in the world. Even at that time, I am sure that his colleagues would have been shocked by his behaviour towards me. The fact that I used this experience to very good effect should not be used to condone this behaviour.

I described earlier how I gave up on therapist-delivered therapy and turned, with good results, to self-help. Why was this experience more effective for me than over one year's therapy delivered by well qualified practitioners? First, I resonated much more with the REBT explanatory model than with the psychoanalytic one, such as I understood it. I liked the fact that when I read Ellis and Harper's (1975) *A New Guide to Rational Living*, the authors, from the very outset, made perfectly clear how they conceptualised emotional disorders. However, even if my therapists had clearly stated the psychoanalytic view of psychopathology, I would still have favoured the REBT view. Why? Because it emphasised the role of cognitive factors which struck a real chord with me in helping to understand not only my own problems, but also those of my clients. Up to that time, I was still practising person centred therapy, but my encounter with this REBT self-help book and my subsequent successful self-help efforts led me to decide to re-train in REBT, a decision I have never regretted.

Second, I resonated with the REBT's direct, clearly understood and, some would say, no-nonsense approach to dealing with one's emotional problems. It was never really clear to me how talking in an open-ended way, as in my psychoanalytic therapies, would help me to overcome my sense of unhappiness, but it was crystal clear to me on reading Ellis & Harper's (1975) book what I needed to do to free myself of these feelings. I needed to identify, examine, and change my rigid and extreme attitudes and act in ways that were consistent with the rational alternatives to these attitudes. Simple, but not easy, as we say in REBT.

For me, one of the problems with these individual therapies was that they were too open-ended with respect to goals. None of my therapists asked me what I wanted to achieve from therapy. When I began to use REBT with myself, I not only asked myself what my problems were, I asked myself where I wanted to be with respect to each of these problems. I saw that my problems at the time were to do with feelings of inferiority and I wanted to be more self-accepting. The REBT position on unconditional self-acceptance (Dryden, 1999a) was a revelation to me. It encouraged me to view myself as equal in humanity to all other humans, to fully acknowledge my weaknesses as well as my strengths and to appreciate that the existence of the former did not mean that I was inferior and that I could address them non-defensively. Carl Rogers' (1957) notion of unconditional positive regard did not have a similar impact on me since it was, as I saw it then, encouraging people to prize rather than to accept themselves.

Having a clear idea of where I was headed on this issue as well as how to work towards getting there were key ingredients to the progress that I made in overcoming my unhappiness. I should add that in my over-enthusiasm I did not appreciate at the time that it is not possible to achieve perfect unconditional self-acceptance. I realise now that this is a life-long process and whereas I am far more self-accepting now that I was then, I still have my vulnerabilities in this area. This fact, however, does not discourage me.

It is perhaps strange to think of developing a bond with yourself, but in self-help that is precisely what happens. In helping myself overcoming my malaise, I developed a more accurate understanding of myself than that shown by my personal therapists towards me. This was because I used the REBT perspective to understand myself. Note that I could not use the psychoanalytic perspective to do this, nor was I helped to do so by any of my personal therapists. Finally, an important aspect of the therapeutic bond is pacing. All of my therapists worked too slowly with me, another feature of the psychoanalytic approach with which I did not resonate. By contrast, when I used REBT to help myself, I was able to do so at my own, quicker rate. From all these experiences, I have learned the following which I routinely implement in my practice as a therapist.

1. I explain to clients exactly what REBT is and outline broadly the kinds of tasks that I am likely to implement and the kinds of tasks they will be called upon to engage in. I elicit their reactions and, if they indicate that REBT is not the type of therapy they are seeking, I refer them to a therapist who is likely to meet their treatment preferences as long as these preferences do not perpetuate the clients' problems.

2. I help my clients to specify their problems and what they want to achieve with respect to each of these problems. Then I focus therapy on helping my clients to achieve their goals.

3. I strive to develop the kind of bond that will facilitate the treatment process and if I consider that any of my colleagues can better develop a preferred bond with any of the people that are seeking my help, I do not hesitate to effect a suitable referral. I am fortunate that financial considerations do not compromise my position on this issue since I am not dependent upon my practice for my livelihood.

Having described and commented on my experiences of both therapist-delivered and self-help therapy, let me move on to my experiences of being a member of a therapy group which I joined in the final year of my undergraduate degree. This experience therefore occurred before I began to train as a counsellor.

One Year of Group Therapy

Actually, the therapeutic experiences I have just related were not my first experience of being a client. In May 1970, towards the end of my second year of my undergraduate degree, I decided to stop working for my exams and to feign illness. I was sent to see the college psychiatrist who decided that I needed to join a psychodynamic group that was being convened at the beginning of the next academic session in October 1970 that he was running with a psychiatrist colleague. In the interim, however, I finally got my act together and re-sat the exams in July which I duly passed.

I dutifully joined the group, which comprised about eight patients and two therapists, who both took a fairly inactive, interpretative role.

I did admit to the group that I had feigned illness after about six months, but since I was well over my crisis by then, this disclosure didn't really help me.

Looking back, I think that my stopping working and feigning illness was an attempt to get out of something that I did not enjoy (second year psychology topics are notoriously tedious) and I hoped that I could go into the final year of the course on the basis of my course work in lieu of passing the exams. Once I had tested the system and realised that I couldn't avoid the second-year examinations, I faced up to my responsibilities and studied hard from that point forward. My decision to take responsibility did not come from my participation in the group since all this happened before I joined the group.

I did learn one thing from the group sessions which proved to be a valuable life lesson. I became friendly with one of the group members and we started to meet socially (which, if I recall, was not prohibited by our group membership). This friendship turned out to be very one-sided and if I did not contact him, he wouldn't contact me. Initially, I disturbed myself about this lack of reciprocity and even confronted him about it in the group. He apologised, promised to initiate contact, but didn't. At this point, I remember changing my attitude about it. I reasoned that he was the person he was and not the person I expected him to be and if I wanted to be friends with him, I had to realise that I would have to initiate contact because he wasn't going to. Once I accepted this grim reality, I calmed down and decided to remain friends with the guy. He never did initiate contact, but I was undisturbed about it. Looking back on this episode, it occurs to me that I never shared my self-authored insight with the group since I tend to work things out in my head rather than through dialogue with other people.

So, what else did I learn from being in the group? Precious little other than psychodynamically-oriented groups were not for me. This was a lesson that I had to relearn several times as I will presently discuss. Of course, some would say that being a member of the group helped me to come to this realisation, and indeed this may be true despite my protestations to the contrary. However, this hypothesis is impossible to disprove. All I can say is that it didn't seem to me either at the time or in retrospect that being in the group had a bearing on my adjustment to my friend's behaviour.

Comments

Looking back, I really don't know why I was referred to this psychodynamic group. Certainly, when I saw the psychiatrist for an assessment interview and he made the recommendation that I join the group, he did not give me any kind of rationale for my joining. My impression is that he needed to get sufficient numbers for the group to be viable and there were no strong contra-indications that would rule me out as a group member. At the time, I was in awe of this psychiatrist (because of his status rather than his personality) and if he thought that I needed to join a group for one year, then he must be right. After all, he was the professional and I was a mere undergraduate. Now, of course, I know different. As a practitioner, I regard giving clients a clear rationale for treatment as paramount and I make sure that they think carefully about my treatment recommendations before accepting them.

One of the features of this group experience was the inactivity of the group therapists. Much of the work was done by the group members who often gave each other fairly inept advice. When the therapists did intervene it was to make interpretations and if these were ignored, as they generally were, they remained silent. From what I could see, very few of the group members derived much benefit from the year of group therapy.

This experience taught me that it was important for a group therapist to encourage interaction between members, and to intervene frequently in the group process. This assists group members to focus on their goals and presents a corrective force when group members give each other bad advice. The way I do this as an REBT group therapist is to highlight any helpful aspects of the proffered advice, and then to focus on the psychological issues that group members often overlook when they advise one another (Dryden, 1999b). In this way, I strive to preserve the motivation of the group members to be helpful to one another, while focusing the members' attention to what they need to do psychologically to achieve their goals. As an REBT group therapist, I see myself as having a gate-keeping role, whereby I encourage fruitful interaction between group members; and an educative role, whereby I encourage members to use REBT techniques to help themselves and one another. The two group therapists running the group that I have just described were rather poor gate-keepers, often allowing unhelpful interactions between group members to develop unchecked and were poor educators in that they did not provide explanations for their interpretations.

Four Tedious Years of Personal Development Groups

In all, I experienced four years of being in three personal develop-ment groups. Frankly, I found them something of a waste of time. Since they were composed of students who saw one another in other contexts (academic, supervisory and social), most of us were on our guard concerning what we said in the group about our lives and about our feelings towards one another. Not that such groups were unhelpful for everyone. From what I could see they especially helped socially inhibited members who learned that they could talk about themselves and even confront other group members and that nothing terrible resulted from such disclosures and confrontations. Since I already knew this, I decided to knuckle down and play the game which seemed to be that one talked about oneself at length every five or six weeks and said something in every other group when others were talking. It seemed that unless you did this, you became the focus of the other group members who wanted to know why you were silent or distancing yourself from the group.

I make no apologies for sounding cynical about these groups, but I do apologise to my past students for making them a mandatory part of counselling programmes that I have run. I did so not because I thought that they were of any value but because professional accrediting bodies expect them to be a part of the training curriculum and I didn't want to disadvantage my students by depriving them of this 'mandatory' experience.

Comments

These personal development groups were strictly speaking not therapy groups, but more like sensitivity groups. Group members were not seen as having personal problems for which they needed help, but developing professionals who needed to become more aware of themselves and their impact on other people. This is quite a reasonable activity for counsellors in training to be engaged in, and I wouldn't have objected to attending one such group for a year. What I objected to was having to attend three such groups over a four-year period. My requests for exemption fell on deaf years for a reason that I can understand being a counsellor trainer myself, but which ultimately cannot be justified, since the raison d'être of a personal development group (PDG) is the 'personal development' of its individual members. It was thought that if trainees could exempt themselves from being a member of a personal development group, then this would produce a schism in the training cohort which would split into 'attenders' and 'non-attenders'. Trainers are very wary of permitting any practices which divide a training cohort and also deprive group members of a forum where they could discuss their feelings about the course and about other course members in a group facilitated by a person external to the course. However, I am not speaking against having a forum for course members to discuss the course, although in my view this needs to be done with the course director present.

It seemed, therefore, that my continuing membership in these personal development groups had more to do with promoting harmony (or at least minimising conflict) in a cohort of trainees than with facilitating the personal development of individual trainees. My argument at the time was that my own particular personal development could have been better promoted outside the group setting, and I still hold to this view.

I mentioned earlier in my description of my personal development groups that many trainees were wary about what they said because they had to see their fellow trainees in other settings. If membership in a personal development group is to be a mandatory training experience, it would be more sensible if such groups were composed of students from different training courses so that each group member of a PDG would only meet with other members in the PDG setting. The practice of putting trainees in patient groups addresses this issue, but raises a number of other issues, a discussion of which is beyond the scope of the present chapter. My suggested alternative would also mean that trainees who had previously attended a PDG would not be obligated to attend another.

If this practice had been in operation when I did my training I would have been spared three tedious years of attending PDG groups and would only have had to put up with one such year!

Preparing for a Mid-Life Crisis That Never Happened: Two Months of Jungian Therapy

As I approached my 40th birthday, I decided to re-enter personal therapy to prepare for my mid-life crisis. I should say that I wasn't experiencing a crisis at the time, nor have I subsequently had the crisis, but I was persuaded by the idea that preparing oneself adequately for a crisis is better psychologically than responding to that crisis after it happens. This time I deliberately chose a Jungian therapist on the basis that Jung's work seemed especially suited to mid-life issues and I wanted to see a female therapist merely because all my previous therapists had been male.

I remained in this therapy for about two months. It became clear to me fairly quickly and, I believe, also to my therapist that I was not suited to a Jungian approach. For one thing, I couldn't remember any of my dreams, which I think my therapist found somewhat frustrating, since it seemed to me that she liked to work with dreams. In addition, I found talking more helpful than her interventions which, to some degree, took me away from my train of thought, but not in a productive way. So, I decided to terminate, an ending which was mutually agreed, well planned and amicable. This ending enabled us to work together on a collegial, professional level much later. These contacts revealed her to be much warmer and more humorous than she ever was as my therapist!

Comments

When I first entered individual therapy, I had just begun to train as a counsellor and therefore it could have been said that I was naïve in deciding to go into psychoanalytic therapy. My knowledge of what was available in the therapeutic scene was fairly limited and my major preoccupation was to find a therapist who came highly recommended. However, sixteen or so years on, I could not be said to be naïve. I had already had a good deal of therapy and had discovered that I was more suited to a cognitive-behavioural approach than a psychoanalytic one. So, you may be wondering: what possessed me to go into Jungian therapy? I have already given one explanation: Jung's approach was said to be particularly suited for those wishing to explore mid-life conflicts and although I hadn't begun to be affected by such issues, I was taking preventative measures. I also wanted to see a woman.

But as I have engaged in writing this chapter, it is also clearer to me that I would not have made a very good client of cognitive-behaviour therapy either, not in the early 1990s at any rate. If I had sought help from a cognitive-behaviour therapist at this point, I would have had to curb my tendency (which, as I write, I see would have been clearly present) to supervise my therapist. If I may humbly say so, I have been a leading proponent of REBT in particular, and of cognitive behaviour therapy in general, for a number of years and had obtained by the early 1990s a reputation in the field. I was probably Britain's leading REBT therapist and could not envisage consulting one of the very small band of trained British REBT therapists. First, I knew them all quite well and had trained most of them, and second, I would have been sorely tempted to supervise them and correct their errors! In addition, I would not have thought of consulting a more generic CBT therapist because they would not have focused on my rigid and extreme attitudes, but chosen instead to focus on my cognitive distortions and the like which I would have found frustrating as I did when I trained in Beck's cognitive therapy in 1981 after I had trained as an REBT therapist a few years earlier.

So, it is a bit rich of me to criticise my Jungian therapist for practising an approach which I must have known in my heart of hearts I would not resonate with. This, of course, turned out to be the case and thus, I do not feel inclined to be too critical of my Jungian therapist.

I will only comment on one further thing. As I mentioned earlier, years after this therapy had ended, I met my ex-therapist in a professional activity and found her to be a charming, warm woman with a good sense of humour. These qualities were not apparent to me when I was her patient. This raises for me an interesting question. In adopting a fairly neutral therapeutic style, do psychodynamic therapists (and I include Jungians here), lose much of the therapeutic potency of their natural interpersonal style and qualities? My experience is that they probably do.

Consulting with Albert Ellis

The final personal 'therapy' experience concerns the consultations that I have had over the years with Albert Ellis, the founder of REBT and the person I most consider a mentor. For over twenty years I have made annual visits to what is now known as the Albert Ellis Institute in New York City. Whenever I go, I arrange to see Albert Ellis in what are known as his lunch time and supper time sessions. These are, in effect, his breaks between therapy sessions. While for the most part I have used these sessions to discuss matters relating to (a) finer points of the theory and practice of REBT; (b) problems that I have had in my clinical practice of REBT; and (c) joint writing projects, I have on various occasions used these sessions to consult with Al on a number of personal issues. Normally, these have been issues where I have failed to identify a subtle factor which has eluded me and thus, I have not been able to get to the heart of the matter. Invariably, Al has helped me to identify this factor and has trusted me to take remedial steps to deal with the clarified problem on my own.

Comments

Of all the therapist-delivered treatment I have had – and when I put together all of them, I am shocked to learn how much therapy I have had (with so little return!) – Albert Ellis, in the sporadic times when I have discussed a personal issue with him, has been by far the best therapist I have ever had. Why is this so? First, our therapeutic discussions over the years have been in the context of him being more of a mentor than a therapist. This for me challenges the wisdom of implementing overly strict boundaries between therapy and non-therapy discussions with the same person. Such boundaries would be constructive for some, but not for me.

Another aspect of therapy with Al Ellis that I appreciated was his use of self-disclosure. I would discuss a personal issue with Al and he would tell me about a relevant experience that he had had with the same issue. Sometimes, he would tell me how he helped one of his clients with a similar problem. Rarely, if ever, would he practise formal, active-directive REBT with me. While I have never discussed this point with him, my sense is that he was quite aware that I knew REBT theory and practice very well and could trust that I had tried to use it with myself before discussing the issue with him. He respected my position as a knowledgeable REBT therapist, and sought to help me in ways that I had perhaps not thought of. His indirect approach here was most beneficial.

As I write this, I am reminded of a remark that one of my REBT colleagues made of supervisory feedback he had received on one of his therapy tapes by an REBT supervisor he had sought help from. 'He treated me as if I knew nothing about REBT,' claimed my colleague, who found this approach to supervision patronising and unhelpful. Al Ellis never once treated me in our therapeutic discussions as if I did not know REBT.

The other helpful aspect of having 'therapy' with Ellis was that his style with me did not change according to the issue we were discussing. I contrast this with the discrepancy between my Jungian therapist's 'inside therapy' style and her 'outside therapy' style. Al was his humorous, raunchy, interesting self no matter what we were discussing. In a phrase, I experienced him to be genuine in all his dealings with me, and this 'genuine informality' is a therapist quality that I find particularly helpful as a client and which I strive to achieve in my own work. I contrast this with the 'non-genuine formal' style of my other therapists.

It is fitting to close this chapter with my therapy experiences with Albert Ellis since I owe him so much as a professional. It is also fitting that I have ended with a discussion of my one positive therapist-delivered treatment that I have had. Although I have been critical of my previous therapists (with the exception of Albert Ellis), I want to end by saying that I would not be a very easy client for most therapists. I have a clear idea of what is helpful to me and what is not, and I have a definite preference for self-help, which makes being in therapy a problematic experience for me if that therapy is not focused sharply on encouraging me to help myself.

And yet, so many of my therapists failed to discover this. As a result, I have learned to consistently ask myself whether or not my

REBT practice best suits the needs of the person who is seeking my help. If it does, then we can proceed; but if not, I am prepared to refer this person to someone else. This is the lasting legacy of my personal therapy experiences and one that helps to keep my feet on the ground and helps me to remain dedicated and humble.

15
My Idiosyncratic Practice of REBT

In this chapter, I concentrate on my idiosyncratic practice of REBT and outline the reasons why I practise it in the way that I do. In particular, I discuss the importance of:

1. Developing relationships with clients based on the principle of 'informed allies';
2. Developing a 'case conceptualisation' with complex 'cases';
3. Developing an REBT-influenced problems and goals list with clients;
4. Working with specific examples of nominated problems at the beginning of therapy;
5. Identifying the adversities at 'A' in the assessment process;
6. Focusing on thinking 'C's as well as emotional and behavioural 'C's;
7. Helping clients to develop and rehearse the full version of flexible and non-extreme attitudes;
8. Encouraging clients to voice their doubts, reservations and objections to REBT concepts and to the REBT therapeutic process;
9. Deliberately instructing clients in the skills of REBT;
10. Encouraging clients to take responsibility for their change process;
11. Using vivid methods to promote change; and
12. Using humour to develop rapport and promote change.

While this list of modes of practice is not designed to be an exhaustive account of my REBT practice, it is meant to indicate what I particularly emphasise in with clients from an REBT perspective.

Introduction

To those outside the cognitive-behavioural therapeutic tradition, all CBT approaches appear the same. This, of course, is far from the truth and while CBT approaches share some important similarities, they also differ from one another in other important ways (cf. Dobson, 2001). For example, while REBT is similar to Beck's cognitive therapy in some respects, it differs from it in others (Dryden, 1984; Haaga & Davison, 1991).

When we consider a specific CBT approach like REBT are we on safe ground in assuming that all REBT therapists practise REBT in the same way? The answer is: it depends. Thus, Robb, Backx & Thomas (1999) found in their survey sample of REBT therapists on the Albert Ellis Institute referral list that when faced with clients who articulated the insight problem (i.e. 'It makes sense, but I don't really believe it yet'), therapists generally responded with cognitive interventions. Warren & McLellarn (1987), in their earlier survey of the same listed therapists, found that 'most RE[B]T therapists follow the philosophies and practices of RE[B]T as espoused and advocated by Ellis' (p. 71). However, they also found that a 'significant number of therapists disagree with Ellis in some of his philosophical views and appeared to adapt the practice of RE[B]T to their own preferred style' (p. 71). On the latter point, Warren & McLellarn found that 36% of their sample reported using inventories designed to identify rigid and extreme attitudes as an assessment procedure; 56% reported using rational role reversal with 38% of clients; and 46% suggest that their clients (38%) listen to audio-recordings of therapy sessions as a homework assignment.

Given that REBT therapists do seem to practise REBT in different ways, while at the same time concurring on some of its main theories and practices, we need to know more about individual differences among REBT practitioners. In this chapter, then, I will take the lead and outline my own practice of REBT, focusing particularly on what I emphasise in my practice and why I do so. Space considerations mean that I am unable to discuss any of these points in depth and I will rarely have an opportunity to detail *how* I make the interventions I discuss (see Dryden, 1999c; Dryden, Neenan & Yankura, 1999 for a more detailed discussion on these points).

Developing Relationships with Clients Based on the Principle of 'Informed Allies'

Although REBT employs a variety of cognitive, emotive, imaginal and behavioural techniques (Ellis & Dryden, 1997), it needs to be stressed that these techniques are used within the context of a therapeutic relationship and as such the development, maintenance and ending of this relationship needs to be considered. It is my view that the REBT literature has tended to underplay the importance of this relationship, a trend that I have tried to counterbalance in some of my own writings (Dryden, 1999c; Dryden, 2001b). In these writings and in my own practice of REBT, I emphasise a concept that I have called the principle of 'informed allies'. This concept comprises the principle of 'informed consent' and the tri-partite idea of the working alliance first introduced by Bordin (1979), which I first introduced into the REBT literature in the late 1980s (Dryden, 1987b). Bordin's conceptualisation of the working alliance highlights the therapeutic bond that develops between therapist and client, the *goals* of the enterprise and the therapeutic tasks that therapist and client undertake during the life of the therapeutic relationship to facilitate goal attainment.

I operationalise the 'informed allies' concept in my practice of REBT in the following ways:

1. Early on in therapy, I outline the REBT model of psychological disturbance and psychological change to my client in bite-sized chunks to facilitate client understanding, using when appropriate the client's presenting problems. I also give them an idea of how I practise REBT and what this means for their participation in this process. I then ask them if they give their *informed consent* to proceed. Three outcomes are possible:

   (a) The client wishes to proceed, so we do;

   (b) The client is unsure; here I usually offer a short-term contract so that the client can experience REBT in action and thus make a more informed decision to proceed or not; and

(c) The client does not wish to proceed. Here I attempt to discover what therapeutic approach may 'fit' the client better and effect a suitable referral.

2. In practising REBT I attempt to develop a suitable *bond* with my client. There are a number of issues that I keep in mind in doing so:

(a) *Informal vs. formal.* Clients differ with respect to their wishes for an informal or formal relationship with their therapists. As long as these wishes are healthy and do not unwittingly perpetuate the clients' problems, I am happy to meet their preferences on this point.

(b) *Directiveness.* While REBT is an active-directive, persuasive approach to therapy, I tend to be less directive and less overtly persuasive with clients who are reactant in personality organisation and who react adversely to attempts to influence them. With these clients I am explicit about REBT concepts and emphasise their choice concerning whether or not they implement these concepts in their life.

(c) *Humour.* Clients differ widely concerning their response to humorous interventions in REBT. While I prefer to practise REBT with a sense of humour (see below), I am quite happy to practise REBT in a more serious vein when this is required. I often have an intuitive 'feel' concerning a client's 'humour quotient', but when I am unsure about whether or not a client will respond well to my brand of humour, I offer 'trial' jokes (in the same way that an analyst makes trial interpretations) and gauge their response to these. I also ask for feedback on my humour and adjust my therapeutic style according to the feedback I receive.

3. In my experience as a supervisor of trainee REBT therapists, I often find that trainees lose sight of their clients' *goals* as they work with their clients over time (Neenan & Dryden, 2001). I am mindful in my own practice to keep my focus and that of my clients on their goals for change. In doing so, I consider that I am being a good role model since one of the ways in which clients maintain their psychological problems is lack of

mindfulness about their healthy goals. I will discuss goals further later in this chapter.

4. I mentioned earlier that the technical aspects of REBT are often highlighted in the literature. From a working alliance perspective, I am particularly concerned about the following issues concerning therapeutic *tasks:*

   (a) That clients understand (i) what their tasks are; (ii) what my tasks are as an REBT therapist; and (iii) the relationship between both sets of tasks;

   (b) That clients understand the relationship between their therapeutic tasks and their therapeutic goals;

   (c) That clients are deemed capable of executing their tasks before they are asked to carry them out;

   (d) That clients are trained to carry out their therapeutic tasks as appropriate;

   (e) That I carry out my therapeutic tasks with skill, care and enthusiasm; and

   (f) That I suggest the use of therapeutic tasks that are potent enough to help clients to achieve their goals.

Developing a 'Case Formulation' with Complex 'Cases'

Beginning with the pioneering work of Persons (1989), cognitive therapists have espoused the value of carrying out case formulations to aid therapeutic intervention. REBT therapists have not embraced this concept as readily and indeed, my work on the subject is the only publication that centrally addresses this issue from an REBT perspective (Dryden, 1999c). Indeed, when I showed a pre-publication copy of this work to Albert Ellis, he questioned the efficiency of making case formulations prior to therapeutic intervention in REBT. His point was that therapists can waste valuable therapeutic time making such formulations and that they could better use such time helping clients to address and overcome their psychological problems. This would be true if therapists carried out lengthy pre-treatment case formulations with all of their clients, but I am not suggesting this, nor is it my practice. My view about conducting a case formulation is this. I will do one when:

1. *The referral is a complex one.* Once the client has given their informed consent to proceed with REBT and if it transpires that the client has complex problems, I will carry out a full case formulation before making any substantive change-based interventions since doing so will help me to understand the complexity of the client's 'case' and help me to save time in the longer run. This meets Ellis's inefficiency argument.

2. *The client isn't making progress as anticipated and/or I am stuck with the client.* When I predict that I can help a client, but the client doesn't make the anticipated progress or I get stuck and don't know why, I will then tend to do a full case formulation with that person. This often helps me to understand why the client isn't making the anticipated progress and/or why I am stuck and suggests avenues for intervention that had not previously occurred to me.

Let me now briefly describe the factors that I consider when I do a formal case formulation. I call this doing a 'UPCP' which stands for 'Understanding the Person in the Context of their Problems' because I do not like referring to a person as a 'case' (Dryden, 1999c). This involves:

1. Obtaining basic information and utilising initial impressions;
2. Developing a problem list;
3. Identifying goals for therapy;
4. Developing a list of problem emotions ('C's);
5. Developing a list of problem adversities;
6. Identifying core rigid and extreme attitudes;
7. Identifying dysfunctional behavioural 'C's;
8. Identifying the purposive nature of dysfunctional behaviour;
9. Identifying ways in which the client prevents or cuts short the experience of problems;

10. Identifying ways in which the client compensates for problems;

11. Identifying meta-psychological problems;

12. Identifying the cognitive consequences of core rigid and extreme attitudes;

13. Identifying the manner of problem expression and the interpersonal responses to these expressions;

14. Identifying the client's health and medication status;

15. Developing an understanding of relevant predisposing factors;

16. Predicting the client's likely responses to therapy;

17. Negotiating a narrative account of the UPCP for consideration with the client.

For more detailed information on how to conduct a UPCP together with a case example see Chapter 5 in Dryden (1999c).

The final point that I wish to make on 'case formulations' is one that Ellis has made informally in many of his professional workshops. This is that competent REBT practitioners build up a working picture of their clients as they proceed in therapy and share this with their clients as a way of fine tuning these more informal case formulations. Albert Ellis is very good at this, as those who have witnessed him conducting therapy or been supervised by him will testify, but he has not written on this subject to any significant degree and this aspect of REBT has tended to be neglected.

Developing an REBT-Influenced 'Problems and Goals' List with Clients

As I listed above, conducting a problem and goals list with clients is an important component of a 'UPCP' or REBT 'case' formulation. It is my practice to develop such a list with virtually all of my clients (and not just when I am conducting a 'UPCP') since this helps both of us to keep on track throughout the therapeutic process. This is probably common practice among REBT therapists. What may be different is the way in which I do this.

Rather than ask my clients to develop a problems and goals list in their own way, I encourage them to use an REBT-inspired formula in doing so (Dryden, 2001b). Usually, I help them to use this formula in a session and then once they have understood it, I suggest that they complete it as a homework assignment. I will now provide this formula and illustrate its use with a client example.

Formula for specifying a problem

Problem = Type of situation + inferential theme + unhealthy negative emotion + unconstructive behaviour/subsequent unrealistic thinking.

Example of specified problem

Whenever my boss asks to see me (type of situation), I think he is going to criticise me (inferential theme) and I feel anxious about this (unhealthy negative emotion). I deal with this anxiety by overworking so that he has nothing to criticise me for (unconstructive behaviour).

In helping clients to set goals, I encourage them in the first instance to keep the type of situation and the inferential theme the same and change the remaining factors. In doing so, I am being consistent with the traditional REBT approach which states that it is important at the outset *not* to change 'A' until clients have achieved a fair measure of change at 'B'. Following the tradition set by Wessler & Wessler (1980), 'A' here incorporates the situation and the inference about the situation.

Formula for specifying a goal

Goal = Type of situation + inferential theme + healthy negative emotion (*rather than* the unhealthy negative emotion) + constructive behaviour/subsequent realistic thinking (*rather than* the unconstructive behaviour/subsequent unrealistic thinking).

Example of specified goal

Whenever my boss asks to see me (type of situation) and I think they are going to criticise me (inferential theme), I want to feel concerned about this (healthy negative emotion) *rather than* anxious. I want to deal with this situation by doing the same level of work as if things were going well (constructive behaviour) *rather than* overworking.

Note that in the goal formula and example that I encourage clients to specify their healthy emotional, behavioural and/or thinking goals as well as what they are going to strive not to feel, act and/or think; hence the emphasis on the phrase '*rather than*' in both formula and example.

I also help clients to distinguish between overcoming psychological problem (OPP) goals and personal development (PD) goals and to set both if relevant. Since this issue is outside the scope of this chapter, I refer interested readers to Dryden (2001b).

Focusing on Specific Examples of Target Problems at the Beginning of Therapy and Working Them Through

In my view, one of the most common errors that trainee REBT therapists make at the beginning of the REBT therapeutic process is to work with clients at an abstract, non-specific level rather than at a specific level (Neenan & Dryden, 2001). Of course, I endeavour to avoid making this error whenever I can. I do so by encouraging clients to identify a problem from their problem list that they would like to work on. The selected problem is known as the 'nominated problem'. Then I encourage clients to identify a specific example of this nominated problem that we can work on and I explain why it is important for us to remain with this example and work it through. I explain that people make themselves disturbed in specific situations or when imagining specific situations and that given this, working with a specific example of their nominated problem will help us both to identify key elements of the ABC framework.

Thus, working with a specific example helps clients to identify with greater clarity than would be the case when working with abstract examples:

1. The aspect of the situation (actual or inferred) they particularly disturbed themselves about (known as the 'adversity' – see below);
2. their primary unhealthy negative emotion (emotional 'C');
3. their unconstructive behaviours or behavioural impulses (behavioural 'C'); and
4. their subsequent distorted thinking (cognitive 'C').

I then encourage my clients to stay with this specific example until I have helped them to identify, examine and change the specific rigid and extreme attitudes that they held in this situation, and encourage them to imagine themselves responding to the critical 'A' while holding their specific flexible and non-extreme attitudes and while acting constructively and thinking realistically. Finally, I encourage them to practise their flexible and non-extreme attitudes and associated constructive behaviour and realistic thinking while facing the situation at 'A' which contains the inferential theme under consideration. When clients have done this, I help them to capitalise on their progress by encouraging them to generalise their learning to other relevant specific situations. Finally, I contend that working with specific examples of nominated problems helps guard against REBT becoming an overly intellectualised enterprise which it can easily become if the therapist works with the client at a general, abstract level.

Identifying the Adversity at 'A' in the Assessment Process

I use the term 'adversity' to represent the aspect of the situation that triggers the person's attitudes at 'B'. In using this term I recognise that there are many possible 'A's in a situation, but only one triggers an attitude which accounts for a particular emotional behavioural-cognitive response at 'C'. To make life even more complex for the REBT therapist, a client can experience several emotions in what Wessler & Wessler (1980) have called an emotional episode – an episode in which the client experiences emotions (and, I would add, behaviours and thinking responses as well) – and that each of these emotions are triggered by its own set of attitudes towards a different adversity.

When 'A's are inferential they have recurring themes when paired with different emotions. This was noted over 25 years ago by Beck (1976), whose thinking on this point has had a decided effect on my own with respect to the nature and role that 'A's play in the ABC model. For instance, when a client reports anxiety, look for the inferential theme of threat or danger in their report; when depression is reported look for loss or failure, etc. (see Dryden, 1995b for an extended discussion of this issue).

In my view and experience, adversities are often inferential in nature. Given this, in identifying the adversity in a specific ABC I often merge the actual with the specified inferential theme in the client's account (e.g. 'I was most anxious about my girlfriend looking over my shoulder' (actual situation) 'in case she found someone else more attractive than me' (inferential theme).

I have devised a number of different ways of identifying adversities (see Dryden, 1995b) and now see the importance of distinguishing between inferences at 'A' and inferences at 'C' (see below). Thus, my practice of REBT features an emphasis on helping the client and myself to identify and work with the adversity in any highlighted emotional episode. This can often be a complex procedure and one which novice REBT therapists struggle to do well and succinctly.

Focusing on Thinking 'C's as Well as Emotional and Behavioural 'C's

I mentioned above that inferences can occur both at 'A' and at 'C' in the ABC framework. When inferences occur at 'C' in this framework they denote the fact that attitudes can not only have emotional and behavioural consequences, but thinking consequences as well. There are a variety of ways of dealing with thinking consequences in REBT. Thus, one can:

1. Deal with them as 'A's rather than as 'C's (e.g. as adversities for a subsequent ABC: let's suppose that everybody in the room does laugh at you, now how would you feel about that? Or as inferences as part of an inference chain: and if everybody in the room does laugh at you, what, for you, would be anxiety-provoking about that?);

2. Examine their distorted nature (e.g. 'What is the likelihood that everybody in the room will laugh at you?); or

3. Educate clients about how they create them and to use them to identify the ABC in which they occur as a 'C'.

I find that while I do, at times, use the first two strategies listed above, I increasingly use the third strategy. Thus, if a client says that they are scared of speaking in public because they fear that everybody in the room will laugh at them, I show the client how they create this distorted inferential 'C'. I ask them questions such as 'what would have to happen for you not to fear that everyone in the room will laugh at you?' If they say: 'For me to have a sense of confidence about what I am talking about', I will show them that the opposite of this is likely to be their critical 'A' and teach them how they create the aforementioned thinking 'C' by using the ABC framework. Thus:

'A' =   Not being confident about what I will be talking about to a group

'B' =   I must be confident about what I am talking about and it is terrible if I'm not

'C'   emotional   =   anxiety
            behavioural   =   urge to cancel the talk
            thinking   =   'If I give the talk everybody will laugh at me'

Helping this client to examine the rigid and extreme attitude in the above example means that it is far less likely that they will create the thinking 'C' than if the rigid and extreme attitude remains unexamined. If the thinking 'C' persists then it can be dealt with by using the other two strategies listed above.

Finally, I want to note that it is a feature of my practice of REBT that I train my clients to identify the cognitive distortions in their inferential thinking so that they can treat these distorted inferences as thinking 'C's rather than to examine them as distorted inferences as cognitive therapists are more likely to do. In this way, my practice of REBT differs from the practice of cognitive therapy.

Helping Clients to Develop and Rehearse the Full Version of Flexible and Non-Extreme Attitudes

As is well known, according to the REBT theory of psychological disturbance and health, rigid and extreme attitudes are at the core of the former and flexible and non-extreme attitudes are at the core of the latter. Consequently, it is a major task of REBT therapists to help their clients to identify, examine and change their rigid and extreme attitudes and to replace them with flexible and non-extreme attitudes which need to be rehearsed and acted on sufficiently often if they are to make a significant difference in the clients' emotional lives. So far, what I have said would feature in the practice of virtually all REBT therapists. What characterises my practice that might not be sufficiently present in the therapeutic work of my colleagues is the emphasis that I place on what I call full versions of flexible and non-extreme attitudes.

As I have noted elsewhere (Neenan & Dryden, 1999), a flexible and non-extreme attitude has two components: one that asserts the presence of the partial flexible/non-extreme attitude and the other that negates the presence of the rigid/extreme attitude. Thus, if my client holds the following demand: 'I must do well in my examination', I help them to develop and rehearse the following alternative full preference: 'I want to do well in my examination (asserted partial preference), but I do not have to do so (negated demand)'. I strive to do this consistently with all forms of flexible/non-extreme attitudes (full flexible attitudes, full non-awfulising attitudes, full bearability attitudes and full unconditional attitudes). I have found that when I do so my client is less likely to transmute their flexible/non-extreme attitudes back into rigid /extreme attitudes than when I work with the partial versions of flexible/non-extreme attitudes (e.g. I want to do well in my examination) (Dryden, 2001b).

Encouraging Clients to Voice Their Doubts, Reservations and Objections Concerning REBT Concepts and the REBT Therapeutic Process

One of the major features of REBT is that it has an explicit model of how people disturb themselves and what they need to do to undisturb themselves. Another major feature of this therapeutic approach is that it endeavours to teach this model to clients whenever possible and whenever appropriate. It is a feature of my practice to encourage clients to voice doubts, reservations and objections they have concerning any of the REBT concepts that I am teaching them or any aspect of the REBT therapeutic process. My clinical experience has been that clients frequently harbour such doubts etc. and if these are not brought to light and examined with clients then they will have a decided negative influence on the therapeutic process. I have found it to be especially important to communicate to clients that I am very open to having REBT criticised in this way and to respond to these criticisms in a non-defensive manner. I also compliment clients for speaking their mind, which is, I have found, a good strategy for unearthing further doubts etc. later in the therapeutic process. Common doubts are too numerous to list here (see Dryden, 1995b, 2001b), but a few examples will suffice:

- Acceptance means resignation
- Accepting others unconditionally means condoning their behaviour
- Musts are motivating
- Because flexible attitudes allow failure, they make it more likely that failure will occur. Rigid attitudes, on the other hand, because they don't permit failure make failure less likely to occur
- REBT is simplistic
- REBT is brainwashing.

From this illustrative list, the deleterious effect of such doubts on the practice of REBT can be clearly seen and reinforces the importance of encouraging clients to reveal their doubts etc. and the importance of dealing with them in a sensitive but authoritative manner.

Deliberately Instructing Clients in the Skills of REBT

I have always remembered a comment that Maxie C. Maultsby Jr. made at the very first workshop on REBT that I attended in 1977. He said that in essence effective therapy is self-therapy. In other words, clients will benefit from psychotherapy to the extent that they apply the principles of the therapeutic approach in their own lives. This fits very well with an educationally-oriented approach such as REBT and over the years I have elaborated this concept to the point that I have recently published a book entitled *Reason to Change: A Rational Emotive Behaviour Therapy (REBT) Workbook* (Dryden, 2001b). While this is a self-help workbook, I use the material with my clients since it gives step-by-step guidance with examples on how to use some of the major REBT techniques. My practice is to devote a portion of each therapy session to the work that clients have done between sessions on the workbook and the rest of the session on clients' nominated problems. In this way, I can monitor the progress that my clients are making on their problems and on their REBT skill development.

Of course, not all clients take to the skills development emphasis of the *Reason to Change* workbook and thus flexibility is the watchword here (as elsewhere). With such clients, I suggest that they do not use the workbook at all and I take a non-workbook approach with them. However, I deliberately instruct most of my clients in the use of core REBT skills and therefore this is an identifiable and key aspect of my practice of REBT.

Encouraging Clients to Take Responsibility for Change

Deliberately instructing clients in the skills in REBT is part of a wider emphasis that I place on encouraging clients to take responsibility for change. Thus, at the outset I outline my tasks as an REBT therapist and their tasks as REBT clients (Dryden, 1995b). These are basically as follows:

- Specify problems
- Be open to the therapist's REBT framework
- Apply the specific principle of emotional responsibility (i.e. acknowledge and act on the idea that I largely make myself disturbed by the holding a set of rigid and extreme attitudes
- Apply the principle of therapeutic responsibility (i.e. acknowledge and act on the idea that in order to undisturb myself I need

to examine my rigid and extreme attitudes, rehearse and deepen my conviction in my flexible and non-extreme attitudes and act and think in ways that are consistent with these developing flexible and non-extreme attitudes and that I commit myself to doing this regularly)
•   Disclose doubts, difficulties and obstacles to change.

In addition, I ask my clients, also at the outset of the therapeutic process, how much time they are willing to devote to helping themselves *per day*. I point out to them that the best predictor of progress in the cognitive therapies is the regular completion of homework assignments.

Throughout therapy, I remind clients that I don't expect them to do my job and I am not able to do theirs. Once again, I want to stress that this emphasis on client responsibility for change is modified according to the client's present capability for taking such responsibility.

Using Vivid Methods to Promote Change

In the early 1980s, I published a series of papers (collated in Dryden, 1986c) on what I called vivid RE[B]T. Vivid interventions are those that bring the therapeutic process to life and I argued then as I still do now that such interventions instigate change more effectively than non-vivid interventions. A good example of this is vivid representations of adversities where such adversities are presented in clear and emotionally impactful ways, enabling clients' attitudes and feelings to be evoked and worked with in therapy sessions.

Thus, my work is still characterised by the use of such methods and I apply the same caveats as I described in the 1986c compilation [e.g. don't overuse vivid interventions in therapy sessions, don't use them with clients with a tendency towards a histrionic response and when you use them with clients use intellectualisation as a defence, introduce such methods gradually and at an initial 'low dose' of vividness, increasing this 'dose' if such clients respond well to the initial 'dose' (see Dryden, 1986c for a fuller discussion of vivid REBT).]

Using Humour to Develop Rapport and Promote Change

The final distinguishing feature of my REBT practice that I want to discuss is my use of humour to develop rapport and to promote change. Although I mentioned the use of humour in the first mode of practice that I discussed in this chapter, I wanted to include it separately since it is such a defining characteristic of my work.

I find it difficult to describe my use of humour in REBT. It is something that one has to observe to understand. However, it is a combination of puns, witticisms, bringing together disparate aspects of a client's experience in humorous fusion, self-mocking and jokes. I don't, on the other hand, make much use of rational humorous songs (Ellis, 1987). Now, I don't want you to get the idea that my sessions are full of humour since this is not the case: I am serious when I need to be and often am. However, I have found that my humorous interventions do lighten the therapeutic atmosphere to good effect, particularly in REBT group therapy. My experience is that humour is a therapeutic factor in that it helps clients to take themselves seriously, but not too seriously. It also serves to remind clients of a therapeutic point between sessions. My clients are wont to say that one of my humorous remarks came into their mind at an appropriate time and reminded them of a salient REBT concept that they were then able to translate into practice. In this sense, humour can also be seen as a vivid intervention.

I hope that I have conveyed in this chapter my idiosyncratic practice of REBT and that this encourages other REBT therapists to discuss their own particular way of practising REBT.

16

Hard-Earned Lessons in Counselling

I became interested in counselling as a direct result of pursuing a PhD in social psychology. My topic was self-disclosure, and many of the papers I was reading at that time concerned self-disclosure in counselling. These articles awakened a powerful response in me, and this, together with my experiences of going to encounter groups in the late 1960s and early 1970s, led me to conclude that I wanted to become a counsellor.

My first major training was a one-year, full-time Diploma in Counselling in Educational Settings at Aston University. This course was basically a training in client-centred counselling, with some emphasis on behavioural techniques for specific problems such as examination anxiety.

For reasons that will become apparent later in this chapter, I came to the conclusion that I needed further training, and enrolled on a two-year, part-time course in psychodynamic psychotherapy. This was an introductory course, and served to convince me that this approach was not for me. During it I developed an interest in rational-emotive therapy (RET) and decided to pursue further training in this approach. This I did part-time from 1977 to 1980 at the Institute for RET in New York. At about the same time I studied for an MSc in psychotherapy at Warwick University with John and Marcia Davis. This eclectic course helped me to integrate some of my previously disparate training and practical experiences, and underscored for me that developing and maintaining a productive working alliance is a crucial ingredient in effective counselling and psychotherapy.

Subsequent training in Aaron Beck's cognitive therapy in Philadelphia, and Arnold Lazarus's multimodal therapy in Princeton, New Jersey extended my practice as an eclectically orientated counsellor, albeit one who is firmly in the rational-emotive and cognitive-behavioural tradition.

My experience of working with clients has been quite broad. I have worked with individuals in a university counselling service, a

GP practice, a clinic which specialises in helping clients who are depressed, and a clinical psychology department. I have worked with couples in Relate, and with groups at the Institute for RET as Albert Ellis's co-therapist. I don't work with families when there are children or adolescents involved, because I believe this work requires special skills which I do not have. As you can imagine, all this training and experience has provided me with many opportunities to learn the hard way.

Thriving on Variety

In April 1981 I went to Philadelphia to begin a six-month sabbatical at the Center for Cognitive Therapy. My intention was to gain a thorough training, and to this end I resolved to restrict myself to clinical practice so that I was not distracted from my purpose.

It is important to stress at this point that I had always had variety in my working life. My first and, at this juncture, only job was as lecturer in counselling at Aston University. My duties there were quite varied, and involved training and supervising counselling trainees, counselling students at the university's counselling service, administration, and academic writing/research. I had never counselled full-time – something I regarded as a lacuna in my career to date, and one I was keen to fill. There was something amiss, I reasoned, when someone whose main job was to train people to work as full-time counsellors had never worked as a full-time counsellor himself. So, I was doubly enthusiastic – first, about immersing myself in an exciting, new approach to counselling, and second, about working as a practitioner. I would take a break from writing and recharge my batteries by refraining from any involvement in training and supervising activities. After all, wasn't that partly what constituted a sabbatical – a break from one's usual duties?

After an initial intensive training in the fundamentals of cognitive therapy, I was deemed to be competent enough to see clients at the Center, and as I had about six years' experience as a counsellor, I was given a reasonably heavy load of about twenty cases. I set off with considerable enthusiasm. I enjoyed the cases I was assigned, and revelled in the expert, one-to-one supervision I received. 'This is the life', I thought, and the idea that I had been missing something fundamental by not working as a full-time counsellor strengthened in my mind.

Then it happened. I began to feel increasingly restless and irritable for no apparent reason. Initially, I couldn't understand what these feelings pointed to, so I decided to apply some of the cognitive techniques I had recently learned and had been applying with my clients on myself, in the hope that this would shed some light on my puzzling experience. In particular, I decided to investigate my automatic thoughts, that is, those thoughts that would pop into my head automatically without any conscious intent. Here is a simple sample of those thoughts and how I responded to them:

I'm just not cut out to be a counsellor.

Response: That's not true. I've been seeing clients now for over six years, and I've never questioned my suitability before. I'm doing reasonably well with the clients with whom I'm working, so I don't think it's true that I'm not cut out to be a counsellor.

I'm not cut out to be a cognitive therapist.

Response: Well, it's true that I have some doubts about cognitive therapy. In lots of ways, I favour RET, which, although similar to cognitive therapy in many respects, is quite different in others. However, I don't think this explains the full extent of my restlessness and irritability, which was now quite marked.

There's something missing in my life.

Response: Now that seems far closer to the heart of the matter. I know there's nothing amiss in my personal life. I've just got married and have my lovely wife with me, so that's not it. However, I do feel there's something missing in my work. What am I not doing that I'm used to and that I enjoy?

It was when I asked myself this last question that the mist began to clear. I missed the other activities that constituted the varied nature of my work at Aston University. It was the variety that I was missing! Once the issue had become clear, the remedy was simple. First, I began to plan an academic paper that compared and contrasted RET with cognitive therapy (Dryden, 1984). Then, I made arrangements to fulfil the trainer and supervisor parts of myself by travelling weekly to the Institute for RET in New York to participate in their training programmes, and serve as one of their supervisors. I did all this while maintaining the same caseload at the Center for Cognitive Therapy.

What this experience taught me was that I thrive on variety in my work, and when this is missing, I very quickly become unfulfilled with consequent feelings of restlessness and irritability. It was a profound learning experience, albeit a difficult one, and I have taken heed of it ever since.

The Importance of Being an 'Authentic Chameleon'

In 1981, Arnold Lazarus published a book entitled *The Practice of Multimodal Therapy,* in which he introduced the concept of the counsellor as 'authentic chameleon'. By this he meant that it is important for counsellors to vary their interpersonal style with different clients, but in an authentic manner. In the same year, and well before I had read Lazarus's book, I learned the hard way about the value of being an 'authentic chameleon'.

At the time that I learned this lesson I was working at the Center for Cognitive Therapy. I was assigned Ian, a forty-two-year-old man who was quite depressed. Early on in counselling he spoke about his previous therapists, but in a pejorative fashion. He complained they were 'a bunch of stuffed shirts', who acted very formally towards him and who sat behind their desks. 'Their dress reflected their manner', he went on, saying that it was as if they wore white coats, such was the interpersonal distance between them and him. In response to my question concerning the type of therapeutic relationship he was seeking, he said he was looking for someone with whom he could loosen up and 'rap'. His preferred image was of the two of us sitting with our feet up on the coffee table discussing his problems in a very informal way, or 'shooting the breeze' as he put it.

Now, I saw no good reason why I could not practise cognitive therapy in this way, and so week after week we would have our 'rap' sessions, as Ian came to call them, while I conceptualised my approach as informal cognitive therapy. I followed all the strategic and technical rules of the therapy, but did so while using a lot of self-disclosure, within a relationship which looked for all intents and purposes as two friends having a heart-to-heart discussion about the problems of one of them. We did indeed take to putting our feet up on the coffee table, and what is more we took turns bringing to the session cans of soda, which we consumed during the therapy hour. The outcome was a salubrious one, and at the end of our work together Ian pointed to our friendly, informal relationship as the most important therapeutic factor, from his vantage point.

Three weeks after I started seeing Ian, I was assigned Mrs G, a fifty-seven-year-old woman who had a considerable problem with anger over what were a number of minor environmental stressors. At our first session, she told me she was looking forward to meeting me because she always found Englishmen very correct and civilised, and fully expected me to observe the protocol of a professional relationship, unlike her previous therapist, who, she claimed, was overly friendly and who she sacked 'in very short order'.

Now, it should be noted that I saw Mrs G an hour before my session with Ian, and it was this temporal proximity that made life difficult for me, but which provided me with the learning that has stayed with me ever since. Every counsellor, I believe, has an interpersonal style which is natural to him or her, and mine was closer to the informality I demonstrated with Ian than to the stark formality demanded by Mrs G; and when I use the term 'demanded' I do so advisedly. For Mrs G reprimanded me for every slip into what she considered to be an inappropriately informal relationship. Before I fully learned my lesson, I made what proved to be the following errors with Mrs G, each of which met with a sharp rebuke: first, I once used her first name, to which she replied, 'Dr Dryden, will you please refrain from calling me by my Christian name'; second, I once tried to illustrate a therapeutic point by making a disclosure about my own similar experience, to which Mrs

G replied, 'Dr Dryden, I am not paying the Center good money to hear about your personal problems'; and, third, I once greeted her at the beginning of the session without my jacket and tie, wrongly thinking (or perhaps hoping!) that I was seeing Ian; her reply was, 'Dr Dryden, will you please put on your jacket and tie.' Once I had fully digested the point, namely that I had to be strictly formal with Mrs G, we got on famously, and she made quite good headway overcoming the problems for which she sought therapy.

What I learned starkly was that different clients benefit from different types of bonds with their counsellor, and that if we are going to take seriously the point that clients are different, we need to acknowledge that one way in which they differ concerns their expectations of what is a helpful counsellor style. Furthermore, I learned that as long as the counsellor has that style in their repertoire, and can be authentic in adopting the style – which, importantly, should not reinforce the client's problems – then there is much to be gained by being an 'authentic chameleon'.

Different Strokes for Different Folks

I have been influenced by the work of Ed Bordin (1979), who has written sensitively about the working alliance in counselling and psychotherapy. He argues that there are three major components of the alliance which need to be considered when appraising our counselling work with clients. These components are bonds, i.e., the relationship between counsellor and client and its vicissitudes; goals, i.e., the objectives that counsellor and client have concerning their work together; and tasks, i.e., the activities in which counsellor and client engage in their quest to help the client achieve their goals.

In the previous section I discussed the lesson I learned in the bond domain of the alliance. In this section I will discuss a similar lesson I learned in the task domain. In fact, I had to learn the lesson several times before I grasped its true message.

As I mentioned, I was originally trained in client-centred counselling. I remember being very enthusiastic about this approach when I was learning about it, and considered that I had found the key to helping people. My first clients responded well to this approach, and this early experience tended to reinforce my unitary view of the counselling universe. Eventually, however, an increasing number of my clients indicated that they wanted more from counselling than the empathy, respect, and genuineness I was offering them. For a time, I thought the fault lay with me. The reason I wasn't helping these clients, I thought, was because I wasn't being empathic, respectful, or genuine enough. This view was in fact reinforced in supervision as my supervisor and I pored over my counselling tapes, looking for instances of my inaccurate empathy.

I remember one case in particular when my client and I struggled for weeks until I broke ranks and, taking a leaf out of Albert Ellis's book, I successfully helped the client by examining her rigidly held attitude that she needed approval in order to be happy. This case proved to be one of the influences that led me to go New York to train in RET.

Again, I thought I had found the Holy Grail. It was clear to me that all clients held rigid and extreme attitudes, and therefore my task was clear – to help them to identify, examine, and change these attitudes using a host of cognitive, emotive, and behavioural techniques. Indeed, I had a lot of success using RET. However, not all clients responded well to this approach.

So how did I initially deal with these expectations? I did what people tend to do when faced with potentially threatening information: I denied it, or I distorted it to protect my unitary view. So the client who kept claiming I was not listening to them closely enough was labelled, I hate to admit it now, a 'resistant client'; the person who wanted to talk at length about their childhood experiences at boarding school was given the standard RET line that it was their present attitudes about these experiences that were the real root of their problem, and if only they would change these then all would be well. A third example of my failure in the task domain of the alliance occurred early in my career when through lack of knowledge I omitted to employ a variant of response prevention with a client with a handwashing compulsion – a task which the research literature clearly demonstrates is indicated for this type of problem. In my naivety, I once again thought that empathy, etc., was all-powerful.

It took quite a bit of disconfirming evidence to disabuse me of my unitary view of the counselling universe. I now believe that different clients need to perform different tasks in counselling at different points in the process. If this idea is correct, then I, as a counsellor, need to be proficient in a wide variety of counselling tasks myself, or refer the client to someone who is better equipped to help them – an issue I take up in my next hard-earned lesson.

Does this mean I am no longer a rational-emotive counsellor? Well, yes and no. I still use rational-emotive theory as a core theoretical framework; however, I am much broader in my use of counselling tasks than I used to be, and much more receptive to my clients' views of what will be of value to them in the counselling process. In short, I now have a pluralistic view of counselling rather than a unitary one.

I May Not Be the Best Person to Help

In my early days as a counsellor, I fluctuated between thinking I had discovered the answer to all clients' problems, to feeling quite uncertain about my ability to help anyone. One way I compensated for the latter was to believe I had to take on anyone who came to me for help. The idea that I might not be the best person to counsel someone was so threatening that the thought rarely, if ever, entered my mind.

Fortunately, I had several experiences with clients that led me to revise this view. One example which stands out in my mind occurred when I lived and worked in Birmingham. I was fairly well known at that time for practising rational-emotive therapy, and in those days, I was far less flexible in its practice than I think I am now.

One evening I received a call from a man who said he had been referred to me for what he called 'RT therapy'. Before rational-emotive therapy was known as 'RET' it was called 'rational therapy', or 'RT' for short. I remember thinking it was a bit odd for someone to call RET by its older abbreviation 'RT'; however, I did not pursue it over the phone, and we proceeded to make an appointment for an assessment session.

After telling me about his various problems, the man asked how I thought I could help him. I responded with a brief overview of RET, how his problems could be traced to a number of faulty attitudes, and how we would work together to help him to identify, examine, and change these attitudes. He listened patiently, but after I had finished he shook his head and said he hadn't heard such a load of intellectualised rubbish in a long time.

Apparently, the person who effected the referral mistook RET for Reichian therapy (RT), a body-orientated approach to therapy which is based on the idea that people's problems are related to energy blockages that are located in various parts of the body, and which require body-orientated interventions such as deep massage. These interventions will, according to the theory, help to free these blockages so that the person's psychic energy can be restored. As you may appreciate, this is a far cry from the theory and practice of RET, so instead of trying to disabuse the man of his ideas of what caused his problems and what he considered he needed to resolve them, I effected a further referral to a local therapist who I knew used Reichian techniques. I heard later that my referral yielded very positive results for the client. This experience led me to begin to question the unquestionable: perhaps I couldn't help everyone.

This tentatively held conclusion was strengthened as my name began to become more widely known in the counselling community. However, as this happened, increasingly I received calls from prospective female clients who either thought my name was 'Wendy' Dryden, or that Windy was a woman's name. A typical conversation would go like this:

Woman: Can I speak to Windy Dryden please?

Me: Speaking. How can I help you?

Woman: No, I'm sorry, you misheard me. I asked for Windy Dryden. She's a female counsellor.

Me: My name is Windy Dryden. I'm often mistaken for a woman because of my first name.

Woman: I'm sorry to trouble you, but I'm looking for a woman counsellor. 'Bye.

I have had this kind of conversation many times now. In fact, I have gained much first-hand experience of numerous women not wanting to see me for counselling because I am a man.

These and similar experiences have led me to conclude that I may well not be the best person to help a client. I am much more comfortable with this idea now, at a time when I am confident in my ability as a counsellor, than I was earlier in my career when I was more uncertain of this ability, and when I had more to prove to myself.

The consequences of realising that I may not be the best person to help is that I now refer prospective clients to other counsellors a lot more than I used to. As Arnold Lazarus has put it (Dryden, 1991), one of our tasks in counselling is to know our own limitations and other counsellors' strengths. By all means, we should work to minimise our limitations, but since we will always have our fallibilities as practitioners, it behoves us to refer clients to others who are better placed to help. I can now do this with satisfaction, whereas earlier in my career, if I did it at all, it was with a sense of failure.

'You Didn't Ask Me!'

One of the most painful lessons I have had to learn as a counsellor is that sometimes I just don't seem to learn – that I seem to make the same mistakes over and over again. When I first discovered this, I thought it applied just to me, since I hadn't read about it in the counselling literature. However, the more I supervised counsellors' tapes, which gave me access to what counsellors actually did in their sessions, as opposed to what they said they did, the more I realised, with relief, that it applied to other people as well.

A vivid example of this stands out in my mind. As I have mentioned, in 1981 I spent a six-month sabbatical at the Center for Cognitive Therapy in Philadelphia. One of the clients I saw there was a forty-two-year-old housewife who was severely depressed. She had had psychoanalytic psychotherapy without any appreciable benefit, and was referred to the Center as it had a growing reputation for the treatment of depression.

The client, whom I will call Phyllis, responded very well to cognitive therapy, and in five months or so her score on the Beck Depression Inventory went from being in the severely depressed range to being in the non-depressed range. At the end of the therapy the client seemed happy with the outcome of our work together. I was also happy, and so was my supervisor. Now, one of the features of the therapy that accounted for its success, or so I thought, was the quality of our relationship. Phyllis and I seemed to get on rather well, and she had a good sense of humour, which I capitalised on during the therapy. At times this humour seemed to be what I called 'overly giggly', but I attributed this to the exuberance of Phyllis's personality. How wrong I was!

A year later I returned to the Center for a visit, and was encouraged to schedule a follow-up session with all the clients I had seen a year previously. Among these was Phyllis. When I met her, she seemed altogether more serious than when I had known her. She had maintained the gains she had made in therapy with me with respect to her depression, but mentioned, almost casually, that in the past year she had had treatment for 'my long-standing alcohol abuse problem'. 'What long-standing alcohol abuse problem? You didn't tell me you had an alcohol problem', I whined pitifully, or so it seems now, many years later. 'Well,' she replied with more than a hint of irony in her voice, *'you didn't ask me!'* As you can imagine, I didn't feel too good about this, which of course is an understatement. I felt wretched. My initial reaction was to write to the University of Aston, which employed me at that time, and tender my resignation. How could I possibly train counsellors if I could make such ridiculous blunder? However, common sense prevailed, and instead I resolved to ask all my subsequent clients about their drinking and drug intake, which I did, or so I thought I did until the episode with Emily.

Emily was an artist who, among other concerns, spoke of feelings of emptiness. I had been working with her for about two years, during which she had begun to extricate herself from being trapped in her vocation by enrolling for a university course. She also had made reasonable progress in overcoming long-standing social and performance-related anxieties. However, we had arrived at an impasse, and Emily came to sessions with increasing anxiety, for which she offered no clear explanation. I realised something was amiss, but couldn't put my finger on what this was. Soon after, Emily came to a session in a state of extreme anxiety and handed me a letter to read. In it, Emily admitted that she had a long-standing drink problem, consuming regularly a bottle of wine a day. Dumbfounded, I again blurted out the question, 'Why haven't you told me before?' I saw my whole counselling life flash before my eyes as I processed her reply, which was, as you may have guessed, *'You didn't ask me!'*

I have several other examples where I mistakenly thought I had learned a lesson from counselling once and for all, but this is the most striking. Of course, there are several important questions to ask about my seeming lapse and, believe me, I have asked them both inside and outside supervision. The point I want to stress here is that as counsellors we don't learn something once and for all. We are human and subject to all the fallibilities this status endows. In counselling this may well mean we have our blind spots. For my own part, while I will of course resolve once again to ask all my clients about their drinking habits, I will be less horrified – but not less chastened – when some future client responds to my enquiry about their failures to disclose a secret drinking problem with the statement, *'You didn't ask me!'*

Conclusion

On re-reading these five hard-earned lessons, two major themes stand out: the importance of variety in counselling, and the inevitability of counsellor fallibility. The variety theme occurs in the first four lessons. In the first, I learned that I thrive on variety in my working life and that I would wilt, to some degree, if I ever had to work full-time as a counsellor for more than a short period of time. In lessons two and three, I learned that clients need a variety of responses from their counsellors in both the bond and task domains of the working counselling alliance. In lesson four I learned that if an individual counsellor has sufficient flexibility and authenticity to provide such varied responses to a broad range of clients, all is well and good; if not, then they should unashamedly refer them on to other practitioners who are more suitable.

The second theme concerns the fact that, being human, all counsellors have limitations. This theme is present in all five lessons. It appears in the first lesson in the guise of my own personal limitations concerning the composition of my working life. Apparently, I function much better in a work setting where there is scope for diversity. If I am to retain my enthusiasm for the field of counselling and to avoid burnout, then one way I can do this is to avoid a restricting range of work tasks. For some, working as a full-time practitioner provides sufficient variety, but not for me.

In lessons two and three I discussed the theme of counsellor limitations more implicitly. If different clients require a different kind of bond with their counsellors, even the most interpersonally flexible of counsellors will not be able to help everyone. Be as flexible as you authentically can, but know your interpersonal limitations is the message of lesson two, while a similar message, but with respect to the use of counselling tasks, is to be found in lesson three. The obvious conclusion in the light of the limitations of individual counsellors occurs in lesson four: don't hesitate to refer to other counsellors when you come up against your own limitations. Having limitations is inevitable, so you don't need to be ashamed of them is a message I would like to convey to beginning counsellors.

Although it is crucial for all counsellors to minimise their errors, the fifth and final lesson demonstrates that we may well come up against blind spots that defy mastery. It might be nice if we could eliminate all our blind spots, but maybe the consequent loss of our humanity would make us less helpful to our human clients. Perhaps that is the most helpful lesson of all.

17

What I Wished I'd Learned During Counsellor Training, What I'm Glad I Did and Didn't Learn and What I'm Sorry that I Did

What I want to do in this chapter is to take a look at my main professional training as a counsellor and consider four things: (a) what I wished I had learned from this training experience; (b) what I am glad I did learn; (c) what I am glad I did not learn and (d) what I'm sorry that I learnt. In reviewing my training, I came to the disconcerting conclusion that I am something of an old timer in the counselling field. I don't 'feel' like an old timer; in fact, I 'feel' like a spring chicken. However, reluctantly, I have to admit that I am an old timer; after all I first trained professionally as a counsellor in 1974.

While I will confine myself to my initial extended training experience, I will refer to my other training experiences which I will briefly outline for you in case you are interested. I began my professional training in counselling with a one-year, full-time course at Aston University, which was basically a person centred counselling course. After this, I did a two-year, part-time course in psychodynamic psychotherapy at the training section of Uffculme Clinic which later became the West Midlands Institute for Psychotherapy. This was basically an introductory course which I did not complete because during the second year of this course I decided to pursue training in Rational Emotive Behaviour Therapy which I did part-time in New York from 1977 until 1979. In 1978, I also took a two-year, part-time MSc course in Psychotherapy at Warwick University. This was a broad, eclectic course which complemented the REBT training that I was pursuing at the same time. Finally, in 1981, I took a sabbatical from my university job and spent six months full-time at the Center for Cognitive Therapy with Aaron Beck in Philadelphia, learning cognitive therapy.

When I initially trained in 1974, training opportunities outside Marriage Guidance were few and far between and they were largely confined to the field of counselling in education. The main courses available at that time were all one-year full-time in nature and were based in the universities of Reading, Keele, Swansea and Aston. The first three named courses were focused on school counselling and were largely open to serving teachers who attended the courses on sabbatical. Yes, that's right, serving teachers were given a year off on full pay and were seconded to train as school counsellors. Happy days! The other course at the University of Aston in Birmingham was focused on counselling in higher educational settings and attracted a generous number of Department of Education and Science (DES) State Bursaries. This meant that the State paid recipients' fees and gave them, in addition, an ample living grant. I was the fortunate recipient of one of these State Bursaries when I took up a place on Aston's one-year Diploma in Counselling in Educational Settings course in the 1974/5 academic year. Prior to this I had done the first year of the South West London College counselling course which later became a self-directed training course (Charleton, 1996), had been a Nightline worker, a Samaritan and worked part-time in the Student Counselling Service at University College, London where Pat Milner was Student Counsellor. So, I had a good introductory grounding in the theory and skills of counselling before I began at Aston.

Two of the strengths of the Aston course were its generous staff–student ratio and the calibre of its trainers. On my course there were seventeen full-time students and the course was staffed by two full-time tutors. The course tutor was Richard Nelson-Jones, who will no doubt be known to you from his books on counselling, and the other tutor was Don Biggs, a Fulbright Fellow. Fulbright Fellows were leading counsellor trainers from North America, seconded to Aston for the purpose of helping Richard Nelson-Jones to provide a professional counsellor training for student counsellors. Previous 'Fulbrights' were C. H. Patterson and Stanley Strong, both internationally known counselling psychologists. So, I was fortunate to be trained by well-respected, experienced trainers who worked under a student–staff ratio of 8.5 to 1. I think that you would be hard placed to find a course in Britain today with these two characteristics.

Another feature of the training course at Aston at that time was that it was full-time. Then, full-time meant full-time. We had one afternoon off for private study, but for the rest of the time we were fully occupied either at college or at our placements which were arranged for us by the course tutor. Nowadays, a full-time counselling course can literally mean full-time, but it more often means far less. Indeed, it is possible today to do a one-year, full-time counselling course by attending college for two days only. In addition, either you have to be in practice already or you have to organise your own placement. So, we got a very good deal at Aston with respect to the amount of training we received over a very full academic year and with respect to the assistance we were given with our placements.

Another good aspect of the Aston training course was that it ran intensive skills-based workshops in the first term where we focused in small groups on basic counselling skills. In these groups, we repeatedly made videos of our peer counselling sessions which were then studied in detail with the purpose of enhancing skill development. What was valuable here was that each individual student made an extended video of their counselling skills and had plenty of time to learn how to improve these skills. At the end of the first term, we had to pass a number of 'readiness to see clients' assessments which comprised a video of our counselling skills and an exam which assessed core knowledge such as being able to identify signs that clients are severely disturbed; being able to articulate the indications and contraindications of counselling and other forms of helping and demonstrating a working knowledge of relevant information about the major psychotropic drugs. These assessments were very useful in helping us to focus our attention on what we had to learn and on understanding why this knowledge and these skills were fundamental to seeing clients.

I mentioned at the outset that the course at Aston at that time was person-centred in orientation. This meant that I did not learn, for example, the importance of taking a history from my clients. I later learned that this was important because it helped me to gain an overall understanding of my clients by discovering amongst other things: (a) the origin and development of my clients' problems, (b) their family background and (c) their use of alcohol and drugs.

I recently wrote an article outlining my approach to a growing area known as case formulation, which involves developing an overall understanding of clients in the context of their problems and where hypotheses concerning the mechanisms underpinning clients' problems are put forward with the purpose of giving a direction and coherence to counselling, thus aiding treatment planning (Dryden, 1999c). This would never have been taught on the Aston course where, in keeping with the views of Rogers (1951), assessment in counselling was not considered to have a valid role. This had the effect of accentuating the confusion many of us experienced when we began to see clients because we didn't have an overall understanding of the clients whom we were seeing. As most of you know, assessment is scorned in person centred counselling because it is seen as emanating from the frame of reference of the counsellor, and the prime directive (if I can borrow a phrase from *Star Trek*) for person centred counsellors is to remain, whenever possible, within the frame of reference of the client. I wish I had learned then that working with clients from *both* an external *and* an internal frame of reference is acceptable and therapeutic and it is more a question of when to work within a particular frame of reference than of which frame of reference to work within.

We also did not learn at Aston how to plan counselling over its course. Although Rogers (1951) did outline the stages that clients tend to go through in person centred counselling, he argued that this occurs as a matter of course if clients experience their counsellors as empathic, warm and genuine. If provision of the core conditions is necessary and sufficient for constructive client change to occur (assuming that these conditions are experienced by the client), then there is no need for treatment planning, a concept which is predicated on the notion that counsellors need to intervene in different ways with different clients. Fortunately, I later learned about this concept on the MSc in Psychotherapy course at Warwick.

Having said all of this, I am glad that we were trained in a model that was systematic even if it does have, in my view, serious limitations. This meant that we could immerse ourselves in the philosophical ideas underpinning the approach, study its model of the person, explore in full its view of psychological health and disturbance, evaluate its view of the acquisition and perpetuation of psychological disturbance and of psychological change and evaluate the influence of all of these ideas on its suggestions for counselling practice. Some of you will recognise some of these points as chapter headings from my textbook *Handbook of Individual Therapy* (Dryden, 1996). I fully acknowledge the influence that the Aston counselling course has had on this book and this, I believe, shows one of the benefits of studying an approach in depth and in a structured way.

There is at present a debate in the literature about the value of studying a core model in professional counsellor training. Its proponents, like myself, argue that doing so enables the trainee to study something in depth and be offered a useful framework for practice even if this framework is limited (Dryden, Horton & Mearns, 1995). In other words, it gives trainees a roadmap for practice. Now, of course, there is the danger that trainees then think that this is the only way to practise, but this standpoint can be elicited and dealt with on the course, particularly if staff members have a flexible attitude towards the core model. Antagonists (e.g. Feltham, 1997) argue that since no one model is more effective than any other it is premature to teach a core model and a more flexible, eclectic approach to counsellor training should be implemented. This makes intuitive sense, but there are real inherent dangers to this approach. First, for such an approach to work, the training has to be delivered by people who are highly experienced in the field and have developed a mature eclectic or integrative approach over many years and can teach this clearly and coherently. The danger, then, lies in training being provided by inexperienced people whose eclecticism or integration has been introjected, rather than developed over time and who are unable to bring the disparate elements of practice into a coherent whole. What is problematic here is the lack of a coherent and systematic approach to training.

In this context, let me say a few words about my concerns about the present approach adopted within counselling psychology training in Britain. In order for a counselling psychology course to be accredited by the British Psychological Society, its trainees have to learn at least two models of counselling as well as take a number of other theory and research modules not centrally related to these two counselling approaches. Such courses are usually two-years part-time. Now, at present I run a two-year, part-time MSc course in Rational Emotive Behaviour Therapy. I find that this duration is just sufficient to enable me to train my students to competence in that one approach to counselling. So, I really wonder what level of competence counselling psychology trainees can attain in learning two counselling approaches at the same time as following other modules. Perhaps it is not the intention of counselling psychology courses to train competent counsellors. If not, who are they trying to train? If so, I wonder how they achieve this because I know that I couldn't. So, in conclusion, I'm glad that I learned from my original course the value of systematic training in a core theoretical model especially when the limits and weaknesses of that model are fully explored.

A counselling course is very much influenced by its trainers and ours was no exception. During the year that I was at Aston, there were initial signs that Richard Nelson-Jones was beginning to move away from person centred counselling and develop his own integrative approach to counselling which he expanded on in much greater detail later (Nelson-Jones, 1984). However, at that time he was still largely influenced by Rogers' ideas and the Aston course was still at heart a person centred one. This is not to say that we did not study other approaches to counselling. Far from it. Richard Nelson-Jones gave a very good counselling theories course and provided extremely useful handouts which were later expanded into his book, *The Theory and Practice of Counselling Psychology* (Nelson-Jones, 1982). We also had a term's course on behavioural counselling which was run by a university lecturer from Birmingham University who was a behaviourally-oriented clinical psychologist. However, there was always the sense that behavioural methods were best used with clients who had specific fears and phobias or study and social skills difficulties while person centred counselling should be used with everybody else.

What I did not learn on the course and wished that I had was the limits of person centred counselling and the importance of a 'horses for courses' approach i.e. which therapeutic methods are best used with which clients experiencing which problems. To be fair to the course, such issues were not actively discussed in the counselling literature in 1974/5 to the extent that they are today. This issue became salient for me because I had a number of clients who wanted more from me than the empathy, warmth and genuineness I was offering them. Because I thought at the time that person centred counselling was the be all and end all of the counselling world, I concluded that the fault must lie within me rather than in the interaction between person centred counselling and the clients themselves. No, because I was sure that person centred counselling did not have limitations, I concluded that the reason that some of my clients wanted more was that I was deficient in offering the core conditions and if only I could be more empathic, warm and genuine then these clients would respond better to my counselling. Now, while I think that there may have been a grain of truth to this analysis, I am more persuaded by the argument that clients respond differently to different therapeutic methods. It took me quite a while to recover from this self-inflicted blow to my confidence, but I am sure that this wouldn't have happened to such a degree if, as I said before, the course was more systematic in dealing with the strengths and weaknesses of person centred counselling. I think that it is so important that any course be rigorous in looking critically at the core model on which the course is based and to help trainees understand that if clients don't improve it may not be due to the counsellor or to the client, but to the fact that the client may be better suited to a different therapeutic approach.

While there are plenty of casebooks in the field of counselling and psychotherapy where brief descriptive information is provided of 'cases' from beginning to end, there is a dearth of material where verbatim transcripts are made available which show in detail the course of therapy. This mirrors many training courses where trainers may discuss their work with different clients, but do not demonstrate this work by allowing their trainees to watch videos or listen to audiotapes of counselling sessions that they have conducted with clients over the entire therapeutic process. This was the case with the course at Aston. Not only did the trainers not demonstrate their work over time with clients, they also did not show us how they worked with clients at all. This meant that we had very little practical idea of how to work with clients over time. We read articles on the therapeutic process and we received supervision on our work with clients from the beginning to the end of the therapeutic process, but we were not shown how to practise counselling over time. This was a significant gap in our education and something that I wished we had covered in that year.

Related to this, since we were not exposed to the work that our Aston trainers actually did with their clients, we were not exposed to helpful role models for effective counselling. Although we did view various videotapes of leading counselling figures working directly with clients in demonstration sessions (notably Rogers, Ellis and Perls working with the now infamous 'Gloria'), this was no substitute for viewing on video or hearing on audio the work of people whom we could then question in depth about why they responded in the way that they did. Fortunately, after Aston I was able to observe master therapists working directly with clients and to discuss with them at length their interventions and why they made them. Thus, in 1978, as part of my REBT training, I served as associate therapist in Albert Ellis's four evening therapy groups during the month of August when his regular associate therapists were on vacation. This was done with the permission of the group members. I found this invaluable not only because it gave me the opportunity to observe closely the originator of REBT working with a number of very different patients, but because it also allowed me to question him later on the nature and purpose of his interventions. I cannot think of a better way of learning to be a group therapist.

Then, a number of years later, I spent two full weeks sitting in with Arnold Lazarus as he conducted his individual sessions. For those of you who do not know Arnold Lazarus he is best known for his pioneering work on technical eclecticism and multimodal therapy. Again, this was done with the expressed permission of his clients. After each day's work I would question Lazarus about the work he was doing with each of his different clients which was more valuable to me than reading two years' worth of counselling and psychotherapy books.

In addition, since I was permitted to intervene in both Ellis's groups and Lazarus's individual sessions, they also gave me valuable feedback on my own interventions. This apprenticeship model of counsellor training is perhaps the best form of training that has been devised and is one that is least used. Of course, it does not easily lend itself to training in psychodynamic counselling and person centred counselling and this perhaps explains why it is so rare. But I would rate these brief episodes of working closely with two master therapists as easily the most valuable form of training that I have received.

Let me now consider what I am glad that I didn't learn in my time as a trainee on the Aston counselling course. First, I did not learn that it was important to study human growth and development in depth in order to practise counselling effectively. While I am not against trainee counsellors learning about human development, it seems to me that on a busy curriculum the in-depth study of this subject has a fairly low priority when practising counselling effectively is the criterion for inclusion and exclusion of a topic. If I practised psychodynamic counselling I would probably have a different view, but in the practice of cognitive-behaviour therapy in general and Rational Emotive Behaviour Therapy in particular this subject is dispensable.

Second, I did not learn that case discussion is a central part of counsellor training. Rather, I learned that it was important to make and present for supervision audio-recordings of my counselling sessions so that I could reflect on what actually happened between my client and myself rather than on my account of what happened. Again, I am not saying that discussion of cases has no useful place in counsellor training. Indeed, I think that it is important when it comes to monitoring case formulation and treatment planning issues. But case discussion to the exclusion of the study of audio-recordings of counselling sessions is not very helpful and I'm glad that I did not learn at Aston that it was.

Third, I am glad that I did not learn at Aston that personal therapy is an essential part of counsellor training. I am not against trainees seeking personal therapy if they do so for personal reasons or if they think that it will help them deal with the stresses of counselling practice. But I am not in favour of such personal therapy being a mandatory part of counsellor training. While there is much evidence that trained therapists think that personal therapy was an important part of their training and even that such therapy made them more effective practitioners, there is little evidence that receiving personal therapy actually makes therapists more effective with their clients. As I have discussed elsewhere, it may well be that the reason why personal therapy does not increase one's effectiveness as a counsellor is that it does not focus on one's work as a counsellor and one's feelings towards one's clients. Rather, it tends to be unrestricted and trainees can talk about anything that they wish to discuss with their personal therapists. I have in mind a form of personal therapy which I have called 'client-centred' personal therapy (Dryden, 1994a) where discussion is focused on client work and the feelings that one experiences in working with clients as a foundation for exploration. I would like to see a research study conducted into the comparative impact of traditional personal therapy and 'client-centred' personal therapy on counsellor effectiveness. Only then will we be able to see the true value of personal therapy in the wider context of counsellor training.

Let me now consider briefly the main thing that I learned during my counsellor training at Aston that I wished that I hadn't learned. This concerned the role that the personal development group has in counsellor training. Even though the personal development group I attended during that year at Aston was not a growthful experience for me and as far as I can tell for any of my fellow trainees, we were frequently assured that this was a very important part of our experience as a counsellor trainee. And I am afraid that I accepted this logic unquestioningly. However, two subsequent types of experience have led me to revise my opinion significantly on this point. The first set of experiences relates to personal development groups that I attended as part of my subsequent training and the second relates to my trainees' experiences of the personal development groups that they attended as part of their training on the courses that I organised.

Let me consider first my further experiences of being a member of personal development groups (see Chapter 14). I attended two groups as part of my psychodynamic training. The first was called a transference group and the second a personal development group although they were to my untutored eyes completely indistinguishable. Once again, I gained little from these groups and so according to their own report did my fellow group members. It was generally thought that seeing one another in other parts of the course served as an inhibiting factor when it came to what we were prepared to disclose about ourselves to one another. Then on the Masters course in Psychotherapy at Warwick I attended a two-year personal development group with similar results and with similar concerns expressed by group members. I have thus attended four personal development groups over a five-year period and cannot say that any of them were personally beneficial experiences. None was harmful, to be sure, but none was particularly helpful and none improved my effectiveness as a counsellor.

When I became a counsellor trainer, I included personal development groups on the curriculum, not because I believed that they are an essential part of counsellor training, but because, in general, the field does. This despite the fact that such groups are routinely given low ratings by students with respect to how useful they are to improving one's competence as a counsellor. If, given the proper resources, I can reorganise my present MSc in Rational Emotive Behaviour Therapy so that it is eligible for BACP and UKCP accreditation, I will still include these groups on the curriculum. But I will do so because they are required for such accreditation and not because I think that they are terribly useful.

If attending a personal development group is to be a mandatory part of counsellor training then it is my view that ideally trainees should join such a group where no other member of their training cohort is present so that they can disclose themselves in the knowledge that they will not meet other group members in other settings. Even then, I am not persuaded of the value of such groups in the counsellor training process, but at least it would meet the oft-repeated criticism by trainees that personal development groups comprising course members inhibit full participation and relevant personal disclosure.

Let me conclude my discussion by considering briefly the impact that practical and contextual constraints have on counsellor training and the compromises that have to be made as a result. In many ways, the Aston counselling course was very well funded. In 1974/5 the phrase 'educational cuts' had not yet been heard and this was reflected in the very generous staff–student ratio that existed then which, as I have already stated, enabled counselling skills workshops to be run giving each individual ample time to practise, to be fully observed and to be given proper feedback. While this funding was generous when compared to that received by counselling courses today, even then the course tutor complained that the Aston course was not funded as a 'clinical' course which, if it had been, would have made the staff–student ratio even more generous. In higher education today, funding on many professional level counselling courses does not often permit staff–student ratios low enough for each student to get sufficient individual attention for skill acquisition and refinement. This applies to the Masters course that I run, so reluctantly I have had to compromise with my own training values. Thus, the skills training workshops that I run have a staff–student ratio of 1:16 when at Aston it was 1:8.5, almost half what it is on my course.

This has meant that I do not have the time to give each of my trainees sufficient attention as they struggle to learn complex practical skills. My dilemma is that if I do reorganise the course to give students the individual attention that they warrant, I could not offer a Masters course since it would not meet university criteria for a Masters course. So, I compromise and struggle as best I can with the resources at my disposal. Sometimes I think that given present funding levels institutions of higher education are not ideal environments for running counsellor training courses. But, were I to run my ideal REBT training course in a private institution, then the fees would be so high that it would exclude all but the most well-off trainee.

Perhaps you would have liked me to have ended on a more optimistic note. I certainly would have liked to have done so. At times like these I look back with envy at my time at Aston; but counselling is about dealing with reality and not about living nostalgically in the past. So, if counsellor trainers like myself are to continue to train counsellors, then we have to work within the means at our disposal. I still have my dreams though and one day I hope to run a training course according to my ideals.

A version of this chapter was given to the Wimbledon Guild on 18 April 1998.

18

Religion, Spirituality and Human Worth

Personal Perspectives

Religious label

I should say at the outset of this chapter that religion plays a peripheral, almost non-existent role in my life and has done ever since I was barmitzvahed. However, my parents are Jewish, I was brought up as a Jew and my wife is Jewish and as such Jewish issues are present in my life. To put it simply, I regard myself as Jewish by culture, but not by religion. If pressed to put a label on my religious orientation I would say that I was a probabilistic atheist and an environmental humanist. By a probabilistic atheist I mean that I very much doubt the existence of a deity, but am not prepared to state this as an absolute fact. By an environmental humanist I mean that I believe that while human affairs and the collective physical and psychological well-being of humans are paramount on this planet, the well-being of other organisms and the environment are to be carefully considered.

Personal position on spirituality

I have always struggled to understand what people mean by the term 'spirituality'. I have always recoiled from it for a number of reasons. First, for me it conjures up matters to do with the 'spirit' and I find it difficult to hear this term without hearing the word 'holy' in front of it. Also, rightly or wrongly, I associate the term 'spiritual' with the term 'transpersonal' and indeed for some transpersonal experiences and one's relationship with whatever one considers to be the 'Ultimate' are defining characteristics of being spiritual. If these are essential characteristics of spirituality, I am not spiritual. However, let me outline part of a definition of spirituality that I can live with, if certain modifications are made to it. Kelly (1995) has said that:

> *the identifiable values of spirituality include confidence in the*
> *meaning and purpose of life, a sense of mission in life and of*
> *the sacredness of life, a balanced appreciation of material*
> *values, an altruistic attitude towards others, a vision for the*
> *betterment of the world and a seriousness of the tragic side of*
> *life.* (p. 4)

Using this as a starting point, I would say that I was spiritual in the sense that there are several major meanings and purposes to my life and that one central one is doing what I can personally and professionally to improve the mental health of my fellow humans. I regard life as something to be cherished but not as sacred and I am aware of the tragic, comic, ironic and romantic sides of life. I, thus, see balance in life and certainly strive to marry my material and non-material interests with those of others and those of the environment.

Religious and spiritual experiences

My *religious* experiences have in the main been negative. I was made to go to Hebrew classes three nights a week and every Sunday morning until I turned 13. I hated virtually every minute of it. If I had a different psychological perspective, I would say that I was religiously abused in that I was forced to go to these classes against my will. My own viewpoint is that I was forced to endure what I saw as hours of meaningless religious study, none of which I took seriously. As soon as I had my barmitzvah, that was that. I stopped going to synagogue and only got married in one because my wife, Louise, would not have married me in any other setting.

When I think of an experience that might be regarded as *spiritual* in nature, I think of one that others might not regard in this category. I was sitting in the kitchen in my boyhood home in 1965 when I heard on the radio the sound of a shotgun followed by a drum roll and a raunchy, soulful saxophone which hit me like a bolt out of the blue. I was transfixed, felt weak at the knees and tingled all over. It was a record called 'Shotgun' by Jr. Walker and the All Stars, which I rushed out there and then to buy. All I can say is that for some reason I deeply resonated to the sounds that I heard that day in a way that defied and still defies understanding. We weren't a musical family and there was no family tradition of listening to blues or soul music that may have prepared the ground for my response. If I had a soul (which I very much doubt), I would say that it was touched that day by Jr. Walker.

The aftermath of this experience is interesting. I was moved by it to take up the saxophone, for which sadly I had no talent. However, I did acquire the nickname 'Windy', from these days and when I changed my surname in the late 1960s I changed my first name too. I went from being David Denbin to Windy Dryden. So that experience 37 years ago has had an enduring impact on me. Not only do I still resonate to the music of Jr. Walker (who sadly passed away in 1993), it led to my name change.

Professional Issues

Impact of personal religious and spiritual background on REBT practice

I am wary of speculating on the impact that the above experiences may have had on my REBT practice with clients since these experiences may have been influenced by factors that may have more of an impact than the experiences themselves. Having said this, I would say that such experiences and their underlying determinants have influenced my clinical work as follows.

1. My negative experiences with Jewish religious education have led me to be particularly alert to situations where clients have accepted the religious and non-religious viewpoints of others without question. This is a delicate area. As an REBT therapist I value independent thinking and would want to facilitate such thinking in clients. Yet I am very aware of the dangers imposing independent thinking on clients, particularly in areas where they have not indicated having a problem. I have found that the way out of this dilemma is to bring such instances of uncritical internalisation of others' viewpoints to the attention of my clients only where it is relevant to their emotional problems and to show them that they have a choice of what to believe. For example, I have seen several orthodox male Jewish clients who have had an emotional problem about masturbation and whose uncritical acceptance of the religious viewpoint that the spilling

of one's own seed is a sin has been centrally involved in their problem. I have shown such clients that: (a) there are other ways of viewing masturbation; (b) there are implications of each viewpoint; (c) they can choose what to believe; and (d) I will work to help them, whatever they choose. If a client chooses to continue to see masturbation as a sin, I will help him to refrain from this activity and highlight for change unbearability attitudes that lead him into temptation. On the other hand, if he decides, after reflection, to view masturbation as a natural male activity and not inherently sinful, I will help him to identify and overcome his guilt-related attitudes about going against his religious teachings. My position is to respect the client's wishes and to work within his (in this case) chosen frame of reference.

2. My Jr. Walker 'spiritual' experience has taught me several things. First, people can deeply resonate to a variety of things and such deep resonance may not be explainable. Second, I respect and take seriously clients' spiritual experiences, whatever they are, even if I don't understand them or if they seem silly from my frame of reference. The experience is more important than the content, and therapist respect for the experience is more important than therapist understanding of the content. Third, looking for historical determinants of 'spiritual' and non-spiritual experiences may not be that helpful from a clinical perspective. This, of course, is echoed in REBT's phenomenological view of client experience.

Human worth and the understanding of evil

I am an REBT therapist for a number of reasons (Dryden, 2001a), but none more so than for its position on human worth. This very much resonates with my humanist leanings. In fact, REBT has two perspectives on human worth. The most radical is that humans are neither worthwhile nor worthless since they are too complex to be globally rated. Rather, they are human and as such they can either accept themselves unconditionally or reject themselves. If they accept themselves unconditionally and others as humans who are all equal in humanity to one another, this will promote the psychological health and well-being of all humans. This position does not prevent humans from rating aspects of themselves (and others) and thus from dealing with the negative aspects of themselves (and others) and capitalising on the positive aspects of themselves (and others). The second, less radical, perspective is that all humans are worthwhile because they are alive, all humans are equal in worth to one another because of their humanity and their aliveness, but they are unequal in rateable aspects of themselves. Again, this position is deemed to promote the psychological health and well-being of humans. See Ellis (1972) for a full discussion of both perspectives.

My own view is that Osama bin Laden, assuming that he was the architect of the September 11 atrocities, is not an evil person, but he is guilty of promoting evil acts that cannot be justified from a humanist perspective (and from many other perspectives too). Viewing people such as bin Laden as evil is easy to do and not doing so may wrongly be seen as failing to condemn what they did. However, viewing them as evil may have several negative consequences:

1. It may prevent us from seeking to understand the thinking behind their actions, understanding which may help us to take action designed to make such atrocities less likely from happening again in the future.

2. It may lead us to view others who act in ways that go against our valued interests as evil.

3. Viewing people such as bin Laden as evil makes it less likely that we will negotiate with them before they commit such atrocities.

4. Public declarations that people such as bin Laden are evil may harden the attitude of their followers and increase the possibility that these followers will commit further atrocities in the future.

5. Viewing people as evil will make it more likely that we will commit atrocities against them which we will then justify as appropriate responses to their atrocities.

6. Treating people as evil and worthless may lead them to regard themselves as worthless and evil and increase the chances that they will act in ways that are consistent with these self-views.

I am not saying that an attitude of unconditional other-acceptance is without negative consequences, but in accordance with REBT theory I would say that such consequences would be fewer and less deleterious to the person holding the attitude, to the object of the attitude and to the world in general.

Issues of self-devaluation and other-devaluation occur in the clinic very frequently, although rarely about people such as Osama bin Laden. The clinical implications of what I have said in this chapter in addressing such issues are as follows:

1. I strive to help clients see the link between self-devaluation (SD)/other-devaluation (OD) and the emotional and behavioural problems that they wish to change.

2. I outline and explain the concepts of unconditional self-acceptance (USA) and unconditional other-acceptance (UOA) and help clients to see what difference holding such attitudes would make to their emotions and behaviours.

3. I outline common doubts, reservations and objections to USA and UOA and engage clients in an open discussion about these and others that they may personally hold about these concepts.

4. I encourage clients to do a thorough cost–benefit analysis about the short-term and long-term advantages and disadvantages to self and others of holding SD vs. USA attitudes and OD vs. UOA attitudes and engage them in an open discussion of these, correcting misconceptions as they are disclosed.

5. I encourage clients to see that they and only they can choose which attitudes to hold, and while I am biased in favour of USA and UOA they should make their own minds up about which attitudes they wish to hold.

6. If clients choose to hold the attitudes of USA and UOA, I encourage them to make a commitment to work towards holding these attitudes and outline the process that this typically

involves: it is a lengthy process which often involves thinking and acting in unnatural ways until they become natural, and like self-actualisation it is a process, not an end state to be achieved once and for all.

Conclusion

In this chapter I have outlined my views on religion, spirituality and evil and discussed some of the clinical implications of these views in my REBT practice. I am surprised about the central role that I have given to encouraging people to think for themselves. On reflection, the negative impact of forced religious instruction was greater than I had thought and helps to explain why I would rather clients thinkingly reject REBT concepts than unthinkingly accept them. I could even say that such a revelation was spiritual in nature!

19

When Being Helped by a Therapist Is Different from Being Helped by a Friend or Loved One

There is quite a lot of concern expressed in the media about the infiltration of counselling and psychotherapy into our personal lives. Some of the imagery that some journalists employ suggest that there is a battle for the psyche going on. Thus, 'armies' of counsellors are portrayed descending on the scene of some tragedy or other, intervening to prevent the masses from developing post-traumatic stress disorder. In other cases, people with more money than sense are pilloried for checking themselves into 'a top private clinic' (usually the Priory Hospital at Roehampton) when they would be far better off, according to one particular journalist, having a few early nights. Thus, people are either portrayed as victims who need protecting from the marauding hordes of counsellors or spoilt brats who counsellors are quite willing to exploit for huge sums of money.

A few years ago, the television consumer programme *Watchdog* arranged for one of its staff to pose as a 'client' and to consult three counsellors for a 'trivial' problem for which counselling was not indicated. Two of the three counsellors recommended ongoing counselling and the other was equivocal. The conclusion that the programme came to was that counsellors were a bunch of opportunists who were looking to make an easy buck. Instead of consulting such charlatans, people are advised to talk to their friends or loved ones.

Leaving aside the question of whether professionally qualified counsellors and psychotherapists are charlatans, can our friends and loved ones provide better help than highly qualified strangers? This question raises a number of complex issues, which I will attempt to address with specific reference to my work as a cognitive-behaviour therapist.

Let me briefly describe cognitive-behaviour therapy before returning to these complex issues. Cognitive-behaviour therapy (CBT) is a tradition in psychotherapy which has its roots in

Epictetus's famous dictum that people are disturbed not by things, but by the views that they take of them. These views (or more commonly, thoughts and attitudes) influence and are sustained by the way we behave in the world. In understanding the way that you feel, therefore, cognitive-behaviour therapists are primarily interested in the way that you think and in the way that you act. In helping you over your emotional problems, CBT therapists will help you (a) to identify, examine and change salient thoughts and attitudes that are manifestly inconsistent with reality, illogical and dysfunctional; and (b) to act in ways that will strengthen an alternative set of thoughts and attitudes that are consistent with reality, logical and functional. Not content with helping you to do this, CBT therapists will help you to do this for yourself so that you can become your own therapist, as it were.

Now your friends and loved ones may well help you in similar ways and sometimes this will be very helpful. You may become so locked into one way of viewing things that you cannot see the wood from the trees because you are emotionally invested in the subject at hand. A well-meaning friend or loved one may listen to you empathically and because they are not so invested in the issue may point out some things that help you to put the matter into a more objective perspective. We have all probably had the experience of saying to a friend or loved one who has helped us in this way: 'Of course! Why didn't I think of that?' When this happens, it is usually with issues that are acute in nature rather than chronic. With more chronic issues, your friends and loved ones may be at a loss once their opening helping gambits have failed to encourage you to see things from a different perspective.

Let me give an example of this latter issue from my clinical practice. I once saw a woman who was racked with guilt over an abortion she had several years earlier. The circumstances were as follows. She became pregnant after a one-night stand and there were several factors. First, she was a staunch Catholic; second, an early scan showed that the child had spina bifida; and third, she was told that if she had the baby, she could risk her life. After much internal struggle and counselling on this issue she decided to have an abortion. However, she was convinced that she was a bad person who had murdered another human being and as a result would rot in hell.

When I saw her, all of her family members, friends and relatives had pointed out to her repeatedly that she had nothing to blame herself for in deciding to have an abortion. After all, they reasoned, what other option did she have? If she had the child there was a good chance that she would die and who would then look after the child? What kind of life would a child with spina bifida have without a caring mother to look after him or her? Virtually every one of her female friends and relatives assured her that faced with this situation they would have opted for the termination. My client's response to these attempts to help was always to feel reassured for a brief period of time and then to return to being racked with guilt.

When I saw her, I took a different tack and one which shows clearly the difference between a lay and a professional response. What did I do that was different and why was it more successful? Instead of encouraging her to focus on the seemingly good reasons for the abortion, I asked her to assume temporarily that she was right and that she had killed another human being. I helped her to see that her extreme feelings of guilt derived not from this 'fact' but from her attitude towards herself for committing this 'crime'. I showed her that underpinning her guilt were two related attitudes. First, she was demanding that she absolutely should not have killed another human being. Second, she viewed herself as an evil person for doing what she absolutely should not have done. Moreover, I helped her to see that the healthy alternative to her feelings of guilt about killing her unborn child was feelings of remorse. In order to feel remorseful, rather than guilty about what she had done, I helped my client to examine and change her demanding and self-condemning attitudes and helped her to think as follows: 'I would have much preferred not to have killed my unborn child, but tragically there is no law of the universe decreeing that I absolutely should not have done so. If there was, then it would have been impossible for me to have had the abortion. I am not an evil person for having the abortion. Rather, I am a fallible human being who, again tragically, did a very bad thing'.

Once I had helped my client to develop these flexible and non-extreme attitudes towards having the abortion and once she had begun to gain real conviction in them a very interesting thing happened. She spontaneously began to take into account the mitigating factors that she could not consider for long when she was consumed with guilt about having the abortion. Accepting herself unconditionally for her 'crime' freed her to realise that as a human being she took a course of action that was the lesser of two evils. Once she had given up the demand that she absolutely should have sacrificed herself for her unborn child and once she realised that she certainly would not have advised any of her close friends to have done the same, she appreciated that human beings are often faced with very difficult dilemmas which have tragic outcomes no matter which course of action one chooses. Her developing unconditional self-acceptance also helped her to see that choosing one's own life over the life of an unborn child is not a despicably selfish act as she had previously thought, but one which reflected a healthy philosophy of enlightened self-interest where one puts one's interests first and those of others a close second.

Herein lies the major difference between a professional response and a lay response. A lay response in this case was to try to convince the person in effect that she hadn't murdered her unborn child and that she had no real choice but to have the abortion. The lay response focuses on the logic of the situation. A professional response, by contrast, focuses on the 'psycho-logic' of the situation. It doesn't set out initially to convince the client that she hadn't murdered her child and that she had no choice but to have the abortion. Rather, it is based on a professional understanding of the dynamics of guilt: that people feel guilty about their perceived wrongdoings not because of the wrongdoings but by their attitudes towards their wrongdoings and that once a person holds a demanding and self-condemning set of attitudes towards a wrongdoing you have very little chance of encouraging them to take an objective and compassionate view of why they did what they did. It follows from this that the best way of encouraging someone to address their guilt constructively is to first have them assume temporarily that they have committed a wrongdoing and then to understand that their feelings of guilt stems from the demanding and self-condemning attitudes that they hold towards the wrongdoing. Helping someone to examine and change these attitudes helps them to take that objective and compassionate view of their behaviour which the lay response attempts to engender. The professional response argues that the lay response is bound to fail in the long term because it does not address the psychological aspects of the situation. Indeed, the lay response is bound to fail because it does not even appreciate the existence of these psychological aspects.

Let me sum up my position so far. I am arguing that in situations where a person does not have chronic problem based on the existence of long-standing rigid attitudes a lay response may be effective, particularly where that response takes into account the psychological aspects of the situation. But in situations where a person does have a chronic problem based on rigid attitudes and where complicated psychological factors are at work then a lay response is almost bound to be ineffective, particularly because it does not understand and therefore cannot address the complex psychological factors that are at work in the situation.

I frequently observe the lay response at work in the therapy groups that I run based on cognitive-behaviour therapy principles and that take place in the setting of a psychiatric hospital. The patients that are on the CBT programme that I am involved with are taught how to assess and intervene with their own problems. They are taught to use the same skills with themselves that therapists are taught to use with their own patients. In teaching the patients how to be their own therapists, it could be said that we are training them to respond professionally with themselves and with other patients on the programme. But here is the rub. When they are in group therapy and talk directly to one another, they tend not to respond at the professional level that I have been discussing. Thus, they tend not to inquire about the attitudes that underpin their respective disturbances. Rather they tend to give one another practical, common-sense advice which might be useful after they have dealt with their underlying rigid and extreme attitudes, but is generally ineffective if these latter attitudes are left intact. This lay response continues even when patients are encouraged to respond at the professional level.

It is perhaps unsurprising that lay people should act like lay people even in a therapy group. My point here is to stress that when lay people make a lay response to someone who has a complex and long-standing psychological problem then such a response has distinct limits. It also has limits with less chronic and complex problems when the response ignores the 'psycho-logical' aspects of the problem and concentrates on the logical aspects of the situation. A lay response is effective, then, when the person being helped can respond productively to the logic being offered by the lay helper. When the person being helped cannot do so then the lay helper tends to run out of ideas and tends to repeat the logical response first offered. An impasse soon ensues. At this point, the lay helper should suggest that the person seek a professional response to their problems.

One area where a lay response is often helpful concerns the offering of an empathic response to another's concerns. When you confide in a friend or loved one and they appear to understand your experience and perhaps even link this to a similar experience of their own while recognising the uniqueness of your own experience, this can be liberating for the discloser. Such a response often serves several purposes at the same time. Apart from the therapeutic value of being understood, there is the recognition that one is being accepted for having the experience and not condemned as one fears one might be. If the empathy is combined with self-disclosure of a similar experience on the part of the listener, the discloser has a sense of connectedness with the rest of humanity. 'I'm not the only person who has experienced this' is a common refrain here. This therapeutic factor is called 'universality' in the professional psychotherapy literature. However, there are instances where the lay person is unable to provide an empathic response to the other where a professional is more capable of doing so. The first of these circumstances relates to out of the ordinary, difficult-to-understand experiences. One of my clients confided in a friend that she hoped that her sister would lose her unborn baby. This was too much for the friend to hear and she quickly made her apologies and left, leaving my client crushed and ashamed. A professional would have recognised the dynamics of unhealthy envy at play and would have been able to help the person to see that she wished her sister to miscarry because she resented the fact that her sister with whom she had always had a rivalrous relationship was pregnant when she was experiencing great difficulty getting pregnant herself. One of the capacities that a professional therapist should ideally have is the ability to hear things that lay persons would find shocking without experiencing shock oneself. Of course, therapists are human beings first and foremost and each of us have our limits in this respect, but I would say that this is a significant area where professionally trained psychotherapists have an advantage over lay people in the helping stakes.

Another area in which therapists have an advantage over friends and loved ones occurs when we consider the dangers of being overinvolved as a helper. Since therapists are not involved in their client's life they can take a far more dispassionate stance towards the person's problems where friends and loved ones, given their investment in the person's life, may be too involved to stand back and be dispassionate. Also, it is a skill to be at once dispassionate and empathic and this dual response is one that needs cultivating over time in training and supervision. Some lay persons can do this spontaneously, but most are not able to do so, particularly if they are significantly involved in what the other person is telling them.

Finally, it is difficult for a friend or loved one to offer someone a therapeutic response if the person's problems relate to oneself. One of my clients recently broke up with her lover who kept ringing her to talk about his feelings about the break-up. As one might expect, my client found this enormously difficult to respond to. As she said to me: 'He wants me to be his therapist while at the same time to be able to express his bitterness to me about the way we ended'. As I often say to people, 'if you are emotionally involved with someone you are probably the last person to be able to help them if their problems are about you'.

Lay people help one another with their emotional problems all the time and long may this continue. To reside all therapeutic responses in the consulting rooms of professional counsellors and therapists would be both dangerous and impossible to achieve and this is not what the profession wants to see either. What I have endeavoured to do in this chapter is to show when a professional response is called for and why it is likely to be more therapeutic than the help offered by lay persons, particularly when the latter are socially or intimately involved in the lives of the person needing help. There is a place for professional therapy. Let's not exaggerate this place, but let's not minimise it either.

20

The Name Change Debate
Ellis's Real Agenda

In this brief chapter, I reveal for the first time Albert Ellis's real agenda for recently changing the name from Rational-Emotive Therapy (RET) to Rational Emotive Behaviour Therapy (REBT).

As is now well known, in 1993 Albert Ellis (1995) changed the name of the therapy that he originally devised from Rational-Emotive Therapy (RET) to Rational Emotive Behaviour Therapy (REBT). In an issue of the *Journal of Rational-Emotive and Cognitive-Behavior Therapy,* Davison (1995) is supportive of this name change, while Franks (1995) and Lazarus (1995) voice their doubts about this new development. Unfortunately, both Davison and Franks fail to discern Ellis's true purpose in changing the name and while Lazarus is on the right track in speculating that REBT is only a forerunner to future name changes, he also fails to determine Ellis's real intention. Ellis, in his article, understandably chooses not to 'come clean'. By closely analysing the content and timing of the name changes that have been made so far, I can reveal for the first time that the next, and penultimate, name change will occur in 1999 and the final change will occur in the year 2031. Here is my reasoning.

Rational therapy was originally devised in 1955 and gained the acronym RT. Note closely that RT are two letters from the name 'Albert'. So we have:

1955 = RT

Six years later, Ellis decided to change the name of Rational Therapy to Rational-Emotive Therapy to reflect the fact that the therapy did not neglect emotions. Thus, RT became RET. Note closely that the addition of the 'E' is yet another letter from the name 'Albert'. Thus we now have:

1961 = RET

Thirty-two years on, Ellis decides on another name change. He argues (Ellis, 1995) that he was wrong not to include RET's decided behavioural emphasis in the name of his therapy; so in 1993 RET became REBT. Note that the inclusion of the new letter 'B' is yet another letter from the name 'Albert'. We now have:

    1993 = REBT

My first hypothesis, based on an examination of the data presented so far, is that in 1999 (i.e. six years from 1993 – remember that the first name change came at the end of a six-year cycle), Ellis will make a fourth change and introduce yet another letter from his name. Recently, Ellis (1991) has claimed that critics have not appreciated that RET/REBT is not only concerned with helping people to overcome their psychological problems, it is also concerned with helping people to ACTUALISE themselves. So my first hypothesis states that in 1999, Ellis will change the name of the therapy to 'Actualising Rational Emotive Behaviour Therapy' or AREBT. Note that subtle introduction of the 'A' – yet another letter from the name 'Albert'. So:

    1999 = AREBT

If my first hypothesis is supported then I can confidently present my second hypothesis which is that: Thirty-two years after the fourth name change, a fifth and final name change will occur (remember that RET became REBT after a gap of 32 years). Ellis has often noted that RET/REBT advocates the use of humour in that it helps people to laugh at their silly ideas (e.g. Ellis, 1987). Humour, then helps people to take themselves seriously, but not too seriously – an important ingredient of psychological health. The use of humour also qualifies as a neglected aspect of REBT. Now, I do admit that there is a problem with this analysis in that the 'H' from humour does not appear in the name 'Albert'. Then it occurred to me. Humour, per se, is not the curative factor here – LAUGHTER is. And 'L' is the missing letter from the name 'Albert'. So finally we have:

    2031 = ALBERT

And what does 'ALBERT' stand for? It stands for:

ACTUALISING LAUGHTER-BASED BEHAVIOURAL
EMOTIVE RATIONAL THERAPY

The fact that Albert Ellis will be 118 years old when he makes this final change is, I admit, problematic. But since he has often claimed that Duracell will some day invent a battery that one can insert up one's behind enabling one to live forever, who knows!

In my next paper, I will reveal the shocking truth about what happened to the hyphen when Rational-Emotive Therapy became Rational Emotive Behaviour Therapy.

21

Albert Ellis

Man of Letters

In this chapter, I reveal that Albert Ellis does actualise his gene for efficiency in the practice of REBT. This is shown in his decreasing use of words and in a corresponding increase in the use of letters and acronyms. A transcript of one of Ellis's therapy sessions is used to demonstrate this in action.

Albert Ellis has often said in workshops that he has a gene for efficiency. This is reflected in his writings on the theory and practice of REBT where there is an increasing use of letters and of acronyms instead of words. Thus, rather than refer to low frustration tolerance, Ellis (and other REBT therapists) use the acronym LFT. Recent additions to this growing list of acronyms is 'USA' (unconditional self-acceptance) and 'PYA' (push your ass). But is Ellis using such acronyms in his therapeutic practice? The following transcript of Ellis conducting therapy with an anxious client provides an affirmative answer.

Albert: What is your first name?

Dee: My first name is Dee.

Albert: OK, Dee, what problem would you like to start with?

Dee: Well, Dr Ellis, I have quite an unusual problem. I really love sailing on the sea, but every time I go I become afraid that I might see a swarm of bees and when I get afraid I shout out 'Ay!'

Ellis: OK, Dee. In REBT we use an ABC model where A is the event and C is your emotional and behavioural response to that event. Now in your case, A is the bees at sea and C is 'Ay'. But, in REBT we say that A doesn't cause C. So, the bees at sea don't cause 'Ay!' Rather it is B, your belief system, that largely

270

	determines C. So, what are you telling yourself at B to make yourself shout out 'Ay!' at C when you see the bees at sea at A, Dee?
Dee:	. . . I'm not sure, Dr Ellis . . .
Albert:	Well, you're not telling yourself: 'I hope I see bees at sea,' are you?
Dee:	Oh, I see. No, I'm not telling myself that. I'm telling myself 'I couldn't bear it if I saw the bees at sea'.
Albert:	That's exactly right. You have LFT at B, about the bees at sea at A that makes you shout out 'Ay!' at C, Dee.
Dee:	So, how do I get over my problem, Dr Ellis?
Albert:	By developing a philosophy of HFT about the bees at sea at A, so you get a healthier response at C, Dee. This new C is your G or goal.
Dee:	What would be my G?
Albert:	Concern about the prospect of seeing the bees at sea or disappointment about actually seeing them.
Dee:	Actually when I'm concerned, I shout out 'Eeee!'
Albert:	Alright. So what you have to do in order to shout out 'Eeee!' at C rather than 'Ay!' at C about the bees at sea at A, Dee, is to dispute your LFT until you develop HFT.
Dee:	That sounds clear, but how do I do this?
Albert:	By going to D, Dee.
Dee:	DD?
Albert:	No, not DD – D, Dee where D stands for disputing.
Dee:	Oh!
Albert:	So where is the evidence that you can't stand to see the bees at sea at A?
Dee:	My feelings tell me that I can't.

Albert	(*sarcastically*): 'Oh, my feelings, my feelings'. Horseshit! Your sacred feelings at C stem from your B about the bees at sea at A and prove that you have LFT rather than that you truly can stand seeing the bees at sea at A, Dee.
Dee:	But it's too hard for me to dispute my LFT at B about the bees at sea at A.
Albert:	Bullshit. That just proves that you are a difficult customer, a DC, Dee, who has LFT about changing her LFT.
Dee:	So, what do I do about that?
Albert:	You push your ass or PYA and force yourself to tolerate your discomfort anxiety or DA while challenging your LFT at B about the bees at sea at A that make you shout out 'Ay!' at C and you keep doing this until you develop HFT at B about seeing the bees at sea at A and achieve your G which is shouting out 'Eeee!' at C instead. Do you see, Dee?
Dee:	I see, Dr. Ellis, but I'm scared to do this in case I fail.
Albert:	That just proves that you have ego anxiety or EA, Dee.
Dee:	So how do I overcome this?
Albert:	By developing a philosophy of unconditional self-acceptance or USA about failing to overcome your LFT at B about seeing the bees at sea at A that leads you to shout out 'Ay!' at C, Dee. Showing yourself that you are a fallible human being or FHB for failing will help you to develop USA.
Dee:	Are there any techniques to help me with this?
Albert:	Yes, rational-emotive imagery or REI. Now, close your eyes and vividly imagine that you are failing to overcome your LFT about seeing the bees at sea at A and make yourself feel depressed at C, Dee. Tell me when you have done that.

Dee: OK.

Albert: Now, while still vividly imagining that you are failing to overcome your LFT about seeing the bees at sea at A, change your feelings from depression to disappointment and tell me when you have done that.

Dee: (*long pause*) . . . OK.

Albert: How did you do that?

Dee: I told myself that I am an FHB for failing to overcome my LFT about seeing the bees at sea.

Albert: Now practise REI for ten minutes a day for 30 days to develop USA about failing to develop HFT and then use it to develop HFT about seeing the bees at sea at A, Dee. OK?

Dee: OK. But that's a lot to take in, Dr Ellis.

Albert: Let me summarise. When you see the bees at sea at A, Dee, you shout out 'Ay!' at C because you have LFT at B. First, go to D and develop HFT at B about the bees at sea at A until you achieve your G or new C which is shouting out 'Eeee!' As you do this you also need to overcome your DA about addressing your LFT. Don't be a DC and PYA. Then, work to develop USA and show yourself that you are an FHB if you fail to overcome your LFT about seeing the bees at sea at A. Then use REI, first to develop USA at B about your ongoing LFT at A, and then to develop HFT at B about seeing the bees at sea at A. OK?

Dee: A-OK, Dr E.

22

The Politically Incorrect Professor
Dave Mearns Interviews Windy Dryden

Preamble

When they were young, both my daughters took an instant liking to Windy Dryden. Not many adults achieve that immediate 'contact' with young people whose appraisal can be the most searching of all. Windy Dryden became Britain's first Professor of Counselling and has been prolific in his publishing, to date, of 115 books. In the course of that astounding output, Dryden has encouraged and developed scores of other counselling authors. I would not hesitate to argue in support of the motion that Windy Dryden has done more to advance the profession of counselling in Britain than any other person. Yet, in the eyes of many within the profession, he is an enigma. Although a leader in counselling he is frequently not really accepted as 'representative' of the profession. Numerous interviews have been done with Windy Dryden – he has even published a book of them! (Dryden & Vasco, 1991). In this interview I wanted to try to get at this apparent paradox between Windy Dryden's contribution and his persona within the profession. Who is this man with whom so many in the profession feel 'uncomfortable'? What is the nature of his 'differentness'? Does the general impression of him tell us more about our profession than about him? After all, were my daughters more accurate in their impression of Windy Dryden as a warm, friendly man who was easy to relate to?

The following interview was recorded on Sunday, 16 May, 1999. The transcript has been tidied rather than edited.

The Interview

Dave: Windy, sometimes when I mention your name to others in the counselling world they raise their eyes. Then, when I say that I'm a friend of yours, they say, 'Are you?' with considerable incredulity in their voice. What do you think this is about, Windy?

Windy: I don't know. I don't really mix that much in counselling circles anymore, partly because I don't enjoy hanging around with lots of counsellors en masse. I would rather watch Tottenham Hotspur than actually go to a BAC conference.

Dave: That must be really bad, Windy, if you'd rather watch Tottenham Hotspur because I know you're an ardent Arsenal fan! How do you think you are seen?

Windy: I don't know, but I could hazard a guess.

Dave: What would that guess be?

Windy: I imagine that I'm seen as an abrupt type who is sort of in the mould of Albert Ellis.

Dave: So, you might be classed with him because you practise the same approach to therapy?

Windy: That could well be the case. However, as I don't hang out that much with counsellors it's difficult for me to know exactly what they think of me. *(pause)* Some people think I'm a woman.

Dave: Of course, 'Wendy'!

Windy: I once had a conversation with somebody in a bookshop. She was holding one of my books and I just said to her: 'Oh yes it's Windy Dryden, he publishes a lot, doesn't he?', so she said to me – 'oh no, she's a woman' – Politely, I added, 'I don't think she is you know' – only to be defeated with, 'Well I've actually seen her lecture'.

Dave: Oh my God!

Windy: I also don't tend to keep in touch with a lot of my ex-students so I don't have a large coterie of followers. Also, I don't have too many friends in the counselling world because I prefer to have a personal life *outside* of that world.

Dave: And do you believe you are, in a way, not very much like most counsellors?

Windy: I would say *yes*, but it's hard for me to tell really because there is a difference between the public persona and the private self of many counsellors. In my view there is not too much of a discrepancy between my public persona and my private self. I can be brusque in my private life and I can also be brusque publicly. I don't have what may be called a public therapeutic 'manner' where I ooze warmth and understanding and no doubt that has permeated the consciousness of the counselling world.

Dave: Would you say that you're not very politically correct?

Windy: That's true. Recently, I received a verbal warning at Goldsmiths College because sometimes I curse in class. Actually, I believe that counselling students need to be comfortable with profanity and I sometimes use profanity in a training setting but never at my students, but certainly *with* them. Anyway, one of my students anonymously complained and the College acted on it, which was strange as it was anonymous. I still hold that it is not the crime of the century but the College deemed otherwise – so that's a very good example of political 'incorrectness'. I do firmly believe that counselling has to be careful in its alignment with political correctness. I believe firmly that counsellors need to create an environment which allows clients to be politically *incorrect*.

Dave: You mean that's what they *should* do.

Windy: I think so.

Dave: Yeah – that it actually should be creating a context which allows clients to behave in a broader range of ways.

Windy: Right, I recently told of my experience at College to someone that I know and he said that he would actually discourage his clients from swearing because he finds that language offensive. I just could not believe that.

Dave: Astonishing.

Windy: It would be interesting to have an open debate about this issue and what annoyed me at College was that this didn't happen. What should have been forum for debate was a forum for censure.

Dave: Gosh, that must have been really sore – I would have felt really sore, particularly with all that happening anonymously.

Windy: Interestingly enough all the students in that year, including presumably the person who complained about me, actually wrote a letter to College saying that they did not find my language offensive at all. In fact, when I told my current group of students the story they said that they would write a letter of complaint about me if I *didn't* swear! Yes, it wasn't an easy time, but I was very naïve in trusting certain people in College who offered a supportive hand and then twisted it and used it against me.

Dave: Let you 'swing' – goodness gracious. That's frightening, because I mean I would have to, for instance, do away with my 'Billy Connolly' routine which is a major part of my lecturing when I'm trying to get people to use their imagination and their perceptiveness – it's really crazy. It's different swearing at someone but just using words, that's different.

Windy: Yes, I certainly don't hold with swearing at students. The other thing which I'm politically incorrect about concerns punctuality. I hold very dear the importance of

punctuality in training students and I have been known
to lock out students who have a terminal lateness
problem. I don't do it immediately, of course. I do talk
to them about it up to three times, but then when I see
that they are not listening to my words, I get them to
learn by action. I am sure that other tutors don't lock out
their students because I'm sure that on most courses
students turn up on time. Although I do recall going up
to Scotland once to work on a certain person centred
course and a sizeable minority of students didn't turn up.

Dave: I know, I know, I know Windy – it was my course. I
spoke with them about it.

Windy: I would have flogged them!

Dave: (*Laughter*)

Windy: So you see I'm hardly a model of political correctness
with all this swearing and locking students going on.

Dave: I like students being punctual too – so I customarily say
at the beginning of a course, 'look I'll start the lectures
on time – even if you are not here I'll start on time'. One
course absolutely got me the next week – *none* of them
were there on time! One of them popped their head
round the door and said, 'Have you started yet?'

Windy: Right, yeah. That's happened to me and I *did* start!

Dave: (*Laughter*)

Windy: I am sure that this kind of behaviour, which is unusual
for a counselling trainer – although it doesn't happen
very often – does travel along the counselling wire and
leaves people making inferences about me rather than
seeing the whole person. I think that counsellors find it
very difficult to see the whole person of other
counsellors.

Dave: You're aware of your controversiality yourself – like in
your book of public lectures, *Are You Sitting
Uncomfortably? Windy Dryden Live and Uncut*

(Dryden, 1998a; see also Part I of this volume). I mean, one of your lectures is the famous, or infamous, 'Dublin' lecture where someone actually walked out very publicly. What was that all about?

Windy: I have no idea. I mean I actually gave a talk which was entitled 'The Counsellor as Educator' and in that talk I discussed the idea that one role, not the only role, that a counsellor can adopt is one where we educate people psychologically. This apparently offended some people – although again you see – one of the things about the counselling world I'm afraid is that very few people will come up to me and say, 'we heard your lecture and we fundamentally disagree with it.' I mean I heard on the grapevine that there were a number of people even arguing that I should not be awarded a Fellowship from the British Association for Counselling because of it. Now it would be nice if people had the guts to come up and talk to me directly or even to write so I can respond. But, that doesn't happen.

Dave: I was at that lecture and perhaps the most controversial thing that I remember was that, at a counselling conference, you were actually saying counselling hadn't helped *you* – what had been helpful, and might be helpful for others, was a good self-help book.

Windy: Yes, and I think that may be seen as a threat – although God knows why, because I'm only talking about my experience. I am not suggesting that we actually replace counsellors with good books, although I'm sure that several of my good books are more effective than some counsellors!

Dave: (*Laughter*)

Windy: It's that kind of remark that gets me into trouble, you see!

Dave: Yes.

Windy: I suppose you won't edit that bit out.

Dave: That's right. But, isn't there something enigmatic about
it – I mean 115 books on counselling and yet you have
nothing good to say about your own experience of being
a client. Four times you've been a client and you've
nothing good to say about any of them?

Windy: No, I wouldn't say 'nothing'. I mean, the second one
was with somebody who was loosely psychodynamic
but also used psychodrama methods and those were
quite useful, the more active methods. The fourth was
with a Jungian therapist who I got on with but we got a
bit bogged down because I couldn't remember any of
my dreams. I don't have the psychological makeup to
benefit from psychoanalytical therapy, I really don't –
I'm not saying therefore that all psychodynamic
therapies are crap because that's obviously not true.

Dave: It's just that the 'fit' wasn't right for you. What does
work for you – I have been picking this up from reading
is, in a sense, being your *own* therapist. It's like you can
give yourself the conditions that are right for you, in
terms of your own . . . I was going to say 'meditation' –
but that's a misleading word – more your
'contemplation' . . .

Windy: But then the old joke is – the only trouble with self-
therapy is with the countertransference! Yes, I mean I
was helped more by reading one of Albert Ellis's books
than I was with the therapists that I actually consulted.

Dave: In reading your book of lectures, the one I enjoyed most
must also have been incredibly controversial. It was the
1997 lecture to the first International Conference on
Counselling Psychology. I mean, you preface the lecture
by saying you think that it is probably your most
controversial and yet I have also talked with someone
who was there and they said there wasn't a murmur, in
the sense that there wasn't a dissenting murmur.

Windy: Well I kind of set it up, after the Dublin experience. In
Dublin, if I had gone in there and said, 'I'm sure that

loads of people are going to be offended by this', then I think everybody would have said, 'oh no I'm far too tolerant and mature to be offended by this!'

Dave: So you pre-empted it?

Windy: I kind of pre-empted it, yes. Not as a deliberate ploy because I really did think that despite this particular 'warning', people would still have been offended.

Dave: One of the things, for instance, you said in that lecture was that women are disturbed not by being raped but by their rigid and extreme views of being raped. I know what you are about there, in terms of Rational Emotive Behaviour Therapy, and you took great care over the presentation, but that is just so against the grain, or against the counselling culture, you knew that you should expect huge reactions.

Windy: Yeah, but you see what I make clear in that lecture is that I didn't then, and do not now, condone rape which I regard as something extraordinarily negative. And that it is healthy for women, in this case, to be, if you like, 'healthily' distressed – *very* distressed about this. However, my point is that some of the conclusions that women make about being raped are not intrinsic parts of that experience and that was the thing I was actually talking about. If it was an intrinsic part of the experience then I would obviously argue that they could not be held responsible for these conclusions. I think that when we talk about 'responsibility' in that area, people often immediately think about 'blame' and, as if I'm blaming rape victims for their own traumatised reaction, which of course I'm not doing. So, I mean, if people were to read the arguments clearly, there would be no difficulty.

Dave: In a sense, if people can read or listen to the argument then it can make sense, but if you only get second hand 'sound bites', then it gets mixed up with people's own irrational thinking in a way.

Windy: That's right.

Dave: I was thinking about this 'enigmatic' quality of Windy Dryden. I wonder if one of the difficulties about you is that you are 'normal', in the sense that you boldly, obstinately refuse to be 'neurotic'. And the norm in our profession *must* be in the direction of neurosis.

Windy: Well that's right, that's why I'm very much ambivalent about the personal therapy requirement. People who attend my courses say, 'oh, do we have to be in personal therapy?', and my response is 'only if you need it'.
           Obviously, I have my vulnerabilities just like anybody else, but I think that I am a reasonably well-adjusted individual in a number of areas.

Dave: And of course 'normality' would be potentially frightening if the norm within the counselling world is 'neurotic'.

Windy: It could very well be.

Dave: You were talking about yourself there, Windy, and I had one or two questions on that. One of the questions is quite simple – are you a 'loner'?

Windy: I wouldn't say that I'm a loner, but I definitely enjoy my own company and I have the ability to be alone and pursue my own personal projects for fairly long periods of time. So yes, in that sense – I'm a loner. Being an only child was a help for that.

Dave: I have always felt that that was fundamental for me too.

Windy: Yeah, but I can also mix with people. Not, as I say, with counsellors that much, particularly en masse – I find them quite a frustrating experience. But certainly going to the Arsenal with my friends and 'laddish' things like around the Leisure Centre where I'm a member, I find interaction with others very enjoyable.

Dave: What 'unhealthy negative emotions' are you prone to, Windy? I mean 'depression', 'guilt', 'anxiety'. Let me guess, 'depression' more than the other two?

Windy: No, you're wrong.

Dave: Interesting.

Windy: I very rarely, if ever, get depressed these days. I was moderately depressed in my early twenties for which I did seek therapy, which as I have said was not very helpful. No, I think of all the unhealthy negative emotions I'm most prone to unhealthy anger.

I think I've inherited, from the male side of my family, a tendency to easily make myself 'unhealthily' angry. On top of that I still do feel 'healthily' angry at times. I think people find it hard to notice the difference and at times it may spill over, from 'healthy' to 'unhealthy', but I'm quite prone to anger in both its forms.

Dave: Yeah, and I can see in that situation that it would be difficult for the other person to know the difference between 'healthy' and 'unhealthy' anger. But 'anger' is your vulnerability more than the others?

Windy: Definitely.

Dave: How about 'rigid and extreme attitudes', any rigid and extreme attitudes that still trip you up?

Windy: Yes, I think one. I have the attitude that other people must not try to shortcut things and if they do they must not get away with it. When people do benefit from taking professional shortcuts I find that most difficult to deal with. For example, a couple of years ago, I was asked to sit on a promotions panel for someone in a field close to our own. I discovered that the person's PhD did not contain any data and I brought this to the attention of the panel at the University. However, they were completely unconcerned about it, which really surprised me. The person eventually was awarded a professorship, which I found difficult to stomach. So it's events like this that I struggle most with.

Dave: Right.

Windy: Anyway, eventually I take myself in hand and accept that things like this are going to happen in our world and that there is no inherent justice in the world to prevent it from happening. So, I strive to tolerate it while actively disliking it.

Dave: That, in a sense, leads neatly on to my next question: what are you *passionate* about in life, Windy? And, by the way, I have already noted down Arsenal! What are you passionate about in life?

Windy: I'm passionate about helping people to live meaningful lives without needlessly disturbing themselves. That's why I spend a lot of my time writing and I am at the moment increasingly writing 'self-help' books, which, in an academic environment, gets you no credit whatsoever. But writing self-help books is one of my abiding passions. I have quite a few other passions – for example I enjoy the Marx Brothers movies, I go over these when I have some time. I'm also a great fan of Al Jolson and Junior Walker and the All Stars. I like Sergeant Bilko, the Billy Bunter novels of Frank Richards. I am passionate about Gregorian music, and steam trains and . . .

Dave: You realise of course, Windy, they are all still in the 'black and white' era – you haven't reached the 'colour' era.

Windy: I know, and I avidly like boxing. Of course, that is another politically incorrect thing for counsellors to follow.

Dave: Which will worry you a lot!

Windy: Right, now I realise that I'm listing my 'interests' rather than my 'passions', but I tend to be passionate about my interests. But, on the whole, my greatest passion is to help people become healthier in a variety of ways. This is the other thing, *variety* is important to me. I think it will be interesting to see what happens with the Internet in the years to come, if we can help some people through that medium.

Dave: As you were talking, what immediately came to my mind was a person who could take the step of buying a self-help book off a railway stand but, by God, would be a hundred miles away from actually seeking contact with another human being for help.

Windy: That's right.

Dave: And the Internet would fit that too, wouldn't it?

Windy: Yeah, that's right.

Dave: Somebody who could make contact through that medium but would find it really difficult to go to counselling. Boy, there must be almost a majority of them – a huge number that counselling never sees.

Windy: That's right. I think that this is where we again get into developing psychological education which, as you know, is one of my passions.

Dave: One of the books I loved in the last year is Firestone's book on suicide (Firestone, 1997). He paints this incredibly vivid picture of the young, often young *male,* who is so cut off from others. And I've often thought, gosh yes, counselling isn't the medium for reaching that person. They would not *engage.*

Dave: Last question, Windy. What *challenges* are there for you in the future? Is it the second century of books?

Windy: Oh no, no, no. I mean I do have writing plans. One of my goals is to have a self-help book for every major emotional disturbance people have. I have brought one out on shame, guilt, anger, jealousy and sulking. I haven't yet touched anxiety and depression, although

I'm going to get around to those. That is one particular goal. But all I really want is just to continue doing the things now I enjoy and find meaningful. One of the things I like about my life is its variety. People often assume, wrongly, that I don't see clients and in fact I see a fair number because I believe that it is important to keep one's skills up to scratch for training purposes. I'm just going to take life as it comes and actually kind of enjoy life a lot and let's see what actually happens. I don't have any particular ambitions and goals because I've achieved quite a lot of them already.

Dave: That's it – Windy, thanks very much indeed.

Windy: Bye.

PART III

STRANGE, BUT RATIONAL

23

Beyond Belief

The Shocking 'ABC's of REBT

If you listen carefully to people talking about matters where disturbed emotions are involved, you will soon get the idea of the model of emotions that people have in their heads that informs their narrative. Let me give you a few examples of what it is possible to hear every day of the week.

- He made me angry
- Losing my job made me feel depressed
- I couldn't do that, it would hurt her feelings
- He brought shame on his family
- My mother guilt trips me

What these snippets have in common is that they assume that events cause people to have certain feelings. Thus, in the first example, the idea is put forward that whatever 'he' did made the narrator feel angry. This might be thought of as the 'event causes feelings' model. Thus:

People's emotions are caused by events

In REBT we have a different model of emotions which can be summed up as follows:

People's emotions are largely determined not by events, but by the attitudes that they hold towards events

So, the narrators of our five snippets, by adhering to an 'event causes feelings' model, are saying that adversities cause disturbed emotions.

The 'Event Causes Feelings' Model

If you think about the 'event causes feelings' model, you will conclude that it is fundamentally pessimistic. Let me show you what I mean by discussing an example.

Maggie wanted to go out with her friends on Friday night and had been looking forward to this outing for many weeks. On Thursday evening, Maggie's mother rang her and told her that she had been let down by a friend who had promised to take her to the pictures. Her mother asked Maggie to take her, but Maggie declined explaining that she was going out with her friends. Then her mother accused Maggie of being selfish and of neglecting her. Maggie felt very guilty about what her mother had said and backtracked saying that she would take her mother to see the film after all.

When talking about this incident later with a friend, Maggie said that the reason that she took her mother to see the film was because her mother had 'made her feel guilty' about going out with her friends.

Maggie's view that what her mother said to her made her feel guilty is pessimistic for the following reasons:

- It implies that every time her mother accuses Maggie of being selfish it is inevitable that Maggie will feel guilty. In the same way as two parts of hydrogen being added to one part of oxygen causes the formation of water, Maggie's mother's accusation causes Maggie's guilt.

- The 'event causes feelings' model deprives Maggie of choice. It is thus false since Maggie, in reality, does have options in this situation. While it is true that she can, and in our example, does adopt an attitude towards her mother's accusation that leads her to feel guilty (as I will explain in greater detail later in this chapter), she has the option of adopting different attitudes, one of which would lead to healthy remorse rather than to guilt.

In addition, Maggie has options about how she views her mother's behaviour. When she feels guilty, it is likely that she infers that her mother is genuinely upset, but she could view her mother's behaviour as a calculated manipulative ploy to control her behaviour. If she viewed her mother's behaviour in this way, she would feel healthily or unhealthily angry depending upon what attitude she took of her mother's presumed manipulative behaviour.

By saying that an adversity causes emotional disturbance, you are also, in fact, arguing that whoever experiences the adversity is bound to be disturbed by it. Thus, if 100 people were faced with their mother's accusation of selfishness, then all 100 people would react with guilt. Statistically, this is highly unlikely. Even if we assume that the majority of this group of 100 people would experience guilt in the face of such an accusation, we would have to concede that a minority would have different reactions to this adversity. Once we acknowledge this point then we are saying that the 'event causes feelings' model of human emotions is wrong.

The 'event causes feelings' model runs counter to what we know about the psychology of human emotion

From the above discussion, we have seen that the 'event causes feelings' model implies that an event can bypass a person's brain and make them feel a certain way. Thus, in our example, when Maggie's mother accuses her of selfishness, this event bypasses Maggie's brain and causes her to feel guilt.

One of the main purposes of the human brain is to process information. The whole idea of processing is that something is done with the information that depends partly on the information to be processed and partly on the individual doing the processing. The 'event causes feelings' model argues that in some way the information slips past the person's brain and directly affects the person's emotional system in ways that can be totally predicted by the information itself. Thus, all we need to know to predict that Maggie will feel guilty is the fact that her mother accused her of being selfish. We do not need to know anything about the way Maggie processes the accusation because, and this is the important point, this information bypasses Maggie's brain.

This goes against what we know about the psychology of human emotion and the factors that influence emotion. Thus, we know that much of human emotion depends upon cognitive appraisal. Such appraisal can only be done by the human brain. Thus, far from bypassing a person's brain, such information is registered by the brain and appraised by it. Such appraisal is a form of information processing that is characterised by evaluation. In the REBT model, we break down this appraisal or evaluative process into two different, but interactive components:

1. an inferential component, and
2. an attitude component

The REBT model, as we will see, allows for quite a bit of variability in cognitive processing. Thus, a person can make a number of different inferences about the same event and can also hold a number of different attitudes towards the event. Even if the 'event causes feelings' model allows for the event to be processed by the person's brain, it follows that the event can only be processed in one way, i.e. in a way that leads to the emotion in question. No variability in processing is possible in the 'event causes feelings' model.

The 'event causes feelings' model versus the REBT model

Before I discuss the REBT model of human emotion in much greater detail, let me briefly compare the 'event causes feelings' model and the REBT model.

The 'event causes feelings' model as I have outlined it states that an event can directly cause an emotion. This means that cognitive processing is bypassed or if such processing takes place it is determined by the event and the person cannot process the event in any other way.

By contrast, the REBT model has at its heart a number of ideas that are different from the 'event causes feelings' model. Thus it argues that:

1. A person processes an event in a unique manner.
2. A person can modify that processing so that they have alternative ways of processing the same event. Crucially for psychotherapy, this means that if the person disturbs themself about an event by the way they process that event, they can 'undisturb' themself about the same event by changing their processing.
3. Different people can process the same event in a variety of different ways.

The REBT Model of Human Emotions

The REBT model is based on what I call the 'situational 'ABC' model'. As I asserted above, this model has, at its heart, the idea that a person processes an event in a particular way and it is the event plus the person's processing of the event that determines how the person feels about the event. This model, thus, is in direct opposition to the 'event causes feelings' model which holds either that processing of the event is not important or that only one way of such processing is possible and that way is determined by the event.

Let me now present the REBT model of human emotions. As I said, I call this the 'situational 'ABC' model' and will expand it to include not only the person's emotional response to an event, but their behavioural response to it as well as their subsequent thinking (i.e. the thinking that they engage in once they begin to feel and act in a certain way).

REBT's 'situational "ABC" model'

Rational Emotive Behaviour Therapy (REBT) is an approach to counselling that can be placed firmly in the cognitive-behavioural tradition of psychotherapy, meaning that it particularly focuses on the way that we think and behave when understanding our emotional responses. REBT was founded in 1955 by Dr Albert Ellis, an American clinical psychologist who brought together his interests in philosophy and psychology which are still present in this approach over 50 years on. I will briefly describe the 'situational ABC' model in its basic form before discussing each element in greater detail.

'Situation'

We do not react in a vacuum. Rather, we think, feel and act in specific situations. The term 'situation' in the 'ABC' model refers to a descriptive account of the actual event to which we respond emotionally and behaviourally.

'A' = Adversity

Within this specific situation, when we have a significant emotional reaction it is usually to a key or critical aspect of this situation. This is known as adversity.

'B' = Basic Attitude

It is a major premise of REBT that while our emotions are usually about an adversity, this 'A' does not cause our emotional reaction. Rather, our emotions are primarily determined by the basic attitudes that we hold towards the adversity. Other REBT therapists refer to 'B' as beliefs but I prefer the term' attitudes'. To preserve the letter B in the 'ABC' framework I formally refer to these attitudes as basic attitudes.

'C' = Consequences of the basic attitudes at 'B' towards the adversity at 'A' (there are three such consequences: emotional, behavioural and thinking)

When you hold an attitude towards an adversity, you will tend to:

- experience an emotion
- act (or be inclined to act) in a certain way, and
- think in certain ways

These three consequences of this 'A x B' interaction are known as emotional, behavioural and thinking consequences respectively.

Let me now discuss each of these elements in greater detail.

'Situation'

Emotional episodes do not take place in a vacuum. Rather, they occur in specific 'situations'. Such situations are viewed in the 'situational ABC' model as descriptions of actual events about which you form inferences (see below).

'Situations' exist in time. Thus, they can describe past actual events (e.g. 'My boss asked me to see her at the end of the day'), present actual events (e.g. 'My boss is asking me to see her at the end of the day'), or future events (e.g. 'My boss will ask me to see her at the end of the day'). Note that I have not referred to such future events as future actual events since we do not know that such events will occur and this is why such future events may prove to be false. But if we look at such future 'situations', they are still descriptions of what may happen and do not add inferential meaning (see below).

'Situations' may refer to internal actual events (i.e. events that occur within ourselves, e.g. thoughts, feelings, bodily sensations, aches and pains, etc.) or to external actual events (i.e. events that occur outside ourselves, e.g. your boss asking to see you). Their defining characteristic is as before: they are descriptions of events and do not include inferential meaning.

'A'

As I said above 'A' stands for an adversity. This is the aspect of the situation about which you experience an emotional reaction. Let me make a number of points about 'A':

1. An 'A' is usually an inference and when it is, it needs to be differentiated from the 'situation' or actual event about which it is made.

An inference is basically an interpretation or hunch about the 'situation', whereas the 'situation' is purely descriptive. Let me provide you with an example to make this distinction clear.

Imagine that you receive a message from your boss to the effect that they want to see you at the end of the day. You think that this means that they are going to criticise your work. The situation or actual event here is: 'My boss wants to see me at the end of the day', while your 'A' is: 'My boss is going to criticise my work'. As can be seen from this example the 'situation' is a description of the facts of the matter whereas the 'A' is a key inference that you have made about the 'situation'. It is key because it is the aspect of the situation to which you have an emotional response. When you have a significant emotional response to an event or 'situation', the 'A' represents the personalised inferential meaning that you give to the situation. As I said earlier I refer to this 'A' as an adversity.

2. Inferences that usually comprise the 'A' can be true or false and as such when you make an inference you need to weigh it against the available evidence.

In the above example, it may be true that your boss is going to criticise your work when you go to see them at the end of the working day or it may be false. All you can do is to consider the available evidence and come up with the 'best bet' about what is going to happen at the meeting with the boss. This involves considering such factors as: (a) what has happened in the past when your boss has asked to see you; (b) the quality of the work that you recently submitted to your boss; and (c) how critical or otherwise your boss is in general.

3. An 'A' can be about a past, present or future event.

When you have an 'A' about a past, present or future 'situation' or actual event you give that event inferential meaning. Thus:

Past 'situation' =	My boyfriend did not return my call
'A' about past 'situation' =	This proves that he doesn't care for me
Present 'situation' =	My father is discussing the value of saving regularly
'A' about present 'situation' =	My father is criticising me for overspending
Future 'situation' =	The hospital will contact me with the results of my blood test
'A' about future 'situation' =	The blood test will show that I am ill

4. An 'A' can be about an event external to you or about an event internal to you.

The defining characteristic of this 'A' is again its inferential nature. For example:

External 'situation' =	Letter with a cheque in it has gone missing
'A' about external 'situation' =	Somebody has stolen my cheque
Internal 'situation' =	Intrusive thought about hitting someone
'A' about internal 'situation' =	I am losing control

'B'

As I said above, 'B' stands for basic attitudes. These attitudes can be rigid and extreme (unconstructive) or flexible and non-extreme (constructive). You can hold attitudes towards descriptive 'situations', but more often you will hold attitudes towards the adversities which represent the inferences that you have made about these more objective 'situations'.

Flexible and non-extreme attitudes

REBT argues that there are four basic flexible and non-extreme attitudes which have the following five major characteristics:

(a) flexible or non-extreme
(b) conducive to your mental health
(c) helpful to you as you strive towards your goals
(d) true
(e) logical

Now let me discuss the four flexible and non-extreme attitudes put forward by REBT theory.

1. Flexible attitude

Human beings have desires and for an attitude to be the cornerstone of healthy functioning it needs to be flexible and incorporate these desires. A flexible attitude has two components The first component is called the 'asserted preference'. Here you make clear to yourself what you want (either what you want to happen or exist or what you want not to happen or exist). The second component is called the 'negated demand'. Here you acknowledge that what you want to occur or exist does not have to occur or exist.

In short, we have:

Flexible attitude = 'asserted preference' component + 'negated demand' component

For example:

Flexible attitude	'Asserted preference' component	'Negated demand' component
I want you to like me, but you do not have to do so	I want you to like me…	… but you do not have to do so

Active versus passive flexible attitude. I make a distinction between an active flexible attitude and a passive flexible attitude. The former leads to action, while the latter does not. Thus, if I hold the attitude that: 'I want you to like me, but you do not have to do so' and this flexible attitude is active, I may think of ways of encouraging you to like me and act appropriately. However, this would not be underpinned by a sense of desperation (which it would be if I held the attitude that you had to like me) and therefore I would be clear what I would do and would not do to encourage you to like me.

However, if my flexible attitude was passive, I would not do anything to try and get what I want (in this case you liking me). When a person's flexible attitude is passive, they decide not to act on this preference. This may be because the person may realise that there is no chance of getting what they want or the effort and/or expense taken to get what the person wants does not merit the achievement of their desire. Thus, I am bald and I would like to have hair, but this isn't necessary for me. My flexible attitude towards having hair is passive, because I am not taking any action to get hair. Why? Because it would involve a lot of expense and inconvenience and I judge that this isn't worth it to me to go to such expense and inconvenience to get what I want in this area of my life.

2. Non-awfulising attitude

When your flexible attitude is not met it is healthy for you to conclude that it is bad that you have not got what you want. It is not healthy to be indifferent about not getting what you desire. As with a flexible attitude, a non-awfulising attitude has two components. The first component may be called 'asserted badness'. Here you acknowledge that it is bad that you have not got what you want or that you have got what you don't want. The second component is called 'negated awfulising'. Here you acknowledge that while it is bad when you don't get your desires met it is not awful, terrible or the end of the world. In short, we have:

Non-awfulising attitude = 'Asserted badness' component + 'Negated awfulising' component

For example:

Non-awfulising attitude	'Asserted badness' component	'Negated awfulising' component
It is bad if you do not like me, but it isn't the end of the world if you don't	It is bad if you do not like me	... but it isn't the end of the world if you don't

3. Bearability attitude

When your flexible attitude is not met it is healthy for you to conclude that it is difficult for you to bear not getting what you want, but that you can bear it. A bearability attitude has five components. The first component may be called 'asserted struggle' because you recognise that it is a struggle to put up with not getting what you want. The second component is called 'negated unbearability'. Here you acknowledge that while it is a struggle to bear not getting your desires met it is not unbearable. The third component is called the 'worth bearing' component and points to the fact that not only can you bear not getting what you want, it is worth doing so. The fourth component is a 'willingness' component and here you assert your willingness to bear the adversity, The fifth and final component is called the 'going to' component and here you assert your commitment to bear the adversity. In short, we have:

Bearability attitude = 'Asserted struggle' component + 'Negated unbearability' component + 'Worth tolerating' component + 'willingness' component + 'going to' component

For example:

Bearability attitude	'Asserted struggle' component	'Negated unbearability' component	'Worth tolerating' component	'Willingness' component	'Going to' component
If you do not like me, that would be hard for me to put up with, but I could bear it and it would be worth it for me to do so. Additionally, I am willing to bear it and I am going to do so	If you do not like me, that would be hard for me to bear...	... but I could bear it...	... and it would be worth it for me to do so	Additionally, I am willing to bear it	... and I am going to do so

4. Unconditional acceptance attitude

When your flexible attitude is not met it is healthy for you to accept this state of affairs. There are three types of unconditional acceptance attitudes: an unconditional self-acceptance attitude where you accept yourself unconditionally for not meeting your desires or for not having them met; an unconditional other-acceptance attitude where you accept another person or other people unconditionally for not meeting your desires and an unconditional acceptance of life conditions attitude where you accept life conditions unconditionally when they don't meet your desires.

There are three components to an unconditional acceptance attitude which I will illustrate with reference to an unconditional self-acceptance attitude. The first component is called the 'negatively evaluated aspect' component. Here you recognise when you have not met your desires or that your desires have not been met by others or by life conditions and you evaluate this particular aspect negatively. The second component is called the 'negated global negative evaluation' component. Here you acknowledge that while you may have acted badly, for example, or experienced a bad event, the whole of you is not bad. The third component is called the 'asserted complex fallibility' component. Whereas in the second component you negated the view that you are a bad person, for example, here you assert what you are: a complex fallible human being. In short, we have:

Unconditional acceptance attitude = 'Negatively evaluated aspect' component + 'Negated global negative evaluation' component + 'Asserted complex fallibility' component

For example:

Unconditional acceptance attitude	'Negatively valued aspect' component	'Negated global negative evaluation' component	'Asserted complex fallibility' component
It is bad if you do not like me but it does not mean that I am worthless. I am the same fallible human being whether you like me or not	It is bad if you do not like me...	... but it does not mean that I am worthless...	... I am the same fallible human being whether you like me or not

In addition to proposing that there are four basic flexible and non-extreme attitudes REBT argues that there are four basic rigid and extreme attitudes which have the following five major characteristics:

(a) rigid or extreme
(b) conducive to psychological disturbance

(c) unhelpful to you as you strive towards your goals
(d) false
(e) illogical

Now let me discuss the four rigid and extreme attitudes put forward by REBT theory.

1. Rigid attitude

REBT theory holds that when you take your desires and turn them into rigid demands, absolute necessities, musts, absolute shoulds and the like, you make yourself emotionally disturbed when you don't get what you believe you must. Even when you do get what you believe you must, you are still vulnerable to emotional disturbance when you hold a rigid demand at the point when you become aware that you might lose what you have and need.

A rigid attitude has two components. The first is known as the 'asserted preference' component and is the same as the asserted preference component of a flexible attitude. Again, you make clear to yourself what you want (either what you want to happen or exist or what you want not to happen or exist). The second component is called the 'asserted demand' component. Here you take what you want and you turn it into a 'rigid demand'
(e.g. 'I want to do well in my examination and therefore I have to do so'). In short, we have:

> Rigid attitude = 'asserted preference' component + 'asserted demand' component

For example:

Rigid attitude	'Asserted preference' component	'Asserted demand' component
I want you to like me and therefore you have to do so	I want you to like me...	... and therefore you have to do so

Because the 'asserted preference' component part of a rigid attitude is often implicit, a rigid attitude is usually expressed just as a rigid attitude without this component being made explicit (i.e. 'You must like me!').

2. Awfulising attitude

When you hold a rigid attitude and you do not get what you think you must get, for example, you will tend to make the extreme conclusion that it is awful, horrible, terrible or the end of the world that you haven't got what you insist you must have. As with a non-awfulising attitude, an awfulising attitude has two components. The first component is the same as that in the non-awfulising attitude – an 'asserted badness' component. Here you acknowledge that it is bad that you have not got what you want or that you have got what you don't want. The second component is called the 'asserted awfulising' component. Here you transform your non-extreme evaluation of badness and transform it into an extreme evaluation of horror (e.g. 'Because it would be bad if I were to fail my exam, it would be horrible were I to do so'). In short, we have:

Awfulising attitude = 'Asserted badness' component + 'Asserted awfulising' component

For example:

Awfulising attitude	'Asserted badness' component	'Asserted awfulising' component
It is bad if you do not like me and therefore it is the end of the world if you don't	It is bad if you do not like me...	... and therefore it is the end of the world if you don't

Because the 'asserted badness' component part of an awfulising attitude is often implicit, an awfulising attitude is usually expressed without this component being made explicit (i.e. 'It's awful if you don't like me!')

3. Unbearability attitude

When you hold a rigid attitude and you do not get what you think you must get, for example, you will tend to make the extreme conclusion that you cannot bear not getting what you demand. Unlike a bearability attitude which has five components, an unbearability attitude has only two components. The first component is again known as the 'asserted struggle' component because you recognise that it is a struggle to put up with not getting what you must. The second component is called the 'asserted unbearability' component. Here you acknowledge that it is not just a struggle to bear not getting your demand met, it is unbearable. Since you think that you cannot bear not getting your demand met the issue of whether or not it is worth bearing does not become an issue. You can't bear it and that's that. In short, we have:

Unbearability attitude = 'Asserted struggle' component + 'Asserted unbearability' component

For example:

Unbearability attitude	'Asserted struggle' component	'Asserted unbearability' component
If you don't like me, that would be hard for me to bear and therefore it would be unbearable	If you don't like me, that would be hard for me to bear...	... and therefore it would be unbearable

Because the 'asserted struggle' component part of an unbearability attitude is often implicit, an unbearability attitude is usually expressed without this component being made explicit (i.e. 'It's unbearable if you don't like me!').

4. Devaluation attitude

When you hold a rigid attitude and you do not get what you think you must get, for example, you will tend to devalue yourself, devalue others or devalue life conditions. Thus, there are three types of devaluation attitude: a self-devaluation attitude where you devalue yourself for not meeting your demands or for not having them met; an other-devaluation attitude where you devalue another person or other people for not meeting your demands; and a devaluation of life conditions attitude where you devalue life conditions when they don't meet your demands.

There are two components to a devaluation attitude which I will illustrate with reference to a self-devaluation attitude. The first component is called the 'negatively evaluated aspect' component. Here you recognise when you have not met your demands or that your demands have not been met by others or by life conditions and you evaluate this particular aspect negatively. The second component is called the 'asserted global negative evaluation' component. Here you give yourself a global negative rating for not meeting your demands, for example. Thus, you may acknowledge that you have acted badly and then evaluate yourself as a bad person for acting badly. In short, we have:

Devaluation attitude = 'Negatively evaluated aspect' component +
'Asserted global negative evaluation' component

For example:

Devaluation attitude	'Negatively evaluated aspect' component	'Asserted global negative evaluation' component
It's bad if you don't like me and proves that I am worthless	It's bad if you don't like me ...	... and proves that I am worthless

Because the 'negatively evaluated aspect' component part of a devaluation attitude is often implicit, a devaluation attitude is usually expressed without this component being made explicit (i.e. 'I am worthless if you don't like me!').

'C'

'C' stands for the consequences that you experience when you hold a basic attitude at 'B' towards 'A'. There are three major consequences which I will consider separately, but which in reality occur together.

Emotional 'C's

When you hold a set of flexible and non-extreme attitudes towards an adversity, your emotional 'C' will be negative but healthy. Yes, that's right; negative emotions can be healthy. Thus, when you face a threat, it is healthy to feel concerned and when you have experienced a loss, it is healthy to feel sad. Other healthy negative emotions (so called because they feel unpleasant, but help you to deal constructively with adversities) are: remorse, disappointment, sorrow, healthy anger, healthy jealousy and healthy envy.

When you hold a set of rigid and extreme attitudes towards an adversity, your emotional 'C' will be negative and unhealthy. Thus, when you face a threat, it is unhealthy to feel anxious and when you have experienced a loss, it is unhealthy to feel depressed. Other unhealthy negative emotions (so called because they feel unpleasant and they interfere with you dealing constructively with negative life events) are: guilt, shame, hurt, unhealthy anger, unhealthy jealousy and unhealthy envy.

Behavioural 'C's

When you hold a set of flexible and non-extreme attitudes towards an adversity, your behavioural 'C' is likely to be constructive. Such behaviour is constructive in three ways. First, it will help you to change the adversity that you are facing if it can be changed. Second, it will help you to make a healthy adjustment if the adversity cannot be changed, and third, it will help you to go forward and make progress at achieving your goals.

When you hold a set of rigid and extreme attitudes towards an adversity, your behavioural 'C' is likely to be unconstructive. Such behaviour is unconstructive in three ways. First, it won't help you to change the adversity that you are facing if it can be changed. Indeed, such unconstructive behaviour will often make a bad situation worse. Second, it will prevent you from making a healthy adjustment if the adversity cannot be changed, and third, it will take you away from pursuing your goals.

Behavioural 'C's can be action tendencies as well as overt behaviours

Strictly speaking, whenever you act in a certain way, most of the time you convert a tendency to act into an overt action. This occurs even though it is happens very quickly and it does not seem to you that you are engaged in such a conversion process. Thus, it is almost always possible for you not to make this conversion and for you not to act in a way in which you feel like acting.

Thus, many times you may feel like doing something, but choose not to do so. Indeed, a central ingredient of facilitating psychological change involves encouraging someone not to do things that they feel like doing when such behaviour is self-defeating.

This distinction between action tendencies and overt behaviour and placing them both under the rubric 'behavioural "C"'s' helps a therapist judge whether a person's attitudes are flexible/non-extreme or rigid/extreme when the person's overt behaviour appears constructive. Asking the person what they felt like doing in the situation but did not do often reveals that the person's action tendencies stem from rigid and extreme attitudes when it appears that their overt behaviour stems from flexible and non-extreme attitudes.

Thinking 'C's

When you hold a set of flexible and non-extreme attitudes towards an adversity, your subsequent thinking (or thinking 'C') is likely to be constructive. Such thinking is constructive in two ways. First, it is realistic and allows you to deal with probable outcomes. Second, it is balanced and recognises, for example, that you will get a range of positive, neutral and negative responses to your behaviour. As a result these thinking 'C's enable you to respond constructively to realistically perceived situations.

When your critical 'A' is negative, but this time you hold a set of rigid and extreme attitudes at 'B' about this 'A', your subsequent thinking (or thinking 'C') is likely to be unconstructive. Such thinking is unconstructive in two ways. First, it is unrealistic in that you will tend to predict the occurrence of low probability, highly aversive outcomes. Second, it is skewed in that you think, for example, that most people will respond to you negatively, a few may respond to you neutrally, but nobody will respond to you positively. As a result these thinking 'C's interfere with your ability to respond constructively to realistically perceived situations.

Let me summarise in the two tables below what I have said about REBT's situational ABC model.

Table 23.1 Situational ABC model of psychological health

Situation =	Objectively described event
'A' = Adversity	Aspect of the situation to which your respond emotionally, behaviourally and cognitively
'B' = Flexible and non-extreme attitude =	Flexible attitude Non-awfulising attitude Bearability attitude Unconditional acceptance attitude
'C' = Consequences	Emotional (healthy negative) Behavioural (constructive) Thinking (realistic and balanced)

Table 23.2 Situational ABC model of psychological disturbance

Situation =	Objectively described event
'A' = Adversity	Aspect of the situation to which your respond emotionally, behaviourally and cognitively
'B': Rigid and extreme attitude =	Rigid attitude Awfulising attitude Unbearability attitude Devaluation attitude
'C' = Consequences	Emotional (unhealthy negative) Behavioural (unconstructive) Thinking (unrealistic and skewed)

REBT's Situational ABC Model:
The Case of Maggie Revisited

You will recall what I said above about Maggie. She wanted to go out with her friends on Friday night and had been looking forward to this outing for many weeks. On Thursday evening, Maggie's mother rang her and told her that she had been let down by a friend who had promised to take her to the pictures. Her mother asked Maggie to take her, but Maggie declined explaining that she was going out with her friends. Then her mother accused Maggie of being selfish and of neglecting her. Maggie felt very guilty about what her mother had said and backtracked saying that she would take her mother to see the film after all.

When talking about this later with a friend, Maggie said that the reason that she took her mother to see the film was because her mother had made her feel guilty about going out with her friends.

As I have already discussed, Maggie held an 'event causes feelings' model of human emotion and this is clearly shown in her statement that the reason that she took her mother to the pictures rather than go out with her friends was down to the fact, as she saw it, that her mother made her feel guilty.

By contrast, the REBT model is at variance with the 'event causes feelings' model. Let me apply REBT's 'situational 'ABC' model' to this event.

'Situation'

It is difficult to know for certain what Maggie's mother actually said to her because we only have Maggie's report of what her mother said. This often happens in counselling and psychotherapy and sometimes we have to assume that the person's description of the situation is objective when we may have our doubts about this objectivity. In this case, since we do not have a record of Maggie's mother's actual words we have to assume that Maggie's account that her mother said that she was selfish and had neglected her was accurate if Maggie said that these were the actual words that her mother used.

'A'

If you recall, an 'A' is the aspect of the situation that the person responds to emotively, behaviourally and cognitively. It is what I refer to as an adversity. We know from Maggie's account that she felt guilty in this episode and took her mother to see a film rather than go out with her friends, which she preferred to do. When we are trying to find 'A', we most frequently use the person's emotional 'C' to do so, in Maggie's case, her guilt. For Maggie what she felt most guilty about was hurting her mother's feelings and therefore this is her 'A'.

'B'

In guilt, the person usually holds a rigid attitude and a self-devaluation attitude towards the 'A'. In Maggie's case her rigid attitude was: 'I must not hurt my mother's feelings' and her self-devaluation attitude was 'I am a bad person for hurting my mother's feelings'.

'C'

We know that Maggie experienced guilt about hurting her mother's feelings. So guilt is her emotional 'C'. We also know that Maggie 'backtracked saying that she would take her mother to see the film after all'. So this 'backtracking' was her behavioural 'C'. From what Maggie said we don't have any information to know what her subsequent thinking (i.e. her thinking 'C') was in this episode. Table 23.3 summarises the ABC analysis of Maggie's guilt.

Table 23.3 Summary of the ABC model of Maggie's guilt

Situational ABC Model of Maggie's Guilt	
Situation =	Maggie's mother told her that she was being selfish and was neglecting her*
'A' (Adversity) =	I have hurt my mother's feelings
'B': Basic rigid/extreme attitude =	I must not hurt my mother's feelings and I am a bad person for doing so
'C' = Consequences	
Emotional =	Guilt
Behavioural =	Taking her mother to the pictures instead of going out with her friends as she had previously arranged
Thinking =	Unknown
* I have assumed here that this is what Maggie's mother actually said to her	

Helping Maggie change

If we use the Situational ABC model as a framework for understanding what an REBT therapist can do and cannot do to help Maggie change, we see the following:

'Situation'

The therapist cannot help Maggie change the situation. It happened and Maggie cannot be helped to make it 'un-happen'.

'A'

The therapist can help Maggie to reconsider her inference that she hurt her mother's feelings. In this respect, the therapist can help Maggie to see that all she did was to say 'no' to her mother and, assuming that her mother's upset was genuine, her mother's feelings and her behaviour stemmed largely from her own attitudes towards her daughter's behaviour and were not caused by Maggie's behaviour. The therapist can help Maggie see, therefore, that by saying that she hurt her mother's feelings, Maggie was adhering to an 'event causes feelings' model and she needs to adopt the REBT model instead. By doing so, she would see that she was responsible for her behaviour and not her mother's reactions to her behaviour.

The therapist can also help Maggie to determine whether her mother's reaction was a genuine distressed reaction or a manipulative attempt to control her daughter through inducing her guilt. This would involve learning something about the history of their relationship and how encouraging or discouraging Maggie's mother has been of her daughter's independence when this conflicts with her own desires.

'*B*'

Here, the REBT therapist can help Maggie change her rigid attitude and self-devaluation attitude towards 'A' to a flexible attitude and an unconditional self-acceptance attitude.

'*C*'

Here the therapist needs to focus on all three 'C's: emotional, behavioural and thinking.

1. *Emotional 'C'*. The therapist can only help Maggie change her guilt by involving other elements of the Situational ABC framework. One cannot change a feeling just by focusing on a feeling. Leaving aside her thinking consequences at 'C' which we don't know anything about, the therapist can help Maggie change her guilt:

- by helping her to change her inference at 'A'
- by helping her not to think about her 'A' or to distract herself from it
- by helping her to change her rigid/extreme attitudes to flexible/non-extreme attitudes at 'B'
- by helping her to change her behavioural 'C'. Here, Maggie could tell her mother that she is not prepared to change her arrangements and in reality to go out with her friends and not backtrack on her plans

1. *Behavioural 'C'*. As noted above, Maggie could stick with her pre-arranged plans and not backtrack on them.

2. *Thinking 'C'*. We do not know what Maggie's thinking consequences of her rigid and extreme attitude were, so I am not able to suggest changes at this level.

REBT's preferred strategy

While I have shown the possible changes that the therapist can help Maggie make, REBT's preferred position would be to suggest that the therapist encourage Maggie to assume temporarily that her 'A' was true – that she did hurt her mother's feelings – and to focus on changing her rigid/extreme attitudes to flexible/non-extreme attitudes. To reinforce this change, Maggie can be encouraged to act in ways that are consistent with her developing flexible/non-extreme attitudes and inconsistent with her established rigid/extreme attitudes.

In Table 23.4, I present a summary of the successful outcome of REBT's preferred strategy with Maggie.

Table 23.4 Situational ABC model of the successful outcome of REBT's preferred strategy

Situation =	Maggie's mother told her that she was being selfish and was neglecting her*
'A' (Adversity) =	I have hurt my mother's feelings
'B': Basic flexible/non-extreme attitude =	I would prefer not to hurt my mother's feelings but I am not immune from doing so, and nor do I have to be. I am not a bad person for hurting her feelings; rather, I am a fallible human being who did something that resulted in my mother's upset
'C' = Consequences	
Emotional = Remorse	
Behavioural = Not taking her mother to the pictures. Instead, going with her friends as she had previously arranged	
Thinking = Unknown	

* I have assumed here that this is what Maggie's mother actually said to her

Does Being Raped Cause Disturbed Emotions?

As we have seen, REBT states that events don't cause emotions. This troubles some people who argue that very negative events like being raped or losing a loved one do cause disturbed emotions. These people are shocked when the 'ABC' model is applied to such adversities. That is why I gave this chapter the subtitle: 'The Shocking "ABC"s of REBT'.

This issue impinges directly on the distinction that REBT makes between healthy and unhealthy negative emotions. Let me take the example of rape. There is no doubt that being raped is a tragic event for both women and men. As such, it is healthy for the person who has been raped to experience a lot of distress. However, REBT conceptualises this distress as healthy even though it is intense. Other approaches to therapy have as their goal the reduction of the intensity of negative emotions. They take this position because they do not keenly differentiate between healthy negative emotions (distress) and unhealthy negative emotions (disturbance).

Now, REBT keenly distinguishes between healthy distress and unhealthy disturbance. Healthy distress stems from flexible/non-extreme attitudes towards an adversity, whilst disturbance stems from rigid/extreme attitudes towards the same adversity. I now have to introduce you to one of the complexities of REBT theory and as I do you will see that REBT is not always as simple as 'ABC'!

REBT theory holds that the intensity of healthy distress increases in proportion to the negativity of the adversity and the strength of the person's flexible/non-extreme attitudes. Now, when a person has been raped, their intense distress stems from their strongly held flexible/non-extreme attitudes towards this very negative event. As virtually everyone who has been raped will have strongly held flexible/non-extreme attitudes towards this event, we could almost say that being raped 'causes' intense healthy distress.

Introducing rigid/extreme attitudes: REBT theory argues that a person, being human, easily transmutes their flexible/non-extreme attitudes into rigid/extreme attitudes especially when the adversities encountered are highly aversive. However, and this is a crucial and controversial point, the specific principle of emotional responsibility states that you are largely responsible for your emotional disturbance because the person is responsible for transmuting their flexible/non-extreme attitudes into rigid/extreme attitudes. That person (and others) retains this responsibility even when they encounter tragic adversities such as rape. So REBT theory holds that when a person has been raped, they are responsible for transmuting their strongly held flexible/non-extreme attitudes into rigid/extreme attitudes, even though it is very understandable that they should do this.

Actually, if we look at the typical rigid and extreme attitudes that people hold towards being raped, we will see that these attitudes are not an integral part of the rape experience, but reflect what people bring to the experience. Examples of rigid/extreme attitudes are:

- I absolutely should have stopped this from happening
- This has completely ruined my life
- Being raped means that I am a worthless person

Whilst it is understandable that people who have been raped should think this way, this does not detract from the fact that they are responsible for bringing these rigid and extreme attitudes to the experience. It is for this reason that REBT theory holds that very negative 'A's do not 'cause' emotional disturbance. This is actually an optimistic position. If highly aversive events did cause emotional disturbance then a person would have a much harder time overcoming their disturbed feelings than they do now when we make the assumption that these feelings stem largely from their rigid and extreme attitudes.

One more point. Some REBT therapists distinguish between disturbed emotions that are experienced when a very negative event occurs and disturbed feelings that persist well after the event has happened. These therapists would argue that being raped does 'cause' disturbed feelings when the event occurs and for a short period after it has happened, but if the person's disturbed feelings persist well after the event then the person who has been raped is responsible for the perpetuation of their disturbances via the creation and perpetuation of their rigid and extreme attitudes. These therapists argue that time-limited rigid and extreme thinking in response to highly aversive adversities is not an unhealthy reaction, but the perpetuation of this thinking is unhealthy. Thus, for these REBT therapists an adversity like rape does 'cause' emotional disturbance in the short term, but not in the long term.

*

In the following chapter, I will consider the role that attitudes play in creating our sense of 'reality'.

24

How Our Attitudes Help
to Create Our 'Reality'

Why is it that some people view the world in a positive light while others view the world through dark-coloured spectacles? Of course personality and temperament play a part here, but since both of these factors are relatively unchangeable, they fall outside the range of this book. Here I am interested in exploring factors that we can change rather than those we can't. So setting aside factors such as personality and temperament, why do some of us see the world (in terms of a glass) as half full and others see the world as half empty? Why do we live in very different, subjectively based worlds?

While the answer to this question is incredibly complex, I am going to simplify matters by focusing on and discussing a small number of factors. However, these factors do have a powerful influence on the ways in which we see the world and, as I have said before, these factors are modifiable, particularly when they have such negative effects on our view of the world.

Attitudes Help to Determine Our 'Reality'

One of the major determinants of the ways in which we see the world is our attitudes. In REBT, we can hold three sets of attitudes: attitudes of indifference, rigid attitudes and flexible attitudes. I will consider each type in turn and consider the impact that each has on our 'reality'. I have put the word 'reality' in quotation marks here to emphasise that our reality is largely subjectively experienced and that your 'reality' is not the same as my 'reality'.

Attitudes of indifference

If you hold an attitude of indifference, you literally do not care about something. For example, Monica holds an attitude of indifference towards whether England qualifies for the next World Cup. She does not care whether England qualifies or not. As a result, Monica does not think about whether England gets into the

World Cup, she does not discuss the issue with anyone and she does not read articles about it. As the example of Monica shows, when you hold an attitude of indifference about something you do not pay attention to it. It is as if it does not exist for you.

Rigid attitudes

When you hold a rigid attitude towards something that is important to you, it not only matters to you, you think that it is absolutely crucial to you. For example, Nell holds the attitude that she must be loved by her boyfriend. His love is important to her, but it is more than this, it is all-important to her. Thus, when she has it she is immediately delirious about it. As time goes on delirium gives way to contentment which in turn fades as Nell goes about her business.

However, if Nell were to begin to think that her boyfriend does not love her and she holds a rigid attitude towards this, then a number of things are likely to happen.

First, Nell's rigid attitude towards being loved by her boyfriend leads her to think a lot about not being loved if this possibility crosses her mind. And once she thinks about her boyfriend not loving her, her rigid attitude means that she will chew it over in her mind and this keeps the issue of not being loved firmly in her head. For example, she may think about recent episodes where her boyfriend acted in ways that may indicate to her that he does not love her.

Second, Nell may well discuss this issue with her friends. This will keep the issue firmly in her mind because they will, for example, give her advice on what to do and phone her up to see how she is feeling about the issue, both of which will keep the issue in her mind.

Third, she may read books on the theme of loss of love and how to rekindle one's relationship. This again will keep the issue of not being loved and what to do about it firmly in her mind.

Flexible attitudes

When you hold a flexible attitude towards something that is important to you, then you indicate that it matters to you, but it is not absolutely crucial to you. For example, imagine this time that Nell holds the attitude that she wants to be loved by her boyfriend, but that his love is not crucial to her. Thus, when she has it she is happy, but not delirious and when she does not have it she is concerned, but not devastated by it.

If Nell were to begin to think that her boyfriend does not love her and this time she holds a flexible attitude towards this, then a number of different things are likely to happen than if her attitude were rigid. First, Nell's flexible attitude towards being loved by her boyfriend leads her to be realistic about not being loved if this possibility crosses her mind. She will consider the evidence at hand and evaluate this evidence carefully before coming to a sensible conclusion about it. If she concludes that her boyfriend loves her then she will forget about her concerns and go about her business. However, if she concludes that he doesn't love her, she will voice her concerns to him, give her evidence, ask for a response from him and then discuss whatever comes up.

Second, Nell may well discuss this issue with her friends, but only after thinking about the issue herself and discussing it, if necessary, with her boyfriend. This will only keep the issue in her mind if there is clear evidence that her boyfriend does not love her.

Third, Nell will tend not to read books on the theme of loss of love and how to rekindle one's relationship unless she has clear evidence that these books are relevant to the actual reality of her situation and if she thinks that such books would be helpful to her. If she does not have such evidence then she would not read such books and thus, the issue of not being loved and what to do about it will not be in her mind.

Creating Realities: The Three Attitudes Compared with Reference to Karen Horney's Three Stances

In her book entitled *Self-Analysis*, Karen Horney (1942), the famous American psychoanalyst, argued that it is possible to take three stances towards people and other factors in life. You can move towards them, move away from them or move against them. Let's compare the three attitude that I have introduced and discussed using Horney's stance model particularly as it is relevant to our current focus, the impact of attitude on the creation of 'reality'.

If you hold an attitude of indifference, you are not motivated to take any of the three stances identified by Horney. Since you do not care about a person or object towards which you hold an attitude of indifference then you will neither move towards them, move away from them nor move against them. The consequence of not taking any stance is that you will not think about the object at all and thus, it doesn't register on your 'reality' radar.

As such, attitudes of indifference play no role in the creation of your version of 'reality' and thus merit no further discussion. On the other hand, if you hold a rigid attitude towards something then you may be motivated to move towards the object of your attitude, away from it or against it depending on the circumstances. However this is also true of holding a flexible attitude towards the same object. The difference is in the extent of the stance taken. It will come as no surprise to you to learn that a rigid attitude leads to the adoption of a rigid stance. Whereas a flexible attitude leads to the adoption of a flexible stance. When considering the three stances I will take each one separately and show how the creation of 'reality' is affected by the adoption of a rigid attitude, on the one hand, and a flexible attitude, on the other.

Rigid attitude: Rigid 'moving towards' stance

Imagine that you hold the attitude that you must have a person in your life and you don't have such a person. In this case you will direct all your energies to finding such a person (i.e. a rigid adoption of the moving towards stance) to the exclusion of other things that you may be interested in. In adopting this stance, you will also find that you will be thinking about meeting a person all the time. The thought will preoccupy you when you are with people since you will be scanning your interpersonal environment in the hope of finding a possible candidate for the object of your need. Also, the thought will preoccupy you when you aren't with people, for you will be dwelling on how you can meet such a person. Your rigid attitude and associated rigid stance of moving towards people means that you create a 'reality' where only one thing is important to you – finding a partner. You will look at the world through 'finding-a-partner' coloured glasses.

Flexible attitude: Flexible 'moving towards' stance

Imagine instead that you hold the attitude that you would like to have a person in your life, but this is not necessary to you and imagine further that you don't have such a person. In this case you will direct some, but not all your energies to finding such a person (i.e. a flexible adoption of the moving towards stance), but certainly not to the exclusion of other things that you may be interested in. Thus, you will try to find a person by allocating time to this pursuit and will be open to the possibility of finding such a person as you go about your daily business. However, you will also allocate time to pursue other interests. In adopting this flexible stance, you will also find that you will be thinking about meeting a person some of the time, but certainly not all the time and your thinking on this issue will be relevant to the situation that you are in. In other words, your thinking will not be dominated by thoughts of meeting someone as it would be if you held a rigid attitude and adopted a rigid stance to the issue, nor would your thoughts about meeting someone overly intrude on your thinking about other matters.

Thinking about finding someone when you are flexible in your attitude and stance on this issue will occupy you to some degree when you are with people, but will not preoccupy you. You may well scan your interpersonal environment in the hope of finding a possible candidate for the object of your desire when it is appropriate to do so (e.g. when you are at a party), but not when it is not appropriate (e.g. when you are at an important business meeting). When you aren't with people, the thought of meeting someone may well fleetingly occur to you, but again it will not preoccupy you and you certainly will not be dwelling on how you can meet such a person. Your flexible attitude and associated flexible stance of moving towards people means that you create a 'reality' where meeting a person is important, but not all-important, to you. You will definitely not look at the world through 'finding-a-partner' coloured glasses, although this issue will influence your vision at the appropriate time.

Rigid attitude: Rigid 'moving away' stance

Imagine that you hold the attitude that you must not see a spider. This attitude will lead you to direct all your energy to avoiding the possibility of seeing a spider (i.e. a rigid adoption of the moving away stance). In adopting this stance, you will also find that you will be thinking about spiders much of the time.

The thought of seeing a spider will preoccupy you when you cannot escape situations where you think you may see a spider and in these situations you will be scanning your environment in dread of seeing one. Also, the thought of seeing a spider will tend to preoccupy you when you are in situations where you might see a spider, for you will be dwelling on how you can avoid seeing one. Your rigid attitude will also lead you to think about avoiding future situations that it is important for you to be in because you might see a spider in these situations. Your rigid attitude and associated rigid stance of moving away from spiders means that you create a 'reality' where one issue dominates – avoiding seeing spiders. You will look at the world through 'spider' coloured glasses.

Flexible attitude: Flexible 'moving away' stance

Imagine instead that you hold the attitude that you prefer not to see a spider, but that it is not necessary that you avoid seeing one. This attitude will lead you to direct some of your energy to avoiding the possibility of seeing a spider, but certainly not all of your energy (i.e. a flexible adoption of the moving away stance). In adopting this stance, you will also find that you will be thinking about spiders some, but not all of the time.

The thought of seeing a spider will to some degree occupy you, but not preoccupy you when you cannot escape situations where you think you may see a spider and in these situations you will be watchful, but not scanning your environment in dread of seeing one. Also, while the thought of seeing a spider will tend to be somewhat on your mind, it will again not preoccupy you when you are in situations where you might see a spider. Your flexible attitude will not lead you to think about avoiding future situations that it is important for you to be in, even though you might see a spider in these situations. Your flexible attitude and associated flexible stance of moving away from spiders means that you won't create a 'reality' where only one thing is important to you – avoiding seeing spiders. Rather, you will create a 'reality' where a number of things are important to you to approach and avoid including spiders. You will not look at the world through 'spider' coloured glasses, although your flexible attitude towards not seeing spiders will influence your vision at the appropriate time.

Rigid attitude: Rigid 'moving against' stance

Imagine that you hold the attitude that others must show you respect and you encounter situations where they do not act respectfully towards you. In such cases, you will make yourself unhealthily angry and act aggressively towards them. You will not be prepared to let any instance of disrespect go (i.e. a rigid adoption of the moving against stance). In adopting this stance, you will also find that you will be thinking about how others treat you much of the time along the dimension of 'respect–disrespect'. The thought of being disrespected will preoccupy you when you are with people since you will be scanning your interpersonal environment in case disrespect is shown to you. Also the thought of being disrespected will be very much on your mind when you aren't with people, for you will be dwelling on how they might treat you when you are next in their company. Your rigid attitude and associated rigid stance of moving against people means that you create a 'reality' where one thing is important to you – being respected. You will look at the world through 'respect–disrespect' coloured glasses'.

Flexible attitude: Flexible 'moving against' stance

Imagine instead that you hold the attitude that you want others to show you respect, but it isn't absolutely necessary that they do so. Imagine further that you encounter situations where others do not act respectfully towards you. In such cases, you will make yourself healthily angry and act assertively, but not aggressively, towards these people. You will stand up for yourself, but will choose when to do so. Thus, you may be prepared to let certain instances of disrespect go, particularly when they are minor (i.e. a flexible adoption of the moving against stance). In adopting this stance, you will tend to think some of the time about how others treat you along the dimension of respect–disrespect, but you certainly will not do so all the time. The thought of being disrespected will be on your mind when relevant, but will not preoccupy you when you are with people since you will be mindful of the way you may be treated, but you will not scan your interpersonal environment obsessively in case disrespect is shown to you. Also, when you are not with people, you may think of how others treat you from time to time, but you will not be preoccupied with the thought of being disrespected. Your flexible attitude and associated flexible stance of moving against people means that you create a 'reality' where being respected is important to you. But it is not the be-all and end-all. You will not look at the world through 'respect–disrespect' coloured glasses, although your flexible attitude towards being respected will influence your vision at the appropriate time.

Rigid and Extreme Attitudes Create Very Distorted Thinking Consequences Which Are Experienced and Accepted as 'Real'

If we take a closer look at 'C' in the 'ABC' framework, we will find that REBT theorists have traditionally argued that there are two main consequences of holding rigid and extreme attitudes: emotional ('You feel the way you think') and behavioural ('You act the way you think'). However, increasingly REBT theorists have come to understand that there are also cognitive consequences of attitudes. At first sight, this is more problematic for people to understand because the maxim, 'You think the way you think' is either a truism or hides a more complex psychological situation. In REBT theory the latter is the case. So, let me try to unravel and clarify this complexity. In doing so I need to distinguish two different types of cognition: attitudes and inferences.

Different types of cognitions: Attitudes and inferences

REBT theory differentiates between attitudes and inferences. Attitudes are evaluative stances that a person takes towards life events, while inferences are interpretations that a person makes about life events. Since much of what we react to are inferences, it can be said that our attitudes are mainly held towards our inferences. For this reason, inferences are put under 'A' in the 'ABC' framework and (basic) attitudes under 'B'.

Flexible/non-extreme versus rigid/extreme attitudes

If you recall, REBT theory differentiates between flexible/non-extreme and rigid/extreme attitudes. Flexible and non-extreme attitudes are consistent with reality. Rigid/extreme attitudes, on the other hand, are inconsistent with reality, illogical, and have largely unconstructive results.

According to the founder of REBT, Albert Ellis (1913–2007), rigid attitudes are at the core of disturbed reactions to adversities and these rigid attitudes spawn a set of extreme attitudes, outlined in Figure 24.1.

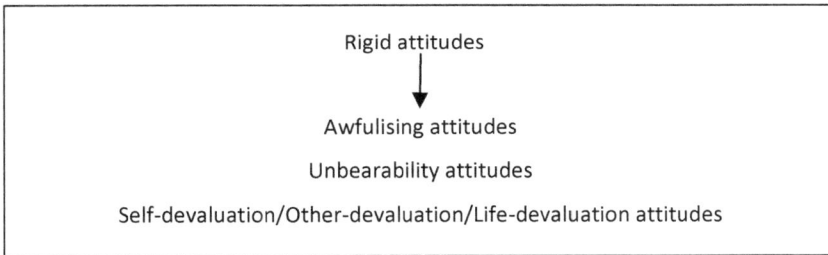

Rigid attitudes

↓

Awfulising attitudes

Unbearability attitudes

Self-devaluation/Other-devaluation/Life-devaluation attitudes

Figure 24.1 Rigid attitudes lead to extreme attitudes

Also, according to Albert Ellis, flexible attitudes are at the core of healthy reactions to adversities and these flexible attitudes spawn a set of non-extreme attitudes. This is outlined in Figure 24.2.

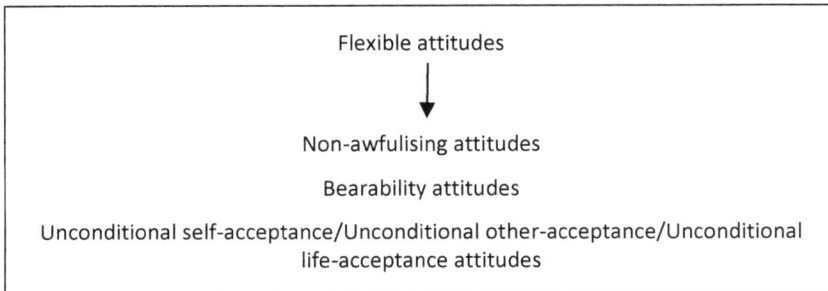

Flexible attitudes

↓

Non-awfulising attitudes

Bearability attitudes

Unconditional self-acceptance/Unconditional other-acceptance/Unconditional life-acceptance attitudes

Figure 24.2 Flexible attitudes lead to non-extreme attitudes

Realistic versus distorted inferences

Inferences are interpretations about life events. As such they are hunches that can be realistic or distorted. Inferences need examining against the available data and the best one can do is to accept them as accurate or inaccurate on probabilistic grounds.

Rigid/extreme attitudes lead to thinking consequences that are highly distorted and skewed

REBT theory argues that when a person holds a set of rigid and extreme attitudes towards an adversity at 'A' then that person will experience three sets of unhealthy responses:

(a) unhealthy negative emotions
(b) dysfunctional behaviours and/or action tendencies, and
(c) highly distorted and skewed thoughts

It is the last of these that I am concerned with in this chapter. The idea that I want to explore here is that when you hold a rigid and extreme attitude then you tend to subsequently think in ways that are highly distorted and skewed. Let me explain how this works.

Shortly, I am going to ask you to imagine that you hold the following rigid attitude: 'Others must find me amusing when I go to a dinner party and it's awful when they do not.' When I do so, I will discuss the thinking consequences of holding this attitude. However, before that, I want to discuss the concept of 'others finding you amusing at the dinner party' from a realistic perspective. Doing so will help you to understand the effect of your rigid and extreme attitude on the way you subsequently think about matters to do with the dinner party and those attending it.

In considering the concept of 'others finding you amusing at the dinner party', the following issues need to be taken into account:

1. The extent to which others at the dinner party find you amusing can be placed on a continuum from 'not at all amusing' to 'extremely amusing'.

2.   The extent to which others at the dinner party find you amusing depends on the interaction between your sense of humour and the sense of humour of the other people present at the time. Some may share your sense of humour while others may not.

3.   Even if all those present share your sense of humour, you may not be in the mood to be humorous or some (or all) of the others might not be in a humorous mood.

As you can see from the above, in reality, there are a number of reasons why others at the dinner party may not find you amusing. Now, when you hold the following rigid/extreme attitude: 'Others must find me amusing when I go to a dinner party and it's awful when they do not', you will see that it has two components.

(a) A rigid component: 'Others must find me amusing when I go to a dinner party …'

(b) An extreme component: '… and it's awful when they do not'

Let me take each component and show how it affects the way in which you are likely to think when this attitude has been activated:

The rigid component

The major effect of the rigid component of your attitude is to polarise matters. Rigidity tends to edit out complexity and leads to black-and-white thinking. Thus, if you cannot convince yourself that others do (did or will) find you amusing, then you will tend to think that they don't (didn't or won't) find you amusing at best and find (found or will find you) decidedly unfunny at worst.

Also, if you do have evidence that the people at the party did not find you amusing, then when you think about future dinner parties you will tend to think that nobody will ever find you amusing again at dinner parties.

The awfulising component

The major effect of the awfulising component of your attitude is to create inferences which are consistent with the concept of 'awful'. These inferences will tend to be highly negative in content. In this context, since you think that it would be awful if others do not find you amusing, you will tend to create inferences like: 'They will tell everybody how boring I am' and 'I will become a social pariah'.

Cognitive and emotional reasoning

While hopefully I have demonstrated the impact of holding rigid/extreme attitudes on the way you subsequently think, in order for you to fully understand how you create 'reality' in this respect, I need to explain the role of two forms of reasoning: cognitive and emotional reasoning.

Cognitive reasoning

The term 'cognitive reasoning' is used to describe the process whereby you conclude that because you have a thought then it reflects 'reality'. For example, let's suppose that you have the following thought: 'My teacher will criticise my essay.' As we have seen, this statement is properly treated as an inference, meaning that it is a hunch about 'reality' which may be accurate or inaccurate and as such it needs to be checked against the available evidence. The best we can do is to say that such a hunch is probably true or probably false since it is rare for inferences to be shown to be definitely true or definitely false. However, when you are operating according to the principle of cognitive reasoning, you conclude that because you have had the thought: 'My teacher will criticise my essay' then this will definitely happen. Why? Because the thought reflects 'reality'.

The principle of cognitive reasoning explains why some people are so frightened of their thoughts. Thus, if you adhere to the principle of cognitive reasoning you will find the prospect of holding the thought 'My child will die soon' terrifying given the awfulising attitude you are likely to hold towards such an event. However, if you do not adhere to the principle of cognitive reasoning then you will more likely conclude that this thought is just a random thought with no predictive powers. Thus, even though you are likely to hold the same awfulising attitude towards such an event as when you operate according to the principle of cognitive reasoning, you will not become anxious because you don't think that the thought reflects 'reality'.

Emotional reasoning

The principle of emotional reasoning is similar to that of cognitive reasoning but, as the name makes clear, it focuses more on your emotions. When you adhere to this principle you think that your emotions reflect 'reality'. Thus, if you are anxious then this proves that the threat you are anxious about is real. For example, if you are anxious about seeing spiders and you find yourself in a room in which you are anxious, then adhering to the principle of emotional reasoning you conclude that your feelings of anxiety prove that spiders are present in the room. Of course, it proves nothing of the sort. What is more likely in this situation is that your anxiety proves that you have an anxiety of spiders and that you are operating according to the principle of emotional reasoning! Your anxiety indicates that you are making yourself anxious about a threat and this threat is an inference about the presence of spiders and, as such, like other inferences it needs to be checked against the available evidence and accordingly accepted as probably true or rejected as probably false.

What happens when you adhere to both cognitive and emotional reasoning

As we have seen, when you use cognitive reasoning you operate on the idea that your thinking indicates reality and when you use emotional reasoning you operate on the idea that your emotions indicate reality. When you adhere to both principles together you operate on the idea that since you have strong feelings and since your associated thoughts are so convincing then this must mean that your feelings and thoughts reflect reality.

If we return, for the moment, to what I was saying about the impact of rigid/extreme attitudes on how you subsequently think and add to this the conjoint application of cognitive and emotional reasoning, then you will appreciate my point that rigid/extreme attitudes influence our sense of 'reality'. Here is an example.

Rigid/extreme attitudes ➝ thinking consequences + emotional reasoning and cognitive reasoning = 'reality'

An example:
> *Peter had applied for job and was called for interview. He was anxious at 'C' about the possibility of not being able to answer some of the questions he might be asked. Peter felt anxious about this because he held the following rigid/extreme attitude: 'I must be able to answer all the questions asked of me and it would be terrible if I can't.'*

Peter's rigid/extreme attitude not only led him to feel anxious as he waited for his interview with some of the other candidates, but also led him to think the following:

- I won't be able answer any of the questions
- All the other candidates will do much better than me
- There is not much point in me staying for the interview

Peter also engaged in both cognitive and emotional reasoning with the consequence that he viewed the thoughts that I have just listed as reflecting 'reality' rather than what they were: inferences that were heavily influenced by his rigid/extreme attitudes towards the possibility of not being able to answer all questions put to him.

Because Peter regarded his thoughts as reflecting reality he decided to leave there and then and was long gone when his name was called for interview.

Cognitive and emotional reasoning: A quick test

As I have described it, when you adhere to both principles of cognitive and emotional reasoning, you are very likely to hold that because you have a strong feeling and because your thoughts seem convincing to you then what you feel and think is real is, indeed, real. However, a moment's reflection will indicate that this is not necessarily the case.

Imagine that you encounter someone who has a very strong feeling and convincing (to them!) thought that the capital of France is Marseille. Now does Marseille become the capital of France just because this individual strongly believes and feels that it is? Of course it doesn't. A strong feeling and convincing thoughts, especially where the feeling is unhealthy and negative (see below) and the thoughts are highly distorted and negatively skewed, are evidence that the person is holding a rigid/extreme attitude at 'B' towards an adversity at 'A' which is giving rise to the emotional and thinking consequences at 'C'.

A List of Thinking Consequences of Rigid and Extreme Attitudes: Cognitive Distortions

In a book that I co-authored with Albert Ellis (Ellis & Dryden, 1997), we showed how rigid and extreme attitudes lead to a variety of highly distorted inferences. In the following, I list each inferential distortion, exemplify it and show how it stems from the person's rigid/extreme attitude. Remember that if the person who has such thoughts adheres to the principles of cognitive and emotional reasoning as discussed above then the person will regard these thoughts as reflecting 'reality'. In what follows I will list the rigid and extreme attitude and italicise the cognitive distortion.

Black-and-white thinking

'I must be in control of my thoughts and *if I begin to lose control of them it will mean that I will completely lose control of them.*'

Jumping to conclusions

'When people see me fail, as they must not do, it's awful *and they will view me as a failure.*'

Fortune-telling

'I must know that I will be accepted into drama school and it's terrible not to know. *If I don't know then I will be rejected.*'

Focusing on the negative

'Because I can't bear things going wrong as they must not do, *I can't see any good happening in my life.*'

Disqualifying the positive

'I must give an excellent presentation and I am worthless when I don't. *When I think I haven't done well and someone compliments me, they do not mean it and are only saying it to be kind.*'

Always and never thinking

'My living conditions must be better than they are and I can't bear them as they are. *They will always be bad and I will never improve them.*'

Minimisation

'I must play well all the time and I am worthless when I don't. *Thus, when I do occasionally play well, it's a fluke.*'

Labelling and over-generalisation

'I must not act selfishly and *when I do I am selfish.*'

Personalising

'When I busk, people who pass by have to take me seriously and it's terrible when they don't. *If some laugh when they pass by, they are laughing at me.*'

Cognitive Consequences of Rigid/Extreme and Flexible/Non-Extreme Attitudes that Underpin Unhealthy and Healthy Negative Emotions

Another way of considering how our attitudes create our 'reality' is to look at the cognitive consequences of attitudes (rigid/extreme and flexble/non-extreme) that underpin negative emotions. REBT theory argues that when you hold an attitude towards an adversity at 'A' then you will experience a negative emotion at 'C'. When your attitude is rigid/extreme at 'B' then that negative emotion will tend to be unhealthy and when your attitude is rational at 'B' then that negative emotion will tend to be healthy. My main point in this chapter is that the cognitive consequences of rigid/extreme attitudes will tend to be highly distorted and skewed in a negative direction whereas the cognitive consequences of flexible/non-extreme attitudes will be more balanced.

In what follows, I will show how attitudes towards emotion-related inferences at 'A' not only determine whether the negative emotion experienced is healthy or unhealthy, but also determine how these attitudes influence subsequent emotion-related inferences at 'C'. If these subsequent inferences are seen to reflect 'reality', you can see the profound effect that attitudes can have on emotion-related 'reality'.

Anxiety versus concern

You experience anxiety or concern when you think that you are facing some kind of threat at 'A'. When you hold a rigid/extreme attitude towards that threat then you will experience anxiety and your subsequent thinking will reflect your tendency to:

- Overestimate the possibility of the threat occurring
- Underestimate your ability to cope with the threat
- Create an even more negative threat in your mind when you reflect on the threat
- Have an increased number of task-irrelevant thoughts

By contrast when you hold a flexible/non-extreme attitude towards this same threat then you will experience concern rather than anxiety and your subsequent thinking will reflect your tendency to:

- Be realistic about the threat occurring
- View the threat realistically
- Make a realistic appraisal of your ability to cope with the threat
- Refrain from creating an even more negative threat in your mind when you reflect on the threat
- Have more task-relevant thoughts than in anxiety

Depression versus sadness

You experience depression or sadness when you infer that you have experienced a loss from your personal domain at 'A', have failed at something important to you, or you or others are facing an unfair plight. When you hold a rigid/extreme attitude towards that loss, failure or plight then you will experience depression and your subsequent thinking will reflect your tendency to:

- See only negative aspects of the loss, failure or plight
- Think of other losses, failures or plights that you have experienced
- Think that you are not able to help yourself (helplessness)
- Only see pain and blackness in the future (hopelessness)

By contrast when you hold a flexible/non-extreme attitude about this same loss, failure or plight then you will experience sadness rather than depression and your subsequent thinking will reflect your tendency to:

- Be able to recognise both negative and positive aspects of the loss, failure or plight
- Acknowledge gains that you have experienced as well as losses; successes you have had in life as well as failures; and good fortune as well as unfair plight
- Be able to help yourself
- Be able to look to the future with hope

Unhealthy anger versus healthy anger

You experience unhealthy anger or healthy anger under the following conditions: (a) when you think that others have transgressed an important personal rule or that you have broken one of your own rules; (b) when your progress towards a goal has been obstructed; (c) when you have been frustrated in some way; or (d) somebody has posed a threat to your self-esteem.

When you hold a rigid/extreme attitude towards one or more of these conditions then you will experience unhealthy anger and your subsequent thinking will reflect your tendency to:

- Overestimate the extent to which the other person has acted in a deliberate manner towards you
- See malicious intent in the motives of others when such intent is not clear
- See yourself as definitely in the right and the other(s) as definitely in the wrong
- Be unable to see the other person's point of view
- Plan to exact revenge

By contrast when you hold a flexible/ non-extreme attitude towards rule transgression, goal obstruction, frustration and threat to self-esteem then you will experience healthy anger rather than unhealthy anger and your subsequent thinking will reflect your tendency to:

- Be realistic in your appraisal of the extent to which the other person acted deliberately
- Not see malicious intent in the motives of others unless this is clear
- See the possibility that you may be wrong and that the other person may be right
- Be able to see the other's point of view
- Not plan to exact revenge

Guilt versus remorse

You experience guilt or remorse when you think that you have broken a moral code (sin of commission), failed to live up to a moral code (sin of omission) or have hurt someone. If you hold a rigid/extreme attitude towards these violations then you will experience guilt and your subsequent thinking will reflect your tendency to:

- Conclude, on reflection, that you have definitely violated your code when there is some uncertainty about this

- Assume more personal responsibility than the situation warrants
- Assign far less responsibility than is warranted to others who are involved
- Not take into account mitigating factors for your behaviour
- Not place your behaviour into an overall context
- Anticipate that you will receive retribution

By contrast when you hold a flexible/non-extreme attitude towards these same violations then you will experience remorse and your subsequent thinking will reflect your tendency to:

- Consider your behaviour in context and with understanding in deciding whether you have violated your code when there is some uncertainty about this
- Assume an appropriate level of personal responsibility
- Assign an appropriate level of responsibility to others involved
- Take into account mitigating factors for your behaviour
- Put your behaviour into an overall context
- Not anticipate that you will receive retribution

Shame versus disappointment

You experience shame or disappointment when you think that (a) you have fallen very short of your ideal; (b) others notice this and think negatively about you; (c) something 'shameful' has been revealed about you or about a group with whom you identify by yourself or by others. When you hold a rigid/extreme attitude towards these inferences then you will experience shame and your subsequent thinking will reflect your tendency to:

- Overestimate the 'shamefulness' of the information revealed
- Overestimate the likelihood that the judging group will notice or be interested in the information revealed
- Overestimate the degree of disapproval you or your reference group will receive

- Overestimate the length of time any disapproval will last

By contrast when you hold a flexible/ non-extreme attitude towards these same inferences then you will experience disappointment rather than shame and your subsequent thinking will reflect your tendency to:

- See information revealed in a compassionate self-accepting context
- Be realistic about the likelihood that the judging group will notice or be interested in the information revealed
- Be realistic about the degree of disapproval you or your reference group will receive
- Be realistic about the length of time any disapproval will last

Hurt versus sorrow

You experience hurt or sorrow when you think that another person has treated you badly and you consider that you don't deserve such treatment. When you hold a rigid/extreme attitude towards this undeserved bad treatment then you will experience hurt and your subsequent thinking will reflect your tendency to:

- Exaggerate the unfairness of the other person's behaviour when you come to think about it again having made yourself feel hurt
- Perceive the other person as showing lack of care or being indifferent
- See yourself as being alone, uncared for or misunderstood
- Think of other past 'hurts'
- Expect the other person to make the first move repairing the relationship

By contrast when you hold a flexible/non-extreme attitude towards the treatment that you think you don't deserve then you will experience sorrow rather than hurt and your subsequent thinking will reflect your tendency to:

- Be realistic about the degree of unfairness in the other person's behaviour
- Perceive the other person as acting badly rather than being uncaring or indifferent
- Not see yourself as being uncared for or misunderstood, but as the recipient of the other person's bad behaviour
- Think of past 'hurts' less frequently than when feeling hurt about the current incident
- Not think that the other person has to make the first move

Unhealthy jealousy versus healthy jealousy

You experience unhealthy jealousy or healthy jealousy when you think that you are facing some kind of threat to your relationship with a significant person (e.g. your partner) from another person. When you hold a rigid/extreme attitude towards that threat then you will experience unhealthy jealousy and your subsequent thinking will reflect your tendency to:

- See threats to your relationship when none really exists
- Think that the loss of your relationship is imminent
- Misconstrue your partner's ordinary conversations as having romantic or sexual connotations
- Construct visual images and other scenarios of your partner's infidelity
- Believe that if your partner admits to finding another person attractive then he (in this case) finds this person more attractive than you and will leave you for the other

By contrast when you hold a flexible/non-extreme attitude towards this same threat then you will experience healthy jealousy and your subsequent thinking will reflect your tendency to:

- Not see threats to your relationship when none exists
- Not misconstrue ordinary conversations between your partner and other women (in this case)

- Not construct visual images and other scenarios of your partner's infidelity
- Accept that your partner will find others attractive without seeing this as a threat to your relationship

Unhealthy envy versus healthy envy

You experience unhealthy envy or healthy envy when you think another person possesses and enjoys something that you desire but do not have. When you hold a rigid/extreme attitude towards this perceived inequality you will experience unhealthy envy and your subsequent thinking will reflect your tendency to:

- Denigrate the value of the desired possession and/or the person who possesses it
- Convince yourself that you are happy with your possessions, although you are not
- Think about how to acquire the desired possession regardless of its usefulness
- Think about how to deprive the other person of the desired possession
- Think about how to spoil or destroy the other's desired possession

By contrast when you hold a flexible/non-extreme attitude towards this same perceived inequality then you will experience concern and your subsequent thinking will reflect your tendency to:

- Honestly admit to yourself that you do actually want what the other person has if this is the case or that you don't actually want it if this is the case
- Not try to convince yourself that you are happy with your possessions when you are not
- Think about how to obtain the desired possession because you desire it for healthy reasons
- Allow the other person to have and enjoy the desired possession without denigrating the possession or the person

As you will see from the above, holding rigid and extreme attitudes lead you to make inferences about salient aspects of the situation that you are in that are highly distorted in nature and are skewed to the negative. On the other hand when you hold flexible and non-extreme attitudes towards the same situation your subsequent inferences are more realistic and balanced in nature.

The Role of Uncertainty and Core Rigid and Extreme Attitudes in the Creation of 'Reality'

So far in this chapter I have explained the role that attitudes play in how people construct 'reality'. In particular, I have considered at some length how holding rigid and extreme attitudes leads a person to think in highly distorted and negatively skewed ways which, when the person operates according to the principles of cognitive and emotional reasoning, they think is reality.

Using REBT's famous 'ABC' framework (see Chapter 23), we may say that when a person holds a specific rigid/extreme attitude at 'B' towards an adversity at 'A' they construct a set of thinking consequences at 'C'. However, there is another way in which holding rigid/extreme attitudes helps to shape our creation of 'reality' this time at 'A' and I will now discuss this. In order for you to understand this process fully, I need to discuss two main principles; the first is fairly straightforward while the second is a little more complex.

Uncertainty

The concept of uncertainty plays an important role in shaping our construction of 'reality'. On its own, this concept plays little role in the creation of 'reality'. However, it is when it is linked to rigid/extreme attitudes and with respect to our purpose here, when it is linked to core rigid/extreme attitudes that it comes into its own in helping us to create 'reality'.

Core rigid/extreme attitudes

So far in this book whenever I have referred to a rigid/extreme attitude, I have considered it as a specific rigid/extreme attitude that a person holds in a specific situation at a specific time about a specific aspect of the situation in which he finds themself.

However, a rigid/extreme attitude can also be a more generally held attitude. When it is, it crops up in specific form in a variety of different contexts but the theme of the attitude remains constant. When a general rigid/extreme attitude has a decided effect on what the person pays attention to in his life it is said to be a core rigid and extreme attitude.

For example, imagine you hold the following core rigid/extreme attitude: 'I must have the approval of significant people in my life.' You will hold specific forms of this core rigid/extreme attitude whenever the theme of the attitude (i.e. approval and the possibility of not having it) becomes salient. Thus you may hold the attitude in different situations that you need the approval of your partner, your parents, your boss, your colleagues etc. and, as such, your core rigid/extreme attitude will be reflected in specific forms of this attitude. This core attitude will lead you to concentrate on the continuum that we might call 'approval–disapproval' and you are likely to see a significant part of the world through 'approval–disapproval' coloured glasses.

Bringing the concepts of 'uncertainty' and 'core rigid/extreme attitudes' together

If we bring the concepts of 'uncertainty' and a 'core rigid/extreme attitude' together, we can see how they help shape 'reality' not at 'C' in the 'ABC' framework but at 'A' in the same framework.

If we take the example of Peter that I discussed earlier in this chapter, we saw that when he held a rigid/extreme attitude about the possibility of not answering all questions put to him at an interview, he created 'reality' where he would not be able to answer any of the interview questions, where he would do far worse than the other candidates and where therefore there would be little point in him staying for the interview. He left the situation before he was interviewed because he considered these thoughts to be 'reality'. But, and this is the main point I want to make here, these thoughts became 'reality' for Peter only after he had processed his 'A' (i.e. 'I might not be able to answer all the questions') with his specific rigid/extreme attitude at 'B'. They were inferences at 'C'. Now, I

342   Windy Dryden Collected! Strange, But Rational

will show you how by bringing your core rigid/extreme attitude to
relevant situations at 'A' which are often shrouded in uncertainty
you create 'reality' at 'A'.

I will first describe how this principle works in general and then
I will illustrate it with an example.

Core Rigid/Extreme Attitude + Uncertainty = Creation of 'Reality' at 'A': The General Principle

When you hold a core rigid/extreme attitude, you bring this to
relevant situations where it is possible for the theme of the attitude
to occur. Since you are likely to be entering a situation where there
will be uncertainty you cannot be sure that the negative strand of the
theme will not occur. Since you cannot convince yourself that this
negative strand will not occur you think that it will occur or at least
you overestimate the likelihood of this happening. You do this
given the rigid black-and-white nature of a core rigid/extreme
attitude (if you recall, rigidity is a main characteristic of a specific
rigid/extreme attitude and this is also true for more general core
rigid/extreme attitudes).

Core Rigid/Extreme Attitude + Uncertainty = Creation of 'Reality' at A': A Specific Example

Susan holds the following core rigid attitude: 'I must not be
criticised by people who are important to me.' She has handed in a
report to her boss at work which her colleagues have read prior to
this and which they all considered to be excellent. However, Susan
cannot be certain that her boss will also find it excellent and won't
criticise it. Because the theme of Susan's core rigid attitude (i.e.
being criticised – being praised) is present in this situation (it is
possible that Susan's boss may criticise or praise her work), Susan
brings this core rigid attitude to the situation. Since she cannot be
sure that her boss will not criticise her work the rigid, black-and-
white nature of her core rigid leads her to think that he will criticise
this and this inference become Susan's 'A' which she then
processes with a specific variant of this core rigid attitude to create
even more negative and distorted inferences at 'C'.

In this way, rigid/extreme attitudes have a decided impact on how we create 'reality' both at 'A' in the 'ABC' framework and at 'C' in the same framework.

The Role of Behaviour in the Creation of 'Reality'

So far in this chapter, I have considered how our attitudes help to create our perception of 'reality'. In this closing section, I will briefly discuss the role that behaviour plays in the 'reality' creation process. As this is actually a very large topic, I will focus on two aspects of behaviour in this respect: safety-seeking behaviour and self-fulfilling prophecies.

Safety-seeking behaviour

When you engage in safety-seeking behaviour, you aim, through your behaviour, to keep yourself safe from threat. I will deal here with a threat that you have already created and will show how your safety-seeking behaviour strengthens your conviction that the threat that you have in fact created is real. Phil was suffering from panic disorder. In his case, these were the factors involved. Whenever Phil began to get anxious he held the attitude that he had to get his feelings under control immediately and if he failed to do so terrible things would happen and that he would have a heart attack if his anxiety increased. When his anxiety did increase then he thought that these feelings and the thoughts that accompanied them were predictors of what was imminent. The processes of cognitive and emotional reasoning strengthened his conviction. So, Phil sought safety and sat down whenever he thought he would have a heart attack. This safety-seeking behaviour in Phil's mind worked as, unsurprisingly, he did not have a heart attack, not because sitting down warded off such an attack, but because he had misinterpreted strong anxiety (which did give him some discomfort in his chest) as evidence of imminent heart failure. Thus, his behaviour helped to maintain his 'reality' that strong anxiety would lead to a heart attack if he did not immediately sit down.

Phil had to learn two things. First, how his rigid attitudes the processes of cognitive reasoning and emotive reasoning helped to create his sense of 'reality' and second, how his safety-seeking behaviour maintained this sense. In therapy, Phil constructed and maintained a flexible attitude towards experiencing anxiety and the related sense of self-control and kept standing when he thought that he was having a heart attack. These two approaches helped him to create a different sense of reality; namely, that strong anxiety and not being in as much control as he liked were signs of anxiety that needed to be understood and tackled and not, in all probability, evidence that he was having a heart attack.

Self-fulfilling prophecies

Finally, I want to show how self-fulfilling prophecies maintain a person's sense of reality. A self-fulfilling prophecy occurs when a person creates a sense of reality (usually from their rigid and extreme attitudes), acts as if that prophecy is true, and the environment and other people in that environment respond in such a manner as to confirm the person's created sense of reality.

For example, Harriet held the attitude that she had to be interesting at social gatherings (rigid attitude) and if she wasn't then nobody would want to talk to her (cognitive consequence of this rigid attitude and created sense of reality). Whenever she went to social gatherings, she kept quiet and did not engage in eye contact with those present because she did not think that she had anything interesting to say (behavioural consequence of her rigid attitude). As a result, nobody spoke to her which she took as evidence that nobody would speak to her if she was not interesting (self-fulfilling prophecy). What Harriet did not appreciate was that people did not speak to her because she seemed to indicate, through her silence and poor eye contact, that she did not invite conversation from others. Her therapist encouraged her (a) to develop a flexible rigid attitude towards others finding her interesting and (b) to initiate conversation with others and to engage in appropriate eye contact. As a result, most people at social gatherings were happy to talk to her and seemed generally interested in what she had to say.

*

In the following chapter, I will outline and discuss the two major forms of psychological disturbance put forward by REBT: ego disturbance and non-ego disturbance.

25

Two Forms of Disturbance

REBT theory argues that we have two major forms of disturbance: ego disturbance and non-ego disturbance. In this chapter I will discuss and illustrate both.

Ego Disturbance

Ego disturbance is so named because when you disturb yourself about some adversity at 'A' the content of your disturbance concerns your negative attitude towards yourself. As in most forms of disturbance, classical REBT theory holds that at the core of ego disturbance lies a rigid attitude. But what defines ego disturbance is the extreme self-devaluation attitude that is derived from this rigid attitude.

Ego disturbance: Three foci

You can experience ego disturbance when your focus is on yourself, on another person (or persons) or on a particular life condition. I will discuss these one at a time.

Ego disturbance: Self-focus

The most common form of ego disturbance occurs when the focus is on yourself. In one case, you have done something that you believe that you absolutely should not have done. Thus, you spent more money than you earned and you held the following attitude: 'I absolutely should not have spent as much money as I did and I'm an idiot for doing so.'

In another case, you did not do something that you think you absolutely should have done. Thus, you failed to inform your friend that his girlfriend was seeing another man and you held the following attitude: 'I absolutely should have told my friend that his girlfriend was cheating on him and I am a gutless bastard for not doing so.'

Ego disturbance: Other focus

A second form of ego disturbance occurs when your focus is on other(s). Two broad scenarios are possible. The first scenario occurs when another person has done something that you hold that they absolutely should not have done, while in the second, the other has not done something that you hold they absolutely should have done. In both these cases you devalue yourself rather than the other person.

Thus, in the first case, your father helped your sister when he did not help you. Your attitude was that he absolutely should not have favoured your sister and the fact that he did proves that you are no good. In the second case, your friend failed to return your calls and you held that he absolutely should have called you back and the fact that he did not do so proves that you are not worth caring about.

Ego disturbance: Life focus

A third form of ego disturbance occurs when your focus is on some aspect of life. Here, you hold that an aspect of life must be the way that it isn't or that it must not be the way that it is. Once again, in both these cases you devalue yourself. For example, in the first case, you failed to get into halls of residence where you held that you absolutely should have got a place. Because you failed to get a place, you concluded that this proves that you are a loser. An example of the second case occurred when you were called for jury service and you held that it absolutely should not have happened to you. Because it did, you concluded that this proves that you are a bad person and this is your punishment.

Ego disturbance in the emotional disorders

In my experience, people come to counselling largely for help with eight emotional problems: anxiety, depression, guilt, shame, unhealthy anger, hurt, unhealthy jealousy and unhealthy envy. In this section, I will show you the role that ego disturbance plays in each of these problems.

Ego disturbance in anxiety

When you experience ego-related anxiety, you think that you are facing a threat to your self-esteem. You hold a rigid attitude and a self-devaluation attitude about this threat to create your anxiety.

Here is an example of ego anxiety. Roger was anxious about losing an important tournament to his arch rival, Peter. Given that he was anxious he began to focus on how he was playing and not on what he needed to do and promptly lost the tournament.

Roger held the following rigid and extreme attitude that underpinned his anxiety: 'I must not lose to Peter. If I do, I am less worthy than I would be if I were to beat him.'

Ego disturbance in depression

When you experience ego-related depression, you have experienced a loss or have failed at something important to you. You hold a rigid attitude and a self-devaluation attitude towards this loss or failure to create your depression.

Here is an example of ego depression. Stephanie became depressed when she received a letter telling her that she failed to get into medical school. As a result she stopped applying for other medical schools thinking that if one turned her down they all would.

Stephanie held the following rigid/extreme attitude that underpinned her depression. 'I must not fail to get into medical school. The fact that I have proves that I am hopeless.'

Ego disturbance in guilt

When you experience guilt, you think that you have broken one of your moral rules, failed to live up to one of your moral rules or have hurt someone's feelings. You hold a rigid attitude and a self-devaluation attitude towards these violations to create your guilt.

Here is an example of guilt. Helen had promised to go out with her friends on an evening when her mother wanted to see her. When she told her mother she could not see her, her mother became very upset. Helen made herself guilty about hurting her mother's feelings and soon after she cancelled her evening out and went to visit her mother instead to ease her conscience.

Helen held the following rigid/extreme attitude that underpinned this guilt: 'I must not hurt my mother's feelings and I am a bad person because I have.'

Ego disturbance in shame

When you experience shame, you think that you have fallen very short of your ideal or that you or a member of your identified reference group have dishonoured that group in some way. In addition, you think that relevant others are evaluating you negatively. You hold a rigid attitude and a self-devaluation attitude about these perceived or actual events to create your shame.

Here is an example of shame. Minal, a young Sikh woman, was discovered talking to a group of young English guys at a party. Her aunt and uncle found out about this and considered that Minal had dishonoured the family name and refused to talk to her. As a result, Minal refused to go out and studied religious texts instead.

Minal held the following rigid and extreme attitude that underpinned her shame: 'I must not dishonour my family and I am a dishonourable person because I have.'

Ego disturbance in unhealthy anger

When you experience ego-related unhealthy anger, you think that someone has acted in a way that you take as a threat to your self-esteem. In common parlance you think that the other person is bad because he has made you feel badly about yourself. You hold a rigid attitude and a self-devaluation attitude towards this threat to create your unhealthy anger as well as an other-devaluation attitude. This type of unhealthy anger is often called ego-defensive anger because by getting unhealthily angry towards the other person you are defending yourself against the threat to your self-esteem.

Here is an example of ego-related unhealthy anger. Simon made himself unhealthily angry about Matthew when he thought that Matthew showed him disrespect. As a result, Simon poured a glass of beer over Matthew in revenge.

Simon held the following rigid and extreme attitude that underpinned his ego-related unhealthy anger: 'Matthew must show me respect and if he does not, I am not worthy of respect. Also, he is bad for making me feel badly about myself.'

Ego disturbance in hurt

When you experience ego-related hurt, you think that you have been treated badly by a significant other when you consider that you do not deserve such treatment. You hold a rigid attitude and a self-devaluation attitude towards this undeserved treatment to create your feelings of hurt.

Here is an example of ego-related hurt. Mel discovered that her friend, Beatrice, had betrayed her trust by telling a third friend about something that Mel asked Beatrice to treat in confidence. Mel thought that she did not deserve to be treated like this. As a result, Mel sulked and refused to speak to Beatrice or respond to her texts.

Mel held the following rigid and extreme attitude that underpinned her feelings of hurt: 'Mel must not betray my confidence. I don't deserve this, but the fact that she has proves that I am not worth caring about.'

Ego disturbance in unhealthy jealousy

When you experience ego-related unhealthy jealousy, you think that you are facing a threat to your relationship. You hold a rigid attitude and a self-devaluation attitude towards this threat to create your unhealthy jealousy.

Here is an example of ego-related unhealthy jealousy. Harriet was unhealthily jealous when she saw her partner talking with an attractive woman at a party. When they got home, Harriet gave her partner the third degree and refused to believe that he was only being friendly to the other woman.

Harriet held the following rigid and extreme attitude that underpinned her unhealthy jealousy: 'My partner must only find me attractive. If he finds other women attractive, it means that I am unlovable.'

Ego disturbance in unhealthy envy

When you experience ego-related unhealthy envy, you focus on something that you prize that another person has that you don't have. You hold a rigid attitude and a self-devaluation attitude towards this inequality.

Here is an example of ego-related unhealthy envy. Petra was unhealthily envious about the fact that her friend Edna had just bought a pair of shoes that when she saw them, Petra really wanted. Being unhealthily envious, and the fact that she could not afford the pair of shoes herself, Petra denigrated the shoes and Edna to anybody who would listen to her.

Petra held the following rigid and extreme attitude that underpinned her unhealthy envy: 'I must have what Edna has. If I don't have it then it proves that Edna has more worth than me.'

Non-Ego Disturbance

Non-ego disturbance is so named because when you disturb yourself about some adversity at 'A' the content of your disturbance does not concern your negative attitude towards yourself. As with ego disturbance, classical REBT theory holds that at the core of non-ego disturbance lies a rigid attitude. But what defines non-ego disturbance is the extreme awfulising and/or unbearability attitudes hat are derived from this rigid attitude.

Non-ego disturbance: Three foci

As with ego disturbance, you can experience non-ego disturbance when your focus is on yourself, on another person (or persons) or on a particular life condition. I will again discuss these one at a time.

Non-ego disturbance: Self focus

The first form of non-ego disturbance occurs when the focus is on yourself. In one case, you have done something that you hold that you absolutely should not have done. For example, you spent more money than you earned and you held the following attitude: 'I absolutely should not have spent as much money as I did and I can't stand being broke.'

In another case, you did not do something that you hold you absolutely should have done. Thus, you failed to inform your friend that his girlfriend was seeing another man and you held the following attitude: 'I absolutely should have told my friend that his girlfriend was cheating on him and it's terrible that I did not do so.'

Non-ego disturbance: Other focus

A second form of non-ego disturbance occurs when the focus is on another or others. Two broad scenarios are again possible. The first scenario occurs when another person has done something that you hold that they absolutely should not have done, while in the second, the other has not done something that you hold they absolutely should have done. In both these cases, you believe that it is awful that these situations have occurred and/or that you can't bear the resultant conditions.

Thus, in the first case, your father helped your sister when he did not help you. You held that he absolutely should not have favoured your sister and that it is unbearable that he did so. In the second case, your friend failed to return your calls and you held that he absolutely should have called you back and that it was terrible that he didn't.

Non-ego disturbance: Life focus

A third form of non-ego disturbance occurs when your focus is on some aspect of life. Here, you hold that an aspect of life must be the way that it isn't or that it must not be the way that it is. Once again, in both these cases you hold that it is awful that these situations exist and/or that you cannot bear the resultant conditions. For example, in the first case, you failed to get into halls of residence and you held that you absolutely should have got a place and that it was awful that you didn't.

An example of the second case occurred when you were called for jury service and you held that it absolutely should not have happened to you and that it was unbearable that it did.

Non-ego disturbance in the emotional disorders

As I said in the section on ego disturbance above, people generally come to counselling largely for help with eight emotional problems: anxiety, depression, guilt, shame, unhealthy anger, hurt, unhealthy jealousy and unhealthy envy. In this section, I will show you the role that non-ego disturbance plays in six of these problems, since shame and guilt are virtually exclusively forms of ego disturbance.

Non-ego disturbance in anxiety

When you experience non-ego-related anxiety you think that you are facing a threat to your domain which does not impact on your self-esteem. You hold a rigid attitude and an awfulising attitude and/or an unbearability attitude towards about this threat to create your anxiety.

Here is an example of non-ego anxiety. Fred was anxious about losing his job because he was underlyingly anxious about losing the comfort of his lifestyle. Given this anxiety, he began drinking and lost his job when he turned up for work drunk.

Fred held the following rigid and extreme attitude that underpinned his anxiety: 'I must not lose the comfort of my lifestyle. If I do, I could not bear giving up what I have come to enjoy.'

Non-ego disturbance in depression

When you experience non-ego-related depression you have experienced a loss or have failed at something important to you. You hold a rigid attitude and an awfulising attitude and/or an unbearability attitude towards this loss or failure to create your depression.

Here is an example of non-ego depression. Ralph became depressed when he lost an important family heirloom. As a result, he avoided talking to family members in case they discovered the loss.

Ralph held the following rigid and extreme attitude that underpinned his depression. 'I absolutely should not have lost the heirloom and it's terrible that I did.'

Non-ego disturbance in unhealthy anger

When you experience non-ego-related unhealthy anger you think that someone has transgressed an important rule or you have been frustrated in some way. You hold a rigid attitude and an awfulising attitude and/or an unbearability attitude or an other-devaluation attitude.

Here is an example of non-ego-related unhealthy anger. Michele made herself unhealthily angry about being stuck in a traffic jam. As a result, she beeped her horn and elicited aggressive responses from others in the traffic jam.

Michele held the following rigid and extreme attitude that underpinned her ego-related unhealthy anger: 'I must not be frustrated when I am late for an appointment and I can't bear it when I am. Others must not get in my way.'

Non-ego disturbance in hurt

When you experience non-ego-related hurt you think that you have been treated badly by a significant other when you consider that you do not deserve such treatment. This is the same as in ego-related hurt. But this time you hold a rigid attitude and an awfulising attitude and/or an unbearability attitude towards this undeserved treatment to create your feelings of hurt.

Here is an example of non-ego-related hurt. Steve was not invited to a party held by one of his friends. He had previously invited that friend to his party. Steve thought that he did not deserve to be treated like this. As a result, he sulked and refused to speak to his erstwhile friend.

Steve held the following rigid and extreme attitude that underpinned his feelings of hurt: 'My friend absolutely should have invited me to his party, particularly when I had invited him to mine. It's terrible to be treated so unfairly when I don't deserve it. Poor me!'

Non-ego disturbance in unhealthy jealousy

When you experience non-ego-related unhealthy jealousy you think that you are facing a threat to your relationship. You hold a rigid attitude and an awfulising attitude and/or an unbearability attitude towards this threat to create your unhealthy jealousy.

Here is an example of non-ego-related unhealthy jealousy. Stuart was unhealthily jealous when his girlfriend did not answer his calls to her mobile phone. When Stuart eventually got hold of his girlfriend he cross-examined her as to what she was doing and who she was speaking to when he could not get hold of her.

Stuart held the following rigid and extreme attitude that underpinned his unhealthy jealousy: 'I must know at all times where my girlfriend is and what she is doing and I can't tolerate not knowing this.'

Non-ego disturbance in unhealthy envy

When you experience non-ego-related unhealthy envy you again focus on something that you prize that another person has that you don't have. But this time you hold a rigid attitude and an awfulising attitude and/or an unbearability attitude towards this inequality.

Here is an example of non-ego-related unhealthy envy. Bernard was unhealthily envious about the fact that his brother had just got a promotion at work when he failed to get his own promotion.

Bernard held the following rigid and extreme attitude that underpinned his unhealthy envy: 'I must have what my brother has and I can't stand the unfairness of him getting what I didn't get.'

*

In this chapter, I have considered the two major types of disturbance separately. In reality, they often interact and people can focus on their ego disturbance problems and disturb themselves with ego-based and/or non-ego-based rigid and extreme attitudes. Similarly, they can focus on their non-ego disturbance problems and disturb themselves again with ego-based and/or non-ego-based rigid and extreme attitudes. This issue is the subject of the following chapter.

26

Every Week's Special Offer
Two Problems for the Price of One

We humans are not the only organisms to feel emotional disturbance. We know from early experiments, for example, that when cats are given a very powerful electric shock then they will avoid the place where they received the shock forever. Dogs can experience depression (or more accurately what we infer is a depressed state) when they learn to become helpless.

However, as far as I am aware, humans are the only organisms with the capacity to make ourselves experience disturbance about our disturbances. The technical term for such secondary disturbance is meta-disturbance and we can be quite creative in doing this as I will discuss later in this chapter. Perhaps a more colloquial way of putting this is the process of getting two problems for the price of one!

As I have already explained from the perspective of REBT (which informs the ideas expressed in this book), when we disturb ourselves we focus on some real or inferred adversity at 'A' in the 'ABC' framework and process this event by holding a rigid and extreme attitude at 'B'. Typically this rigid/extreme attitude has at least two attitude components – a rigid attitude component and an extreme attitude component. The consequences of this 'A' x 'B' interaction are emotional, behavioural and thinking responses that occur at 'C'. Since the attitude in this situation is rigid and extreme your responses at 'C' are likely to be unconstructive.

The part of our response system that is uniquely human is our ability to focus on any of these unconstructive responses (which then becomes a new 'A' which I will call 'A2') and to hold flexible/non-extreme or rigid/extreme attitudes towards these responses at 'B'. When this set of attitudes is rigid/extreme at 'B' (or 'B2') then your responses at 'C' (or 'C2') are also likely to be unconstructive. This process is presented in Figure 26.1.

```
'A' = Adversity

'B' = Rigid and Extreme Attitude

'C' = Unconstructive Consequences
          Emotional
          Behavioural
          Cognitive
                  |
                  ↓
'A2' = Unconstructive Consequence (see above)

'B2' = Rigid/Extreme or Flexible/Non-Extreme Attitude

'C2' = Unconstructive or Constructive Consequence
          Emotional
          Behavioural
          Cognitive
```

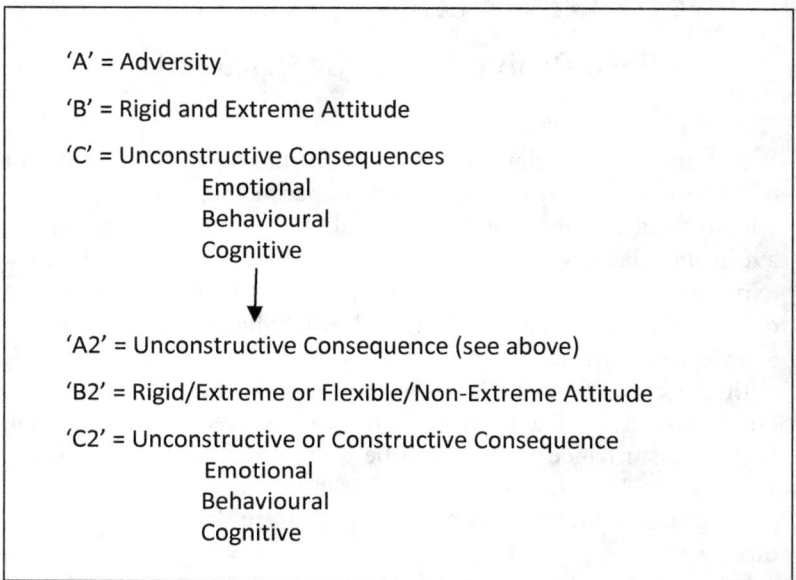

Figure 26.1 People can disturb themselves or 'un-disturb' themselves about their original disturbance

Before I discuss the three major forms of meta-disturbance, I suggest that you re-read Chapter 23 where I discussed the two major forms of disturbance: ego disturbance and non-ego disturbance.

Disturbing Yourself about Your Emotional Disturbance

Perhaps the most common form of meta-disturbance occurs when you experience a disturbed emotion at 'C', focus on it at 'A2' and then disturb yourself about it at 'C2' by holding a rigid/extreme attitude at 'B2'.

Emotions and transformations

When you disturb yourself about a disturbed emotion, the most common reason for this concerns the inference that you make about the emotion rather than the emotion itself.

What actually happens is quite complicated. So let me try to simplify matters by outlining the steps involved:

1. You make yourself disturbed at 'C1'
2. You focus on this disturbed emotion
3. You bring a core rigid/extreme attitude to this disturbed emotion, the content of which informs the inference that you make about this disturbed emotion at 'A2'
4. You hold a rigid/extreme attitude (at 'B2') towards this inference at 'A2'
5. You create a new disturbed emotion at 'C2'

Below I discuss some examples of disturbed emotions and the inferences that people make of them due in large part, as I have just shown, to the core rigid/extreme attitudes that they bring to these emotions (see Chapter 24 for a full discussion of the role of core rigid and extreme attitudes in the formation of inferences at 'A').

These inferences, then, serve as a new 'A' (here called 'A2') about which you disturb yourself with a new set of rigid/extreme attitudes (at 'B2') to create meta-disturbance at 'C2'.

Disturbing yourself about anxiety

As I have noted above, we largely disturb ourselves about our emotions by first forming a personalised inference about that emotion and then holding a rigid/extreme attitude towards that inference. In this section, I will discuss and illustrate how people disturb themselves about their anxiety. Common inferences that people form about anxiety include the following:

1. Anxiety is a personal weakness
2. If I feel anxious it means that I am losing control
3. If I am anxious, others will look down on me (e.g. I will be seen as unreliable)
4. Anxiety will hamper my career if it becomes known that I am anxious

Nathan and Harry

Let me show how two people transformed their commonly experienced anxiety differently to create different meta-disturbances. Two colleagues, Nathan and Harry were both anxious about public speaking because they feared that they would not perform well at forthcoming presentations and they both held the same rigid and extreme attitude that they must do well at their respective presentation. They both also had meta-disturbance about their anxiety, but this meta-disturbance had different roots as we shall now see.

Nathan was anxious about the prospect of being anxious because he saw his original anxiety as evidence that he was losing control. Nathan transformed his original anxiety into the inference ('I am losing control') because he brought the following core rigid attitude to his original anxiety: 'I must retain complete control of my emotions at all times.'

Nathan's meta-disturbance about his anxiety is shown below:

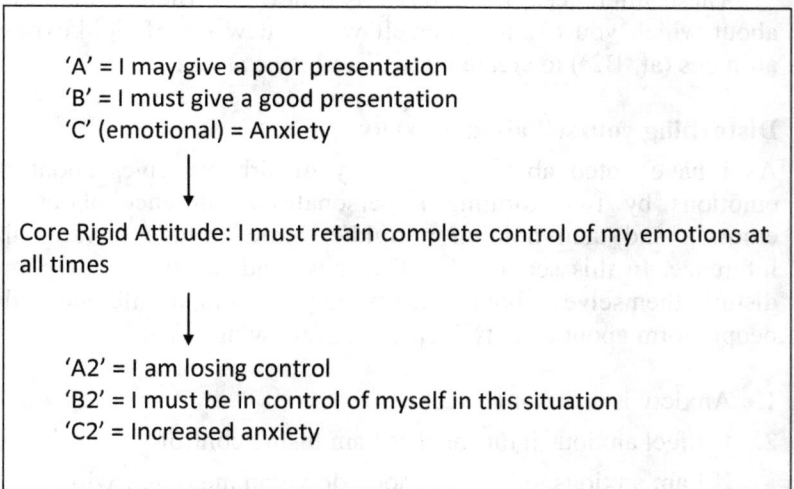

'A' = I may give a poor presentation
'B' = I must give a good presentation
'C' (emotional) = Anxiety

$\downarrow$

Core Rigid Attitude: I must retain complete control of my emotions at all times

$\downarrow$

'A2' = I am losing control
'B2' = I must be in control of myself in this situation
'C2' = Increased anxiety

Notice that Nathan's rigid/extreme attitude at 'B2' is a specific example of the core rigid/extreme attitude that Nathan brought to his anxiety at 'C' to create his inference at 'A2'.

Harry, on the other hand, was anxious about the prospect of being anxious because he feared that others would spot his anxiety and think less of him. Harry transformed his original anxiety into the inference ('People at the presentation will spot that I am anxious and think less of me') because he brought the following core rigid attitude to his original anxiety: 'Others must not spot that I am anxious and think less of me.'

Harry's meta-disturbance about his anxiety is shown below:

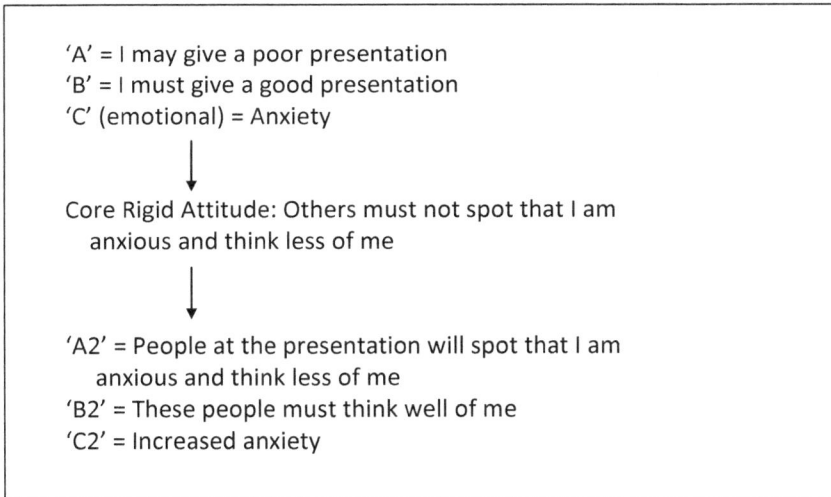

'A' = I may give a poor presentation
'B' = I must give a good presentation
'C' (emotional) = Anxiety

Core Rigid Attitude: Others must not spot that I am
   anxious and think less of me

'A2' = People at the presentation will spot that I am
   anxious and think less of me
'B2' = These people must think well of me
'C2' = Increased anxiety

Notice in this case that Harry's rigid attitude at 'B2' is a specific example of the core rigid attitude that he brought to his anxiety at 'C' to create his inference at 'A2'.

It is important to note two important points here. First, note the role that Nathan's and Harry's different core rigid attitudes played in the different inferences they formed at 'A2' of their common original anxiety at 'C'. Second, the specific rigid attitudes that Nathan and Harry held at 'B2' towards their transformed inferences at 'A2' were specific examples of the different rigid attitudes that they brought to their common anxiety at 'C'.

Disturbing yourself about depression

In this section, I will discuss and illustrate how people disturb themselves about their depression. Common inferences that people form about depression include the following:

- Depression is a personal weakness
- If I am depressed I am being self-indulgent
- If others discover that I am depressed I will be judged as unreliable
- If others discover that I am depressed, I will be stigmatised
- If others discover that I am depressed, I will be judged as being needy
- Depression is dependency
- If I am depressed it will hamper my career if this is discovered

Samantha and Fiona

Let me show how two people transformed their commonly experienced depression differently to create different meta-disturbances. Two friends, Samantha and Fiona, were both depressed about failing to get jobs that they had applied for, and they both held the same rigid and extreme attitude that they must succeed to get the jobs and if not they are failures. They both also had meta-disturbance about their depression but this meta-disturbance had different roots as we shall now see.

Samantha was ashamed about feeling depressed because she saw her original depression as evidence that she had an emotional weakness. Samantha transformed her original depression into the inference ('I have an emotional weakness') because she brought the following core rigid attitude to her original depression: 'I must be emotionally strong at all times.'

Samantha's meta-disturbance about her depression is shown below:

'A' = I failed to get a job that I wanted
'B' = I must succeed at getting the job
'C' (emotional) = Depression

↓

Core Rigid Attitude: I must be emotionally strong
    at all times

↓

'A2' = I have an emotional weakness
'B2' = I must be emotionally strong
'C2' = Shame

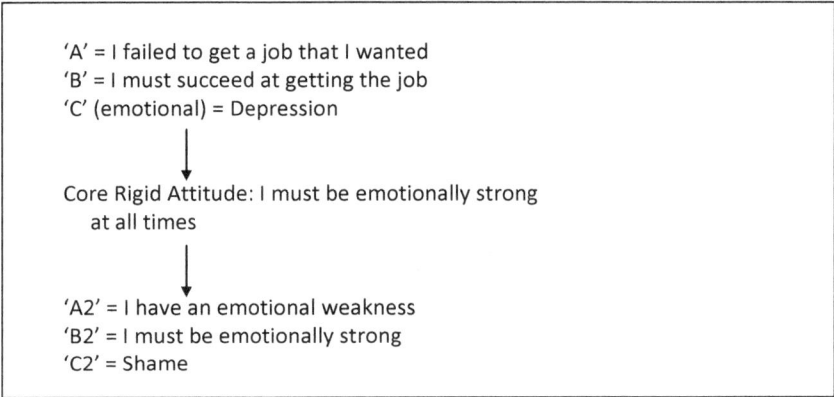

Notice again that Samantha's rigid attitude at 'B2' is a specific example of the core rigid attitude that she brought to her depression at 'C' to create her inference at 'A2'.

Fiona, on the other hand, was anxious about being depressed, because she feared that others would think that she was unreliable. Fiona transformed her original depression into the inference 'People will think that I am unreliable' because she brought the following core rigid attitude to her original depression: 'I must be seen to be reliable at all times.'

Fiona's meta-disturbance about her depression is shown below:

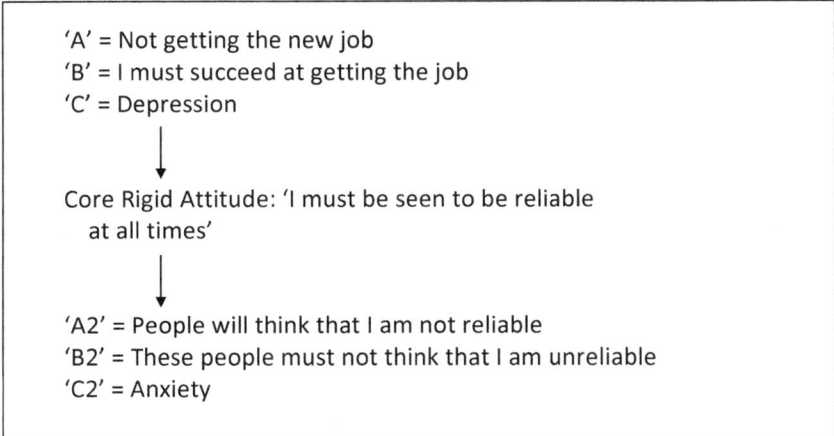

'A' = Not getting the new job
'B' = I must succeed at getting the job
'C' = Depression

↓

Core Rigid Attitude: 'I must be seen to be reliable
    at all times'

↓

'A2' = People will think that I am not reliable
'B2' = These people must not think that I am unreliable
'C2' = Anxiety

Notice again that Fiona's rigid attitude at 'B2' is a specific example of the core rigid attitude that she brought to her depression at 'C' to create this inference at 'A2'.

Again, note two important points here. First, note the role that Samantha's and Fiona's different core rigid attitudes played in the different inferences they formed at 'A2' of their common original depression at 'C'.

Second, the specific rigid attitudes that Samantha and Fiona held at 'B2' about their transformed inferences at 'A2' were specific examples of the different rigid attitudes that they brought to their common depression at 'C'.

Disturbing yourself about guilt

In this section, I will discuss and illustrate how people disturb themselves about their feelings of guilt. Common inferences that people form about guilt include the following:

- Guilt means that I am oversensitive
- Guilt means that I put myself last
- Guilt is a useless emotion
- Guilt is evidence that I am being stupid

Oliver and Toby

Let me now show how two people transformed their commonly experienced guilt differently to create different meta-disturbances. Two people, Oliver and Toby, who did not know one another, had wives who had recently become very ill and could not leave the house. Oliver and Toby both felt guilty about leaving their wives on their own because they held the same extreme attitude that they were bad for neglecting them. They both also had meta-disturbance about their feelings of guilt but this meta-disturbance had different roots as we shall now see.

Oliver was angry with himself for feeling guilty because he saw his original guilt as evidence of oversensitivity. Oliver transformed his original guilt into the inference ('My guilt proves that I am being oversensitive') because he brought the following core rigid attitude to his original guilt: 'I must not be oversensitive in any walk of life.'

Oliver's meta-disturbance about his guilt is shown below.

As with previous examples of meta-disturbance, Oliver's rigid attitude at 'B2' is a specific example of his core rigid attitude that he brought to his guilt at 'C' to create his inference at 'A2'.

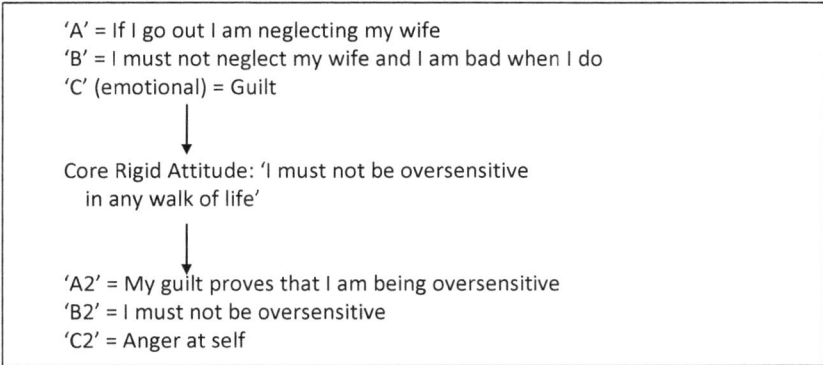

```
'A' = If I go out I am neglecting my wife
'B' = I must not neglect my wife and I am bad when I do
'C' (emotional) = Guilt

        |
        v

Core Rigid Attitude: 'I must not be oversensitive
   in any walk of life'

        |
        v

'A2' = My guilt proves that I am being oversensitive
'B2' = I must not be oversensitive
'C2' = Anger at self
```

Toby, on the other hand, was ashamed about feeling guilty because he viewed guilt as a useless emotion. Toby transformed his original guilt into the inference 'Guilt is a useless emotion' because he brought the following core rigid attitude to his original guilt: 'My emotions must be productive.'

Toby's meta-disturbance about his guilt is shown below.

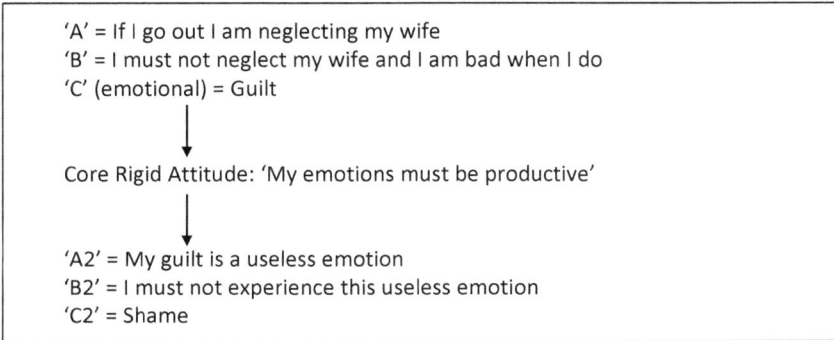

```
'A' = If I go out I am neglecting my wife
'B' = I must not neglect my wife and I am bad when I do
'C' (emotional) = Guilt

        |
        v

Core Rigid Attitude: 'My emotions must be productive'

        |
        v

'A2' = My guilt is a useless emotion
'B2' = I must not experience this useless emotion
'C2' = Shame
```

Notice yet again that Toby's rigid attitude at 'B2' is a specific example of the core rigid attitude that he brought to his guilt at 'C' to create his inference at 'A2'.

Again, and for the last time, note the role that Oliver's and Toby's different core rigid attitudes played in the different inferences they formed at 'A2' of their common original guilt at 'C'.

And also, for the last time, the specific rigid attitudes that Oliver and Toby held at 'B2' about their transformed inferences at 'A2' were specific examples of the different core rigid attitudes that they brought to their common guilt at 'C'.

Disturbing yourself about shame

In this section, I will discuss and illustrate how people disturb themselves about their feelings of shame. Common inferences that people form shame include the following:

*   It is weak to feel shame
*   Shame means that I care too much what other people think
*   Shame means that I have ridiculously high standards for myself
*   My feelings of shame indicate that I am being oversensitive

Lenny and Henrietta

Let me now show how two people transformed their commonly experienced shame differently to create different meta-disturbances. Two people, Lenny and Henrietta, who did not know one another, had in their estimation fallen very short of the high standards that they had set for themselves by getting drunk at the same corporate event.

Lenny and Henrietta both felt ashamed of their behaviour because they held the same extreme attitude that they were disgraceful people for acting disgracefully. They both also had meta-disturbance about their feelings of shame but this meta-disturbance had different roots as we shall now see.

Lenny was ashamed about feeling shame because he saw his original shame as evidence of weakness. Lenny transformed his original shame into the inference 'It is weak to feel shame' because he brought the following core rigid attitude to his original shame, 'I must not be weak in dealing with adversity'.

Lenny's meta-disturbance about his shame is shown below:

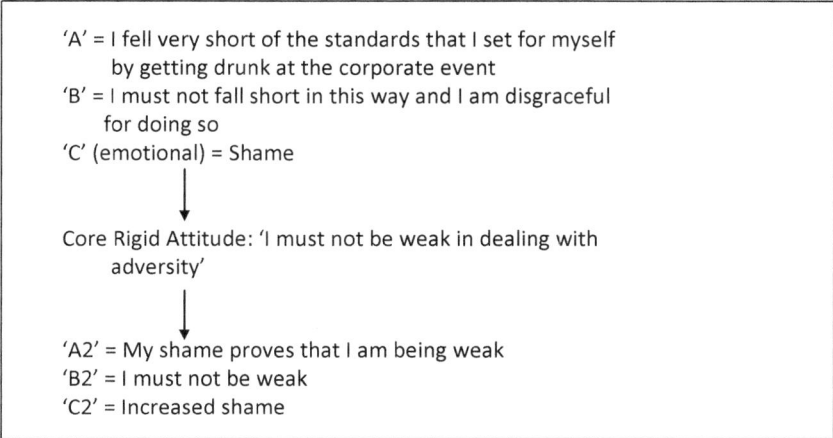

```
'A' = I fell very short of the standards that I set for myself
      by getting drunk at the corporate event
'B' = I must not fall short in this way and I am disgraceful
      for doing so
'C' (emotional) = Shame

          ↓

Core Rigid Attitude: 'I must not be weak in dealing with
      adversity'

          ↓

'A2' = My shame proves that I am being weak
'B2' = I must not be weak
'C2' = Increased shame
```

Henrietta, on the other hand, was angry with herself for feeling shame because she saw her original shame as evidence of her being oversensitive. Henrietta transformed her original shame into the inference 'Shame means that I am being oversensitive' because she brought the following core rigid attitude to her original shame: 'I must not be oversensitive in dealing with adversity.' Henrietta's meta-disturbance about her shame is shown below:

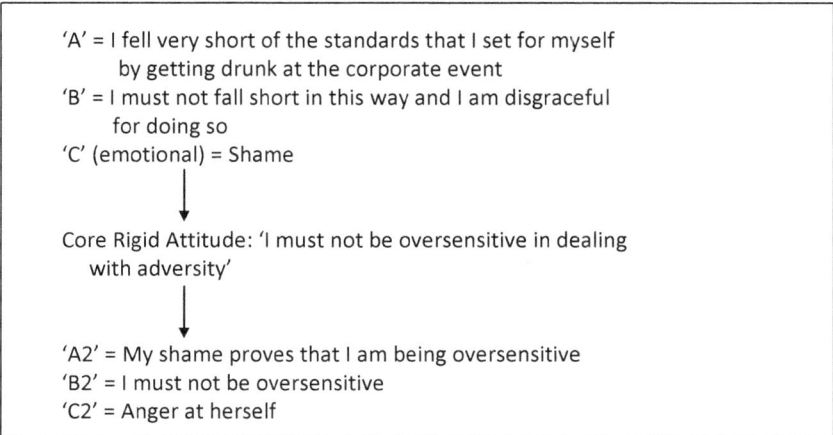

```
'A' = I fell very short of the standards that I set for myself
      by getting drunk at the corporate event
'B' = I must not fall short in this way and I am disgraceful
      for doing so
'C' (emotional) = Shame

          ↓

Core Rigid Attitude: 'I must not be oversensitive in dealing
   with adversity'

          ↓

'A2' = My shame proves that I am being oversensitive
'B2' = I must not be oversensitive
'C2' = Anger at herself
```

Disturbing yourself about unhealthy anger

In this section, I will discuss and illustrate how people disturb themselves about their feelings of unhealthy anger. Common inferences that people form about unhealthy angry include:

- Anger is a sign of immaturity
- Anger is a sign of weakness
- Anger means that I am not in control of myself
- Anger is morally wrong
- Being angry is not socially appropriate
- Being angry is not culturally appropriate
- If I am angry I will get into trouble
- Anger leads to conflict

Zara and Lionel

Zara and Lionel experienced unhealthy anger about the same event, but experienced different meta-emotional disturbances as shown below. I will present Zara's situation first.

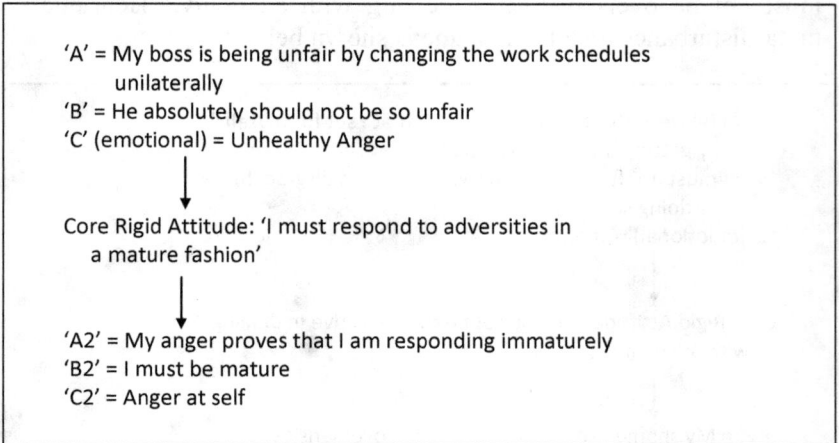

'A' = My boss is being unfair by changing the work schedules
     unilaterally
'B' = He absolutely should not be so unfair
'C' (emotional) = Unhealthy Anger

$\downarrow$

Core Rigid Attitude: 'I must respond to adversities in
    a mature fashion'

$\downarrow$

'A2' = My anger proves that I am responding immaturely
'B2' = I must be mature
'C2' = Anger at self

Here is Lionel's situation:

'A' = My boss is being unfair by changing the work schedules
     unilaterally
'B' = He absolutely should not be so unfair
'C' (emotional) = Unhealthy Anger

$\downarrow$

Core Rigid Attitude: 'I must avoid conflict at all times'

$\downarrow$

'A2' = My anger will lead to conflict with my boss
'B2' = I must avoid conflict with my boss
'C2' = Anxiety

Disturbing yourself about hurt

In this section, I will discuss and illustrate how people disturb themselves about their feelings of hurt. Common inferences that people form about hurt are:

Hurt is a sign of immaturity

Hurt is a sign of childishness

Hurt is a sign of weakness

Hurt is sign of oversensitivity

When I feel hurt I am being over-emotional

Paula and Laura

Paula and Laura experienced hurt about the same event, but experienced different meta-emotional disturbances as shown below. I will present Paula's situation first.

'A' = My friend betrayed my trust by telling our common
      friend what I told her in confidence.
'B' = She absolutely should not have betrayed my trust
'C' (emotional) = Hurt

↓

Core Rigid Attitude: 'I must respond to adversities
      in an adult fashion all the time'

↓

'A2' = My feelings of hurt prove that I am being childish
'B2' = I must not be childish
'C2' = Shame

Now here is Laura's situation:

'A' = My friend betrayed my trust by telling our
      common friend what I told her in confidence
'B' = She absolutely should not have betrayed my trust
'C' (emotional) = Hurt

↓

Core Rigid Attitude: 'I must maintain a degree of
      emotional equilibrium at all times'

↓

'A2' = My feelings of hurt means that I am being
      over-emotional
'B2' = I must regain my emotional equilibrium
      immediately and it will be terrible if I don't
'C2' = Anxiety

Disturbing yourself about unhealthy jealousy

In this section, I will discuss and illustrate how people disturb themselves about their feelings of unhealthy jealousy. Common inferences that people form about unhealthy jealousy are:

- Jealousy is a sign of insecurity
- Jealousy is a sign of possessiveness
- Jealousy is a sign of weakness
- Jealousy is a sign of neediness

Paul and Laurence

Paul and Laurence each experienced jealousy about a very similar threat to their relationship with their respective partners, but experienced different meta-emotional disturbances as shown below. I will present Paul's situation first.

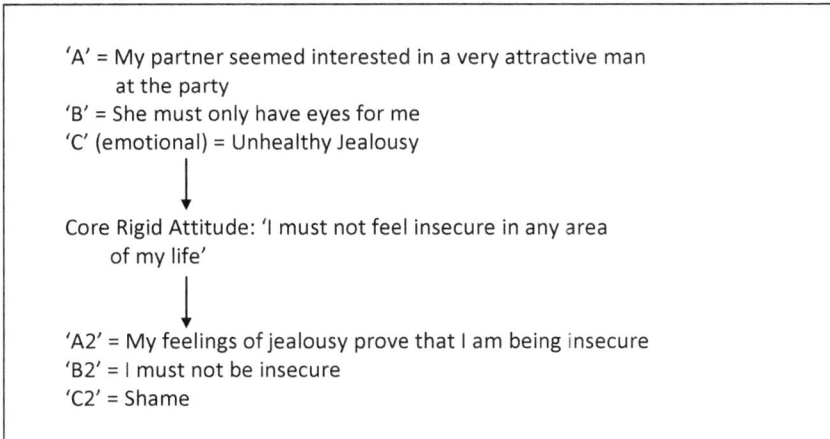

'A' = My partner seemed interested in a very attractive man
at the party
'B' = She must only have eyes for me
'C' (emotional) = Unhealthy Jealousy

Core Rigid Attitude: 'I must not feel insecure in any area
of my life'

'A2' = My feelings of jealousy prove that I am being insecure
'B2' = I must not be insecure
'C2' = Shame

Now here is Laurence's situation:

'A' = My partner seemed interested in a very attractive
    man at the party
'B' = She must only have eyes for me
'C' (emotional) = Unhealthy Jealousy

↓

Core Rigid Attitude: 'I must allow people to be themselves
    and not try to possess them'

↓

'A2' = My feelings of jealousy prove that I am
    being possessive
'B2' = I must not be possessive
'C2' = Anger at self

Disturbing yourself about unhealthy envy

In this final section, I will discuss and illustrate how people disturb themselves about their feelings of unhealthy envy. Common inferences that people form about unhealthy envy are:

- Envy is an ugly emotion
- Envy is a sign of insecurity
- Envy is selfishness
- When I am experiencing envy, I am being shallow
- When I am feeling envy, I am deluding myself
- Envy means that I am being materialistic

Jane and Jill

Jane and Jill experienced envy over their friend's promotion. However, they had different meta-emotional disturbances as shown below. I will present Jane's situation first.

'A' = My friend has been promoted and got what I
        wanted but have not got
'B' = This inequality must not exist
'C' = Unhealthy envy

↓

Core Rigid Attitude: 'I must only have noble emotions'

↓

'A2' = My feelings of envy are ugly
'B2' = I must not experience this ugly emotion
'C2' = Shame

Now here is Jill's situation:

'A' = My friend has been promoted and got what I
        wanted but have not got.
'B' = This inequality must not exist
'C' = Unhealthy envy

↓

Core Rigid Attitude: 'I must not be materialistic'

↓

'A2' = My feelings of envy mean that I am being materialistic
'B2' = I must not be materialistic
'C2' = Shame

Disturbing yourself about the pain of disturbed emotions

So far in this section, I have focused on and discussed the phenomenon where a person makes themselves disturbed in the first place and then makes an inference about that disturbed emotion, whereupon they then disturb themself about this inference in the second place. I discussed this phenomenon for each of the eight emotional problems for which people routinely seek help.

However, people can also disturb themselves about their original disturbed emotions because they hold rigid and extreme attitudes towards the pain of these emotions. Here is a typical example where Laura originally experiences the emotion of hurt.

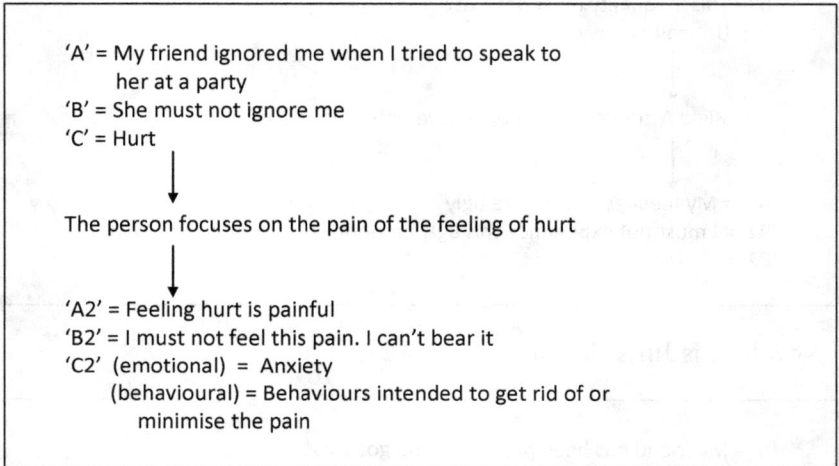

'A' = My friend ignored me when I tried to speak to
        her at a party
'B' = She must not ignore me
'C' = Hurt

$\downarrow$

The person focuses on the pain of the feeling of hurt

$\downarrow$

'A2' = Feeling hurt is painful
'B2' = I must not feel this pain. I can't bear it
'C2' (emotional) = Anxiety
        (behavioural) = Behaviours intended to get rid of or
            minimise the pain

One of the consequences of holding a rigid/extreme attitude towards the pain of a disturbed emotion is that this attitude and the additional disturbance it creates motivate the person to avoid the pain of the original disturbance rather than bearing it long enough to deal with it productively.

Thus, Laura, in the example above, focuses on the pain of the emotion of hurt (rather than making an inference about what it means to her to experience this emotion as described above on p. 368), and disturbs herself about the pain of this emotion because she holds a rigid/extreme attitude towards this pain and is thereby motivated to attempt to eliminate or minimise it as soon as she can.

I call the process where a person holds the attitude that she must not experience a particular disturbed emotion and it is unbearable to experience it because of the pain of the disturbance, 'disturbed emotional pain unbearability', a concept which is specific to the experience of the pain of the disturbed emotion.

There is a related concept, which I call 'negative emotional pain unbearability', which points to the person's perceived inability to bear emotions when they are negative, whether they are disturbed or healthy!

It is important to note that both forms of emotional pain unbearability may be specific to a particular emotion or general across emotions. The more general they are, the more disturbed a person is likely to be in life. It is interesting to note in this regard that the person who has what might be called 'general negative emotional pain unbearability' is likely to be more psychologically disturbed and impaired than the person who has what might be called 'general disturbed emotional pain unbearability'. This is because the person in the first case is disturbed and motivated to avoid all forms of negative emotion, healthy and unhealthy while the person in the latter case is disturbed and motivated to avoid only all forms of unhealthy negative emotions. I will not consider the former type in the remainder of this discussion.

The Effects of Meta-Emotional Disturbance

So far in this discussion of meta-emotional disturbance, I have considered two types of such disturbance:

1. *'Meaning-focused meta-emotional disturbance'*
   Here, the person transforms their original emotional disturbance at 'C' into an inference at 'A2' which they then process with a rigid/extreme attitude at 'B2' to create the meta-emotional disturbance at 'C2'.

2. *'Emotional pain-focused meta-emotional disturbance'*
   Here the person experiences the original emotional disturbance at 'C' and focuses on the emotional pain aspect of the experience at 'A2' which he then processes with a rigid/extreme attitude at 'B2' to create the meta-emotional disturbance at 'C2'.

In this section of the chapter, I will discuss two major consequences of these two types of meta-emotional disturbance: (a) avoidance of emotional disturbance, and (b) elimination or minimisation of emotional disturbance. Both serve to perpetuate the original emotional disturbance and create further disturbance for the person concerned.

Avoidance of emotional disturbance

When you avoid emotional disturbance you avoid (a) encountering situations in which you think you would disturb yourself if you did actually encounter them, and (b) thinking about events which if you did think about you would disturb yourself. Let me elucidate these by providing some examples.

Situationally-based avoidance of emotional disturbance: Some examples

1. Lucy would avoid supermarkets in case she felt anxiety after disturbing herself about feeling anxious one day in a supermarket.
2. Bob avoided getting involved with women after disturbing himself about feeling hurt when his last girlfriend rejected him out of the blue. He would go out with them, but would end the relationship if he felt he was beginning to develop feelings for the woman.
3. Larry would avoid situations in which there was the slightest chance of him making himself unhealthily angry since he found the experience of anger unbearable.
4. Brenda avoided relationships with men because she would disturb herself if she experienced unhealthy jealousy.
5. Henry was invited to a party thrown by his friend to celebrate an award he received from work. He did not go because he knew that he would feel unhealthily envious if he did go, an emotion that he found unacceptable.

Thinking-based avoidance of emotional disturbance: Some examples

1. Frank would change the subject every time someone mentioned Paris. If he thought about Paris, he would feel depressed about losing a girlfriend to his best friend many years ago and he was ashamed of still feeling depressed about the loss.
2. David would not read poetry because it made him think about an occasion when he was ridiculed by a teacher after he read out a poem in class. He still feels unhealthily angry about this event and is ashamed about feeling this way.

3. Susanna avoids the subject of politics because it reminds her of an affair she had with a married man who was a politician. She still feels ashamed about the affair and anxious about feeling ashamed because she fears losing control if she does.
4. Bill won't talk of his experiences in the war because it leads him to remember feeling afraid and he feels depressed about this fear reaction.
5. Ferdinand tries not to think about his late father because he has unresolved feelings of unhealthy anger towards of him about which he feels guilty. He has a variety of distractions that he uses every time he begins to think of his father.

Elimination/minimisation of emotional disturbance

As the name implies, when you avoid emotional disturbance, you are attempting to prevent the onset of emotional disturbance. So, when you attempt to eliminate or minimise emotional disturbance, you have already started to experience the disturbed feeling.

Once you have started to experience a disturbed emotion about which you have meta-emotional disturbance, an important element of your response is that it is designed to eliminate the disturbed emotion or reduce its intensity as quickly as possible. This is reflected in the person's rigid/extreme attitude. Not is only the person demanding that they must not experience the disturbed emotion, they are also demanding that they must get rid of it at best or minimise it at worst immediately. Given this, the person seeks quick methods of achieving their end.

The following (with examples) are the most common forms of quick elimination or minimisation of emotional disturbance.

Withdrawal

When you are in a situation where you begin to experience a disturbed emotion that you find unacceptable or unbearable in some way, one very quick way of eliminating it is to withdraw from the situation as quickly as you can. Kevin did this whenever he began to make himself anxious in big groups. Because he was ashamed of his anxious feelings, he would make his excuses to leave without unduly drawing attention to himself.

Distancing oneself from the adversity

If you can't leave a situation in which you experience an unacceptable or unbearable disturbed emotion, then one way of minimising the disturbed emotion is to attempt to distance yourself from the aspect of the situation about which you are disturbing yourself. This is, of course, the 'A' in the 'ABC' assessment of your disturbance. So, if you can't leave the physical situation in which 'A' occurs, what are your options if you wish to eliminate or minimise your unacceptable or unbearable disturbed feelings as quickly as possible? There are two ways of achieving this:

1. *Physically distancing yourself from 'A'* Martha was anxious about talking to strangers in a party situation and ashamed about feeling anxious. She did not avoid parties, but would distance herself from the possibility of being in a situation where she was in a group where she did not know anyone. Thus, she made sure that she was always with one person she knew.

2. *Psychologically distancing yourself from 'A'* Here, you attempt to distance yourself from 'A' by focusing on another aspect of the situation you are in or by distracting yourself by thinking about something else. For example, Victor distracted himself every time someone in his therapy group started to talk about sex. He was anxious about sex himself and ashamed that he was anxious about it. He was quite successful at seeming to pay attention to what group members were saying while replaying scenes from some of his favourite movies in his mind.

Changing 'A' while remaining in the situation in which 'A' occurred

If you are in a situation where you have disturbed yourself and you find this emotion unacceptable or unbearable, then one way of eliminating or minimising the disturbed emotion is to change the 'A' while remaining in the situation where the 'A' has occurred. For example, Walter was talking to a colleague about work when the colleague brought up the subject of a presentation that Walter did the previous week. The presentation had not gone well and Walter had felt depressed about it. He also felt anxious about the 'losing control' aspect of depression as he saw it. Consequently, when he began to feel depressed about the presentation in the conversation, he quickly, but subtly changed the topic of the conversation away from his presentation to the more general topic of the use of PowerPoint in presentations.

Use of alcohol, drugs and food

People with meta-emotional disturbances often use a variety of mood-altering substances to quickly eliminate or minimise the unacceptable or unbearable disturbed emotions. It is recognised by all those who counsel people with drug, alcohol and food abuse problems that a major reason why these people abuse their preferred substance(s) is for mood-altering purposes. While these substances can have the desired effects, in the short term, people often use them because they think that they will have the desired effect, whether or not it does. Leaving this aside for a moment, the main problem is that the use and abuse of these substances to eliminate or minimise the experience of unacceptable and/or unbearable emotions lead to the possibility of the person becoming addicted to their preferred substance(s) and/or developing additional mental and physical problems as the consequence of such prolonged use and abuse.

Disturbing Yourself about Your Unconstructive Behaviour

So far in this chapter I have focused on our ability as humans to disturb ourselves about our disturbed emotions. However, 'C' in the 'ABC' framework does not only stand for emotional consequences of rigid/extreme attitudes, it also stands for behavioural consequences of rigid/extreme attitudes.

In the present context, then, once we hold rigid/extreme attitudes at 'B' about an adversity at 'A', we tend to act in unconstructive ways at 'C' and can either convert these urges into overt actions or not.

Disturbing Yourself about Your Actual Behaviour

Let's first take the case where we convert our action tendencies into overt actions. We can then focus on these actions and make inferences about them coloured by core rigid/extreme attitudes that we bring to these behaviours.

Here are a couple of examples of inferences that it is possible to form about our behavioural disturbance at 'C'. In these examples I will only give the behavioural consequences of rigid/extreme attitudes (at 'B').

The case of Sharon

'A' = A traffic warden unfairly gave me a parking ticket
      even though she was wrong to do so
'B' = She absolutely should not have been so unfair to me
'C' (behaviour) = Swore angrily at the warden

$\downarrow$

Core rigid attitude: I must be polite and caring at all times

$\downarrow$

'A2': I was rude to the traffic warden
'B2': I absolutely should not have been rude to her
'C2': Guilt

The case of Dylan

'A' = Not knowing if the mole on my arm is cancerous or not
'B' = I must know for sure that it is not cancerous
'C' (behaviour) = Keep seeking reassurance

$\downarrow$

Core rigid attitude: I must not be irrational in the way
I respond to things

$\downarrow$

'A2' = Checking my wart is evidence that I was irrational
'B2' = I absolutely should not have been irrational
'C2' = Anger at self

Disturbing yourself about your action tendencies

Now let's first take the case where you focus on your unconstructive action tendencies. You may consider it strange to think of a tendency to act that has not been converted into overt action as unconstructive. After all, it is only an urge and surely only overt action can be considered constructive or unconstructive. While there's some validity to this argument, I still think it is useful to think of an action tendency that stems from a rigid/extreme attitude as being unconstructive. First, it alerts you that you need to do something to help yourself before you act and indeed that you can do something to help yourself before you act. Second, as I will show, people do disturb themselves about their action tendencies and they would not do that if they did not deem them to be unconstructive. Attempting to convince them that their action tendencies are not constructive when they think that they are is not usually an effective strategy.

Once you have disturbed yourself at 'A' you will experience an urge to act or what I call here an action tendency. You can then focus on this action tendency and make an inference about it again coloured by a relevant core rigid/extreme attitude that you bring to this tendency.

Here are a couple of examples of inferences that it is possible to form about unconstructive action tendencies at 'C'. In these examples I will only give the action tendency consequences of rigid/extreme attitudes (at 'B').

The case of Luke

'A' = Thinking I wasn't impressing the girl at the party
'B' = I must impress her
'C' (action tendency) = Felt like running away, but didn't

↓

Core rigid attitude: 'I must always face up to things'

↓

'A2' = Feeling like running away is cowardly
'B2' = I absolutely should not have been cowardly
'C2' = Shame

The case of Delia

'A' = My child was rude to me
'B' = He must not be rude to me
'C' (action tendency) = Felt like hitting him but didn't

↓

Core rigid attitude: 'I must feel in control of myself
   with my children at all times'

↓

'A2' = I will lose control of myself with Jimmy
'B2' = I must feel in control right now
'C2' = Anxiety

Disturbing yourself about your distorted subsequent thinking

When we talk about REBT's 'ABC' framework, we usually consider 'C' to be the emotional consequences or the behavioural consequences of rigid/extreme attitudes. However, as I discussed in Chapter 24, 'C' can also be the thinking consequences of rigid/extreme attitudes and when it is, these thoughts are usually highly skewed to the negative and grossly distorted.

Thus, when you disturb yourself at 'C' about an adversity at 'A', you can focus on the thinking consequences of your rigid/extreme attitudes and make inferences about them coloured by the core rigid and extreme attitude that you bring to these thoughts.

Here are a couple of examples of inferences that it is possible to form about thinking consequences at 'C'. In these examples I will only give the thinking consequences of rigid/extreme attitudes.

The case of Emily

'A' = My mother criticised my dress sense in front
    of my friends
'B' = She must not criticise me in public
'C' (thinking) = 'I hope she rots in hell'

↓

Core rigid attitude: 'I must not think badly about people
    that I am close to'

↓

'A2' = I was horrible to my mother by thinking that way
'B2' = I absolutely should not have been horrible to her
'C2' = Guilt

The case of Freda

'A' = My mother criticised my dress sense in front
    of my friends
'B' = She must not criticise me in public
'C' (thinking) = 'I hope she rots in hell'

↓

Core rigid attitude: I must be in control of the way I think
    act and feel at all times with people I am close to

↓

'A2' = I am losing control of myself by thinking that way
'B2' = I absolutely should be in control of my thoughts
'C2' = Anxiety

I will bring this chapter to a close by discussing the concept of 'rigid/extreme attitude focused meta-disturbance'.

Rigid/extreme attitude focused meta-disturbance

This concept points to the process whereby you learn that you disturb yourself by holding one or more rigid/extreme attitudes and then you focus on these rigid/extreme attitudes and you disturb yourself for continuing to hold them. Here are a few examples of rigid/extreme attitude focused meta-disturbance:

Ira

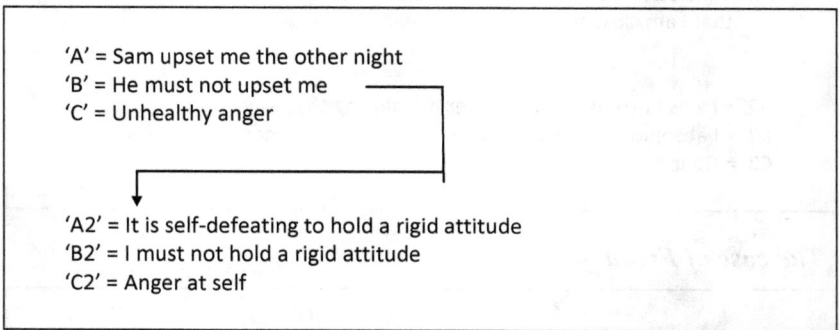

Carol

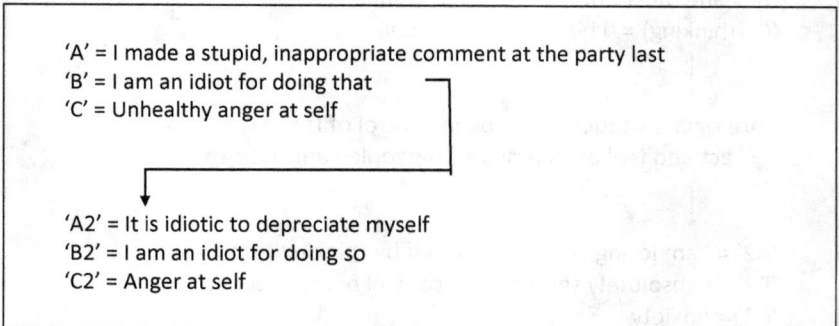

The two examples of rigid/extreme attitude focused meta-disturbance that I have given have illustrated meta-rigidity (rigidity about rigidity) and meta-self-devaluation (self-devaluation about self-devaluation). However there are many possibilities and Figure 26.2 below spells out these possibilities.

Rigidity	Awfulising

Rigidity about
    Rigidity
	Rigidity about
	    Awfulising

Awfulising about
    Rigidity
	Awfulising about
	    Awfulising

Unbearability about
    Rigidity
	Unbearability about
	    Awfulising

Depreciation about
    Rigidity
	Devaluation about
	    Awfulising

Unbearability	**Devaluation**

Rigidity about
    Unbearability
	Rigidity about
	    Devaluation

Awfulising about
    Unbearability
	Awfulising about
	    Devaluation

Unbearability about
    Unbearability
	Unbearability about
	    Devaluation

Devaluation about
    Unbearability
	Devaluation about
	    Devaluation

Figure 26.2   Sixteen types of rigid/extreme attitude focused meta-disturbance

*

In the next chapter, I will differentiate between bad feelings and disturbed feelings and argue that it is often good for a person to experience the former.

27

Feeling Bad Can Be Good

Recently, there has been quite a lot of interest in the science of happiness and in positive psychology. These areas developed in part because it was clear that while counsellors and psychotherapists have a lot to say about how best to address psychological problems, they don't have as much to say about how people can be happy and be optimistic, for example.

As the average life span marches beyond three score years and ten to four score years and ten, it is important that we spend as much time as we can experiencing happiness and other positive emotions. If happiness scientists and positive psychologists can learn about how we can promote such positive states and teach us to maximise them, then they will get no argument from me. To the contrary, I fully support their endeavours.

However, in the rush towards such positive states of mind and happy living, there is a real risk that we gloss over, forget and even denigrate the value of feeling bad. What, I hear you start; the value of feeling bad. Is this a misprint or has Dryden finally taken leave of his senses? Well, it is not a misprint and as far I know I am as sane as I ever have been! My argument is that at times it is good to feel bad. While I am not saying that we should pursue feeling bad in the same way as we pursue happiness (although some people argue that to pursue happiness is not to experience it), I will argue that under certain circumstances feeling bad is the healthiest option on offer to us and thus, we should come to appreciate the benefits of bad feelings. I shall expand on and discuss this thesis in this chapter.

Feeling Good or Neutral about Life's Adversities

I will argue in this chapter that it is healthy to feel bad, but not disturbed, in the face of life's adversities. Before I discuss this topic, I need to consider and dispense with two other possible responses to adversities: to feel good and to feel neutral.

Let me first consider feeling good about life's adversities. In order to do this you would have to hold an attitude such as 'I want bad things to happen and it is good when they do'. Now, this might make sense under a few specialised conditions. Thus, if you want to build your resilience, you need adversities in your life to do this, so then this attitude might make sense. However, you would not feel good about the adversity itself, but about the opportunity that it provides you to build your resilience. A second specialised condition under which you might feel good about life's adversities is as follows. Imagine that an eccentric uncle tells you that every time you experience a life adversity, he will give you £5,000, as long as you do nothing to bring that about. If you do, he will pay you nothing. Well, if you needed the money you would probably hope that an adversity befalls you and if it did you would probably feel pleased. However, on closer examination, we would see it was not the adversity that you would feel good about, but the money that accompanies it.

Other than these specialised conditions, and even then we have seen that it is not the adversity itself that you have good feelings about but the opportunity for resilience building it gives you in the first case and the money awarded to you in the second, it is unrealistic for you to feel good about something bad happening. That does not mean that when you focus on other more pleasant aspects of your life that you would not feel good about them, but when your focus is on the adversity itself, then it would be unhealthy for you to feel good about it.

It would also be unhealthy for you to feel neutral about an adversity. In order to achieve this you would have to believe something like: 'I don't care if this adversity happens to me or not.' Now, such attitudes of indifference are accurate if you truly do not care if something happens or not. For example, I don't care if one US ice hockey team beats another one as I have no interest in ice hockey. However, if you truly do have a preference about something happening and it doesn't happen, trying to convince yourself that you don't care when you do involves you lying to yourself: your preference proves that you care. People are much more likely to try to convince themselves that they don't care about an adversity when they are disturbed about it than when they have bad feelings about it. They employ the 'I don't care' philosophy as a defence against the pain of their disturbed feelings, to lessen their pain if you will. So when you hear someone say that they don't care about something that they can realistically be expected to care about then they usually hold a rigid/extreme attitude towards the adversity, one that leads to their disturbed feelings.

Bad Feelings versus Disturbed Feelings

The essays in this book are informed by the theoretical ideas that underpin Rational Emotive Behaviour Therapy, the first approach to be developed in what I call the cognitive behaviour therapy (CBT) tradition. One of the cornerstones of REBT theory is that rigid/extreme attitudes are at the core of psychological disturbance while flexible/non-extreme attitudes are at the core of psychological health (see Chapter 23). REBT further argues that when a person faces one of life's adversities, then they will experience negative feelings whether they hold a rigid/extreme attitude or a flexible/non-extreme attitude towards adversity. However, as rigid/extreme attitudes are qualitatively different from flexible/non-extreme attitudes in the sense that they are not at opposite ends of a single continuum, then the negative feelings that stem from these different attitudes are also qualitatively different from one another. In REBT, we call the negative feelings that stem from rigid/extreme attitudes 'unhealthy negative feelings' and those that stem from flexible/non-extreme attitudes 'healthy negative feelings'. In this chapter, I will call the former 'disturbed feelings' and the latter 'bad feelings'.

So REBT theory argues that when you are actually facing an adversity or think that you are, then you will either feel bad or disturbed, based on the attitude that you hold towards this adversity. In Chapter 28, I will discuss the ideas people hold about eight different disturbed emotions that interfere with their efforts to address them constructively. I will also consider the bad feeling alternatives to these disturbed feelings. Table 27.1 summarises these below.

Basically, what this table shows is that when you are facing an adversity of whatever type then you have two choices: to feel bad about the adversity or to feel disturbed about it.

My argument here is that to feel bad about an adversity is healthy, but to feel disturbed about it is unhealthy. This is best shown by considering the behaviours and thinking that accompany bad and disturbed feelings respectively. As we do so, remember that feelings, behaviours and thinking are all consequences of rigid and extreme attitudes and flexible and non-extreme attitudes and that these consequences are likely to be constructive when the attitudes are flexible and non-extreme and unconstructive when the attitudes are rigid and extreme.

Table 27.1 Adversities, disturbed feelings and bad feelings

Adversity	Disturbed Feeling	Bad Feeling
• Threat	Anxiety	Concern
• Loss • Failure • Undeserved plight (to self/others)	Depression	Sadness
• Broken moral code • Failed to live up to moral code • Harmed or hurt someone	Guilt	Remorse
• Falling short of your ideal in front of others or with these others in mind • Others view self negatively • Member of reference group disgraces that group	Shame	Disappointment
• Others have let you down • Others have betrayed you • Others or have failed to reciprocate [Self is undeserving in these scenarios]	Hurt	Sorrow
• Frustration • Goal obstruction • Self or other transgresses personal rule • Other shows self disrespect or threatens self-esteem	Unhealthy anger	Healthy anger
• Threat to relationship with partner posed by another person	Unhealthy jealousy	Healthy jealousy
• Another person possesses and enjoys something you desire and do not have	Unhealthy envy	Healthy envy

Behaviours and action tendencies associated with bad and disturbed feelings

In Table 27.1 I listed the terms that REBT theory employs to differentiate between disturbed feelings and bad feelings, but these terms on their own do not give a clear idea concerning why bad feelings about adversities are largely healthy and why disturbed feelings about the same adversities are largely unhealthy. In my view there are two better ways of making this point: looking at the behaviours that accompany these feelings and looking at the associated subsequent thinking linked to them. I will first consider the behavioural dimension. Before I do so, it is important to make a distinction between overt behaviours and action tendencies. Overt behaviour concerns actual behaviour while the latter concerns the urges we feel to act in a certain way which we do not act on. Thus, when a person has not acted in the face of adversity and it is not clear whether the person's feelings are disturbed or bad, an examination of his action tendencies may be revealing. For example, Peter was angry when a cyclist cut him up, but he did nothing about it. All he could say was that he felt angry which did not clarify whether his feelings were bad or disturbed feelings. However, when asked what he felt like doing but suppressed, Peter replied that he felt like killing the cyclist, a clear indication that his anger was disturbed. Tables 27.2 and 27.3 provide examples of the overt behaviours and action tendencies associated with each of the eight disturbed and bad feelings that occur when different types of adversities occur.

Subsequent thinking associated with bad and disturbed feelings

The second way of differentiating bad from disturbed feelings is to examine the thinking associated with them. This thinking is actually a consequence of the flexible/non-extreme and rigid/extreme attitudes at 'B' towards the adversity at 'A'. The former is characterised by being realistic and balanced while the latter is characterised by being distorted and skewed. Tables 27.4 and 27.5 provide examples of the thinking associated with each of the eight disturbed and bad feelings that occur when different types of adversities occur.

I hope you can see by inspecting Tables 27.2 to 27.5 that the behaviours, action tendencies and subsequent thinking associated with bad feelings show why these feelings are constructive. They reflect a flexible response to an adversity and encourage realistic thinking and constructive behaviour which will encourage people to change adversities that can be changed and to adjust constructively to adversities that cannot be changed.

Table 27.2   Disturbed feelings and examples of dysfunctional behaviours/action tendencies

Disturbed Feeling	Examples of Dysfunctional Behaviours and Action Tendencies
Anxiety	Withdrawing from threat; avoiding threat; seeking reassurance even though not reassurable; seeking safety from threat
Depression	Prolonged withdrawal from enjoyable activities
Guilt	Begging for forgiveness
Shame	Withdrawing from others; avoiding eye contact with others
Hurt	Sulking
Unhealthy anger	Aggression (direct and indirect)
Unhealthy jealousy	Prolonged suspicious questioning of the other person; checking on the other; restricting the other
Unhealthy envy	Spoiling the other's enjoyment of the desired possession

Table 27.3   Bad feelings and examples of functional behaviours/action tendencies

Bad Feeling	Examples of Functional Behaviours and Action Tendencies
Concern (as opposed to anxiety)	Confronting threat; seeking reassurance when reassurable
Sadness (as opposed to depression)	Engaging with enjoyable activities after a period of mourning or adjustment to the loss
Remorse (as opposed to guilt)	Asking, not begging, for forgiveness
Disappointment (as opposed to shame)	Keeping in contact with others, maintaining eye contact with others
Sorrow (as opposed to hurt)	Assertion and communicating with others
Healthy anger (as opposed to unhealthy anger)	Assertion
Healthy jealousy (as opposed to unhealthy jealousy)	Brief, open-minded questioning of the other person; neither checking or the other nor restricting them
Healthy envy (as opposed to unhealthy envy)	Striving to gain a similar possession for oneself if it is truly what you want

Table 27.4 Disturbed feelings and examples of subsequent distorted thinking

Disturbed Feeling	Examples of Subsequent Distorted Thinking
Anxiety	Overestimating the negative consequences of the threat if it occurs
Depression	Hopelessness; helplessness
Guilt	Assigning too much responsibility to self and too little to others
Shame	Overestimating the negativity of others' reactions to self and the extent of these reactions
Hurt	Thinking that the other has to put things right of their own accord
Unhealthy anger	Thinking that the other has malicious intent; thoughts of exacting revenge
Unhealthy jealousy	Tending to see threats to one's relationship in the absence of evidence
Unhealthy envy	Tending to denigrate the value of the desired possession

Table 27.5 Bad feelings and examples of subsequent realistic thinking

Bad Feeling	Examples of Subsequent Realistic Thinking
Concern (as opposed to anxiety)	Realistically appraising the negative consequences of the threat if it occurs
Sadness (as opposed to depression)	Viewing the future with hope; seeing self as able to cope with adversity
Remorse (as opposed to guilt)	Assigning appropriate level of responsibility to self and to others
Disappointment (as opposed to shame)	Realistically appraising others' reactions to self and the extent of these reactions
Sorrow (as opposed to hurt)	Not thinking that the other has to put things right of their own accord. Thinking that one can initiate the healing process oneself
Healthy anger (as opposed to unhealthy anger)	Only thinking that the other has malicious intent when there is clear evidence of this; thoughts of assertion rather than of exacting revenge
Healthy jealousy (as opposed to unhealthy jealousy)	Tending to see threats to one's relationship only when there is clear evidence that such threats exist
Healthy envy (as opposed to unhealthy envy)	Honestly admitting to oneself that one wants the desired possession for its own sake and not because the other person has it

I also hope you can see by inspecting Tables 27.2 to 27.5 that the behaviours, action tendencies and subsequent thinking associated with disturbed feelings show why these feelings are unconstructive. They reflect a rigid response to an adversity and encourage distorted thinking and dysfunctional behaviour which will impede people from changing adversities that can be changed and from adjusting constructively to adversities that cannot be changed.

Feeling Bad When Things Can't Be Changed: An Example

Let me first consider an example of the healthiness of bad feelings as opposed to disturbed feelings about an adversity which a person cannot change. Adam had been diagnosed with tinnitus and after several consultations with experts in the field, he concluded that there was no treatment for this condition. He became depressed and anxious about this and stayed in just in case he encountered sudden loud noises which would exacerbate his tinnitus. When he had to go out, he first rang the local council to determine whether and where road works were being undertaken so he could plan his route to avoid these works again in case they made his hearing problem worse. The unintended consequence of such strategies was to keep the subject of his tinnitus at the forefront of his mind and to keep Adam away from activities that he had previously enjoyed.

When Adam was referred for counselling, he was quite resistant to the idea. In his mind, his problem was his tinnitus and no amount of counselling would do anything about that. He also considered that his anxious and depressed feelings were perfectly natural responses to tinnitus and could not see how any counsellor could help. However, because his GP was quite insistent that he at least gave counselling a try and because he respected this doctor, he sought help.

Fortunately for Adam, the counsellor to whom he was referred knew a lot about tinnitus and had a lot of experience counselling people in Adam's situation. The counsellor first helped Adam to see that while his tinnitus was an adversity, it did not directly cause him feelings of anxiety and depression. Rather, these feelings were largely determined by the rigid and awfulising attitudes that he held towards salient aspects of his condition. Before the counsellor encouraged Adam to examine these rigid and extreme attitudes, they outlined the flexible and non-awfulising attitude alternatives so that Adam could see that he had a choice of which attitude to hold towards issues to do with his tinnitus. The counsellor also helped Adam to see that his avoidance actually reinforced his rigid and extreme attitude and if he was to think constructively about his tinnitus he would need to re-engage with life and face up to situations that he had come to avoid. In this respect, no expert that Adam had consulted about dealing with his tinnitus from a medical point of view had recommended such avoidance.

While Adam understood the points that his counsellor was making he was still apprehensive about applying these ideas. So, his counsellor recommended that he 'try these ideas on for size' so to speak and for a month he agreed to think rationally and stop avoiding activities and the possibility of hearing a loud noise. As his counsellor said he could always go back to his old ideas and avoidant lifestyle if the new way of thinking and acting bore no fruit or, as Adam feared, made his tinnitus worse.

However, as the counsellor predicted, and to Adam's amazement, Adam stopped feeling depressed and anxious about his tinnitus-related issues. Instead his developing flexible and non-extreme attitudes led him to feel disappointed and concerned about these issues. In addition, he reported that because he was re-engaging with life again he was thinking far less about his tinnitus than when he avoiding going out. This process was aided by him refraining from plotting his routes when he went out to avoid the possibility of hearing loud noises. When this did happen, he practised his non-awfulising attitude which helped him to keep such incidents in proportion.

This example shows that Adam's disturbed feelings about aspects of his adversity that could not change and the associated behaviour that accompanied them gave him two problems for the price of one (see Chapter 26): the practical problem of dealing with tinnitus and a psychological problem about this practical problem. On the other hand, Adam's bad feelings about these same aspects and the associated behaviour that accompanied them freed him to deal with the practical elements of living with tinnitus.

Feeling Bad When Things Can Be Changed as a Prelude to Taking Steps to Change Them: An Example

In this example, I will show how Neelam's bad feelings about something helped her to take steps designed to change them while her disturbed feelings paralysed her. Neelam was doing very well at work and was expecting to be promoted when her old boss who had been very supportive of her left and was replaced by a new boss who was anything but. Indeed, there were racist undertones about how her boss spoke to her. Neelam reacted to this situation with unhealthy anger. She had thoughts of attacking her boss physically and she was so scared of these thoughts that she decided to sit on her feelings and did nothing about them. As a result this issue dominated Neelam's existence and she could think of nothing else. A routine medical check revealed that Neelam was suffering very high blood pressure and her doctor, who knew Neelam well, discovered the root of the problem and referred her for counselling.

The counsellor helped Neelam to discover the rigid/extreme attitudes that underpinned her anger and enabled her to see that healthy anger, based as it was on a set of alternative flexible/non-extreme attitudes, was a healthy and realistic alternative to her unhealthy anger. Neelam did, at first, say that she wanted to be indifferent to her boss, but her counsellor suggested that this was unrealistic since she really did care about how her boss treated her and that an indifferent response would have been based on her lying to herself.

As part of this discussion, Neelam's counsellor showed her that it was her unhealthy anger and the rigid/extreme attitudes that underpinned it that were the reasons why she had aggressive retaliatory fantasies towards her boss. Most importantly he encouraged her to see that the major behaviour associated with healthy anger was assertion. Crucially, Neelam saw that her unhealthy anger led her not to do anything to try and change the situation that could, at least theoretically, be changed. On the other hand, if she felt healthy anger instead, she at least had the option of asserting herself first with her boss and then more formally with Human Resources (HR) if the situation with her boss did not improve.

Neelam worked steadily to develop and strengthen flexible and non-extreme attitudes that facilitated action-based assertion. She first asserted herself with her boss and told him that she would report him if he continued to make racist remarks to her. When he continued to do so, she made a formal complaint against him to HR and presented written evidence that she had collected at the suggestion of her union. The outcome of this complaint was that Neelam was promoted and transferred to another part of the company and her former boss was formally disciplined.

Why Change 'Feels Wrong'

In this final section of the chapter, I will consider the idea that when a person begins to experience psychological change this experience is accompanied by a sense of discomfort. If you think about it, this is inevitable. When a person maintains a problem they experience two things: a sense of discomfort associated with the emotional pain of the problem and a sense of comfort associated with the familiarity of having a problem that has been there for some time. Consequently, when the person does things that bring about change on the problem it is to be expected that they begin to experience discomfort associated with the unfamiliarity of change.

As I sometimes put it: 'If it ain't strange, it ain't change.' This means that when you start to experience psychological change initially it will feel strange. Let me make this point by telling you how I explain the discomfort of change to my clients. Here I am explaining it to Sharon.

Windy: Imagine that you want to play tennis well. You save up your money to get tennis lessons from a professional. On your way to your first lesson, you meet an uncle who tells you that he is a good tennis player and will teach you free of charge. This appeals to you because you get to learn to play tennis and spend your money on other things that you want, so you agree.

So, he teaches you to play tennis, but unfortunately he teaches you to do all the wrong things. You don't know this so you practise diligently and learn many bad habits which become entrenched. Armed with these bad habits, you enter local competitions, but much to your dismay you keep getting beaten easily by other players. Feeling dejected, someone suggests that you go to a tennis professional for a diagnostic session which you do. At that session, the tennis professional diagnoses all your faults, and impressed, you decide to book some sessions with him.

At these sessions, the tennis professional shows you, one at a time, all the things you are doing wrong and demonstrates all the things you need to do to correct these faults. Now when you begin to try to implement a correct shot when you are used to playing it incorrectly, is it going to feel natural?

Sharon: No.

Windy: Why not?

Sharon: Because I would have practised my bad shots so much they would have become habits.

Windy: Therefore, how are you going to feel when you begin to play the correct shots?

Sharon: I am going to feel very uncomfortable.

Windy: So, what attitude will you need to develop towards this discomfort if you are to learn to play the shots correctly and if they are to become second nature to you?

Sharon: I will have to think that it's uncomfortable but it's worth persisting with because I want to play tennis well.

As this interchange shows, change feels bad in that it is almost always associated with the discomfort of unfamiliarity. If you bear this discomfort and do the things that you need to do to solve a problem, be it a tennis problem or a psychological problem, then you will move beyond the strangeness of change and experience eventually the familiarity of change.

*

In the next chapter, I will consider and discuss some of the ideas that people hold about their disturbed feelings and their bad feeling alternatives that lead them to be ambivalent or resistant to change the former in favour of the latter.

28

Of Course I Care, I'm Jealous!

In Chapter 26, I discussed the fact that when people disturb themselves in the first place, they often disturb themselves about their disturbed emotions in the second place. This phenomenon, which is known as meta-emotional disturbance in the professional literature, serves to help perpetuate a person's disturbed feelings because by disturbing himself about his primary disturbed feelings he is impeded from working constructively to change them.

However, people can also have ideas about their disturbed emotions that lead them to be ambivalent about targeting them for change at best or to be resistant to the idea of changing them at worst. If REBT therapists do not understand these ambivalence-creating or resistance-creating ideas then they will not be best placed to help their clients examine these ideas in a way that gives them an opportunity to discuss them fully. In this chapter, I am going to consider the main ideas that people hold about their disturbed emotions that promote such ambivalence or resistance. I will do so for each of the disturbed emotions that I discussed in Chapter 24:

anxiety
depression
shame
guilt
hurt
unhealthy anger
unhealthy jealousy
unhealthy envy

In considering these ideas, I will deal with one or two of the most common doubts, reservations or objections that people express with respect to giving up each of the eight unhealthy negative emotions listed above and to adopting each of the eight alternative healthy negative emotions (or what I called bad feelings in Chapter 27) listed below:

concern (as opposed to anxiety)
sadness (as opposed to depression)
disappointment (as opposed to shame)
remorse (as opposed to guilt)
sorrow (as opposed to hurt)
healthy anger (as opposed to unhealthy anger)
healthy jealousy (as opposed to unhealthy jealousy)
healthy envy (as opposed to unhealthy envy)

What I will do is to list the main doubt or doubts that people express about giving up their disturbed emotion and working towards the healthy alternative. I will then respond to the doubt.

Doubts, Reservations and Objections to Feeling Concern and to Stopping Feeling Anxious

Doubt 1: Anxiety helps to motivate me to do well, while concern doesn't provide me with much motivation. So if I give up feeling anxious in favour of concern, I will lose motivation to do things.

Response

Anxiety can gear up your system and motivate you, but it often does so at a price. Useful motivation comprises arousal that anxiety does provide and reflective thinking which anxiety often impedes. So when you are anxious, you are geared up for action, but can't think clearly about what constitutes productive action. Thus, when you are anxious you are often rushing around like a headless chicken, motivated and geared up enough to take action, but flooded with many, often competing, thoughts about what action to take.

By contrast when you feel concern, you have both the motivation to take action and the presence of mind to think clearly about what constructive action to take. So, if you feel concern as opposed to anxiety then you are motivated to take action, but can take full advantage of that motivation to deal with the threat you are facing in a considered, constructive way. Anxiety may give you the former, but it doesn't give you the latter.

Doubt 2: Anxiety keeps me on my guard, while if I am concerned I am lulled into a false sense of security. So, I need to feel anxious in order to be alert to threat.

Response

It is true that anxiety keeps you on your guard, but it often leads you to overestimate both the presence of threat and the extent of the threat. Thus, if you tend to feel anxious about what people think of you, then, when you meet a new group of people, you tend to think that many of these people will not like you. You may then focus on evidence in the environment that you think confirms your perception (e.g. you may infer that because a person does not smile at you it is evidence that they do not like you) and edit out or distort evidence that is inconsistent with your perception (e.g. you may think that a person being nice to you is evidence that they feel sorry for you). One might say that when you are anxious you lull yourself into a false sense of insecurity.

By contrast, when you feel concerned rather than anxious, you are a lot more realistic in your perception of threat. You tend to see threat when it actually exists and not when it does not exist. Thus, if you tend to feel concerned but not anxious about what people think of you, then, when you meet a new group of people, you tend to think a person does not like you only when they give you just cause to make that conclusion. Otherwise, you think that they are neutral towards you until they get to know you better. You don't necessarily think that everyone will like you until you get evidence to the contrary. This realistic appraisal means that when you are concerned, you do not lull yourself into a false sense of security.

402 Windy Dryden Collected! Strange, But Rational

Doubts, Reservations and Objections to Feeling Sad and To Stopping Feeling Depressed

Doubt 1: Feeling depressed is an appropriate response to a significant loss. Feeling sad minimises the significance of my loss. So in order for me to do justice to my loss, I need to feel depressed.

Response

If you have experienced a significant loss in your life, you may well think that depression is an appropriate response to that loss, but fortunately you would be wrong. I say fortunately here because depression is a disorder of mood that leads to withdrawal from life and despair about the future. This is not a healthy response to loss.

Your doubt about sadness being an appropriate response to a significant loss is based on the idea that sadness is of mild or moderate intensity. And that such a 'low-level' of intensity does not do justice to a 'high-level' of significant loss. However, sadness can be an intense emotion and can enable you to digest and adjust to your loss without withdrawal from life or despair about the future. As such, sadness is both an appropriate and a healthy emotional response to your significant loss and one that does full justice to the significance of that loss.

Doubt 2: Feeling depressed is evidence that I am sensitive, whereas feeling sad means that I am less sensitive. Thus, my depression enables me to keep my sensitivity.

Response

Luckily you are wrong about this. Depression is a response to a loss from your personal domain that is based on rigid/extreme attitudes towards that loss. Sadness is a response to the same loss that is based on flexible/non-extreme attitudes. As I have shown you in previous chapters, unconstructive attitudes are characterised by rigid and extreme thinking. Thus, rather than being a sensitive response to a significant loss, depression is more accurately viewed as an oversensitive response to that loss. On the other hand, constructive attitudes are characterised by flexible and non-extreme thinking. This means, in this context, that the strength of your constructive attitude will vary according to the significance of your loss. Thus, when you experience a significant loss, the strength of your constructive attitude will be great and thus you will react sensitively (rather than insensitively or oversensitively) to your loss. In short then, sadness is a better sign of your sensitivity than depression which is a sign of your oversensitivity. Thus, you will not lose your sensitivity if you work towards feeling sad rather than depressed.

Doubts, Reservations and Objections to Feeling Disappointed and to Stopping Feeling Ashamed

Doubt 1: Because I have done something that has seriously broken an accepted social code, it is appropriate for me to feel ashamed about what I have done. Feeling disappointed about my behaviour doesn't do it enough justice.

Response

When you feel ashamed about your behaviour that you say seriously broke an accepted social code, you are holding a self-devaluation attitude. You hold that you are an inadequate person for what you have done. According to REBT theory this is neither an appropriate nor a healthy response to your socially inappropriate behaviour because you are rating your entire 'self' on the basis of your behaviour (see Chapter 28 for a discussion of self-devaluation attitudes). Remember also that you can feel intensely disappointed about the way you have behaved without devaluing yourself for your behaviour and we argue in REBT that this intense but healthy feeling does do justice to your socially inappropriate behaviour.

Doubt 2: The prospect of feeling ashamed about falling short of my ideal helps me to reach my ideal. The prospect of feeling disappointed about falling short of my ideal doesn't motivate me in the same way. So I need to have the threat of feeling ashamed to help me to maintain my high standards of behaviour.

Response

This doubt is based on the idea that the threat of devaluing yourself in a shame-based way is an effective way of motivating yourself to achieve your ideal. The prospect of feeling ashamed does have some motivating properties in this sense, but more often it impedes your striving to reach your ideal. As with anxiety, shame (and the threat of experiencing shame) frequently affects your task-oriented behaviour by hijacking your attention with shame-related thoughts. It is difficult to focus on what you are doing (a crucial feature of high-level task performance) when your mind is flooded with shame-related thoughts.

When you are motivated by the prospect of feeling disappointed rather than ashamed about falling short of your ideal, you are able to concentrate on what you need to do to achieve your ideal (which you will do because it is important for you to achieve your ideal) without the interference of shame-based self-devaluing thoughts hijacking your attention.

You may not have had the experience of being motivated by the prospect of feeling disappointed about failing to achieve your ideal, but this does not mean that it is not a more effective motivator than the threat of feeling shame in the same circumstances. It is a more effective motivator, but you need to practise acting on your flexible/non-extreme attitudes to appreciate this point.

Doubts, Reservations and Objections to Feeling Remorse and to Stopping Feeling Guilt

Doubt 1: Feeling guilty about wrongdoing helps prevent me from breaking my moral code. Feeling remorse about wrongdoing wouldn't have the same effect on me. So I need to feel guilty to keep me on the straight and narrow.

Response

When you feel guilty about doing something wrong, you think that you are a bad person for breaking your moral code. When you think that you are a bad person, you make it more rather than less likely that you will do bad things. Why? Because if you are a bad person, how can you fail to act badly, now and in the future? You can't. On the other hand, when you feel remorseful, but not guilty about breaking your moral code, you do not think of yourself as a bad person. Rather, you accept yourself as a fallible human being and as such you are capable of doing bad, good and neutral things. Since this self-acceptance attitude acknowledges you are capable of acting morally, you are more likely to act well than you are when you depreciate yourself as a bad person. Thus, remorse is more likely to keep you on the straight and narrow than guilt.

Doubt 2: If I don't feel guilty about my wrongdoing then I might turn into a psychopath. Guilt is evidence that I have a conscience.

Response

You seem to think that you have two choices in the moral domain: either to feel guilty or be a psychopath. However, there is a third, more constructive option – to feel remorse. Let me illustrate what I mean by referring to the following scenarios:

In each case I want you to imagine that you have broken a generally accepted moral code.

1. I have done something wrong – I am a bad person for doing wrong (Guilt)
2. I haven't done anything wrong (Psychopathy)

3. I have done something wrong – I am a fallible person who has done wrong (Remorse)

In the guilt scenario, you demonstrate that you have a conscience by acknowledging that you have done something wrong, but you needlessly disturb yourself by globally rating yourself as a bad person. In the psychopathy scenario, you demonstrate that you have no conscience in that you do not acknowledge that you have done anything wrong. In the remorse scenario as in the guilt scenario, you also demonstrate that you have a conscience, but unlike in the guilt scenario, you do not needlessly disturb yourself in that you accept yourself as a complex, fallible human being capable of good and bad acts (as well as neutral acts).

Thus, remorse prevents you from turning into a psychopath, but it also prevents you from needlessly disturbing yourself.

Doubts, Reservations and Objections to Feeling Sorrow and to Stopping Feeling Hurt

Doubt: Feeling hurt when I feel betrayed is perfectly normal. So why should I give it up? I don't understand what feeling sorrowful about being betrayed means.

Response
Your doubt touches upon the issue that in the English language we do not have very clear, generally agreed terms that keenly distinguish between unhealthy negative emotions (like hurt) and healthy negative emotions (like sorrow). Consequently, the terms that I use (e.g. hurt versus sorrow) may not be meaningful to you. If this is the case, you can come up with your own words once you have understood the major differences between (what I call) hurt and sorrow. Let me use a common example to make my point.

Imagine that you have told a friend something in confidence and they have agreed to keep your secret to themself. You then discover that they have revealed your secret to several other people. You correctly conclude that your friend has betrayed you. Now when you feel hurt about this betrayal:

1. You hold one or more of the following rigid and extreme attitudes:
   (i) My friend absolutely should not have betrayed me
   (ii) It's terrible that they betrayed me
   (iii) I can't bear the fact that they betrayed me
   (iv) I have been treated in a way that I didn't deserve. Poor me!

2. You tend to act in the following ways:
   (i) You withdraw from your friend and (to a lesser extent) the other people they have told
   (ii) You refuse to talk to your friend and (to a lesser extent) the others when they approach you
   (iii) If you do talk to your friend, you do so aggressively
   (iv) You plan to exact revenge on your friend

3. You tend to think in the following ways:
   (i) 'People are not trustworthy'
   (ii) 'I'll never confide in anyone again'
   (iii) You tend to think about the betrayal obsessively

Now when you feel sorrowful about this betrayal:

1. You hold one or more of the following flexible and non-extreme attitudes:
   (i) It is very undesirable for my friend to have betrayed me, but I'm not exempt from being treated in this way, and nor do I have to be exempt
   (ii) It's very unfortunate that they betrayed me, but it isn't the end of the world
   (iii) My friend betraying me is difficult to bear, but I can bear it and it's worth bearing. I am willing to bear it and I am going to do so.
   (iv) I have been treated in a way that I didn't deserve. This behaviour is poor but I'm not a poor pitiable creature

2. You tend to act in the following ways:
    (i) You are wary about approaching your friend and (to a lesser extent) the others they have told, but are prepared to do so
    (ii) You are prepared to talk to your friend to discover why they did it and to tell her your feelings and to the others involved when they approach you
    (iii) If you do talk to your friend, you do so assertively rather than aggressively
    (iv) You don't plan to exact revenge on your friend, but you are reluctant to tell her any more secrets until you have repaired your relationship and they have regained your trust

3. You tend to think in the following ways:
    (i) 'Some people are not trustworthy, but others are'
    (ii) 'I will confide in someone again. I won't tar everyone with the same brush. But I will be more circumspect'
    (iii) You tend to think about the betrayal from time to time, but not obsessively

From the above, I hope that you can see that while hurt might be a statistically normal response to being betrayed, it is not a particularly healthy one. Also, I hope that you can now understand what constitutes sorrow as a response to betrayal and that it is, from a longer-term perspective, a healthier response.

Doubts, Reservations and Objections to Feeling Healthy Anger and to Stopping Feeling Unhealthy Anger

Doubt 1: If someone crosses me I'd be a wimp if I responded with what you call healthy anger. The other person is a bastard and needs to be taught a very severe lesson. So, don't ask me to give up my unhealthy anger.

Response

At the heart of your criticism is the idea that a response to the person who you say has crossed you that is based on healthy anger is bound to be a weak response and would prove that you were a wimp if you made it. Responses based on unhealthy anger tend to be aggressive and show no respect for the other person. They may well 'teach the other person a lesson' but either provoke an aggressive response back or intimidate the other person so that they are scared of you. On the other hand, responses that are based on healthy anger are strong, but respectful. These responses tend to be assertive in nature and provoke a dialogue between you and the other person and tend to elicit a respectful response from the other person.

So, healthy anger in the form of assertion is not a weak response. It is both strong and yields better interpersonal results for you. So you will not be 'a wimp' if you work towards healthy anger.

Doubt 2: I feel very powerful when I am unhealthily angry. I don't get that same buzz with healthy anger. So, if I give up my unhealthy anger, I'll lose that buzz.

Response

Yes, when you feel unhealthy anger, you may well experience a sense of power and while healthy anger will give you a sense of power it may well not be as intense as with unhealthy anger. So, you may well lose the intense buzz that accompanies unhealthy anger if you work towards healthy anger. However, this is a price that is probably worth paying for two reasons. First, as I discussed in my response to the previous doubt, healthy anger yields more productive longer-term results than unhealthy anger and second, the power that you experience with unhealthy anger is uncontrolled rather than controlled as is the case with healthy anger. So, the question you need to ask yourself is this? Are you willing to give up the intense but short-term buzz that you get with unhealthy anger in exchange for the better results that you get with healthy anger?

Doubts, Reservations and Objections to Feeling Healthy Jealousy and to Stopping Feeling Unhealthy Jealousy

Doubt 1: Unhealthy jealousy motivates me to do things that reassure me that my partner isn't having an affair. If I give it up, then I won't know for sure what's happening and I can't bear not knowing.

Response

Your unhealthy jealousy partly stems from the attitude that you need reassurance that your partner isn't having an affair. If you then give up your unhealthy jealousy, you will have done so by examining and changing your rigid/extreme attitude that you need to know that your partner isn't involved with anyone else and not knowing what's happening is unbearable. When you work towards feeling healthy jealousy (which you will experience only when you have clear-cut evidence that your partner is having an affair with someone else), you will still face not knowing for sure what your partner is up to, but you will able to bear this and learn not to seek reassurance, which in turn will enable you to think more objectively about what your partner is doing when they are out of contact.

Doubt 2: My unhealthy jealousy is a sign of how much I care for my partner.

Response

When you are unhealthily jealous, you are correct in saying that this may be based on caring. After all, if you did not care for your partner, you may not be that concerned about losing them. However, in the main, unhealthy jealousy is based on disturbance not healthy caring. When you are unhealthily jealous, you think the worst of your partner. You think that they will be off with any person as soon as someone comes along. Is that a sign of caring? When you are unhealthily jealous, you may cross-examine your partner about their movements and who they have spoken to during the day and about what, you may follow them surreptitiously or set traps for them. Are these signs of caring?

No, I hope you can see that unhealthy jealousy and the behaviours that it leads to are signs of rigid/extreme attitudes rather than evidence of how much you care for your partner.

Doubts, Reservations and Objections to Feeling Healthy Envy and to Stopping Feeling Unhealthy Envy

Doubt: What you call unhealthy envy motivates me to get the things that others have that I want. If I give up feeling this kind of envy then I won't try to get what I want.

Response

Your point that unhealthy envy motivates you to get what you want may be true on occasion, but when you get it you soon move on to coveting something else that someone has that you don't have. In other words, you don't get over your problem of unhealthy envy by pursuing what you don't have. In fact, the more you act according to the attitudes that underpin your unhealthy envy, the more you operate according to this unhealthy negative emotion.

Your implication that healthy envy won't motivate you to get what you want is false because in healthy envy you have the desire to get what you want and this desire will motivate you. Also, when you are motivated by healthy envy, you are pursuing something that you genuinely want and that when you get it you don't immediately switch your attention to coveting other things that others have that you don't have. So healthy envy is motivating and helps you to pursue things that you genuinely want and won't get tired of as soon as you have obtained them.

*

As I have said throughout this book, according to REBT theory, rigid attitudes are at the core of emotional disturbance. However, the language of rigid demands sometimes causes problems. One such problem concerns the many meanings of the word 'should' which I will fully discuss in the following chapter.

29

Shoulds to the Right of Me, Shoulds to the Left of Me ...

As we have seen throughout this book, Rational Emotive Behaviour Therapy (REBT) theory holds that at the root of psychological disturbance lies a set of rigid/extreme attitudes. It further holds that at the core of this root (if this is not mixing metaphors!) lies a rigid attitude. So the essence of psychological disturbance is rigidity.

So far, so good – until we consider the language of rigidity. Rigid attitudes that are at the core of psychological disturbance can be expressed using the following terms, to name but a few:

- Unconditional musts
- Absolute shoulds
- Absolute have to's
- Absolute got to's

You will note that I have used the terms 'unconditional' and 'absolute' in the above list. This is to underscore that I am referring to concepts that are rigid in nature. This is the central point of this chapter: that REBT therapists are only interested in targeting absolute shoulds for change and not any other shoulds. And herein lies the problem, because the word 'should' has several different meanings and if the therapist is not careful they may inadvertently try to encourage the client to change a non-absolute should which may be perfectly legitimate in the context in which the client has been using it.

In this chapter, therefore, I will consider ten different meanings of the word 'should' so that you know what they are when you encounter them. Such knowledge will help you to only target absolute shoulds – your own or anyone else's – for change.

The Recommendatory Should

If I say to you 'You should try the Italian restaurant that has just opened in town', what do I mean? Well, it has the word 'should' in it so am I demanding that you do so and damning you to hell if you don't? Of course not! What I mean by this is that because I enjoyed it when I ate there, I recommend that you eat there as well. As such this 'should' can be referred to as the 'recommendatory should'. It is not rigid, nor absolute, nor unconditional. It merely puts forward a suggestion to you based on my own experience which you are free to act on or ignore. If a therapist heard this, treated it as absolute should and began to examine it, the person making the recommendation would be very perplexed about the challenge. They would rightly claim that they were not being rigid, merely making a helpful recommendation to a friend.

The Advisory Should

Imagine that you have been out late several times in a row and as a consequence you have had less sleep than you require. A friend telephones you and asks you to go out with him for a drink that evening. Foreseeing another late night, you are tempted, but you decline. Your friend tries to get you to change your mind, but you hold firm saying: 'Thanks for the offer, I would really like to join you for a drink, but I really should get an early night tonight.' It is clear that you are not making a demand here. Thus, you are not saying that you absolutely have to get an early night and that you are damnable and/or that it is awful if you don't. Thus, your should is not absolute.

So, what do you mean when you say, in this context, that 'I really should get an early night'? You mean that you have determined that this is the best course of action for you to take in the circumstances and on this occasion you have decided to take your own advice. Now, you could easily decide to ignore this advice and go out, but whether you follow your own advice or not, this does not change the nature of the 'should' as you are using it with yourself.

I call this should the 'advisory' should, because it involves the person giving others or themself advice. This advice usually involves what the person considers the best course of action for self and/or others. When it is used with others the person using this 'should' may well be saying 'this is what I would do if I was in your shoes'.

Advisory shoulds, therefore, usually – although not always – outline the healthiest option for the person. However, since humans frequently do not take the healthiest course of action, advisory shoulds are often not followed. Thus, we often say things like 'I know I should go home and study ..., but I am going to stay and have one more drink' or 'I know I shouldn't ... but I am going to have one more of these delicious cakes'. Thus, advisory shoulds (or should nots) often point to what is in our longer-term interests and when we don't follow them, it is often due to a philosophy of unbearability attitudes.

The Hopeful Should

Similar to the advisory should is what might be termed the 'hopeful should'. This should points to what you consider to be desirable or undesirable and outlines what you hope will or will not happen based on these preferences. It lacks the advisory nature of the advisory should. In particular, the hopeful should is directed to life conditions which may be deemed to be desirable or undesirable, but which fall outside the domain of what is advisable. The hopeful should tends not to be based on blind faith however. Rather it is based on some evidence that the hoped-for condition will happen, but there is also some doubt in the person's mind.

So when I say that hopefully it should be sunny in Bermuda when I go on holiday there, I am outlining the conditions that I would like to exist at that point. I am also saying that research has shown me that it is likely to be sunny at the time I am going there, but it may not be. However, I am certainly not advising that it be sunny in Bermuda because there is nobody to advise!

Also, as briefly noted above, when I hold a hopeful should towards others, I am not advising them, particularly when I don't have contact with them at the time when I hold the hopeful should. Here are a few examples of other-directed hopeful shoulds which lack the advisory nature of the advisory should.

- *My teacher hopefully should give me good grades*
- *If I look nice, the doorman should hopefully let me into the club*
- *If I work hard, my boss should hopefully reward me*
- *If I refrain from shouting at him, hopefully he should refrain from shouting at me*

In all of these examples, the person is indicating that there is a reasonable chance of getting what they want or of avoiding what they do not want, but it is not cut and dried in that there is still a chance that the person won't get what they want or will get what they do not want – hence, the hope.

Finally, hopeful shoulds can be directed towards oneself and when they are, they again have the same two qualities: (a) there is a reasonably good chance of me getting what I want, and (b) there is some doubt about this happening. This is shown in the following examples of self-directed hopeful shoulds.

- *Hopefully, I should pass my exam if I study hard*
- *Hopefully, if I brush my teeth, I should be able to avoid large dental bills*
- *I should hopefully get to heaven if I am a good Christian*

The Preferential Should

In Chapter 23 of this book, I outlined the two components of a non-dogmatic preference (also known as a flexible attitude). I said there that such an attitude has an 'asserted preference' component (e.g. 'I want it to happen ...') and a negated demand component ('... but it doesn't have to happen'). I see the preferential should as being synonymous with the asserted preference component as in the phrase 'preferably this should happen'. The preferential should is different from the hopeful should in that while the latter is based on some evidence that the desired condition may well occur, although there is some doubt that it will, when you hold a preferential should you are indicating what you want whether or not it is likely to occur. For example, if you say 'Preferably I, rather than Jay-Z, should have married Beyoncé', you are indicating what you would have liked to have happened despite the fact that it would be highly unlikely that you would have fulfilled your desire.

As with other preferences, the stronger your preferential should is the more likely it is that you will transform it into an absolute should, for example, if you say, 'Beating you at chess is very important to me and therefore I must do so.' However, if I say I mildly want to beat you at chess, I am far less likely to transform my desire into a demand, as the strength of my desire is weak.

The Ideal Should

The ideal should refers to the situation that where ideal conditions exist then 'x' (whatever 'x' is) should happen. So, when I say that this train should arrive at 8pm tonight, I am not demanding that it absolutely has to. Rather, I am saying that if ideal conditions exist then the train will arrive at 8pm tonight.

I once had a client who had come to me for 'anger management'. He reported to me in one of our counselling sessions that he would get furious with people getting in his way from his office to the train station. He had calculated that it 'should' take 18 minutes from door to door and therefore, he said, that is how long it 'should' take. After some discussion, we decided that he meant the following: 'Because it ideally should take me 18 minutes from my office to the station, therefore it absolutely should take me 18 minutes.' What was particularly interesting in this case was that the ideal conditions that my client had calculated should (ideally) exist were where there were no people around and all traffic lights were in his favour! As is often the case, ideal conditions rarely existed and he was continually faced with the disconfirmation of his ideal. But he continually demanded that the ideal must exist with predictably unhealthy results! This case shows that one can hold absolute shoulds about ideal shoulds (as well as other shoulds, as we shall see).

The Deserving Should

When a person uses the deserving should they specify what 'should' occur on the basis of their sense of justice or fairness. For example, the statement 'Campbell should be imprisoned for five years for what he did' specifies a relationship between what Campbell did and what the person thinks should happen if justice were to prevail. It goes without saying that the sense of justice is subjective and will vary from person to person. 'He should get five years for what he did', 'No, I think should be hanged for it!' is an exchange between two people indicating different ideas of justice-based shoulds.

When a person disturbs himself about a deserving should not being met, this indicates that the person also holds an absolute should. Let's consider Harry who has worked very hard for a promotion. The day before he was to find out whether or not he had been promoted, Harry told his friend, 'Well, I should be promoted if there is any justice in the world.' When he found out that he hadn't been promoted, Harry felt hurt and angry. He did so not because he did not get what he believed he should (or deserved to) get, but because he implicitly believed that justice (as he saw it) absolutely should have prevailed! His boss obviously believed that Harry should not have been promoted in the sense that they considered that Harry did not deserve promotion.

The Predictive Should

Every time Naomi went to her mother for support, she got criticised instead. Her mother told her that she needed to stand on her own two feet and refused to offer any comfort to her daughter. From Naomi's perspective, she was standing on her own two feet, but was looking for motherly support and an opportunity to discuss her concerns and get what she saw was appropriate encouragement from her mother. Needless to say she did not get it. Naomi would disturb herself about this state of her affairs because (a) she held an ideal should about the situation: 'My mother is supposed to give me support' and (b) she brought an absolute should to her ideal should: 'My mother must do what she is supposed to do.'

If only Naomi held a predictive should in this situation she would have been much less likely to disturb herself. A predictive should involves, as the term suggests, a prediction about the future based on the reality of the past. Naomi had accumulated much data to indicate that every time she went to her mother for support then her mother criticised her. These data strongly suggest that the next time Naomi goes to her mother for support, she will receive criticism instead. Thus, Naomi would have been wiser to say: 'If I go to my mother for support, she should criticise me.' While this statement sounds strange, it does accord with the most probable outcome based on past data.

Now it is important to realise that predictive shoulds are best regarded as hypotheses about the future that can be disconfirmed. Let's suppose that Naomi's mother sees a play about an unsupportive mother, sees herself in the mother character and resolves from that point onwards to be supportive to Naomi rather than critical of her. If she does so then Naomi's predictive should, based as it is on past experience, will be disconfirmed.

The Conditional Should

The next meaning of the word 'should' that I want to discuss and illustrate is what might be called the conditional should. Here, certain conditions are specified that have to be met if a result is to be achieved. There is no sense that these conditions have to be met in an absolute sense, just that there will be one set of consequences if they are met and another set of consequences if they are not met. Here are a few examples of conditional shoulds:

* *You should have a passport if you want to fly abroad*
* *I overslept and missed my first appointment at work. I should have set the alarm to wake myself up.*
* *You should have a first degree to get onto the Masters programme*

Sometimes, there are exceptions to the 'conditional should' rule. When this occurs the word 'normally' qualifies the conditional should. Thus, if I tell a prospective student that he should normally have a degree to get onto the Masters programme, I am saying that there may be some exceptions to this rule and he may or may not qualify as such an exception.

The Empirical Should

Sometimes when I am teaching the different meanings of the word to a professional audience, I say to them that in my view the Holocaust should have happened. The discomfort in the room can be palpably felt as the audience seems to bridle at my remarks.

I deliberately use the phrase 'the Holocaust should have happened' to get people's attention before I explain that the 'should' in this statement is what we call in REBT theory the 'empirical should'. The empirical should here indicates that all the conditions were in place for the Holocaust to happen and therefore empirically the Holocaust should have happened.

Actually, this point becomes more acceptable to people if appropriate adverbs are introduced. In this case, I might say: 'Tragically, all the conditions were in place for the Holocaust to happen and sadly and regretfully therefore the Holocaust should have happened.'

In summary, the empirical should makes the obvious point that reality should be reality. This is illustrated by the statement: If we take two particles of hydrogen and add one particle of oxygen we should [empirically] get water.

The Absolute Should

I will end this chapter in a similar manner to the way I started it by focusing on the absolute should. This tenth meaning of the word 'should' is the only should that REBT theory argues is involved in the client's disturbance. As the descriptor 'absolute' indicates, this should is rigid and gives the person no room to manoeuvre. As a result, when you hold an absolute should you disturb yourself when you don't get what you believe you absolutely should get and you are vulnerable to self-disturbance when you do get what you absolutely should get because the demanded conditions might change.

*

In closing, let me reiterate that it is important for therapists to clarify the meaning of their clients' shoulds. It is only absolute shoulds that should advisedly be targeted for change. In this context, it is important to appreciate that people may hold absolute shoulds about other kinds of shoulds (e.g. 'Because my father ideally should be nice to me therefore he absolutely should do so') and in such cases therapists are advised to clarify the different shoulds being held, carefully help their clients to differentiate their absolute shoulds from the other kinds of shoulds and target only the former for change.

Sometimes when people hold shoulds, whether they are preferential or absolute, and they do not get what they believe they should get, they hold an attitude towards themselves. In the next chapter, I will discuss the two possible stances one can take towards the self: self-devaluation and unconditional self-acceptance.

30

How Humanistic Are You?

The attitude that you take towards human beings is an important determinant of how you feel about yourself and others in a range of situations. It is useful to stand back and consider the attitude towards self and others advocated by Rational Emotive Behaviour Therapy (REBT) theory as this is the attitude towards humans that at first glance seems attractive, but on closer inspection raises a lot of issues for people in its application and these issues make it difficult for some to embrace the view of humans on offer.

I will begin this discussion by considering what it means to be human.

What It Means To Be Human

Let's consider humans and see what we can say about them that is beyond dispute and that will not change until they die. I believe that we can say the following about humans which conveys what it means to be human. First of all, it is worth noting, although it is a truism to say, that once born human, people will remain human for the rest of their lives. It is very unlikely that any person will wake up one day as if in a Kafkaesque short story and metamorphose into a verminous bug. No, once a person becomes human, they will remain human until they die.

1. Humans are complex

Humans are complex organisms. While I will consider this complexity by considering humans' functioning in different systems as if these systems were separate, in reality, humans function holistically and this functioning reflects a very complex interaction between the following systems:

Cognitive

Humans' cognitive system is itself complex and comprises descriptive thoughts, inferences, beliefs, attitudes and values and these cognitive subsystems reciprocally influence one another.

Cognitions can either be verbal in form or occur as images. When they appear as images, these often contain meaning that gives them their influence. Please note that while some would consider spiritual matters to warrant a separate section, I consider such matters to be a reflection of a person's beliefs, attitudes and values and thus, I include them here.

Behavioural

Humans' behavioural system compromises overt actions and action tendencies. The latter are, in effect, urges to behave which are not acted on for one reason or another. While humans' behaviour occurs in social and non-social contexts, even when other people are not physically present, their psychological presence exerts an influence on our behaviour. If you watch someone talking on the phone, you will see that they are engaging in similar non-verbal behaviour to what they would if the other person were present.

Emotional

Humans' emotional system contains our ability to experience different emotions, both negative and positive in tone. Within the negative emotional dimension, it is possible to identify at least eight negative emotions which can take a healthy form (healthy negative emotions or HNEs) or an unhealthy form (unhealthy negative emotions or UNEs). In Chapter 27, I called the former, 'bad feelings' and the latter 'disturbed feelings'.

It should be noted that healthy negative emotions do not have universally agreed names. Having made this point, the following are eight pairs of negative emotions with the UNE listed first:

Unhealthy negative emotions (UNES)	Healthy negative emotions (HNEs)
Anxiety	Concern
Depression	Sadness
Guilt	Remorse
Shame	Disappointment
Hurt	Sorrow
Unhealthy anger	Healthy anger
Unhealthy jealousy	Healthy jealousy
Unhealthy envy	Healthy envy

Within the positive emotion dimension, one can also identify emotions that can take a healthy form (e.g. satisfaction) or an unhealthy form (e.g. mania).

Personality traits

Humans can be placed along a series of continua of personality traits. While these traits are relatively stable, they are not fixed for all time and changes in personality dispositions do happen, but when they do, they tend not to be profound. Thus, while it is possible for people to become less introverted, someone who scores highly on introversion will not usually change to become very extrovert.

There are numerous personality traits that humans can be said to have. Here I will list five 'super-traits' which are known in psychology as the 'Big 5' (e.g. McCrae & Costa, 2002). These represent an emerging consensus in psychology concerning how personality can be best viewed in terms of a collection of traits. I will first list the 'Big 5' and then also list the six subordinate traits (or facets) that are used to measure each super-trait. A person can be located on a continuum for each super-trait and rated for each facet.

1. Neuroticism ⟷ Emotional Stability
   - Anxiety (tense)
   - Angry hostility (irritable)
   - Depression (not contented)
   - Self-consciousness (shy)
   - Impulsiveness (moody)
   - Vulnerability (not self-confident)

2. Extraversion ⟷ Introversion
   - Warmth (outgoing)
   - Gregariousness (sociable)
   - Assertiveness (forceful)
   - Activity (energetic)
   - Excitement-seeking (adventurous)
   - Positive emotions (enthusiastic)

3. Openness to Experience ⟷ Closedness to Experience
   - Fantasy (imaginative)
   - Aesthetics (artistic)
   - Feelings (excitable)
   - Actions (wide interests)
   - Ideas (curious)
   - Values (unconventional)

4. Agreeableness ⟷ Disagreeableness
   - Trust (forgiving)
   - Straightforwardness (not demanding)
   - Altruism (warm)
   - Compliance (not stubborn)
   - Modesty (not show-off)
   - Tender-mindedness (sympathetic)

5. Conscientiousness ⟷ Lack of conscientiousness
   - Competence (efficient)
   - Order (organised)
   - Dutifulness (not careless)
   - Achievement striving (thorough)
   - Self-discipline (not lazy)
   - Deliberation (not impulsive)

Talents and abilities

In the same way that people can be placed on continua of personality characteristics, they can also be placed on continua according to what talents and abilities they have. When we say that a person has a talent for something, we tend to mean that they easily show that they are good at something. They may well need to be trained to make the most of such talent, but that training builds on something that is already there in the person. Interestingly, when we talk of a person having 'raw' talent, we are saying that the person shows talent at something without having received any substantial training in the talent. We also mean that without such training the person will not fully realise their potential.

If we take two children with differential talent for playing the piano for example, we will note that the child with talent learns the piano far more easily than the child without talent. With equal tuition the child with talent will progress further, with greater ease and far more quickly than the child without talent. The extent to which the child with talent will realise their potential depends on that child developing and maintaining a disciplined approach to learning the piano over time. It may be that a child with lesser talent develops more skill at playing the piano in the longer run than the child with greater talent if they devote more time to learning and practising what they learn than their more talented colleague.

People will generally demonstrate greater inherent talent in some areas than in others, although a small number of people may demonstrate such talent in a great many areas and others will demonstrate such talent in only a very small number of areas. One of my students once told me that he realised that he wasn't very talented at anything, so he accepted that he had to work hard for what he achieved in life. This is exactly what he did, and he went a long way to fulfilling his limited potential.

It is important to realise that the expression of talents and abilities is what counts in life, and this is done through the development and maintenance of behaviourally-based skills underpinned by tacit cognitive processes. It may be comforting to know that one has a raw talent for something, but one is usually happier if one translates one's talents into behaviourally-based skills.

Physiological functioning

Humans are capable of a full range of physiological responses in emotional episodes and particularly when they are experiencing an unhealthy emotion (such as anxiety). Thus, when they are anxious, humans may shake, sweat, go blotchy, experience an urge to urinate, their heart may beat faster or they may experience symptoms in their stomach. However, it is unlikely that they will experience all these at once.

Bodily aspects

In one episode of *Star Trek: The Next Generation*, an alien described humans as 'ugly bags of mostly water'. Such a description focuses on our bodies (bags) and its constituents (mostly water) and indeed, without our bodies we would die and no longer be human. So, our bodies are a central part of being human. While we have a tacit understanding of the prototypical features of our bodies (i.e. normally we have two eyes, two ears, one nose, one head etc.), we also recognise, often with some disgust, that it is possible to be human and have a body which in some respect(s) is very different from the prototype (i.e. one ear, no nose, more than ten toes). In times gone by such people were regarded as 'freaks' and some would earn a living from being a 'freak'. Even though it is politically incorrect to regard such humans as 'freaks', our feelings of disgust often reflect our unexpressed views that people who differ radically from the prototype are not quite human.

As I say our bodies and its aspects are important to us. We tend not to think about our bodies when they are in good working order, but when something goes wrong, we do focus on the aspect that has gone wrong and take steps to remedy whatever it is that is wrong either by taking appropriate self-care steps or by seeking help.

We become very attached to an aspect of our bodies when this aspect is threatened. If you ask someone how central their big toe is to them, they will probably reply that it is not very central. However, you are likely to get a very different answer if you threaten to cut the person's toe off!

Sensations

It is generally agreed that humans have five main senses: touch, taste, sight, hearing and smell. Other writers argue that additional senses include balance, temperature, kinaesthetic sense and pain. Human beings differ to the extent to which we experience sensations within these modalities. However, all humans can be profiled on these senses so that an individualised profile can be developed for each person concerning how powerful their experience is in each of these sensory domains.

2. Humans are fallible

There is a song by the group Human League entitled 'Human' which includes these lyrics: 'I'm only human, born to make mistakes'. Fallibility is an inherent design feature of humans which, as far as we know, will always be a defining feature of being human. As the rational psychiatrist Maxie C. Maultsby Jr. once said: 'Humans have an incurable error-making tendency.' It is ironic, then, that so many people strive to be perfect since they will rarely reach perfection or if they do, it will be fleeting. Torvill and Dean, the British ice skaters who won the Olympic gold medal for ice dancing in 1984 did so by being awarded perfect scores by the judges on both technical ability and artistic merit. However, would they have received perfect scores from the judges if they had to dance the same routine immediately afterwards? This is doubtful as fatigue would have set in and their level of concentration would probably have been less focused the second time around.

Indeed, it is ironic to note that striving for enduring perfection rather than for fleeting performance perfection is itself evidence of fallibility as it is a mistake to strive for enduring perfection and thus the person who does so is demonstrating his or her fallibility!

3. Humans are unique

'You are unique. Just like everyone else.' This humorous quip does point to something serious: that while we share uniqueness at the conceptual level, we differ from one another at the level of the individual. As the song goes: 'There will never be another you'.

Let's consider the uniqueness of a specific individual and imagine that this individual was cloned at birth. Would the person still be unique and therefore distinct from their clone? I think the answer would be 'yes', for although the person and their clone would share the same genetic substrate, they would have different experiences and these would have some differential impact on the person and their clone.

4. Humans are constantly in flux

One unalterable fact is that from the day we are born until the day we die, human beings are in flux. We are constantly changing. Now, certain things about us change more than others. For example, while we can change our gender by surgery, we cannot as yet alter the chromosomal structure that determines our gender. On the other hand, we can change the way we think more easily, particularly about matters in which we have a strong personal investment. While our personality traits probably have a large biological substrate, we can change ourselves within these constraints. REBT is based on the theory of soft determinism which means that change is possible within biological constraints. Thus, although you will experience continuity in your identity, you are not the same person now as you were, say 20 years ago.

What Stance Can We Best Take Towards Humans?

I have devoted a lot of space in this chapter to considering what it means to be human, particularly focusing on what is common among humans. I have done so because when we come to consider what stance we can best take towards humans, it is important to base this discussion on a keen understanding of human nature.

Can humans be rated?

Perhaps the most common stance that we take towards ourselves and others is based on the idea that it is possible to assign a global rating to a person. If you listen carefully to what people say about themselves and others, then such ratings are easily identified. Here are a few that you may have heard:

- *I'm worthless*
- *They are a bad person*
- *I would be a better person if I had worked harder*
- *They are a complete idiot*
- *They are scum*

While it is obviously possible to assign global ratings to humans, I want to argue here when we do so we do the following:

1. We are ignoring the truth about humans
2. We are being illogical
3. We achieve some possible benefits from doing so, but in the main the consequences of rating people are largely negative

Let me consider these points one at a time.

Rating people is false

When we rate people, we use a global rating to evaluate an organism of great complexity. In doing so we are not reflecting the truth about humans. For how can we legitimately use a single global rating to reflect the complexity of humans? The answer is that we cannot.

Let me explain why by considering one of the person-rating statements presented above, in this case a self-devaluation statement.

1. Self-devaluation: It is false to devalue the 'self'

When I say that I am worthless (which is a common form of self-devaluation) I am saying that my total being has no worth at all. I am implying that I can rate all the different aspects that comprise me as a person and assign that complexity a single rating of worthlessness. Can I do that in a way that reflects the truth about me as a person? The answer is a resounding 'No'! As I explained in the section on 'What it means to be a person', I have had numerous cognitions in my lifetime, acted in many ways, experienced many emotions, have a myriad of different personality characteristics and talents/abilities. In addition, I have experienced an unquantifiable number of sensations. My body is a highly complex 'bag' and my physiological functioning is complex. If it were true that I was worthless, then I would be a single cell amoeba whose cell was worthless. I hope that I have made the point that when I say that I am worthless, I have made an evaluation of myself that does not reflect the truth about me as a highly complex being, which defies the legitimate applicability of a single rating to account for my complexity. Even if I could apply such a rating, as soon as I apply it, it would be out of date because of the fact that I would have changed and had additional thoughts, feelings and behaviours that would have to be rated and included in the evaluation of my 'self'.

Also, when I say that I am worthless it is usually as a result of one or more of four situations:

a. I have done something that I believe I absolutely should not have done (e.g. *I absolutely should not have let my father down. I am a bad person for doing so.*)

b. I have failed to do something that I believe I have absolutely should have done (e.g. *I failed my exam which I absolutely should not have done. I did so and this proves that I am a failure.*)

c. Something happened to me that I believe absolutely should not have happened (e.g. *My friend criticised me which they absolutely should not have done. Their criticism proves that I am unlikeable.*)

d. Something did not happen to me that I believe absolutely should have happened (e.g. *My friends did not ask me to join them. They absolutely should have asked me and the fact that they didn't proves that I am not worth knowing.*)

In each of the above situations, you will note that the person concerned is making a demand. Albert Ellis, in his characteristically colourful manner captured this relationship between rigid attitudes and self-devaluation attitudes when he said: 'Shouldhood leads to shithood. You are never a shit without a should.' I would put it somewhat differently: 'Rigid attitudes lead to self-devaluation. You will rarely devalue yourself without holding a self-related rigid attitude.'

Let's consider one of these situations and see why it is false for the person to rate themself as a consequence of failing to comply with a rigid attitude held towards themselves. The person in the first situation, whom I will call Bob, said the following: 'I absolutely should not have let my father down. I am a bad person for doing so.'

Now let's assume that Bob had let his father down and that it was bad of him to do so. It is certainly legitimate for Bob to rate his action as being 'bad'. But is it true that he is a bad person for acting badly? Clearly not! It is unrealistic for Bob to judge his total self as being bad as a consequence of doing something bad. If it were true that Bob was a bad person then everything about him would have to be bad. 'I am a bad person' means that Bob is using the adjective 'bad' to describe his personhood and 'I am' denotes his identity. However, clearly this is not the case. The truth is that Bob is a complex, fallible, unique, unrateable human being who has done something wrong.

2. Self-devaluation: Devaluing the 'self' is illogical

When Bob, in the above example, says that he is a bad person for doing a bad thing (in this case letting his father down), he is also thinking illogically. He is, in fact, committing the part–whole error. He is saying that a part of him (in this case his behaviour whereby he let his father down) defines the whole of him (i.e. 'I am a bad person'). Now in logic the part cannot define the whole. However, it is perfectly logical for the whole to incorporate the part as in the statement: 'I am a complex, fallible, unrateable, unique human who has acted badly by letting my father down.' Here the part of Bob (his bad behaviour) is incorporated into the whole of him.

3. Self-devaluation: Devaluation of the self is largely unhelpful

Again I will use the case of Bob who felt guilty about letting his father down. When Bob believes that he is a bad person for letting his father down what are the consequences of this attitude? First of all, Bob is going to feel guilt about his behaviour. Second, he is going to either act or have an urge to act in one or more of the following unhelpful ways. He may:

* Escape the pain of guilt in unhealthy ways
* Beg for forgiveness from his father (rather than ask for it)
* Promise unrealistically that he will not 'sin' again
* Punish himself physically or by deprivation
* Disclaim responsibility for wrongdoing
* Reject offers of forgiveness

Third, Bob may subsequently think in a number of ways including:

- On reflection, he immediately assumes that he has definitely done the wrong thing
- Assumes more personal responsibility than the situation warrants
- Assigns far less responsibility to others than is warranted
- Does not think of mitigating factors for his behaviour
- Does not put his behaviour into an overall context
- Thinks that he will receive retribution

Now sometimes devaluing oneself may be helpful. Thus, Bob may, by devaluing himself, take responsibility for letting his father down, learn why he did so, and put this learning into practice in the future. However, these positive outcomes, while they can be achieved through self-devaluation, are better achieved by self-acceptance (to be discussed below).

Unconditional acceptance as the alternative to person rating

We have seen that when you engage in person rating your rating is false in that it does not do justice to the complexity, fallibility, unrateability and uniqueness of the person being rated. Second, your rating is illogical in that normally when you rate someone you focus on one or a few aspects of that person and then assign the person a global rating. In doing so, you make the illogical part–whole error. Finally, when you rate someone, the consequences to you in doing so are normally unconstructive. Luckily, there is an alternative to person rating, and this is known as unconditional person-acceptance. This comes in two forms: unconditional self-acceptance and unconditional other-acceptance.

Unconditional person-acceptance (UPA) is based on the idea that it is not possible to assign a global rating to a person. The (UPA) alternatives to the person-rating statements are presented below:

- *I'm worthless.* I am not worthless. I am a complex, fallible, unrateable and unique.

- *They are a bad person.* They are not a bad person. They are a fallible person who has done a bad thing.

- *I would be a better person if I had worked harder.* It would be better for me if I worked harder, but I would not be a better person.

- *They are a complete idiot.* They are not a complete idiot or any kind of idiot. They may have acted idiotically but that proves that they are fallible.

- *They are scum.* I may dislike intensely certain aspects of them, but they are decidedly not scum. They are human.

When we accept people unconditionally, we do the following:

a. We state the truth about humans
b. We are being logical
c. We achieve largely positive consequences from doing so

Let me consider these points one at a time.

Unconditionally accepting people reflects the truth about people

When we accept people unconditionally, we refrain from using a global rating to evaluate them. Indeed, we do not evaluate them at all. Instead, we may rate aspects of them, but assert the truth of who they are.

Let me explain why by considering one of the person-acceptance statements presented above, in this case a self-acceptance statement.

1. Unconditional self-acceptance is based on the truth about you

When I say 'I am not worthless; I am complex, fallible, unrateable and unique', I am negating the idea that I am worthless and asserting certain truths about me that do not change about me in my lifetime no matter what I do, fail to do or no matter what happens to me or fails to happen to me.

Also, when I accept myself, it is usually about the following four situations:

a. I have done something that I would have preferred not to have done, but that I do not demand that I absolutely should not have done (e.g. *I would have preferred not to have let my father down, but that does not mean that I absolutely should not have done so. I am not a bad person for doing so. Rather I am a complex, fallible, unique, unrateable human being who has done the wrong thing*).

b. I have failed to do something that I would have preferred to have done, but recognise that there is no reason why I had to have done it (e.g. *I failed my exam which I wish I had not done, but there is no reason why I absolutely should have passed it. I failed, but this does not prove that I am a failure. It proves that I am a fallible human being*).

c. Something happened to me that I believe preferably rather than absolutely should not have happened (e.g. *My friend criticised me which I wished they had not done, but recognise that there is no reason why they absolutely should not have done so. Their criticism does not prove that I am unlikeable. Rather, it proves that I am fallible and still able to be liked*).

d. Something did not happen to me that I wish had happened, but do not demand absolutely should have happened (e.g. *My friends did not ask me to join them. I wish they had asked me, but there is no reason why they absolutely should have done so. The fact that they did not do so does not prove that I am not worth knowing. It proves that I am fallible and may have done something that dissuaded them from asking me*).

In each of the above situations, you will note that the person concerned holds a flexible attitude. When this is the case a good aphorism might be: 'Flexible attitudes lead to unconditional self-acceptance. You will rarely devalue yourself when you surrender your self-related rigid attitudes.'

Let's consider one of these situations and see why it is false for the person to rate themselves as a consequence of failing to comply with a rigid attitude held towards themself. The person in the first situation whom we have called Bob said the following: 'I absolutely should not have let my father down. I am a bad person for doing so.'

Now let's again assume that Bob did let his father down and that it was bad of him to do so. It is certainly legitimate for Bob to rate his action as being 'bad'. And it is also true that he is not a bad person for acting badly. Bob can prove that he is a complex, fallible, unique and unrateable human being.

2. Unconditional self-acceptance is logical

When Bob says that he is not a bad person for doing a bad thing (in this case letting his father down), rather, he is a complex, fallible, unique, unrateable human being, he is thinking logically. In particular, he is avoiding committing the part–whole error. Bob is saying that a part of him (in this case his behaviour whereby he let his father down) can be incorporated into the whole of him and that it does not define him. This is a logical position for Bob to take.

3. Unconditional self-acceptance leads to largely helpful consequences

When Bob believes that he is not a bad person for letting his father down, rather he is a complex, fallible, unique and unrateable human being, what are the consequences of this attitude? First of all, Bob is going to feel remorse about his behaviour rather than guilt. Second, he is going to either act or have an urge to act in one or more of the following helpful ways. He:

- Faces up to the pain or remorse without acting in unhealthy ways
- Asks for forgiveness from the person wronged (rather than begs for it)
- Does not promise unrealistically that he will not 'sin' again. Rather, he promises to stand back and reflect on the reasons for his behaviour and learn the appropriate lessons
- Does not punish himself physically or by deprivation

- Takes appropriate responsibility for wrongdoing
- Accepts offers for forgiveness

Third, Bob subsequently thinks in a number of ways. Thus, he:

- Takes into account, on reflection, all the relevant factors before assuming that he has definitely done the wrong thing
- Assumes the appropriate amount of personal responsibility warranted by the situation
- Assigns the appropriate level of responsibility to others warranted by the situation
- Does think of mitigating factors for his behaviour
- Does put his behaviour into an overall context
- Does not think that he will receive retribution

Now sometimes unconditional self-acceptance may be unhelpful. Thus, Bob may, by accepting himself unconditionally, think that he does not have to take responsibility for letting his father down and thus may not learn why he did so, thus increasing the chances that he will act in similar ways in the future.

However, these negative outcomes tend to stem from a misunderstanding of the true meaning of unconditional self-acceptance and are most often associated from the defence mechanism known as denial, which stems much more often from self-devaluation than from unconditional self-acceptance. I will now discuss the most common doubts, reservations and objections to the concept of unconditional self-acceptance.

Doubts, Reservations and Objections to Adopting an Unconditional Acceptance Attitude and to Giving Up a Devaluation Attitude

Here, I will discuss the most commonly expressed doubts that people have about embracing unconditional person-acceptance and relinquishing person devaluation. I will also present how I usually respond to such doubts, which are usually based on misconceptions about the meaning of the concept of unconditional person acceptance and the so-called positive aspects of person devaluation.

Doubt 1: Accepting myself unconditionally means that I don't need to change aspects of myself that I am not happy with or that I can't do so. Devaluing myself, on the other hand, motivates me to change. Therefore, adopting an unconditional self-acceptance attitude discourages personal change, while keeping my self-devaluation attitude encourages such change.

Response

You are confusing the term unconditional 'acceptance' with the terms 'resignation' and/or 'complacency'. Accepting yourself unconditionally means acknowledging that you are a complex, unique fallible human being with good aspects, bad aspects and neutral aspects. It means that you can and are advised to identify aspects of yourself that you are not happy with and to change them if you can. Indeed, adopting an unconditional self-acceptance attitude will help you to change these aspects because it will enable you to devote all your energies to understanding the factors involved and what you can do to change them (e.g. 'I tend to procrastinate and this proves that I am a fallible human being with good, bad and neutral aspects. Since procrastination is a negative aspect, let me see why I do it and what I can do to stop doing it'). Resignation, on the other hand, means not trying to change negative aspects of yourself because you are sure that you cannot change them (e.g. 'I tend to procrastinate and there is nothing that I can do to change this'). This is very different to what is meant by unconditional self-acceptance. Finally, 'complacency' means having an 'I'm alright, Jack' philosophy which discourages self-change because there is no need to change anything about you. Again, this is very different from self-acceptance.

Holding a self-devaluation attitude actually discourages self-change. Devaluing yourself means treating yourself as if you were a simple being whose totality can be rated rather than as a complex, unique fallible human being who cannot legitimately be given a global rating. It means that when you identify a negative aspect of yourself that you wish to change you devalue yourself for having this aspect (e.g. 'I tend to procrastinate and this proves that I am an incompetent fool'). Adopting a self-devaluation attitude will stop you from changing your negative aspects because rather than devoting all your energies to working to change them, you focus on your negativity as a person. Thus, instead of focusing on reasons why you tend to procrastinate and figuring out a way of dealing with these factors you dwell on what an incompetent fool you are.

Thus, your unconditional self-acceptance attitude has the opposite effect to what you think it has. It motivates you to change aspects of yourself that you dislike rather than thinking that you don't need to change them or that you can't change them. Your self-devaluation attitude also has the opposite effect to what you think it has. It prevents you from changing negative aspects of yourself rather than motivating you to change them.

Doubt 2: Adopting an unconditional other-acceptance attitude means that I am condoning that person's bad behaviour. Devaluing that person shows that I am not condoning his (in this case) behaviour.

Response

When you accept another person unconditionally, you are taking the same stance towards them as you are taking towards yourself when you hold an unconditional self-acceptance attitude. It means that you are acknowledging that the other person is a complex, unique fallible human being with good aspects, bad aspects and neutral aspects.

Thus, you can accept the other person without condoning their behaviour. Thus, you can acknowledge that your boss is a fallible human being for treating you unfairly without condoning their unfair treatment of you. This attitude will lead you to take constructive action towards your boss if you think that it is appropriate for you to do so.

When you devalue another person, it is true that you are not condoning his bad behaviour, but it is also true that you are condemning the person for their bad behaviour. Returning to our example, when you hold an other-devaluation attitude you don't condone your boss's unfair treatment of you, but you do regard them as a rotten person for treating you badly. This attitude will stop you from taking constructive action towards your boss and may lead you to take action that is harmful to both you and your boss.

In summary, holding an unconditional other-acceptance attitude does not mean that you are condoning another person's bad behaviour. It also has the advantage of promoting constructive action with the person who is acting badly. Holding an other-devaluation attitude also does not lead to you condoning the bad behaviour of the other person, but may lead you to act in unconstructive ways towards that person.

Let me end this chapter by inviting you to take part in a quiz which will show you how humanistic you are!

Looking for the Good in Hitler and Acknowledging the Bad in Mother Teresa

I will close this chapter by quoting from a lecture I gave in 1997 where I argued that Hitler was not all bad, nor Mother Teresa all good. We may need to see Hitler as all bad and Mother Teresa as all good, but this says more about us than it does about them. This is what I said in that lecture (see Chapter 12):

Let me briefly review some of Hitler's better qualities. He was a very good organiser and a very good public speaker. He showed great bravery in the First World War, capturing several enemy soldiers single-handedly. He was capable of love and was kind to animals. Please do not think that by saying these things that I am a Neo-Nazi or an apologist for Hitler. He did, of course, do immense harm to Jews, of whom I am one, to Gypsies and to homosexuals. I do not absolve him from the responsibility for any of this, but the fact of the matter is that he was not all bad. If he was, he would not have been human.

You may have heard that Mother Teresa is on the fast-track to being made a saint by Rome. Her name is synonymous with goodness, and there is no doubt that her

devoted efforts have brought succour to countless people
over the years. But was she all good? Far from it. Her
hospitals were poorly stocked with medical supplies and
were often kept in a bare and frozen state – this despite the
fact that her mission received very generous financial
support from many quarters.

Also, despite publicly stating that she would not accept
money from the rich, she received donations amounting to
$1.25 million from Charles Keating, who was sent to prison
for ten years for fraud. Mother Teresa sent an unsolicited
letter to the trial judge to ask for clemency. When the deputy
district attorney in Los Angeles County wrote to Mother
Teresa explaining the facts of the case and requesting that
she return the money donated to her by Keating, money he
stole from ordinary, working people, Mother Teresa did not
respond.

In addition, perhaps because of her respected position,
Mother Teresa's accounts were never audited, and thus,
large sums of money sent by her to her 'headquarters in
Rome' have never been explained. I could go on and those
of you who are interested in learning more should read a
book entitled The Missionary Position: Mother Teresa in
theory and practice by Christopher Hitchens (1995).
Unfortunately, in his zeal to expose the 'sins' of Mother
Teresa, Hitchens takes an either/or approach and fails to
consider and evaluate her good works. My purpose in
mentioning this lesser-known side of Mother Teresa is not
to discredit her, but to place her in full context, to
acknowledge the bad in her as well as the good.

My point is that Hitler was not evil and Mother Teresa
was not a saint. Hitler had his good side and Mother Teresa
her bad. In taking this stance I do not for one minute wish to
excuse Hitler for his crimes against humanity, nor do I wish
to detract from Mother Teresa's good works. Rather, I wish
to make the point that both were human and have features
that we all share.

In conclusion, let me say that one of our tasks as human
beings is to accept that we are capable of experiencing the

entire range of human reactions and responses. We are all capable of the greatest of good and the vilest of evil. To use jargon for a moment, we all have a Hitler inside us as well as a Mother Teresa. If we fully accept ourselves as such, we can learn to maximise the good in ourselves and to minimise the bad. However, if we try to expel our bad unwanted side, and in particular if we attempt to do so in a rigid manner, we create problems for ourselves and for those with whom we come into contact. If we accept ourselves as fallible human beings capable of experiencing the entire range of human functioning, and if we accept others as similar to ourselves in this respect, such acceptance will promote understanding and compassion.

Let me now invite you to take a brief quiz to see how humanistic you are. Here are the questions:

1. Having the love of a significant other makes you a more worthwhile person. *True or False?*

2. If someone you admire is better than you at an important activity, he or she is a better person than you. *True or False?*

3. If you fail at something really important, you are not a failure but a fallible human being. *True or False?*

4. You can give a human being a single global rating which completely accounts for them. *True or False?*

5. Someone who rapes a child is wicked through and through.

   True or False?

6. Mother Teresa and Adolf Hitler are of equal worth as humans. *True or False?*

The humanistic answers are as follows:

1. False
2. False
3. True

4. False
5. False
6. True

If you gave any other answer, you are operating on the idea that humans can legitimately be assigned a global rating.

As the following dialogue from one of my self-acceptance groups shows, giving the non-humanistic answer often reveals an objection to the concept of unconditional person-acceptance.

Here is what happened when Carol gave a non-humanistic answer to question 5.

Windy: So, Carol, you think that someone who rapes a small child is wicked through and through?

Carol: That's right.

Windy: What do others think?

Betty: Well, my immediate strong reaction to that question was that anyone who rapes a small child is wicked through and through, but then I thought that if I believed that then I would also have to believe that you can give a human being a single global rating that completely accounts for them, which I most definitely don't.

Lionel: I had the same reaction, but I thought that if the answer to question 4 was false the answer to question 5 would also have to be false.

Carol: But what if it were your child who was raped?

Fiona: I thought about that, and I concluded that I would probably think that the person who raped her was wicked through and through, but I'd be wrong.

Carol: I see.

Brian: Do you think that if you said that such a person wasn't wicked through and through then you would be condoning the crime in some way?

Carol: Not condoning it, but not condemning it as much as I should.

Liam: Aha! But why can't you condemn the crime as an act of great wickedness without condemning the person as wicked through and through?

Carol: I guess you can.

Windy: So what's the answer to question 5?

Carol: False, but it will take some getting used to.

In the following chapter, I will discuss the application of the philosophy of unconditional self-acceptance (USA) and show how I would have helped Oedipus keep his eyesight by helping him to put the philosophy of USA into practice.

31

Unconditional Self-Acceptance Applied
Or 'Oedipus keeps his eyesight!'

You may think that the concept of unconditional self-acceptance as discussed in Chapter 30 is an interesting theoretical concept and you would be right. But it is not just a theoretical concept. It has real practical applications and can protect against self-harm. 'Really?' I hear you ask. 'Really!' is my reply. Let me explain what I mean by considering the case of Oedipus and how I would have helped him if he came to me for counselling.

Oedipus Schmoedipus: Why You Don't Have to Gouge Your Eyes Out When You Have Discovered that You Have Killed Your Father and Married Your Mother

Most of you will be familiar with the story of Oedipus. For those of you who are not, let me briefly relate this tragic tale. The Chambers Biographical Dictionary (Magnusson, 1990: 1098) states that Oedipus was the:

> ... Greek legendary figure, who killed his father, Laius, and married his mother, Jocasta ... An oracle had warned Laius, King of Thebes, that he would be killed by his son. Laius therefore exposed the infant Oedipus to die on the mountains after piercing his feet with a spike (hence the name Oedipus, which in Greek means 'with swollen feet'). The young Oedipus was rescued and adopted by Polybus, King of Corinth, and grew up with the belief that the rulers of Corinth were his parents. When told by an oracle that he was fated to kill his father and marry his mother, he left Corinth in an attempt to avoid fulfilling the prophecy. On his way through Boeotia, he was involved in a quarrel with his (to him unknown) father Laius, and killed him. He freed Thebes from the scourge of the Sphinx by solving her

riddles, and in return married the now-widowed Jocasta, his mother, and became King of Thebes. At length, the terrible truth about his origins and parenthood was revealed to him. Jocasta took her life and Oedipus blinded himself.

As you all know, this tale inspired Sigmund Freud, who coined the term 'Oedipus complex' to describe a young boy's longing to oust his father and have his mother for himself. I want to focus on a different part of the story and argue that Oedipus's act of self-blinding stemmed from a rigid and extreme attitude. I am going to show you that there was no need for Oedipus to gouge his eyes out and no need for him to feel guilty about what he did.

Let's assume that I was alive at the time and practising REBT and that Oedipus, in an obvious state of disturbance, consulted me. This is how I would have endeavoured to help him.

Session 1

Windy: OK, Oedipus, what's your problem?

Oedipus: I'm in a terrible state. I have committed three terrible sins.

Windy: What are they?

Oedipus: I've killed my father, married and slept with my mother and when she discovered this, she killed herself and I am responsible for that too.

Windy: Did you know that they were your mother and father before you killed the former and married the latter?

Oedipus: No, but that doesn't help me. People have tried to comfort me by reminding me that I didn't know this, but I still want to gouge my eyes out.

Windy: OK, which crime shall we discuss first?

Oedipus: Let's start with the murder of my father, Laius.

Windy: OK, how do you feel about killing your father?

Oedipus: Very guilty.

Windy: Right. Let me put this into REBT's 'ABC' framework. 'A', which stands for the adversity, is murdering your father, and 'C', which stands for your emotional consequence, is guilt.

Oedipus: What's 'B'?

Windy: 'B' stands for the basic attitudes that you hold towards murdering your father which account for your guilt. In REBT, 'A' (i.e. in this case you murdering your father), does not cause 'C' (i.e. your guilt). Rather your 'B' is at the core of your feelings of guilt.

Oedipus: So what are my basic attitudes?

Windy: Well, let me put forward a couple of hunches and you correct me if I'm wrong. First, I think you are demanding that you absolutely should not have killed your father and second, I think that you think that you are a thoroughly rotten person for killing him. Am I right?

Oedipus: That's exactly right. But aren't I a rotten person for killing my father?

Windy: Of course not. Let's leave aside for a moment that you didn't know that he was your father and accept that you did a rotten thing. How are you a rotten person for doing this rotten thing?

Oedipus: Well, I killed my father.

Windy: I'm not disputing that. Killing your father was wrong, it was a rotten deed, but how are you rotten through and through for doing this rotten thing?

Oedipus: I guess I'm not.

Windy: Why not?

Oedipus: Because as you say, one rotten deed does not make me rotten through and through.

Windy: That's right. If you were rotten through and through, you could never do anything good, but we know that you freed Thebes from the scourge of the Sphinx. Wasn't that a good deed?

Oedipus: Yes, it was.

Windy: But if you were a rotten person how could you have done such a noble deed?

Oedipus: You're right, I couldn't.

Windy: So, if you aren't a rotten person, what are you?

Oedipus: I'm a fallible human being who can't be rated by my actions. Being fallible means that I can do good deeds and bad deeds.

Windy: That's exactly right. Now, it's healthy to feel badly about your bad deeds, and consequently it would be healthy if you were to feel very remorseful about killing your father. But guilt is an unhealthy emotion which could lead you to blind yourself. Is that clear?

Oedipus: So, remorse is healthy and guilt isn't.

Windy: That's right, remorse stems from your unconditional self-acceptance attitude and guilt from your self-devaluation attitude. Now let's look at the other part of your attitude: 'I absolutely shouldn't have killed my father.' Where is the law of the universe that states that you absolutely should not have done that?

Oedipus: Well it was very, very wrong.

Windy: You'll get no argument from me on that score, but being human are you immune from doing very, very, bad acts and do you have to have such immunity?

Oedipus: No, I don't have that immunity and nor do I have to have it. But I was warned that I would kill my father. I absolutely should have known what I was doing and refrained from doing it.

448 *Windy Dryden Collected! Strange, But Rational*

Windy: Well, that would have been highly desirable, but does it follow that because it would have been highly desirable that you knew it was your father, therefore you absolutely should have known? Are you an oracle in your spare time?

Oedipus: Point taken.

Windy: And incidentally, if there was a law of the universe forbidding you from killing your father, there's no way that you could have killed him because you would have had to follow that law.

Oedipus: Right, reality should be reality however tragic it is.

Windy: Well put. Now I suggest that you go over these ideas for homework and next week I'll help you to get over your disturbed feelings about marrying your mother and about your part in her suicide.

Oedipus: And also, can we deal with my feelings of shame when others view me as an object of disgust?

Windy: We can indeed.

Oedipus: Great. How much do I owe you?

Windy: £200.

Oedipus: That's a small price to pay for saving my eyesight.

Windy: See you and be seen by you next week.

I wish to stress two points from this interchange. First, it is important that I agree with Oedipus that his 'crimes' were heinous. It is fundamental to REBT strategy that I do not try to show him what he had already acknowledged, albeit intellectually: that he neither knew his father before he killed him nor knew his mother before he married her. Oedipus will be more open to this type of intervention once he has made strides in accepting himself unconditionally for his 'crimes'. Second, it is important to distinguish between normal, understandable responses on the one hand and healthy responses on the other. While it is very understandable and statistically normal for Oedipus to condemn himself for his actions, this does not mean that it is healthy for him to do so. If I do not target for change his guilt-producing, self-condemnatory attitude, he will remain vulnerable to deliberate self-harm.

Session 2

Windy: Well, Oedipus, did you go over the ideas we discussed last session for homework?

Oedipus: Yes, and it was very helpful. I can now see that I did two very bad things in killing my father and marrying my mother. But rather than excusing myself from these sins, I faced up to them and practised the philosophy of unconditional self-acceptance.

Windy: Can you be more explicit?

Oedipus: OK. As we discussed last week, I first took responsibility for killing my father and reasoned that while that was a heinous act which I very much regret doing, I am not a heinous person for committing this sin.

Windy: Good. So, you reasoned that you were not a heinous person, but what kind of person are you for committing this sin?

Oedipus: What you called last week a fallible human being, too complex to be rated.

Windy: Some would say that that is a cop out.

Oedipus: I realise that. But I am fully prepared to take responsibility for what I did and take the consequences.

Windy: Now, how do you feel about marrying your mother?

Oedipus: Well, again I held off from reassuring myself that I did not know that she was my mother and took responsibility for committing another grave sin. Then I used the same reasoning as before. I convinced myself that even though marrying one's mother is incest and heinous, this act, however bad, does not define me as a person. I am still a fallible human being even though I married my mother and killed my father.

Windy: You also mentioned last week that you felt guilty about your mother taking her own life when she found out what had happened. Did you also deal with that?

Oedipus: Well, I applied the same reasoning to this tragedy as well. I first assumed that her suicide was my fault and examined the idea that I am bad because she killed herself. I again accepted myself unconditionally for the full part that I played which helped me to stand back and rethink what I was responsible for and what she was responsible for.

Windy: And the outcome of that?

Oedipus: I still feel terribly remorseful about my part and of course I am grieving her death, but I no longer think that I am a bad person.

Windy: Excellent.

Oedipus: However, I still feel like gouging my eyes out.

Windy: Oh, really. Why?

Oedipus: Well, I may be able to accept myself unconditionally, but the national tabloids have just gotten hold of the story and are going to publish it this weekend.

Windy: And if they do?

Oedipus: Well, people will regard me as a disgusting human being.

Windy: Well, again. Let's suppose they do. Not all of them will, of course, because the more intelligent among them will realise that you did not know the man you killed was your father and the woman you married was your mother. But let's suppose that a significant majority do regard you as a disgusting human being, why would you have to blind yourself?

Oedipus:	Because I could not bear to see the look of disgust on their faces when they look at me.
Windy:	Because, if you saw that disgust, how would you feel about their disgust?
Oedipus:	Well, I would feel deeply ashamed and that's why I would want to gouge out my eyes.
Windy:	But can you see the link between your feelings of shame and your wish to gouge your eyes out?
Oedipus:	Yes, I can.
Windy:	So, before you blind yourself, can we address your feelings of shame about their disgust of you?
Oedipus:	Certainly, but I don't think it will help.
Windy:	Well, it may not, but there is no harm in trying is there?
Oedipus:	No, none at all.
Windy:	Let's put this into REBT's 'ABC' framework as we did last week. What is 'A'?
Oedipus:	A is the expression of disgust shown towards me by those who have discovered that I have killed my father and married my mother. 'C' is my feelings of shame.
Windy:	And 'B'?
Oedipus:	'B' stands for my basic rigid and extreme attitudes towards this disgust that is at the root of my shame.
Windy:	So, if you want to address your feelings of shame, what do we need to examine?
Oedipus:	My rigid and extreme attitudes.
Windy:	And what are your rigid and extreme attitudes?
Oedipus:	Well, I remember from last week that there are two: a rigid attitude and a self-devaluation attitude.
Windy:	Well remembered. Let's take them one at a time and apply them to the present situation where you think

people are disgusted with you and you feel shame. Now what is your rigid attitude here?

Oedipus: I guess that people must not be disgusted with me.

Windy: And your self-devaluation attitude?

Oedipus: That I am a disgusting person if they are disgusted with me.

Windy: Good: Now let me invite you to stand back and examine these two attitudes. Let's start with your rigid attitude that people must not be disgusted with you for killing your father and marrying your mother. Well, why must they not be disgusted with you?

Oedipus: Well, I guess because I'm King and they must respect the King and not be disgusted with him.

Windy: Well, that would be very nice but what's the reality?

Oedipus: The reality is that they are disgusted with me.

Windy: And you are demanding that reality must not be reality. What do you think of that idea?

Oedipus: It's ridiculous because if reality is that way that's the way it should be.

Windy: Now let's look at the alternative attitude. It's in two parts. The first part outlines your desire: 'I really don't want them to be disgusted with me ....' Now is that true or false?

Oedipus: That's perfectly true.

Windy: Now the second part is: '... but that doesn't mean that they must not find me disgusting'. Is that part true or false?

Oedipus: That is also true.

Windy: So your rigid attitude is false and your flexible attitude is true. Which of these attitudes is the least constructive for you?

Oedipus: My rigid attitude is the least constructive.

Windy: Why?

Oedipus: Because it leads me to feel deeply ashamed and makes me want to gouge my eyes out.

Windy: And your flexible attitude, what are the consequences of holding that attitude?

Oedipus: Well, I wouldn't feel ashamed of myself, but I would still be deeply disappointed that they think that way of me.

Windy: And would you feel like gouging your eyes out?

Oedipus: No, I don't think I would.

Windy: Now let's look at your self-devaluation attitude. If they find you disgusting for killing your father and marrying your mother does that make you a disgusting person?

Oedipus: No.

Windy: Why not?

Oedipus: Because my identity is not defined by how people view me no matter what I have done.

Windy: So, if you are not a disgusting person for killing your father and marrying your mother, who are you?

Oedipus: Well, I am a fallible human being who finds himself in a very difficult situation.

Windy: How credible are your flexible and unconditional self-acceptance attitudes?

Oedipus: Well, they make perfect sense, but I don't really believe them yet.

Windy: That is perfectly understandable. For to really believe them you need to act in ways that are consistent with them. Now what can you do between now and next week to cement your flexible and unconditional self-acceptance attitudes?

Oedipus: Well, I can go out with my head held high and talk to people rather than hide away.

Windy: Do that while you are actively rehearsing your flexible and unconditional self-acceptance attitudes and that will enhance its effects.

Oedipus: OK. See you next week.

Would Oedipus have been as well known if he had accepted himself unconditionally and gotten on with his sighted life rather than gouging his eyes out? I doubt it since rigid and extreme thinking leads to dramatic events that remain in the public psyche. But maybe forgetting such figures as Oedipus is a small price to play if we are to pursue psychologically healthy lives.

*

In the following, and final, chapter of this Collection, I consider two rigid attitudes that have interesting effects on the way our minds work and on the way we function in the world: the rigid demands for certainty and self-control.

32

On Taking Improper Precautions and On Thinking the Unthinkable

For ten years I had a peer supervision arrangement with Dr Ruth Wessler (sadly deceased) where we sent one another audiotapes by mail for each other to supervise. For example, I would listen to an audiotape of one of Ruth's therapy sessions and record my supervisory comments on the other side of the tape. And Ruth would do the same with my tapes. We could not meet regularly for Ruth lived in Downers Grove, near Chicago in Illinois and I lived in England. Indeed, I only met Ruth twice in person, but in the ten years in which we knew one another we got to know each other's work very well and my practice as an REBT therapist is still very much influenced by Ruth's supervisory comments and the relaxed way in which she practised REBT.

On Taking Improper Precautions

For my present purpose, I will discuss a client who was in therapy with Ruth and whose sessions I had the privilege to supervise. One session is particularly memorable and is relevant to the theme of the current chapter. The client, who I shall call Valerie, was discussing with Ruth her fear of getting pregnant. Two important points to note: that she was a Roman Catholic, but she did use contraception.

As the interview unfolded, Ruth asked Valerie what contraception she used with her partner. Here is her reply and the ensuing dialogue.

Valerie: Well, I am on the pill, but as that is not completely safe, I also insist that my partner (who I shall call Roger) wear a condom. And just to be on the safe side I use some spermicidal cream which I find works well with the coil that I had fitted about a year ago. Oh, and I

Valerie: know that this might sound a bit excessive, but I also insist that Roger withdraws before he ejaculates.

Ruth: And you are still anxious about getting pregnant?

Valerie: Petrified!

Ruth: Help me to understand why.

Valerie: Well, this is how I see it. As I said before the pill is not totally safe, and we have all heard stories that condoms split or come off so, although I have asked Roger to withdraw before he ejaculates, he might not do so or some pre-ejaculate might leak into me, get through the spermicidal cream barrier and find a tiny way through my diaphragm, And bingo! I'm pregnant!

Ruth: Just as a matter of interest, when you are anxious, what are the chances in your mind that you will get pregnant even with taking so many precautions?

Valerie: In my mind? A very good chance.

How do we explain why an intelligent woman like Valerie (who worked as Head of Department in a community college) thought that there was a good chance of getting pregnant when she and her partner employed five different forms of contraception at the same time?

The answer can, in fact, be found in some of the previous chapters of this book, but let me draw together these disparate pieces of information to explain this strange phenomenon, at least from an REBT perspective.

Valerie held a rigid attitude towards getting pregnant

It is probable that Valerie held a rigid attitude towards getting pregnant. At another point, she told Ruth that she found getting pregnant 'inconceivable' (no pun intended!) and that it would be 'awful' for her if she did. Her use of the words 'inconceivable' and 'awful' and the anxiety that accompanied them indicated to me that these extreme evaluations and the anxiety are consequences of a rigid attitude towards getting pregnant.

Valerie held a rigid attitude towards uncertainty with respect to the threat of getting pregnant

Having said this, the number of contraceptive methods that Valerie employed and encouraged her partner to use indicates the presence of another rigid attitude, one that is more subtle than her rigid attitude towards getting pregnant, but one which exerted a powerful influence on Valerie's behaviour nonetheless. Let's see how Ruth helped Valerie to identify this second rigid attitude.

Ruth: So even though you are using five methods of contraception at the same time, you still feel anxious and think that there is a good chance of getting pregnant when you feel anxiety. Is that right?

Valerie: Yes, that is right.

Ruth: Other than a sixth form of contraception what would you need to get rid of your anxiety at that point?

Valerie: Well, I would need to know that it was not possible for me to get pregnant.

Ruth: Oh, I see. So, if a family planning expert said to you: 'Good news! With the forms of contraception that you are using, you only have a 0.5% chance of getting pregnant', how would you feel?

Valerie: I would still be anxious.

Ruth: And still think that you had a good chance of getting pregnant under these circumstances?

Valerie: Yes. I know it sounds mad, but yes, I would still think that there is a good chance of getting pregnant.

Ruth: So, the only condition that would lead you to not feel anxious in these circumstances would be a cast-iron guarantee that you could not get pregnant.

Valerie: Well, yes, but it would have to be a guarantee that I would believe.

Ruth: Indeed!

So, there is much evidence that Valerie held a rigid attitude towards getting pregnant. First, she used five different forms of contraception at the same time. The purpose of contraception is to prevent pregnancy. However, Valerie was using contraception to try to prevent anxiety about getting pregnant. Her clear-thinking mind told her that it was very, very unlikely that she would get pregnant, but she was not using her clear-thinking mind when she held a rigid attitude towards uncertainty. Her rigid mind led her to attempt to reassure herself (by using yet another form of contraception) at a time when she was not reassurable. As such, the use of a further contraceptive method actually perpetuates Valerie's anxiety, in the longer term, even though it alleviates her anxiety in the very short term. It does so because it reinforces Valerie's rigid attitude that she needs absolutely certainty at that time that she is not going to fall pregnant.

Valerie held a rigid attitude towards having a sense of comfort accompanying her rigid attitude towards for uncertainty with respect to the threat of getting pregnant

In the above section, I argued that Valerie held a rigid attitude where she held that she had to know for certain at any given point in time (and usually just before making love to her partner!) that she would not get pregnant. The ingredient 'certainty–uncertainty' may be regarded as largely a cognitive factor in that Valerie's focus is on knowledge. However, it also emerged in dialogue with Ruth that Valerie held a second distinct, but related rigid attitude. Let's return to the appropriate point in the dialogue between Ruth and Valerie.

Ruth: So, we have looked at the fact that you are demanding that you know for certain that you will not get pregnant. Are you making any other demands in this situation where you are about to make love with your partner?

Valerie: Well, I'm not sure if it's the same, but when I get to feel uncomfortable in the situation, I either check that all the precautions are in place or I don't make love.

Ruth: So you don't only react to the thought that you are in an uncertain situation regarding getting pregnant, but you also react to the uncomfortable feelings that accompany the uncertainty?

Valerie: In a strange way, I see that discomfort as evidence that I am going to get pregnant.

As Ruth discovered, Valerie held the rigid attitude that she had to feel comfortable before making love and that in some way she related this to the uncertainty she considered that she was facing.

People who hold a rigid attitude that they have to be certain in a given situation tend also to hold a rigid attitude that they 'feel' safe or feel comfortable and that when they do have these feelings of discomfort they associate it with the cognitive state of uncertainty that they are facing.

Valerie's rigid attitudes towards certainty and comfort lead her to black-and-white thinking

Realistically, there are four possibilities related to uncertainty/discomfort and Valerie becoming pregnant:

1. Valerie is certain and feels comfortable that she won't get pregnant and she does not get pregnant
2. Valerie is certain and feels comfortable that she won't get pregnant and she gets pregnant
3. Valerie is not certain and is not comfortable that she won't get pregnant and she does not get pregnant
4. Valerie is not certain and is not comfortable that she won't get pregnant and she does get pregnant

Again realistically, what determines whether or not Valerie gets pregnant depends on the following factors:

a. Valerie and her partner having sexual intercourse without using contraception where her partner ejaculates inside of her
b. The fertility of Valerie and her partner

You will note that I have not listed Valerie's level of uncertainty and discomfort about getting pregnant here because as far as we know, it is not a relevant factor. Valerie's anxiety level may be a factor here, but this depends on a number of other factors including the two that I have just listed.

Because Valerie holds rigid attitudes towards certainty and comfort about not getting pregnant, these attitudes lead to black-and-white thinking. If Valerie would articulate her rigid attitudes and the black-and-white thinking that stems from them she would probably express them like this:

> I must know for sure I will not get pregnant and have a sense of comfort that this will not happen and I can't bear not having such certainty and comfort

These rigid/extreme attitudes then lead to Valerie thinking the following: 'If I do not have such certainty and comfort then there is a good chance that I will get pregnant.'

If we return the four conditions listed above, Valerie's rigid attitudes lead her to think that uncertainty and discomfort related to getting pregnant means that she will get pregnant. What Valerie needs to understand is that given her excessive use of contraception here she is much more likely to associate uncertainty and discomfort with her getting pregnant than with her not getting pregnant. But she can only really process this once she operates on a set of flexible/non-extreme attitudes rather than a set of rigid/extreme attitudes towards certainty and comfort with respect to her getting pregnant.

The role of behaviour in perpetuating and addressing Valerie's problem

Valerie may examine her rigid attitudes towards certainty and comfort with respect to getting pregnant and form a more realistic association in her mind between uncertainty, discomfort and pregnancy. But if she continues to use five concurrent forms of contraception then she will perpetuate her problem and undo all the good work that she did to examine her attitudes and re-think the probabilities of getting pregnant in light of uncertainty and the felt sense of discomfort. What Valerie needs to do is to use the one safest form of contraception for her and her partner. Doing so will help her to function in healthy ways in her attitude, cognitive and behavioural systems. If she keeps this consistency in place then eventually her feelings of anxiety will change to healthy concern.

For the record, Ruth helped Valerie do exactly this and she was able to enjoy a healthy, anxiety-free sex life with her partner while only using the contraceptive pill.

On Thinking the Unthinkable

Rosemary was a 48-year-old widow who was a pillar of her community. She was a very religious woman who was very active in her local church and gave freely of her time to church-sponsored voluntary activities. However, recently, Rosemary retreated into her house and avoided anything to do with religion and especially anything to do with Jesus Christ. Her friends were concerned about her, especially as she did not respond to their attempts to contact her. So, what happened that resulted in Rosemary transforming herself from an active churchgoer to a virtual recluse?

One day, Rosemary was in church praying and was in a state of reverie. She suddenly became aware that she was looking at a painting of Christ and found herself looking at his crotch. She was horrified about this, and she responded by trying not to look at the painting, but as is usual in such instances, she began to have involuntary, unwanted thoughts about Christ's crotch. Feeling ashamed about her thoughts, but desperate to be forgiven by God for what she regarded as blasphemy she tried to go to a different church in her area, but to no avail. As soon as she went into the church, she scanned her environment hoping not to see any images of Christ which, given the context, was unlikely.

She then tried to go to churches outside her area, but all the time she engaged in one of two unhelpful strategies. The first strategy was hyper-awareness of the presence of an image of Christ. Here, Rosemary scanned her environment trying to locate images of Christ so that she could prepare herself not to look at his crotch, nipples and lips, with the result that she was drawn to looking at these erogenous zones which she regarded as taboo. The second strategy was avoidance. Initially, Rosemary tried to go to church determined not to look at any images of Christ. However, this resulted in her seeing such images in her mind's eye and in doing so she was drawn to looking at these taboo areas and then repelled by her blasphemy.

When it was clear to Rosemary that these two strategies were making matters worse, not better, she decided to avoid going to church and to pray from home. However, every time she closed her eyes to pray a naked image of Christ came to mind and she again was drawn to looking at Christ's erogenous zones and at the same time repelled by what she was looking at. So, Rosemary tried to pray with her eyes open, but when she did this she thought about the images of Christ and such phrases as 'Christ's crotch', 'The penis of Christ', 'Jesus's nipples' kept coming into her mind. The more she tried to dismiss these thoughts, the more they came into her mind.

After this, Rosemary started to avoid praying altogether and she ended up avoiding anything to do with her religion. As virtually everyone she knew was associated with her religion this meant avoiding these people as well, with the result that Rosemary became a virtual recluse. It was at this point that she went to her doctor who referred her for professional help.

Rosemary's rigid attitudes

During the course of counselling, Rosemary was helped to identify a number of rigid attitudes that she held towards her own psychological processes. She acknowledged that she held the rigid attitude that while in church she must only have thoughts that were consistent with being in the house of God and with the activity of prayer. When she suddenly caught herself looking at Christ's crotch this violated her demand and she concluded that she was a bad person for having such thoughts.

The effects of Rosemary's rigid attitudes on her thinking and behaviour

As I have just noted, Rosemary reacted to her looking at Christ's crotch by holding the rigid attitude that she must not have such thoughts while praying in church. The major effect of this rigid attitude was to make it more likely rather than less likely that she had such thoughts. Once she made such thoughts taboo and insisted that she not have them, her mind scans for the existence of such thoughts, thus increasing their frequency. Remember that Rosemary used increased scanning as a strategy when she attempted to solve her problem by trying different churches to pray in, all to no avail.

Try this simple experiment that counsellors are fond of using with clients like Rosemary: 'Close your eyes and think of a white polar bear. Now instruct yourself to banish all thoughts of the bear. Really force yourself not to think of it. Now what are you thinking of?' In all probability, you are thinking of a white polar bear. Some people manage to change the bear's colour in their mind, but they are still thinking of the bear! This is how the mind works. It is not under our complete control and often operates as if it is a wilful teenager, doing the opposite of what it is instructed to do. This process is exacerbated when the person does not just instruct themself not to think of something, but demands rigidly that they must not do so.

Rosemary's rigid attitude that she must not have 'inappropriate' thoughts of Christ led her to try to eliminate such thoughts by avoiding looking at images of Christ in church. Here, Rosemary was putting into practice a kind of 'out of sight, out of mind' policy. However, as before, the reverse happened. Her underlying rigid attitude towards her 'inappropriate thoughts' led these thoughts to come into her mind even when she was avoiding looking at ecclesiastical images of Jesus Christ.

Rosemary first tried to help herself while in church. As she failed to do so in her local church, she went from church to church hoping that a change of venue would solve the problem. However, this strategy was doomed to failure because Rosemary took her thought-related rigid attitude with her from church to church.

Reluctantly, Rosemary then decided to see if she could solve her problem by avoiding going to church altogether. However, she couldn't because the problem was not to be found in the location of a church, but in the location of her attitudinal system. Indeed, the more Rosemary tried to avoid reminders of church, Christ and religion including stopping praying and avoiding seeing anybody who was connected to the church or to religion (which, in Rosemary's case was almost everybody), the more involuntary 'inappropriate' thoughts intruded into her mind. In this way, Rosemary unwittingly generalised her problem until she sought help.

How Rosemary reintegrated herself back into her religion

Fortunately, Rosemary was referred to someone who understood the role of attitudes and behaviour on her problem and knew what she needed to do it to address the problem correctly. Here are the therapeutic ingredients that contributed to Rosemary's recovery and reintegration into her religion and church life.

Normalising 'inappropriate' thoughts

Rosemary learned that it is normal for people to have thoughts that they would rather not have and that it is not necessary to understand the precise reason why the person has such thoughts for them to be accepted by the person. Rosemary and her counsellor speculated why she might have been drawn to Christ's crotch. They considered amongst other hypotheses that it may have been a random thought or evidence that Rosemary was feeling sexually frustrated at the time. They came to no firm conclusions and Rosemary was helped to see that she did not need to know the precise reason. Her important task was to accept (not like) the existence of such thoughts.

Developing a flexible attitudes towards her 'inappropriate' thoughts

The most important thing that Rosemary learned from therapy was to develop a flexible attitude towards her thoughts rather than the rigid one that was largely responsible for creating the problem in the first place. Thus, Rosemary came the view that while she would prefer only to have thoughts that were consistent with prayer and being in church, she did not have to be immune from having such thoughts. She came to regard them as irritants to be endured rather than 'horrors' to be immediately expunged from her mind.

Understanding how her mind works when she is being rigid and when she is being flexible

Rosemary was helped to understand how her mind worked when she held a rigid attitude towards thinking 'inappropriate' things about Christ, initially in church and then elsewhere. She saw how this led her to switch between becoming hypervigilant about the presence of images of Christ and trying to avoid looking at these images. She also was helped to see the relationship between trying to avoid thinking about something and an increase in these unwanted thoughts (e.g. through the white polar bear exercise described above) and how this relationship became much stronger when she held a rigid attitude towards having such thoughts in the first place and immediately getting rid of them in the second place.

She was helped to see how her mind works when she holds a flexible attitude towards unwanted thoughts. Initially she had to take this on trust as she had no experience of it. However, she began to experience this difference having repeated the white polar bear exercise several times while holding a flexible attitude towards this thought. She found that while she was honest with herself and would prefer not to have her unwanted thoughts about Christ, when she did not insist that she did not have them in the first place and did not have to get rid of them in the second place, she found that they usually went after a time when she just 'let them be' in her mind, as I will discuss further below.

Accepting scanning and reversing avoidance

Rosemary was helped to understand that mental scanning was a consequence of holding a rigid attitude towards a threat, in her case seeing an image of Jesus Christ. When she identified that she was beginning to do this, she learned to rehearse her flexible attitude towards her unwanted thoughts and go about her business in the church, praying normally. She also learned that when she felt the urge to avoid looking at an image of Christ she was to rehearse her flexible attitude first and while doing so look at the image.

Rosemary also learned that it was important for her face up to what she had been avoiding. Armed with her new understanding of the problem and her developing alternative flexible attitude towards her unwanted thoughts, Rosemary step-by-step returned to her local church and step-by-step met all the people that she had come to avoid. This 'avoidance of avoidance' as she came to call it was a key factor in Rosemary's recovery.

Developing and practising REBT-oriented mindfulness

Rosemary learned that the goal of therapy was not to eliminate her unwanted, 'inappropriate' thoughts about Christ, but to go about her business even though she had these thoughts. To this end she learned several techniques based on the principles of mindfulness, all of which helped her to be mindful of these thoughts and to let them be rather than to try to get rid of them or to engage in an inner dialogue of what they indicated about her. She realised that such an inner dialogue was based on the idea that once she understood why she had them, they would go. However, her developing mindful approach was based on an honest admission that she would rather not have these thoughts. She was able to use the techniques of mindfulness as long as she did not transform this desire into an implicit rigid attitude. If she did engage in such a transformation, she acknowledged that she had done this, reminded herself that she did not have to be immune from these thoughts and that she did not have to eliminate them and then went back to employing her mindfulness methods.

At the end of therapy, Rosemary fully reintegrated herself into church life. She still had her unwanted thoughts from time to time, but did not disturb herself about having them. She still felt bad about having such thoughts, but as they were unwanted, she could hardly be expected to feel good or neutral about them, could she?

*

In the Postscript that follows, I reflect on the personal contributions that I have made to the theory and practice of REBT. I think doing so is a fitting way to bring to a conclusion this very personal collection of my writings.

Postscript

Personal Contributions to Rational Emotive Behaviour Therapy[4]

Overview

In this Postscript, I will outline some of my major contributions to the development of theory and practice in Rational Emotive Behaviour Therapy (REBT). I will focus on my contribution to the professional therapy literature and will not refer to any of the many REBT-inspired self-books that I have written over the years or to the recent work I have done to develop Rational Emotive Behaviour Coaching. While ultimately it is for others to pass judgment on my contributions to REBT, I have valued the opportunity to look back over my 40-year career as an REBT therapist and reflect on what I think I have contributed. Amongst other things I have done the following:

1. I have changed some of the language of REBT concepts to make them clearer and less pejorative.

2. I have endeavoured both to highlight its distinctive features and to connect it to the broader context of psychotherapy.

3. I have shown how working alliance theory can inform the effective practice of REBT and have developed a variety of therapist and client training materials to achieve the same end.

4. I have tried to implement Ellis's principle of therapeutic efficiency by developing a variety of REBT-based approaches to brief therapy and single session interventions and have been in the vanguard of developing what I have called 'Vivid REBT'.

5. I have, over the course of my career, published pieces of a rather controversial nature to show what light REBT can shed on

---

[4] Revised from a talk given to the Societa Italiana Terapia Comportmentale Cognitiva at the Sigmund Freud University, Milan on 13/10/2017.

difficult topics, which are featured in Parts I, II and III of this Collection.

6. I end this Postscript by making the point that the most effective REBT therapists are those that embody the theory in their everyday life and show how this has been the case for me.

Introduction

As I outlined earlier in this Collection, I was first introduced to what was known at that time as Rational-Emotive Therapy (RET) in 1974 while studying on the one-year, full-time, Diploma in Counselling in Educational Settings course at the University of Aston in Birmingham where a year later I joined the lecturing staff. The course I was on was heavily rooted in person centred therapy. While I resonated with this approach's theory I did not resonate with its suggestions about practice. By contrast, I was drawn to both the theory and practice of REBT and had an opportunity in 1977 to do some training with Maxie C. Maultsby and Virginia Anne Church, two proponents of Rational Behaviour Therapy (RBT), which was closely identified with REBT but not synonymous with it. My appetite having been whetted, I decided to train at what is now known as the Albert Ellis Institute in New York. A year later I did several training courses during the summer of 1978 and had the unique opportunity of serving as Albert Ellis's co-therapist for four nights a week during August. A few years later, I had become a fully trained REBT therapist and an REBT supervisor.

However, largely due to the training I had received at Aston University, I considered that it was important for me also to be trained in psychotherapy from a broader perspective and in 1978 I began a two-year Master of Science degree in Psychotherapy at the University of Warwick, qualifying in 1980. This course was highly eclectic and encouraged students to consider therapeutic issues from a broad and varied perspective. Thus, while I have continued to be highly influenced by REBT's distinct view of psychological disturbance and its remediation, I have also drawn from the best of what other therapeutic approaches have to offer. This 'both-and' rather than 'either-or' standpoint is a hallmark of pluralism in psychotherapy (Cooper & McLeod, 2011; Cooper & Dryden, 2016).

Therefore, I consider that the concepts of 'rationality' and 'pluralism' are defining features of my therapeutic career and as such, these two concepts form the title of my volume of selected works that appears in the 'World Library of Mental Health' published by Routledge (Dryden, 2013a).[5] In this Postscript, I set out to map what I consider to be my major contributions to the theory and practice of REBT within a pluralistic perspective.

Preserving the Distinctiveness of REBT and Its Classical Views

The first contribution I would like to discuss concerns what I call preserving the distinctiveness of REBT. My interest in this topic was sparked by the row that occurred when Albert Ellis was prevented from working at the Institute that bore and still bears his name. At that time, Albert was claiming that professionals at the Institute were 'watering down' REBT to the point that it was becoming indistinguishable from CBT. At that time, I had taught on the Institute's professional training courses for many years and was aware that some trainers were not as 'classical' in their REBT teaching and supervision as others, but this had always been the case and was not a recent phenomenon. And of course, other trainers, including myself, were classical in teaching REBT, particular on the Institute's 'primary certificate' programme. Thus, in my view, Ellis's perception that there was a general 'watering down' of REBT at the Institute was wrong and needed a response.

The Distinctive Features of REBT

On thinking about how I could respond to Ellis's unfounded criticism, I decided that there needed to be a clear statement concerning the nature of REBT. Ellis (e.g. 1980a) himself had muddied the waters on this issue by claiming that there were, in

---

[5] However, I have never been happy with the terms 'rational' and 'irrational' in REBT theory and practice and have changed them as I will presently discuss.

fact, two REBTs: sometimes diplomatically referred to as specific vs general REBT and at other times more pejoratively as elegant vs inelegant REBT. Ellis (1980a) said that general (or inelegant) REBT could be regarded as synonymous with cognitive behaviour therapy (CBT). Thus, in my view, there needed to be a clear statement of what is 'non-watered-down' REBT, so I set about writing a paper on this subject.

As I began work on this paper, it quickly became apparent that the task was too big for an article and thus I set about writing a book on the subject which was published with the title *Rational Emotive Behaviour Therapy: Distinctive Features* (Dryden, 2009a, 2015, 2021a). By 'distinctive features' I meant the theoretical and practical features aspects of REBT that taken together would indicate the nature of this therapeutic approach and would distinguish it from other CBT approaches (see Table P.1).

REBT's Unique ABC Models of Psychological Disturbance and Health

Thinking now about which of these features are unique to REBT – meaning those features that only appear in REBT - I think that these are encapsulated in REBT's ABC models of psychological disturbance and health. Let me briefly outline these here:

Situation

The 'situation' refers to a descriptive account of what happened in the emotional episode that the therapist and client are investigating. Maultsby (1975) referred to this as the 'camera check'. While the 'situation' variable is not a mandatory part of the ABC models, I have found it useful to include it for two reasons. First, it helps a client to select a specific example of their 'target' problem (i.e. the problem that they have targeted for change). Second, it helps the client to examine, at the appropriate time, the distortions that they may have made at 'A'. This variable is, of course, not unique to REBT.

Table P.1   REBT's distinctive features (Dryden, 2021a)

The Distinctive Theoretical Features of REBT

- Terminology and theory
- Post-modernism, relativism and other emphases: REBT's distinctive theoretical heritage
- REBT's distinctive ABC model
- Rigid and extreme attitudes are at the very core of psychological disturbance
- Flexible and non-extreme attitudes are at the very core of psychological health
- Distinction between unhealthy negative emotions (UNEs) and healthy negative emotions (HNEs)
- REBT's key principle of emotional responsibility
- Explaining why clients' inferences are highly distorted
- Position on human worth
- Distinction between ego and discomfort disturbance and health
- Focus on meta-psychological disturbance
- The biological basis of human irrationality
- REBT's position on the origin and maintenance of psychological problems
- REBT's position on psychological change
- Position on good mental health

The Distinctive Practical Features of REBT

- The therapeutic relationship in REBT
- Position on case formulation
- Psycho-educational emphasis
- Dealing with problems in order: i) disturbance; ii) dissatisfaction; iii) development
- Early focus on rigid and extreme basic attitudes (R/EBs)
- Helping clients to change their rigid and extreme attitudes to flexible and non-extreme attitudes
- Variety of therapeutic styles
- REBT encourages clients to seek adversity when carrying out homework assignments, but does so sensibly
- Change is hard work and the use of therapist force and energy
- Emphasis on teaching clients general flexible and non-extreme attitudes and encouraging them to make a profound philosophic change
- Compromises in therapeutic change
- When to use a change-based focus (CBF) and when to use an acceptance-based focus (ABF)
- Focus on clients' misconceptions, doubts, observations and objections to REBT
- Therapeutic efficiency
- Theoretically consistent eclecticism

'*A*'

'A' represents the aspect of the situation that the client responded to in the emotional episode under investigation. Traditionally, 'A' has stood for 'activating event', but I prefer to use the term 'adversity'. I do so for three reasons. First, the term 'activating event' is confusing. It does not help both therapist and client to see clearly that the latter has responded to some aversive aspect of the situation and not to the situation itself. Second, it does not make clear what is activated. Is it 'B' or is it 'C'. Finally, it does not make clear that the ABC models are, in essence, explanations of how clients handle adversity. The term 'activating event' does not make clear that the 'A' is negative while the term 'adversity' does.

Most commonly, 'A' is inferential, which means that the client has interpreted what happened in the situation to which they have responded. This inference may be accurate or inaccurate. In my view, it is a unique feature of REBT that, the therapist encourages the client to assume, at least temporarily, that 'A' is true unless there is a good reason not to do so. The purpose of this strategy is to help the person to identify the basic attitudes at 'B' that largely account for their responses at 'C'. Other approaches to CBT which advocate the examination and change of problematic cognitions are more likely initially to help the client to examine and change cognitive distortions at 'A' rather than use them as a way of identifying problematic, self-defeating basic attitudes at 'B'.

While, of course, in REBT we advocate a 'B–C' explanation of psychological disturbance and health rather than an 'A–C' explanation, 'A's help us to understand what emotions the person experienced at 'C'. REBT is a good example of a transdiagnostic approach to understating and dealing with psychological disturbance. This means in our case that all disturbance rests on the activation of a set of rigid and extreme attitudes. However, an understanding of the inferential theme at 'A' is necessary for us to understand the type of emotional disturbance experienced by the client.

In the work that I have done on clarifying the REBT position on the major emotional problems for which clients seek help (Dryden, 2009c, 2022a), I have extended Beck's (1976) work in specifying these inferential themes at 'A' (see Table P.2). Given that the specification of such emotional themes has been done by Beck (1976) and others, it is not a unique feature of REBT although it is an important one.

Table P.2   Inferences and Negative Emotions (Unhealthy and Healthy)

Inference	Emotion (UNE/HNE)
• Threat	Anxiety/Concern
• Loss • Failure • Undeserved plight	Depression/Sadness
• Broken moral code • Failure to live up to moral code • Hurt or harmed someone	Guilt/Remorse
• Revelation of highly negative information about self or reference group • Falling very short of ideal • Others look down on or shun you (or a group with whom you identify)	Shame/Disappointment
• Others undeservedly treat you badly • Another person indicates that their relationship with you is less important to them than the relationship is to you	Hurt/Sorrow
• Frustration; goal obstruction • Bad treatment from others • Transgression of personal rule • Disrespect; threat to self-esteem	Unhealthy Anger/Healthy Anger
• A threat is posed to your relationship with your partner from a third person. • A threat is posed by uncertainty you face concerning your partner's whereabouts, behaviour or thinking in the context of the first threat	Jealousy/Non-Jealous Concern about Relationship
• Another person possesses and enjoys something desirable that you do not have	Unhealthy Envy/Healthy Envy

'B'

Most of the unique features of REBT can be seen in its view that disturbed responses to adversity can be largely accounted for by the presence of a set of rigid and extreme basic attitudes and that healthy responses to adversity can be largely accounted for by the presence of a set of flexible and non-extreme attitudes.

In 2016, I wrote explaining why I had difficulties with the terms 'belief' and rational/irrational and announced that instead of 'beliefs' I was going to use the term 'attitudes' and instead of irrational and rational as they pertain to attitudes I was going to use the terms rigid/extreme and flexible/non-extreme (Dryden, 2016). While I refer the reader to that text for a full explanation for my reasoning and decision, briefly my points are as follows:

- The term 'belief' can refer to an inference (e.g. 'I believe that you do not like me) or to faith, both religious (e.g. 'I believe in God) or in a person ('I believe in you'). As such it can be confusing for clients. The term 'attitude' is closer to what Ellis mean by the word 'belief'. It means adopting an evaluative stance to something like an adversity and tends not to have other meanings that may serve to confuse clients (Colman, 2015). Because the term 'attitude' begins with the letter 'A' to preserve it under 'B', I suggested in the 2016 book that I will use the term 'basic attitude' when formally referring to the ABC framework and the term 'attitude' at other times.

- The term 'irrational' is problematic in my view because clients often think it means 'crazy' or stupid' as well as lacking reason. Women, in particular, find the term 'irrational' insulting since it is a pejorative term that has been used to put down women for years. Because 'irrational beliefs' are rigid and extreme in nature, I decided to use these terms when describing attitudes and throughout this book, I have referred to 'rigid and extreme attitudes' rather than 'irrational beliefs'.

    The term 'rational' is problematic in my view because clients often think it means 'cold', 'unemotional' or 'robot-like'. Since 'rational beliefs' recognise the importance of passion in the strong desires that people have, the term 'rational' conjures up the opposite of what is meant. Because 'rational beliefs' are flexible and non-extreme in nature, I decided to use these terms when describing attitudes and throughout this book, I have referred to 'flexible and non-extreme attitudes' rather than 'rational beliefs'.

Ellis (1994) was quite clear that while there are (what I call) four rigid/extreme attitudes, rigid attitudes lie at the core of psychological disturbance and the remaining three: awfulising attitudes, unbearability attitudes and devaluation attitudes are derived from this rigid attitudinal core. Similarly, Ellis was clear that while there are (what I call) four flexible/non-extreme attitudes, flexible attitudes lie at the core of psychological health and the remaining three: non-awfulising attitudes, bearability attitudes and unconditional acceptance attitudes are derived from this flexible attitudinal core.

I think that one of my contributions to this unique feature of REBT theory has been to ensure, in my writings, that the differences between rigid/extreme attitudes and flexible/non-extreme attitudes are clearly defined. I have emphasized that while a rigid attitude comprises a preference that the person makes rigid (e.g. 'I want to do well, and therefore I have to do so'), a flexible belief comprises the same preference, but which the person keeps flexible (e.g. 'I want to do well, but I don't have to do so'). Thus, when someone says that a preference such as 'I want to do well' is a flexible attitude, my response is that without knowing whether the person keeps the preference flexible or makes it rigid, we just don't know whether this is the case or not. This is important because in many authored textbooks on counselling and psychotherapy, preferences on their own are described as rational beliefs (or what I call flexible/non-extreme attitudes) which is not the case (Dryden, 2013b). In many of my books, I have ensured that I fully delineate the components of each rigid/extreme attitude and its flexible/non-extreme alternative. My view is that if someone is going to critique this unique feature of REBT theory, then it is important that they need to understand it fully.

'C'

In REBT, 'C's are the consequences of holding attitudes at 'B'. These consequences can be emotional, behavioural and thinking. REBT's view of negative emotions follows logically from its position on the differences between rigid/extreme attitudes and flexible/non-extreme attitudes and is thus also one of its unique features. This view is that the negative emotions that stem from rigid/extreme attitudes are largely unhealthy in effect, whereas those that stem from flexible/non-extreme attitudes are largely healthy in effect (see Table P.2 above). Clients are often puzzled about the idea that a negative emotion can be healthy, so the therapist needs to explain why this is the case. Here the therapist explains that when a client faces an adversity at 'A', then their emotion is bound to be negative, and when their attitude is flexible/non-extreme, then this helps to ensure that this emotion is healthy and encourages them to take constructive action to change the adversity if it can be changed. I have written several books whose main focus has been to outline REBT's view of negative emotions (e.g. Dryden, 2009c, 2022a) and how to deal with them (Dryden, 2012a, 2012b).

REBT's view of the behavioural consequences of basic attitudes at 'B' also follows logically from its position on the differences between rigid/extreme and flexible/non-extreme attitudes. It is that when a person holds a set of rigid/extreme attitudes towards an adversity at 'A', then their behaviour tends to be unconstructive and when the person holds a set of flexible/non-extreme attitudes then their behaviour tends to be constructive.

In our book, *The Practice of Rational Emotive Behavior Therapy*, Ellis and I argued that the cognitive distortions popularised by David Burns (1980) stem from rigid and extreme attitudes (Ellis & Dryden, 1987, 1997). I have done a number of research studies that support this view (Bond & Dryden, 1996b; Bond & Dryden, 1997; Dryden, Ferguson & Clark, 1989; Dryden, Ferguson & McTeague, 1989; Dryden, Ferguson & Hylton, 1989). These studies routinely showed that in a variety of contexts when someone holds a set of rigid/extreme attitudes towards an adversity, then they make adversity-related inferences that are much more distorted and biased to the negative than when they hold a set of flexible/non-extreme attitudes towards the same adversity. In the latter case, the inferences that they make tend to be balanced and realistic. Consequently, one of my contributions to REBT has been to ensure that cognitive consequences of rigid/extreme attitudes and flexible/ non-extreme attitudes are given equal status to the emotional and behavioural consequences of the same beliefs in any explication of the ABCs of REBT (Dryden, 2013b).

One of my interests has been on how the ABCs of REBT have been portrayed both within the REBT community and in the wider field of psychotherapy. Thus, I have researched how the ABC model has been represented in counselling and psychotherapy textbooks, by a sample of qualified REBT therapists and in Albert Ellis's posthumously published book co-authored with his wife (Ellis & Joffe Ellis, 2011). In the book that summarises this research (Dryden, 2013b), I consider all the errors made and confusions shown about the ABC model and supply corrections to them all. In this way, I consider that one of my major contributions to REBT has been as the gatekeeper of Ellis's classical views.

REBT from a Broad Perspective

Despite my roles as the custodian of Ellis's classical views and the preserver of REBT's distinctiveness, I have always sought to connect it with the broader therapeutic zeitgeist. In presenting this work here I will do so using the Piagetian terms of assimilation and accommodation. Accommodation involves making changes to REBT's schema as a result of new information and assimilation involves fitting new information within REBT's existing schema.

Accommodation

As I said above, accommodation in REBT involves changes being made to the REBT schema as a result of new information coming to light. My main contribution here has been recent and involves my suggestion that the term 'belief' is replaced by the term 'attitude' in and the terms 'irrational' and 'rational when referring to 'beliefs' are replaced by the terms 'rigid/extreme' and flexible/non-extreme (see above and Dryden, 2016).

Assimilation

As outlined above, assimilation involves incorporating new information within REBT's existing schema. It involves giving an REBT 'spin' on matters therapeutic. Albert Ellis did this a lot during his lifetime.

My contributions to the REBT literature from the perspective of assimilation began early in my career as an REBT therapist, influenced as I was by the eclectic nature of the MSc in Psychotherapy that I took between 1978 and 1980 at the University of Warwick. My first paper in this genre was entitled 'Past Messages and Disputations' (Dryden, 1979). This piece was one of the first articles that I wrote on REBT and the first of mine to be published in *Rational Living,* the house organ of the currently named Albert Ellis Institute which is now the *Journal of Rational-Emotive & Cognitive-Behavior Therapy.* The basic thesis of this article was that while REBT therapists do not routinely take their clients back to their past, they can certainly do this, particularly when clients think that this will be therapeutic for them. However, as they do this, therapists need to guard against teaching clients that the past can cause present disturbance. Rather the past or more accurately the inferences that one has formed of past events can and often do contribute to such disturbance. How this is dealt with is then explored in the article.

REBT as theory-consistent eclecticism

A year later, I published a paper that was focused on REBT as a form of what I came to call theoretically-consistent eclecticism (Dryden, 1982). In that paper, I argued that it is possible for REBT therapists to select styles, strategies and techniques originated from other therapeutic approaches but to do so in ways that are consistent with REBT theory. I outlined the following theory-inspired guidelines for choosing such therapeutic procedures:

Helping clients get better rather than feel better. Numerous therapeutic procedures help people feel better in the short-term and REBT therapists would use them, but only if they also help them to get better. This means using procedures that encourage attitude change at 'B' in the longer term.

Helping clients to accept themselves rather than to raise their self-esteem. One of the unique features of REBT is its position on encouraging clients to accept themselves unconditionally rather than on encouraging them to raise their self-esteem. In considering whether to use a therapeutic procedure, it is important to avoid, wherever possible, using one which does the latter rather than the former unless there is a good reason to do so.

Helping clients to feel healthily angry rather than unhealthily angry. As already noted earlier, a unique feature of REBT is its position on the difference between healthy and unhealthy negative emotions. In the 1982 paper, I argued that in selecting therapeutic procedures in the treatment of unhealthy anger, REBT therapists need to avoid those that maintain unhealthy anger and use those that promote healthy anger. However, the same is true when promoting all healthy negative emotions, not just healthy anger.

Helping clients to expose themselves fully to adversity rather than gradually face it. Ellis (e.g. 1983) argued that it was important to encourage clients to face adversity as fully as possible rather than to face it gradually. His point was that the use of desensitisation procedures unwittingly reinforce clients' unbearability attitudes. The implicit message is: 'go slowly and avoid feeling too uncomfortable because you may not be able to bear it'. Exposure methods, if clients are prepared to use them, by contrast, help people deal with adversity without reinforcing the above attitudes. However, not all clients will opt for full exposure, and in such circumstances, I recommend that they choose tasks that are 'challenging, but not overwhelming' for them (Dryden, 1985). This is one of several compromises with the ideal practice of REBT that its therapists are called upon to make and in 1987, I wrote a piece on this point which indicates that the best REBT therapists are those prepared to be flexible (Dryden, 1987a). The theme of therapist flexibility can be found throughout my writings on REBT to the present day (Dryden, 2018a).

Therapist self-disclosure

I did my PhD thesis on self-disclosure and I was awarded my doctorate in 1974. I returned to the subject in 1990 when I was invited to write a chapter on self-disclosure in REBT. In that chapter (Dryden, 1990), I outlined the advantages and potential dangers of therapist self-disclosure and made the point that perhaps the most valuable aspect of such disclosure is to show the client that it is possible to have a problem and use REBT to address it effectively. I briefly returned to this subject many years later where I stressed the importance of the therapist asking the client for permission to self-disclose before doing so (Dryden, 2018a).

Case formulation

In developing REBT, Ellis (1962) eschewed the practice of engaging clients in a lengthy period of assessment and diagnosis before offering treatment. He related his experiences when he had to do this and noted that clients would often drop out before treatment began. Consequently, therapeutic efficiency – bringing about change in the briefest time possible (Ellis, 1980b) – became one of REBT's distinctive features (Dryden, 2009a, 2015, 2021a). This is why Ellis counsels REBT therapists to adopt an early focus on clients' rigid/extreme attitudes and to encourage their clients to tackle their problems full on, if possible.

Ellis's position helps to explain why REBT advocates a problem assessment approach to treatment rather than a case formulation approach, as is more common in CBT. Ellis argued that you can build up a formulation of a 'case' over time as you focus on helping a client to address their problems and that to base therapy on the practice of doing a case formulation before initiating treatment is less efficient. While this idea remains to be testedempirically, it has not encouraged most REBT therapists to use a case formulation approach when taking such an approach may be indicated.

While I agree that the routine practice of doing a case formulation before embarking on therapy is not an efficient one, I also hold that at times taking a case formulation can be helpful (e.g. in complex cases and where clients have previously failed to benefit from therapy). Consequently, over twenty years ago, I published an REBT approach to case formulation (Dryden, 1998b) which I called

'Understanding a Person in the Context of their Problems' (UPCP). As far as I am aware it is the only formal approach to REBT case formulation that has been developed. The approach suggests a number of factors that need to be considered in developing a UPCP (see Table P.3).

Table P.3   Understanding the Person in the Context of their Problems (UPCP): An REBT Approach to Case Formulation (Dryden, 1998b)

- Basic information and initial impressions
- Identify therapeutic goals
- Develop a list of problem emotions (Cs)
- Identify dysfunctional behaviours (Cs)
- Identify the purposive nature of dysfunctional behaviour
- Develop a list of adversities (As)
- Identify core rigid and extreme basic attitudes (Bs)
- Identify ways in which the person prevents or cuts short the experience of problems
- Identify ways in which the person compensates for problems
- Identify meta-problems
- Identify the cognitive consequences of core rigid and extreme basic attitudes
- Identify the manner of problem expression and the interpersonal responses to this expression
- Predict the person's likely responses to therapy
- Negotiate a narrative account of the UPCP with the client

482   *Windy Dryden Collected!*

Self-compassion

In recent years, CBT has been influenced by developments in the fields of mindfulness (see Crane, 2017) and compassion (see Gilbert, 2007). In the latter area, Kristen Neff's (e.g. 2003) writings on self-compassion have attracted a lot of interest among CBT therapists. In 2012, I was invited by Michael Bernard to contribute to his edited volume on self-acceptance – a key concept in REBT theory (Bernard, 2013). In response to this invitation, I decided that I would write a piece on the relationship between unconditional self-acceptance (USA) and self-compassion (Dryden, 2013c). This chapter again shows how a concept that was developed outside REBT (self-compassion) can be related to a concept that was developed within REBT (unconditional self-acceptance) to create a more sophisticated understanding of how to help people more effectively, in this case with problems of self-criticism and low self-esteem. My basic thesis in this chapter was that to help clients to be compassionate towards themselves it is best to help them first to accept themselves unconditionally. Thus, it is difficult for people to show themselves compassion when they devalue themselves.

The Importance of the Working Alliance in REBT

During the Master's programme that I took in Psychotherapy at the University of Warwick from 1978 till 1980, I became interested in working alliance theory put forward by Ed Bordin (1979). In his view, the old psychoanalytic concept of the 'working alliance' could be reformulated and serve to explain the outcome of psychotherapy. Bordin argued that a good outcome was dependent on the strength of the working alliance between therapist and client and when the two had a good bond, agreed on therapeutic goals and carried out their respective goal-directed tasks then the chances of a good outcome was increased. Later, I added a fourth component of the alliance that I called 'views' (Dryden, 2006a, 2011). These were the understandings that the therapist and client had about the nature of the client's problems and how they could be best tackled as well as about the practical aspects of the therapeutic contract.

I published my first paper on the working alliance in REBT in the 1980s (Dryden, 1986b) and over twenty years later I used it as a structure for an REBT skills-oriented book that I wrote (Dryden, 2009c). I have included the working alliance in REBT in all of my chapters on REBT and have thus done my best to show that REBT is not just a collection of strategies and techniques, but can be best viewed as a purposeful therapeutic endeavour within the context of a developing alliance-based relationship between therapist and client. As such, I regard it as one of my most important contributions to the REBT literature. My current thinking on this topic is outlined in Dryden (2021b).

Language and Meaning in REBT

REBT theory comprises a number of concepts, all of which have a specific meaning in that theory. This meaning is often at variance with how these concepts are generally understood and as such, if the therapist does not take care to ensure that the client understands and agrees with the REBT meaning of a particular concept then therapeutic misunderstanding and miscommunication is likely to ensue. This was the subject of a paper that I wrote entitled 'Language and Meaning in RET' (Dryden, 1986a). Using the working alliance framework, which became a feature of my later publications, language and meaning in REBT theory is a topic that can be best placed in the 'views' domain of the alliance. When the therapist clarifies the client's understanding of REBT-based concepts he or she is carrying out important work within the 'tasks' domain of that alliance.

In that paper, I discussed among other issues that (i) both unhealthy and healthy negative emotions need to be clarified; (ii) unqualified shoulds should ideally not be used when referring to rigid attitudes; (iii) the terms 'catastrophic' and 'awful' are not synonymous; (iv) the term 'acceptance' is particularly open to misunderstanding and does not mean resignation, for example. As I have pointed out in my work on the working alliance, it is very important for the therapist and client to develop a shared vocabulary when discussing concepts that are open to misinterpretation and this was the key message of that paper.

Vivid REBT

REBT can be practised in a manner that is flat, boring and mechanical and when it is, it is rarely effective since clients are not encouraged to participate in an emotionally engaging process. By contrast, when REBT is practised in a way where its concepts come to life then clients do seem to benefit a lot more. They remember the concepts better and are thus able to retrieve and apply them when they need to. In the early 1980s, I published three linked articles on what I called 'Vivid RE[B]T' and outlined a number of ways in which therapists could make the practice of REBT more therapeutically stimulating for their clients.

Thus, I discussed ways in which the following aspects of REBT could be made more vivid: (i) problem assessment; (ii) disputing; and (iii) working through. These three articles were combined in a chapter that was published in Dryden (1986c). I now see this work as representing the therapist's contribution to the task domain of the working alliance.

Idiosyncratic REBT

One of the unfair criticisms of REBT has centred on the misconception that all REBT therapists practise in the argumentative, abrasive style wrongly attributed to Albert Ellis. While Albert could be abrasive, most of the available videotapes and audiotapes of him doing therapy do not show this. Rather, they demonstrate him being keen to help, focused and problem-solving in style. His lack of undue warmth is consistent with his views that this therapeutic ingredient fosters client dependency and is to be avoided (Ellis interview in Dryden, 1997b).

The Albert Ellis Institute has sought to correct the idea that there is only one way of practising REBT by releasing DVDs of a variety of REBT therapists doing demonstration sessions of REBT in a variety of different styles. Each therapist shows their unique way of developing a working alliance particularly in the bond and task domains of the alliance.

My own approach to addressing this important misconception was to edit a book entitled *Idiosyncratic REBT* where I invited several leading therapists to write about their own way of practising

REBT (Dryden, 2002). This collection shows the diversity of ways that REBT therapists initiate, maintain and suitably end the REBT-based working alliance.

Windy Dryden's idiosyncratic practice of REBT (see also Chapter 15)

My own idiosyncratic practice of REBT as presented in this book is marked by:

- Developing relationships with clients based on the principle of 'informed allies'
- Developing a 'case formulation' with complex 'cases'
- Developing an REBT-influenced problem and goals list with clients
- Working with specific examples of target problems at the beginning of therapy
- Identifying the critical 'A' (what I call the 'adversity') in the assessment process
- Focusing on thinking 'Cs' as well as emotional and behavioural 'C's
- Helping clients to develop and rehearse the full version of flexible/non-extreme attitudes
- Encouraging clients to voice their doubts, reservations and objections to REBT concepts and therapeutic process
- Deliberately instructing clients in the skills of REBT
- Encouraging clients to take responsibility for their change process
- Using vivid methods to promote change and
- Using humour to develop rapport and promote change.

Development of Training Materials
for Therapists and Clients

My career has been characterised by my carrying out several roles at the same time. These roles are: working in part-time independent practice, training therapists and executing a variety of academic tasks. I have found that each role enriches the other and variety has been the spice of my working life. From the beginning of my career, I have been interested in developing materials to help train therapists to practise REBT efficiently, and I have also done the same to help clients get the most out of REBT.

Developing Training Material for Therapists

In looking back at the work I have done developing training materials for REBT therapists over the years, I think I have contributed in the following ways.

Step-by-step guides

I have devised a number of step-by-step guides that were written to outline the various steps that therapists need to take when using REBT with clients. Perhaps the best known of these is 'the REBT primer' that has appeared in three editions (Dryden& DiGuiseppe, 1990; Dryden, DiGiuseppe & Neenan, 2003, 2010). The second edition was used by Dryden, Beal, Jones & Trower (2010) in the development of an REBT competency scale for clinical and research purposes. The latest edition of the primer outlines and discusses a 20-step treatment sequence that REBT therapists are encouraged to use with flexibility and sensitivity (see Table P.4).

I wrote a much simpler step-by-step guide that was designed to be used by therapists enrolled in the Albert Ellis Institute's 'Primary Certificate in REBT' programme. Participants would use it as a guide when they were serving as 'therapist' in the daily peer counselling sessions that form a central part of this programme. As such the 'First Steps Guide', as it has come to be known (Dryden, 2006b), outlines five major steps that participants need to learn and practice throughout the practicum: (i) define the problem and be goal-oriented; (ii) assess a concrete example of the client's target problem; (iii) preparing the client for the attitude examination process; (iv) examine the client's attitudes and (v) help the client to strengthen conviction their flexible/non-extreme attitudes and weaken conviction in their rigid/extreme attitudes.

Table P.4   The Rational Emotive Behavioural Treatment Sequence (Dryden, DiGiuseppe & Neenan, 2010) – with modifications to allow for use of the terms 'basic attitudes' and 'rigid/extreme' and 'flexible/non-extreme)

Step 1	Ask for a problem
Step 2	Clarify and select the target problem
Step 3	Formulate the target problem
Step 4	Set a goal with respect to the formulated target problem
Step 5	Ask for a specific example of the formulated target problem
Step 6	Assess the 'Situation'
Step 7	Assess 'C'
Step 8	Assess 'A'
Step 9	Agree upon a goal with respect to the assessed problem
Step 10	Help your client to see the link between the goal with respect to the formulated target problem and the assessed problem
Step 11	Identify and assess any meta-emotional problems if relevant
Step 12	Teach the 'B'–'C' Connection
Step 13	Assess 'rigid and extreme basic attitudes'
Step 14	Connect 'rigid and extreme basic attitudes' and the emotional problem and 'flexible and non-extreme attitudes' and the emotional goal
Step 15	Examine 'rigid and extreme attitudes' and 'flexible and non-extreme attitudes'
Step 16	Prepare your client to deepen conviction in 'flexible and non-extreme attitudes'
Step 17	Check the validity of 'A'
Step 18	Negotiate a homework assignment
Step 19	Check homework assignments
Step 20	Facilitate the working-through process

Note: 'A' = adversity; 'B' = basic attitude; 'C' = consequence of rigid and extreme attitude

The Masters-level training text

In 1995, I developed a Masters course in Rational Emotive Behaviour Therapy at Goldsmiths University of London which ran until I retired in 2014. I wrote with my colleague, Rhena Branch, a book which served as the course text for an intensive 12-week (one day a week) training module in the skills of REBT (Dryden & Branch, 2008). This text has a lot of illustrative dialogue and exercises and served as the foundation for the rest of the Master's course.

More advanced texts

I have also written some more advanced texts for REBT therapists wishing to extend their REBT skills set. 'Learning from Mistakes in REBT' helps trainees to identify and avoid common mistakes in practising REBT (Dryden & Neenan, 2011a). 'How to Think and Intervene like an REBT Therapist' spells the clinical thinking that effective REBT therapists engage in and how this guides their use of clinical strategies and techniques (Dryden, 2009d).

In most of my training texts, I encourage therapists to ask clients for their doubts, reservations and objections (DROs) to REBT concepts and, indeed, any aspect of the REBT therapy process. It is my view that clients who harbour such DROs subsequently 'resist' the efforts of their therapists to help them. A core skill of the REBT therapist is to ask for, elicit and deal effectively with these DROs if 'resistance' to change is to be effectively addressed. I explore this in another advanced text called 'Working with Resistance in Rational Emotive Behaviour Therapy' (Dryden & Neenan, 2011b).

Bite-sized points for therapists

While a full and nuanced understanding is central to practising REBT effectively and I believe that the training books that I have mentioned do just that, sometimes the busy REBT therapist needs access to what I call bite-sized points which each very briefly summarise an important aspect of REBT theory and practice. To this end, my colleague, Michael Neenan and I wrote a book entitled *Rational Emotive Behaviour Therapy: 100 Key Points and*

Techniques, which presents such points in the following nine sections: (i) therapeutic alliance issues; (ii) educational issues; (iii) dealing with clients' misconceptions about REBT; (iv) technical issues; (v) encouraging clients to work at change; (vi) disputing; (vii) dealing with obstacles to client change; (viii) creativity; (ix) develop yourself personally and professionally (Dryden & Neenan, 2015, 2021).

I produced an even more economical approach to providing therapists with important therapeutic points when I produced, again with Michael Neenan, *The REBT Therapist's Pocket Companion*. This book contains 240 pithy points of therapy wisdom for therapists and literally fits into one's pocket or purse (Dryden & Neenan, 2003).

Developing Training Material for Clients

Albert Ellis often said that a major goal of REBT should ideally be to help clients to become their own REBT therapists. While this is often done towards the end of therapy, my view has long been that if we are going to do this, then why not do it in a structured way and at the outset of therapy. Consequently, inspired by the well-known cognitive therapy text for clients called *Mind Over Mood*, which first came out in the mid-1995s (Greenberger & Padesky, 1995), I wrote a structured REBT manual for clients (Dryden, 2001b). I designed this book, entitled *Reason to Change: A REBT Workbook* so that clients could use it on their own or as an adjunct to therapy. However, I did not write a companion clinician's guide showing therapists how to incorporate the client workbook into therapy as was the case with *Mind Over Mood*. This proved to be a mistake which I rectified when I wrote linked client and therapist guides that were focused on helping clients to deal with one or more of the eight emotional problems for which clients seek therapeutic help (Dryden, 2012a, 2012b).

While *Reason to Change* was well received and clients with an obsessive-compulsive orientation to structured self-help loved it, I came to the view that most clients would benefit more from a smaller and less comprehensive approach to structured REBT self-help. So, I wrote *Getting Started with REBT: A Concise Guide for Clients* (Dryden, 2006c) which interestingly did not sell nearly as many copies as *Reason to Change*. Consequently, I recently wrote a second edition of the latter text (Dryden, 2022b).

Encouraged by the favourable reception given to The *REBT Therapist's Pocket Companion* I decided to write one for clients entitled, *The REBT Client's Pocket Companion* (Dryden, 2003). Again, this book contains 240 pithy points of therapy wisdom for clients and was also designed to fit into their pocket or purse.

Ever Briefer Interventions

Like Albert Ellis (1980b), I value therapeutic efficiency and have contributed to developing brief REBT in three ways.

Brief REBT in Eleven Sessions

My first major writing on brief REBT was to develop an eleven-session approach to REBT (Dryden, 1995a). I chose eleven sessions because in field testing the model, that was the number of sessions that I decided I needed to carry out all my tasks with clients who were seeking or were referred for brief therapy. In retrospect, while specifying the number of sessions and outlining what should ideally occur in each session, I made several mistakes. First, I assumed that other therapists work at the same rate as me with clients and this is not the case. Second, I did not stress clearly enough that not all the outlined therapy tasks needed to be covered with all clients. Some therapists, thus wrongly, but understandably assumed that they had to do all the tasks and in the specified session or they were not doing REBT properly. I realise now that I had developed a therapy manual which while valuable lacked the flexibility of how I would approach the task of writing a book on brief REBT now.

Single-Session Therapy

When I retired from my academic position at Goldsmiths University of London in 2014, I wanted a fresh therapeutic challenge. After much thought, reading and experimentation, I decided to develop an REBT-inspired approach to single-session therapy (Dryden, 2017, 2019). I was particularly inspired to do so by the work of Moshe Talmon (1990) and Michael Hoyt (Hoyt & Talmon, 2014). As the literature on single-session therapy (SST) makes clear, the goal is not to offer one session and that's that, but to treat the first session as if it could be the one and only session the client has. It may be the case that the client decides to come back for another session. Using the SST mindset (see Hoyt, Young & Rycroft, 2020), I would then conduct this new session as if it could be the last, and so forth. For the record, when people want a single session of therapy from the outset, my way of working is to offer them a 30-minute pre-session telephone call where the client and I set out to discuss how the latter can get the most from the session that follows soon after.[6] After the session (either face-to-face session or by online video platform), I carry out a follow-up telephone session at an agreed time with the client later to evaluate their progress the SST process and my contribution to it.

Very Brief Therapeutic Conversations in 30 Minutes or Less

Over the years, I have carried out more than many hundreds of live demonstrations of REBT in front of a professional or mixed professional and lay audience. I record each session and have it transcribed and then share these with the volunteer. These sessions are very much like the ones that Albert Ellis used to do at his Friday Night Workshop at the Albert Ellis Institute.[7] I have recently completed a book on my work in this context where I show what can be realistically achieved in 30 minutes or less by using a very focused REBT approach (Dryden, 2018b). This book contains the transcripts and commentary of eight very brief therapeutic conversations (VBTCs).

After Covid-19, online training events in the field of counselling and psychotherapy exploded in number and I have expanded the range of my live REBT-based therapy demonstrations. I now do a weekly 'Windy Dryden Live!' slot for the REBT Facebook Group, convened by Matt Walters where I do up to three extremely brief

---

[6] This was the case before Covid-19. Subsequently, I ask clients to complete a pre-session questionnaire which covers the same ground.
[7] This event still continues, but is now called 'Friday Night Live'.

demos in an hour, each lasting less than 18 minutes (Dryden, 2021c).

It is too early to judge how the last three developments will be received by the REBT community and, thus, only time will tell if I will consider them important contributions to REBT.

The Personal and the Controversial

I will bring this Postscript to a close by briefly discussing writings that are more controversial and personal in nature. I will begin with the controversial.

Controversial Writings

There is something in my personality that enjoys being controversial, not for its own sake, but to stimulate debate. To this end, I have published a number of my controversial writings and lectures in book form (Dryden, 1998a, 2002b, 2010).[8] Examples of pieces in this genre include: 'Looking for the Good in Hitler and acknowledging the Bad in Mother Teresa' (Dryden, 1998a) – see Chapter 12 in this Collection, 'On Taking Improper Precautions and Thinking the Unthinkable' (Dryden, 2010) – see Chapter 32 in this Collection, and 'Life's Bitter Pills: Dealing with Difficult Issues in Abuse' (Dryden, 2014).

My lecture 'Rationality, Outrageous Ideas and Sensitivity', published in Dryden (1998a) – see Chapter 11 in this Collection, sums up my approach here in that I show how rationality can be applied sensitively to controversial issues, without shying away from difficult truths. I like to do this in ways that capture the audience's attention. Thus, a section in the aforementioned lecture is entitled: 'Oedipus Schmoedipus: Why You Don't Have to Gouge Your Eyes Out When You Have Discovered That You Have Killed Your Father and Married Your Mother'. It contains an imaginary dialogue between myself and Oedipus which gives a flavour of my humorous approach to such matters.

---

[8] These form the three parts of this Collection.

Personal Writings

Although as far as I am aware, there is no research on this point, I believe that the best REBT therapists are those who use it with themselves at various points in their life. While it is true that some REBT therapists see it as a collection of techniques, others see it almost as a way of living. I would place myself in the latter camp. I am an REBT therapist partly because I used self-help techniques well before I became a therapist that were very similar to its current methods. Thus, I used to be very anxious about speaking in public because I was fearful of stammering. After listening to the comedian, Michael Bentine discuss on the radio how he overcame his fear of stammering in public (he basically used an anti-awfulising technique), I used something similar and helped myself enormously. While I was teased badly at school because of my stammer, I did not unduly disturb myself because I could see that the boys who teased me were only doing this to impress their friends and were nice to me on a one-to-one basis. I saw that while it was painful to be teased, I did not take it to mean that it reflected badly on me as a person. If anything, I saw that it reflected badly on my teasers, although I do not recall feeling hostile towards them. I discussed much of this in what I consider to be my best chapter in an edited collection (Dryden, 2001a) – see Chapter 13 in this Collection. The book it featured in is called *Embodied Theories*, edited by Spinelli & Marshall (2001) and contains accounts by therapists from different orientations reflecting on the question: 'To what extent do I practise with myself what I use to help others?'

Another personal piece of writing details my own experiences of being in therapy as a client or group member, much of which was not particularly helpful (Dryden, 2005) – see Chapter 14 in this Collection. I reflected in that chapter on the difficulty of being helped by a therapist who held a different view of my problems and what accounted for them than I did. This, of course, shows that the problem was in the 'views' domain of the working alliance. Indeed, the most effective help I received was by Albert Ellis himself with whom I discussed some personal issues in his lunchtime and supper sessions.

It is fitting that I end with Albert Ellis. Despite the fact that his final days were difficult and that he fell out with me and several others during those days, if it wasn't for Albert, I would not be here reflecting on my personal contributions to REBT. I owe him an enormous debt.

Appendix

Windy Dryden's 250 Books

1984

1. Dryden, W. (1984). *Rational-Emotive Therapy: Fundamentals and Innovations*. London: Croom Helm. [Reprinted in the Psychology Revivals series by Routledge, 2014.]

2. Dryden, W. (ed.). (1984*). Individual Therapy in Britain*. London: Harper & Row.

1985

3. Dryden, W. (ed.). (1985). *Marital Therapy in Britain. Volume 1: Context and Therapeutic Approaches.* London: Harper & Row.

4. Dryden, W. (ed.). (1985). *Marital Therapy in Britain. Volume 2: Special Areas.* London: Harper & Row (pp. 350).

5. Dryden, W. (1985*). Therapists' Dilemmas*. London: Harper & Row.

1986

6. Dryden, W., & Golden, W.L. (eds). (1986). *Cognitive-Behavioural Approaches to Psychotherapy*. London: Harper & Row.

1987

7. Dryden, W. (ed.). (1987). *Key Cases in Psychotherapy.* London: Croom Helm. [Also published by New York University Press, New York, 1987.] [Reprinted in the Psychology Revivals series by Routledge, 2014.]

8. Dryden, W. (1987). *Counselling Individuals: The Rational-Emotive Approach.* London: Taylor & Francis.

9. Dryden, W. (1987). *Current Issues in Rational-Emotive Therapy.* London: Croom Helm (pp. 221). [Reprinted in the Psychology Revivals series by Routledge, 2014.]

10. Ellis, A., & Dryden, W. (1987). *The Practice of Rational-Emotive Therapy.* New York: Springer.

1988

11. Dryden, W., & Trower, P. (eds). (1988). *Developments in Cognitive Psychotherapy.* London: Sage.

12. Dryden, W., & Trower, P. (eds). (1988). *Developments in Rational-Emotive Therapy.* Milton Keynes: Open University Press (pp. 234). [Initially published as Dryden, W., & Trower, P. (eds). (1986). *Rational-Emotive Therapy: Recent Developments in Theory and Practice.* Bristol: Institute for RET (UK).]

13. Trower, P., Casey, A., & Dryden, W. (1988). *Cognitive-Behavioural Counselling in Action.* London: Sage.

14. Rowan, J., & Dryden, W. (eds). (1988). *Innovative Therapy in Britain.* Milton Keynes: Open University Press.

15. Cole, M., & Dryden, W. (eds). (1988). *Sex Therapy in Britain.* Milton Keynes: Open University Press.

16. Aveline, M., & Dryden, W. (eds). (1988). *Group Therapy in Britain.* Milton Keynes: Open University Press.

17. Street, E., & Dryden, W. (eds). (1988). *Family Therapy in Britain.* Milton Keynes: Open University Press.

18. Epstein, N., Schlesinger, S., & Dryden, W. (eds). (1988). *Cognitive-Behavioral Therapy with Families.* New York: Brunner/Mazel.

1989

19. Dryden, W. (ed.). (1989). *Key Issues for Counselling in Action.* London: Sage.

20. Dryden, W. (ed.). (1989). *Howard Young – Rational Therapist: Seminal Papers in Rational-Emotive Therapy.* London: Gale Centre Publications.

21. Cole, M., & Dryden, W. (1989). *Sex Problems: Your Questions Answered.* London Macdonald Optima.

22. Dryden, W., & Spurling, L. (eds). (1989*). On Becoming a Psychotherapist.* London: Routledge.

23. Dryden, W., & Trower, P. (eds). (1989). *Cognitive Psychotherapy: Stasis and Change.* London: Cassell. (pp. 198). [Also published by Springer Publishing Co., New York, 1989.]

24. Dryden, W., Charles-Edwards, D., & Woolfe, R. (eds). (1989*). Handbook of Counselling in Britain.* London: Routledge.

1990

25. Dryden, W. (1990). *Rational-Emotive Counselling in Action.* London: Sage.

26. Dryden, W. (1990). *Creativity in Rational-Emotive Therapy.* London: Gale Centre Publications.

27. Dryden, W. (ed.). (1990). *Individual Therapy: A Handbook.* Milton Keynes: Open University Press.

28. Dryden, W., & Gordon, J. (1990). *Think Your Way to Happiness.* London: Sheldon.

29. Mearns, D., & Dryden, W. (eds). (1990). *Experiences of Counselling in action. London: Sage.*

30. Dryden, W., & Gordon, J. (1990). *What is Rational-Emotive Therapy? A Personal and Practical Guide.* London: Gale Centre Publications.

31. Dryden, W., & DiGiuseppe, R. (1990). *A Primer on Rational-Emotive Therapy.* Champaign, IL: Research Press.

32. Dryden, W., & Scott, M. (eds). (1990). *Introduction to Cognitive Behaviour Therapy: Theory and Applications.* London: Gale Centre Publications.

33. Dryden, W., & Norcross, J.C. (eds). (1990). *Eclecticism and Integration in Counselling and Psychotherapy.* London: Gale Centre Publications.

34. Dryden, W. (1990). *Dealing with Anger Problems: Rational-Emotive Therapeutic Interventions.* Sarasota, FL: Professional Resource Exchange.

35. Yankura, J., & Dryden, W. (1990). *Doing RET: Albert Ellis in Action.* New York: Springer Publishing Co.

36. Dryden W. (ed.). (1990). *The Essential Albert Ellis: Seminal Writings on Psychotherapy.* New York: Springer Publishing Co.

1991

37. Dryden, W. (ed.). (1991). *The Essential Arnold Lazarus.* London: Whurr Publishers.

38. Dryden, W. (1991). *Reason and Therapeutic Change.* London: Whurr.

39. Dryden, W., & Rentoul, R. (eds). (1991). *Adult Clinical Problems: A Cognitive-Behavioural Approach.* London: Routledge.

40. Dryden, W. (1991). *Dryden on Counselling. Vol. 1: Seminal Papers.* London: Whurr.

41. Dryden, W., & Branco Vasco, A. (1991). *Dryden on Counselling. Vol. 2: A Dialogue.* London: Whurr.

42. Dryden, W. (1991). *Dryden on Counselling. Vol. 3: Training and Supervision.* London: Whurr.

43. Dryden, W. (1991). *A Dialogue with John Norcross: Toward Integration.* Milton Keynes: Open University Press.

44. Dryden, W. (1991). *A Dialogue with Arnold Lazarus: 'It Depends'.* Milton Keynes: Open University Press.

45. Dryden, W. (1991). *A Dialogue with Albert Ellis: Against Dogma.* Milton Keynes: Open University Press.

46. Heap, M., & Dryden, W. (eds). (1991*). Hypnotherapy: A Handbook.* Milton Keynes: Open University Press.

47. Hooper, D., & Dryden, W. (eds). (1991). *Couple Therapy: A Handbook.* Milton Keynes: Open University Press.

48. Dryden, W., & Gordon, J. (1991). *How to Untangle Your Emotional Knots.* London: Sheldon Press.

49. Dryden, W., & Thorne, B. (eds) (1991). *Training and Supervision for Counselling in Action.* London: Sage.

1992

50. Dryden, W. (ed.). (1992). *Integrative and Eclectic Therapy: A Handbook.* Buckingham: Open University Press.

51. Dryden, W. (1992). *The Dryden Interviews: Dialogues on the Psychotherapeutic Process.* London: Whurr.

52. Dryden, W. (1992). (ed.). *Hard-Earned Lessons from Counselling in Action.* London: Sage.

53. Dryden, W. (1992). *The Incredible Sulk.* London: Sheldon Press.

54. Dryden, W., & Feltham, C. (1992). *Brief Counselling: A Practical Guide for Beginning Practitioners.* Buckingham: Open University Press.

55. Dryden, W., & Feltham, C. (eds). (1992). *Psychotherapy and Its Discontents.* Buckingham: Open University Press.

56. Dryden, W., & Yankura, J. (1992). *Daring to Be Myself: A Case Study in Rational-Emotive Therapy.* Buckingham: Open University Press.

57. Walen, S.R., DiGiuseppe, R., & Dryden, W. (1992). *A Practitioner's Guide to Rational-Emotive Therapy* (2nd edition). New York: Oxford University Press.

1993

58. Dryden, W. (1993). *Reflections on Counselling.* London: Whurr.

59. Dryden, W. (ed.). (1993). *Questions and Answers on Counselling in Action.* London: Sage.

60. Dryden, W., & Gordon, J. (1993). *Beating the Comfort Trap.* London: Sheldon Press.

61. Cole, M., & Dryden, W. (1993). *Sex: Why It Goes Wrong and What You Can Do About It.* London: Optima.

62. Dryden, W., & Gordon, J. (1993). *Peak Performance: Become More Effective at Work.* Didcot, Oxfordshire: Mercury.

63. Dryden, W., & Hill, L.K. (eds). (1993). *Innovations in Rational-Emotive Therapy.* Newbury Park, CA: Sage.

64. Feltham, C., & Dryden, W. (1993). *Dictionary of Counselling.* London: Whurr.

65. Thorne, B., & Dryden, W. (eds) (1993). *Counselling: Interdisciplinary Perspectives.* Buckingham: Open University Press.

66. Dryden, W., & Watts, A. G. (eds). (1993). *Guidance and Counselling in Britain: A 20-year perspective.* Cambridge: CRAC/Hobsons.

67. Dryden, W., & Yankura, J. (1993). *Counselling Individuals: A Rational-Emotive Handbook. 2nd edition.* London: Whurr.

1994

68. Dryden, W. (1994). *Progress in Rational Emotive Behaviour Therapy.* London: Whurr.

69. Dryden, W. (1994). *Overcoming Guilt.* London: Sheldon Press.

70. Dryden, W. (1994). *10 Steps to Positive Living.* London: Sheldon Press.

71. Dryden, W. (1994). *Invitation to Rational-Emotive Psychology.* London: Whurr.

72. Dryden, W., & Gordon, J. (1994). *How to Cope When the Going Gets Tough.* London: Sheldon.

73. Yankura, J., & Dryden, W. (1994). *Albert Ellis.* London: Sage.

74. Dryden, W., & Feltham, C. (1994). *Developing the Practice of Counselling.* London: Sage.

75. Feltham, C., & Dryden, W. (1994). *Developing Counsellor Supervision.* London: Sage.

76. Dryden, W., & Feltham, C. (1994). *Developing Counsellor Training.* London: Sage.

1995

77. Dryden, W. (1995). *Brief Rational Emotive Behaviour Therapy.* Chichester: John Wiley & Sons.

78. Dryden, W. (ed.). (1995). *Rational Emotive Behaviour Therapy: A Reader.* London: Sage.

79. Dryden, W. (ed.). (1995). *The Stresses of Counselling in Action.* London: Sage.

80. Dryden, W. (1995). *Preparing for Client Change in Rational Emotive Behaviour Therapy.* London: Whurr.

81. Dryden, W. (1995). *Facilitating Client Change in Rational Emotive Behaviour Therapy.* London: Whurr.

82. Scott, M.J., & Stradling, S.G., & Dryden, W. (1995*). Developing Cognitive-Behavioural Counselling.* London: Sage.

83. Dryden, W., & Yankura, J. (1995). *Developing Rational Emotive Behavioural Counselling.* London: Sage.

84. Dryden, W., & Gordon, J. (1995). *How to Cope with Difficult Parents.* London: Sheldon.

85. Palmer, S., Dryden, W., Ellis, A., & Yapp, R. (eds). (1995). *Rational Interviews.* London: Centre for Rational Emotive Behaviour Therapy.

86. Dryden, W., & Neenan, M. (1995). *Dictionary of Rational Emotive Behaviour Therapy.* London: Whurr.

87. Palmer, S., & Dryden, W. (1995). *Counselling for Stress Problems.* London: Sage.

88. Dryden, W., & Feltham, C. (1995). *Counselling and Psychotherapy: A Consumer's Guide.* London: Sheldon Press.

89. Traverse, J., & Dryden, W. (1995). *Rational Emotive Behaviour Therapy: A Client's Guide.* London: Whurr.

90. Dryden, W., Horton, I., & Mearns, D. (1995). *Issues in Professional Counsellor Training.* London: Cassell.

1996

91. Dryden, W. (1996). *Overcoming Anger: When Anger Helps and When It Hurts.* London: Sheldon Press.

92. Dryden, W. (1996). *Rational Emotive Behaviour Therapy: Learning from Demonstration Sessions.* London: Whurr.

93. Dryden, W. (ed.). (1996). *Research in Counselling and Psychotherapy: Practical Applications.* London: Sage.

94. Dryden, W. (ed.). (1996). *Handbook of Individual Therapy.* London: Sage.

95. Dryden, W. (ed.). (1996). *Developments in Psychotherapy: Historical Perspectives.* London: Sage.

96. Woolfe, R., & Dryden, W. (eds). (1996). *Handbook of Counselling Psychology.* London: Sage.

97. Steinberg, D., & Dryden, W. (1996). *How to Stick to a Diet.* London: Sage.

98. Cole, M., & Dryden, W. (1996). *Sex – How to Make it Better for Both of You: A Practical Guide to Overcoming Sex Problems.* London: Vermilion.

99. Neenan, M. & Dryden, W. (1996). *Dealing with Difficulties in Rational Emotive Behaviour Therapy.* London: Whurr.

100. Dryden, W. (1996). *Inquiries in Rational Emotive Behaviour Therapy.* London: Sage.

101. Palmer, S., & Dryden, W. (eds). (1996). *Stress Management and Counselling: Theory, Practice, Research and Methodology.* London: Cassell.

1997

102. Dryden, W. (1997). *Therapists' Dilemmas. Revised Edition.* London: Sage.

103. Dryden, W. (1997). *Overcoming Shame.* London: Sheldon.

104. Ellis, A., & Dryden, W. (1997). *The Practice of Rational Emotive Behavior Therapy. 2nd edition.* New York: Springer. [Also published by Free Association Books, London, 1999.]

105. Dryden, W., Gordon, J., & Neenan, M. (1997). *What is Rational Emotive Behaviour Therapy? A Personal and Practical Guide.* Loughton, Essex: Gale Centre Publications.

106. Yankura, J., & Dryden, W. (eds). (1997). *Using REBT with Common Psychological Problems: A Therapist's Casebook.* New York: Springer.

107. Yankura, J., & Dryden, W. (eds). (1997). *Special Applications of REBT: A Therapist's Casebook.* New York: Springer.

1998

108. Dryden, W. (1998). *Developing Self-Acceptance: A Brief, Educational, Small Group Approach.* Chichester: John Wiley & Sons.

109. Dryden, W. (1998). *Are You Sitting Uncomfortably: Windy Dryden Live and Uncut.* Ross-on-Wye: PCCS Books.

110. Dryden, W. (1998). *Overcoming Jealousy.* London: Sheldon.

1999

111. Neenan, M., & Dryden, W. (1999). *Rational Emotive Behaviour Therapy: Advances in Theory and Practice.* London: Whurr.

112. Dryden, W. (1999). *A Positive Thought for Every Day.* London: Sheldon.

113. Dryden, W., & Mytton, J. (1999). *Four Approaches to Counselling and Psychotherapy.* London: Routledge.

114. Dryden, W. (1999). *Rational Emotive Behavior Therapy: A Training Manual.* New York: Springer.

115. Dryden, W. (1999). *Rational Emotive Behaviour Therapy: A Personal Approach.* Bicester: Oxon: Winslow Press.

116. Dryden, W (1999). *Rational Emotive Behavioural Counselling in Action. 2nd edition.* London: Sage.

117. Dryden, W., Neenan, M., & Yankura, J. (1999*). Counselling Individuals: A Rational Emotive Behavioural Handbook. 3rd edition.* London: Whurr.

118. Dryden, W. (1999). *How to Accept Yourself.* London: Sheldon.

2000

119. Neenan, M., & Dryden, W. (2000). *Essential Rational Emotive Behaviour Therapy.* London: Whurr.

120. Dryden, W. (2000). *Invitation to Rational Emotive Behavioural Psychology.2nd edition.* London: Whurr.

121. Dryden, W. (2000). *Overcoming Procrastination.* London: Sheldon.

122. Neenan, M., & Dryden, W. (2000). *Essential Cognitive Therapy.* London: Whurr

123. Dryden, W. (2000). *Overcoming Anxiety.* London: Sheldon.

124. Dryden, W., & Matweychuk, W (2000). *Overcoming Your Addictions*. London: Sheldon.

2001

125. Neenan, M., & Dryden, W. (2001). *Learning from Errors in Rational Emotive Behaviour Therapy*. London: Whurr.

126. Dryden, W. (2001). *Reason to Change: A Rational Emotive Behaviour Therapy (REBT) Workbook*. Hove, East Sussex: Brunner-Routledge.

127. Dryden, W. (2001). *How to Make Yourself Miserable*. London: Sheldon.

2002

128. Neenan, M., & Dryden, W. (2002). *Life Coaching: A Cognitive-Behavioural Approach*. Hove, East Sussex: Brunner-Routledge.

129. Neenan, M., & Dryden, W. (2002). *Cognitive Behaviour Therapy: An A-Z of Persuasive Arguments*. London: Whurr.

130. Bond, F. W., & Dryden, W. (eds), (2002). *Handbook of Brief Cognitive Behaviour Therapy*. Chichester: Wiley.

131. Dryden, W., & Neenan, M. (eds), (2002). *Rational Emotive Behaviour Group Therapy*. London: Whurr.

132. Dryden, W. (2002). *Overcoming Envy*. London: Sheldon.

133. Dryden, W. (ed.). (2002). *Handbook of Individual Therapy*. 4th edition. London: Sage.

134. Dryden, W. (2002). *Fundamentals of Rational Emotive Behaviour Therapy: A Training Manual*. London: Whurr.

135. Dryden, W. (2002). *Up Close and Personal*. Ross-on-Wye: PCCS Books.

136. Dryden, W. (ed.). (2002). *Idiosyncratic Rational Emotive Behaviour Therapy*. Ross-on-Wye: PCCS Books.

2003

137. Dryden, W. (ed.). (2003). *Rational Emotive Behaviour Therapy: Theoretical Developments.* Hove, East Sussex: Brunner-Routledge.

138. Dryden, W., DiGiuseppe, R., & Neenan, M. (2003). *A Primer on Rational Emotive Behavior Therapy. 2nd edition.* Champaign, IL: Research Press.

139. Woolfe, R., Dryden, W., & Strawbridge, S. (eds). (2003). *Handbook of Counselling Psychology. 2nd edition.* London: Sage.

140. Dryden, W., & Opie, S. (2003).*Overcoming Depression.* London: Sheldon.

141. Dryden, W., & Neenan, M. (2003). *The REBT Therapist's Pocket Companion.* New York: Albert Ellis Institute.

142. Dryden, W. (2003) *The REBT Pocket Companion for Clients.* New York: Albert Ellis Institute.

143. Dryden, W., & Ellis, A. (2003). *Albert Ellis Live!* London: Sage.

144. Dryden, W. (2003*). Letting Go of Anxiety and Depression.* London: Sheldon.

145. Dryden, W. (2003). *Managing Low Self-Esteem.* London: Whurr.

2004

146. Dryden, W. (2004). *Rational Emotive Behaviour Therapy: Clients' Manual.* London: Whurr.

147. Dryden, W., & Neenan, M. (2004*). Counselling Individuals: A Rational emotive Behavioural Handbook. 4th edition.* London: Whurr.

148. Dryden, W., & Neenan, M. (2004*). The Rational Emotive Behavioural Approach to Therapeutic Change.* London: Sage.

149. Dryden, W., & Constantinou, D. (2004). *Assertiveness Step by Step*. London: Sheldon Press.

150. Dryden, W., & Neenan, M. (2004). *Rational Emotive Behavioural Counselling in Action. 3rd edition*. London: Sage.

151. Neenan, M., & Dryden, W. (2004). *Cognitive Therapy: 100 Key Points and Techniques*. Hove, East Sussex: Brunner-Routledge.

152. Feltham, C., & Dryden, W. (2004). *Dictionary of Counselling. 2nd edition*. London: Whurr.

2006

153. Neenan, M., & Dryden, W. (2006). *Cognitive Therapy in a Nutshell*. London: Sage.

154. Neenan, M., & Dryden, W. (2006). *Rational Emotive Behaviour Therapy in a Nutshell*. London: Sage.

155. Feltham, C., & Dryden, W. (2006). *Brief Counselling: A Practical Integrative Approach. 2nd edition*. Maidenhead: Open University Press.

156. Dryden, W. (2006). *Counselling in a Nutshell*. London: Sage.

157. Dryden, W. (2006). *First Steps in REBT: A Guide to Practising REBT in Peer Counseling*. New York: Albert Ellis Institute.

158. Dryden, W., & Neenan, M. (2006). *Rational Emotive Behaviour Therapy: 100 Key Points and Techniques*. Hove, East Sussex: Routledge.

159. Dryden, W. (2006). *Getting Started with REBT: A Concise Guide for Clients*. Hove, East Sussex, East Sussex: Routledge.

160. Dryden, W. (2006). *Helping Yourself with REBT: First Steps for Clients*. New York: Albert Ellis Institute.

2007

161. Dryden, W. (ed.). (2007*). Dryden's Handbook of Individual Therapy. 5th edition.* London: Sage.

162. Dryden, W. (2007). *Overcoming Hurt.* London: Sheldon.

2008

163. Dryden, W., & Branch, R. (2008). *The Fundamentals of Rational Emotive Behaviour Therapy: A Training Handbook. 2nd edition.* Chichester: Wiley.

164. Dryden, W., & Reeves, A. (eds). (2008). *Key Issues for Counselling in Action. 2nd edition.* London: Sage.

165. Branch, R., & Dryden, W. (2008). *The Cognitive Behaviour Counselling Primer.* Ross-on-Wye: PCCS Books.

2009

166. Dryden, W. (2009). *Rational Emotive Behaviour Therapy: Distinctive Features.* Hove, East Sussex, East Sussex: Routledge.

167. Dryden, W. (2009). *Understanding Emotional Problems: The REBT Perspective.* Hove, East Sussex, East Sussex: Routledge.

168. Dryden, W. (2009). *How to Think and Intervene Like an REBT Therapist.* Hove, East Sussex, East Sussex: Routledge.

169. Dryden, W. (2009*). Skills in Rational Emotive Behaviour Counselling and Psychotherapy.* London: Sage.

170. Dryden, W. (2009). *Self-Discipline: How to Get It and How to Keep It.* London: Sheldon Press.

2010

171. Woolfe, R., Strawbridge, S., Douglas, B., & Dryden, W. (eds). (2010). *Handbook of Counselling Psychology. 3rd edition.* London: Sage.

172. Dryden, W. (2010). *Strange, but Rational.* Ross-on-Wye: PCCS Books.

173. Dryden, W., DiGiuseppe, R., & Neenan, M. (2010). *A Primer on Rational Emotive Behavior Therapy. 3rd edition.* Champaign, IL: Research Press.

174. Dryden, W. (2010). *Coping with Life's Challenges: Moving on From Adversity.* London: Sheldon Press.

175. Dryden, W. (2010). *Coping with Envy.* London: Sheldon Press.

2011

176. Dryden, W. (2011). *Dealing with Emotional Problems in Life Coaching: A Rational-Emotive and Cognitive Behaviour Therapy (RECBT) Approach.* Hove, East Sussex: Routledge.

177. Dryden, W. (2011). *Understanding Psychological Health: The REBT Perspective.* Hove, East Sussex, East Sussex: Routledge.

178. Neenan, M., & Dryden, W. (2011). *Rational Emotive Behaviour Therapy in a Nutshell. 2nd edition.* London: Sage.

179. Neenan, M., & Dryden, W. (2011). *Cognitive Therapy in a Nutshell. 2nd edition.* London: Sage.

180. Dryden, W. (2011). *Counselling in a Nutshell. 2nd edition.* London: Sage.

181. Trower, P., Jones, J., Dryden, W., & Casey, A. (2011). *Cognitive-Behavioural Counselling in Action. 2nd edition.* London: Sage.

182. Dryden, W. (2011). *How to Develop Inner Strength*. London: Sheldon Press.

183. Dryden, W. (2011). *First Steps in Using REBT in Life Coaching*. New York: Albert Ellis Institute.

184. Dryden, W. (2011). *Be Your Own CBT Therapist*. London: Hodder Education.

185. Dryden, W. (2011). *Manage Your Anxiety Through CBT*. London: Hodder Education.

186. Dryden, W. (2011). *Coping with Manipulation: When Others Blame You for Their Feelings*. London: Sheldon.

2012

187. Dryden, W. (2012). *Dealing with Emotional Problems Using Rational-Emotive Cognitive Behaviour Therapy: A Client's Guide*. Hove, East Sussex, East Sussex: Routledge.

188. Dryden, W. (2012). *Dealing with Emotional Problems Using Rational-Emotive Cognitive Behaviour Therapy: A Practitioner's Guide*. Hove, East Sussex, East Sussex: Routledge.

189. Dryden, W., & Neenan, M. (2012). *Learning from Mistakes in Rational Emotive Behaviour Therapy*. Hove, East Sussex: Routledge.

190. Dryden, W., & Neenan, M. (2012). *Working with Resistance in Rational Emotive Behaviour Therapy*. Hove, East Sussex: Routledge.

191. Dryden, W., & Branch, R. (eds). (2012). *The CBT Handbook*. London: Sage.

192. Dryden, W. (ed.). (2012). *Cognitive Behaviour Therapies*. London: Sage.

193. Dryden, W. (2012). *CBT Tips for a Fulfilling Life.* London: Hodder Education.

194. Dryden, W. (2012). *Transforming Eight Deadly Emotions into Healthy Ones.* London: Sheldon Press.

195. Still, A., & Dryden, W. (2012). *The Historical and Philosophical Context of Rational Psychotherapy: The Legacy of Epictetus.* London: Karnac Books.

196. Dryden, W. (2012). *How to Come Out of Your Comfort Zone.* London: Sheldon Press.

2013

197. Dryden, W. (2013). *The ABCs of REBT: Perspectives on Conceptualization.* New York: Springer.

198. Dryden, W. (2013*). Rationality and Pluralism: The Selected Works of Windy Dryden.* Hove, East Sussex: Routledge.

199. Dryden, W. (2013). *Coping with Guilt.* London: Sheldon Press.

200. Neenan, M., & Dryden, W (2013). *Life Coaching: A Cognitive Behavioural Approach.* Hove, East Sussex: Routledge.

2014

201. DiGiuseppe, R.A., Doyle, K.A., Dryden, W., & Backx, W. (2014). *A Practitioner's Guide to Rational Emotive Behavior Therapy. 3rd edition.* New York: Oxford University Press.

202. Dryden, W., & Reeves, A. (eds). (2014). *The Handbook of Individual Therapy. 6th edition.* London: Sage.

203. Dryden, W., & Spurling, L. (eds). (2014). *On Becoming a Psychotherapist. Classic Edition.* Hove, East Sussex: Routledge.

204. Dryden, W. (2014). *Ten Steps to Positive Living. 2nd edition.* London: Sheldon Press.

2015

205. Neenan, M., & Dryden, W. (2015). *Cognitive Behaviour Therapy: 100 Key Points and Techniques. 2nd edition.* Hove, East Sussex: Routledge.

206. Dryden, W., & Neenan, M. (2015). *Rational Emotive Behaviour Therapy: 100 Key points and Techniques. 2nd edition.* Hove, East Sussex: Routledge.

207. Dryden, W. (2015). *Rational Emotive Behaviour Therapy: Distinctive Features. 2nd edition.* Hove, East Sussex: Routledge.

208. Dryden, W. (2015). *How to Get the Most Out of CBT.* Hove, East Sussex: Routledge.

209. Dryden, W. (2015). *How to Help Your Clients Get the Most Out of CBT.* Hove, East Sussex: Routledge.

2016

210. Trower, P., Jones, J., & Dryden, W. (2016). *Cognitive-Behavioural Counselling in Action. 3rd edition.* London: Sage.

211. Cooper, M., & Dryden, W. (eds). (2016). *The Handbook of Pluralistic Counselling and Psychotherapy.* London: Sage.

212. Dryden, W., & Aebi, J. (2016). *Four Approaches to Counselling and Psychotherapy. Classic Edition.* Abingdon, Oxon: Routledge.

213. Dryden, W. (2016). *Attitudes in Rational Emotive Behaviour Therapy: Components, Characteristics and Adversity-Related Consequences.* London: Rationality Publications.

214. Dryden, W. (2016). *When Time is at a Premium: Cognitive-Behavioural Approaches to Single-Session Therapy and Very Brief Coaching.* London: Rationality Publications.

2017

215. Dryden, W. (2017). *Single-Session Integrated CBT (SSI-CBT): Distinctive Features.* Abingdon, Oxon: Routledge.

216. Dryden, W. (2017). *Very Brief Cognitive-Behavioural Coaching (VBCBC).* Abingdon, Oxon: Routledge.

217. Matweychuk, W.J., & Dryden, W. (2017). *Rational Emotive Behaviour Therapy: A Newcomer's Guide.* Abingdon, Oxon: Routledge.

218. Dryden, W. (2017). *The Coaching Alliance: Theory and Guidelines for Practice.* Abingdon, Oxon: Routledge.

2018

219. Dryden, W. (2018). *Cognitive-Emotive-Behavioural Coaching: A Flexible and Pluralistic Approach.* Abingdon, Oxon: Routledge.

220. Dryden, W. (2018).*Rational Emotive Behavioural Coaching: Distinctive Features.* Abingdon, Oxon: Routledge.

221. Dryden, W. (2018). *A Practical Guide to Rational Emotive Behavioural Coaching.* Abingdon, Oxon: Routledge.

222. Dryden, W. (2018). *Flexibility-Based Cognitive Behaviour Therapy.* Abingdon, Oxon: Routledge.

223. Dryden, W. (2018). *Very Brief Therapeutic Conversations.* Abingdon, Oxon: Routledge.

224. Dryden, W. (2018). *The Relevance of Rational Emotive Behaviour Therapy for Modern CBT and Psychotherapy.* Abingdon, Oxon: Routledge.

2019

225. Dryden, W. (2019). *Single-Session Therapy: 100 Key Points and Techniques.* Abingdon, Oxon: Routledge.

226. Dryden, W. (2019). *Single-Session 'One-At-A-Time' Therapy: A Rational Emotive Behaviour Therapy Approach.* Abingdon, Oxon: Routledge.

227. Dryden, W. (2019). *Single-Session Therapy: Distinctive Features.* Abingdon, Oxon: Routledge.

228. Dryden, W. (2019). *Rational Emotive Behaviour Therapy in India: Very Brief Therapy for Problems of Daily Living.* Abingdon, Oxon: Routledge.

229. Bernard, M.E., & Dryden, W. (eds). (2019). *Advances in REBT: Theory, Practice, Research, Measurement, Prevention and Promotion.* Switzerland AG: Springer Nature.

230. Dryden, W., & Bernard, M.E. (eds). (2019). *REBT with Diverse Client Problems and Populations.* Switzerland AG: Springer Nature.

231. Dryden, W. (2019). *Helping Clients Deal with Adversity by Changing Their Attitudes.* Abingdon, Oxon: Routledge.

2020

232. Dryden, W. (2020). *Single-Session Coaching and One-At-A-Time Coaching: Distinctive Features.* Abingdon, Oxon: Routledge.

233. Neenan, M., & Dryden, W. (2020). *Cognitive-Behavioural Coaching: A Guide to Problem-Solving and Personal Development. 3rd edition.* Abingdon, Oxon: Routledge.

234. Dryden, W. (2020). *The Single-Session Therapy Primer: Principles and Practice.* Monmouth: PCCS Books.

2021

235. Dryden, W. (2021). *Dealing with Emotional Problems in Coaching: A Rational-Emotive and Cognitive Behavioural Approach. 2nd edition.* Abingdon, Oxon: Routledge.

236. Dryden, W. (2021). *Single-Session Therapy and Its Future: What SST Leaders Think.* Abingdon, Oxon: Routledge.

237. Dryden, W. (2021). *Help Yourself with Single-Session Therapy.* Abingdon, Oxon: Routledge.

238. Neenan, M., & Dryden, W. (2021*). Cognitive Behaviour Therapy: 100 Key Points and Techniques. 3rd edition.* Abingdon, Oxon: Routledge.

239. Dryden, W., & Neenan, M. (2021). *Rational Emotive Behaviour Therapy: 100 Key Points and Techniques. 3rd edition.* Abingdon, Oxon: Routledge.

240. Dryden, W. (2021). *Seven Principles of Good Mental Health.* London: Rationality Publications.

241. Dryden, W. (2021). *Rational Emotive Behaviour Therapy: Distinctive Features. 3rd edition.* Abingdon, Oxon: Routledge.

242. Dryden, W. (2021). *Seven Principles of Rational Emotive Behaviour Therapy.* London: Rationality Publications.

243. Dryden, W. (2021). *Seven Principles of Single-Session Therapy.* London: Rationality Publications.

244. Dryden, W. (2021). *Windy Dryden Live!* London: Rationality Publications.

245. Dryden, W. (2021). *The Working Alliance in Rational Emotive Behaviour Therapy.* Abingdon, Oxon: Routledge.

246. Dryden, W. (2021). *Seven Principles of Doing Live Therapy Demonstrations.* London: Rationality Publications.

247. Dryden, W. (2021). *Single-Session Therapy @ Onlinevents.* Sheffield: Onlinevents Publications.

2022

248. Dryden, W. (2022). *The Single-Session Therapist's Pocket Companion.* London: Rationality Publications.

249. Dryden, W. (2022). *Reason to Change: A Rational Emotive Behaviour Therapy (REBT) Workbook. 2nd edition.* Abingdon, Oxon: Routledge.

250. Dryden, W. (2022). *Windy Dryden Collected!* London: Rationality Publications.

References

Bannister, D. (1983). The internal politics of psychotherapy. In D. Pilgrim (ed.), *Psychology and Psychotherapy: Current Trends and Issues*. London: Routledge & Kegan Paul.

Beck, A. T. (1976). *Cognitive Therapy and the Emotional Disorders*. New York: International Universities Press.

Bernard, M.E. (ed.). (2013).*The Strength of Self-Acceptance: Theory, Practice and Research*. New York: Springer.

Bond, F. W., & Dryden, W. (1996a). Modifying irrational control and certainty beliefs: Clinical recommendations based upon research. In W. Dryden (ed.), *Research in Counselling and Psychotherapy: Practical Applications*. London: Sage.

Bond, F.W., & Dryden, W. (1996b). Testing an REBT theory: The effects of rational beliefs, irrational beliefs, and their control or certainty contents on the functionality of inferences, II: In a personal context. *International Journal of Psychotherapy, 1*(1), 55-77.

Bond, F.W., & Dryden, W. (1997). Testing a REBT theory: The effects of rational beliefs, irrational beliefs, and their control and certainty contents on the functionality of inferences. I: In a social context. *Journal of Rational-Emotive and Cognitive-Behavior Therapy, 15*(2), 157–88.

Bordin, E. S. (1979). The generalizability of the psychoanalytic concept of the working alliance. *Psychotherapy: Theory, Research and Practice, 16*, 252–60.

British Psychological Society. (1997). *Code of Conduct, Ethical Principles & Guidelines*. Leicester: BPS.

Burns, D. D. (1980). *Feeling Good: The New Mood Therapy*. New York: Morrow.

Charleton, M. (1996). *Self-Directed Learning in Counsellor Training*. London: Cassell.

Colman, A. (2015). *Oxford Dictionary of Psychology*. 4th edn. Oxford: Oxford University Press.

Cooper, M., & Dryden, W. (eds). (2016). *The Handbook of Pluralistic Counselling and Psychotherapy*. London: Sage.

Cooper, M. & McCleod, J. (2011). *Pluralistic Counselling and Psychotherapy*. London: Sage.

Crane, R. (2017). *Mindfulness-Based Cognitive Therapy: Distinctive Features. 2nd edition*. Abingdon, Oxon: Routledge.

Davison, G. C. (1995). Personal reflections on Albert Ellis and rational emotive behavior therapy. *Journal of Rational-Emotive and Cognitive-Behavior Therapy, 13*, 81–4.

Dobson, K. S. (ed.) (2001). *Handbook of Cognitive-Behavioral Therapies*, 2nd edn. New York: Guilford.

Dryden, W. (1979). Past messages and disputations: The client and significant others. *Rational Living, 14*(2), 26–8.

Dryden, W. (1980). The relevance of research in counselling and psychotherapy for the counselling practitioner. *British Journal of Guidance and Counselling, 8*(2), 224–32.

Dryden, W. (1982). Rational-emotive therapy and eclecticism. *The Counsellor, 3*(5), 15–22.

Dryden, W. (1984). Rational-emotive therapy and cognitive therapy: A critical comparison. In M.A. Reda & M.J. Mahoney (eds), *Cognitive Psychotherapies: Recent Developments in Theory, Research and Practice* (pp. 81–99). Cambridge, MA: Ballinger.

Dryden, W. (1985). Challenging but not overwhelming: A compromise in negotiating homework assignments. *British Journal of Cognitive Psychotherapy, 3*(1), 77–80.

Dryden, W. (1986a). Language and meaning in RET. *Journal of Rational-Emotive Therapy, 4*(2), 131–42.

Dryden, W. (1986b). Some aspects of the therapeutic alliance in rational-emotive therapy. *British Journal of Cognitive Psychotherapy, 4*(2), 78–82.

Dryden, W. (1986c). Vivid methods in rational-emotive therapy. In A. Ellis & R. Grieger (eds), *Handbook of Rational-Emotive Therapy, Volume 2* (pp. 221–45). New York: Springer.

Dryden, W. (1987a). Compromises in rational-emotive therapy. In W. Dryden, *Current Issues in Rational-Emotive Therapy* (pp. 72–87). London: Croom Helm.

Dryden, W. (1987b). The therapeutic alliance in rational-emotive individual therapy. In W. Dryden, *Current Issues in Rational-Emotive Therapy* (pp. 59–71). London: Croom Helm.

Dryden, W. (1990). Self-disclosure in rational-emotive therapy. In G. Stricker & M. N. Fisher (eds). *Self-Disclosure in the Therapeutic Relationship* (pp. 61–74). New York: Plenum.

Dryden, W. (1991). *'It Depends': A Dialogue with Arnold Lazarus.* Buckingham: Open University Press.

Dryden. W. (1994a). Possible future trends in counselling and counsellor training: A personal view. *Counselling: The Journal of BAC, 5*(3), 194–7.

Dryden, W. (1994b). *Ten Steps to Positive Living.* London: Sheldon.

Dryden, W. (1995a). *Brief Rational Emotive Behaviour Therapy.* John Wiley, Chichester

Dryden, W. (1995b). *Preparing for Client Change in Rational Emotive Behaviour Therapy.* London: Whurr.

Dryden, W. (ed.) (1996). *Handbook of Individual Therapy.* London: Sage.

Dryden, W. (1997a). *Overcoming Shame.* London: Sheldon.

Dryden, W. (1997b). *Therapists' Dilemmas. Revised edition.* London: Sage.

Dryden, W. (1997c). Why I no longer practise person centred therapy and psychodynamic therapy: Some personal reflections. Lecture given to the MSc Counselling Psychology course, University of East London, 25 April.

Dryden, W (1998a). *Are You Sitting Uncomfortably? Windy Dryden Live and Uncut.* Ross-on-Wye: PCCS Books.

Dryden, W. (1998b). Understanding persons in the context of their problems: A rational emotive behaviour therapy perspective. In M. Bruch & F.W. Bond (eds), *Beyond Diagnosis: Case Formulation Approaches in CBT* (pp. 43–64). Chichester: John Wiley & Sons.

Dryden, W. (1999a). *How to Accept Yourself.* London: Sheldon Press.

Dryden, W. (1999b). Friend or therapist? In S. Greenfield (ed.), *Therapy on the Couch: A Shrinking Future?* London: Camden Press.

Dryden, W. (1999c). *Rational Emotive Behaviour Therapy: A Personal Approach.* Bicester, Oxon: Winslow Press.

Dryden, W. (2000). *Overcoming Procrastination.* London: Sheldon.

Dryden, W. (2001a). How rational am I?: Self-help using rational emotive behaviour therapy. In E. Spinelli & S. Marshall (eds), *Embodied Theories* (pp. 28–42). London: Continuum.

Dryden, W. (2001b). *Reason to Change: A Rational Emotive Behaviour Therapy (REBT) Workbook.* London: Brunner/Routledge.

Dryden, W. (ed.). (2002). *Idiosyncratic Rational Emotive Behaviour Therapy.* Ross-on-Wye: PCCS Books.

Dryden, W. (2003). *The REBT Pocket Companion for Clients.* New York: Albert Ellis Institute.

Dryden, W. (2006a). *Counselling in a Nutshell.* London: Sage.

Dryden, W. (2006b). *First Steps in REBT: A Guide to Practising REBT in Peer Counseling.* New York: Albert Ellis Institute.

Dryden, W. (2006c). *Getting Started with REBT: A Concise Guide for Clients.* Hove, East Sussex: Routledge.

Dryden, W. (2009a). *Skills in Rational Emotive Behaviour Counselling and Psychotherapy.* London: Sage.

Dryden, W. (2009b). *Rational Emotive Behaviour Therapy: Distinctive Features.* Hove, East Sussex: Routledge.

Dryden, W. (2009c). *Understanding Emotional Problems: The REBT Perspective.* Hove, East Sussex: Routledge.

Dryden, W. (2009d). *How to Think and Intervene Like an REBT Therapist.* Hove, East Sussex: Routledge.

Dryden, W. (2011). *Counselling in a Nutshell. 2nd edition.* London: Sage.

Dryden, W. (2012a). *Dealing with Emotional Problems Using Rational-Emotive Cognitive Behaviour Therapy: A Client's Guide.* Hove, East Sussex: Routledge.

Dryden, W. (2012b). *Dealing with Emotional Problems Using Rational-Emotive Cognitive Behaviour Therapy: A Practitioner's Guide*. Hove, East Sussex: Routledge.

Dryden, W. (2013a). *Rationality and Pluralism: The Selected Works of Windy Dryden*. Hove, East Sussex: Routledge.

Dryden, W. (2013b). *The ABCs of REBT: Perspectives on Conceptualization*. New York: Springer.

Dryden, W. (2013c). Unconditional self-acceptance and self-compassion. In M.E. Bernard (ed.), *The Strength of Self-Acceptance: Theory, Practice and Research*(pp. 107-120). New York: Springer.

Dryden, W. (2015). *Rational Emotive Behaviour Therapy: Distinctive Features. 2nd edition*. Hove, East Sussex: Routledge.

Dryden, W. (2016). *Attitudes in Rational Emotive Behaviour Therapy: Components, Characteristics and Adversity-Related Consequences*. London: Rationality Publications.

Dryden, W. (2017). *Single-session Integrated CBT (SSI-CBT): Distinctive Features*. Abingdon, Oxon: Routledge

Dryden, W. (2018a). *Flexibility-Based Cognitive Behaviour Therapy: Insights from Forty Years of Practice*. Abingdon: Oxon: Routledge.

Dryden, W. (2018b). *Very Brief Therapeutic Conversations*. Abingdon: Oxon: Routledge.

Dryden, W. (2019). *Single-Session 'One-At-A-Time' (OAAT) therapy: A Rational Emotive Behaviour Therapy Approach*. Abingdon, Oxon: Routledge.

Dryden, W. (2021a). *Rational Emotive Behaviour Therapy: Distinctive Features. 3rd edition*. Abingdon, Oxon: Routledge.

Dryden, W. (2021b). *The Working Alliance in Rational Emotive Behaviour Therapy*. Abingdon, Oxon: Routledge.

Dryden, W. (2021c). *Windy Dryden Live!* London: Rationality Publications

Dryden, W. (2022a). *Understanding Emotional Problems and Their Healthy Alternatives: The REBT Perspective.2nd edition*. Abingdon, Oxon: Routledge.

Dryden, W. (2022b). *Reason to Change: A Rational Emotive Behaviour Therapy (REBT) Workbook, 2nd Edition*. Abingdon, Oxon: Routledge.

Dryden, W., Beal, D., Jones, J. & Trower, P. (2010). The REBT competency scale for clinical and research applications. *Journal of Rational-Emotive & Cognitive Behavior Therapy, 28*, 165–216.

Dryden, W., & Branch, R. (2008). *The Fundamentals of Rational Emotive Behaviour Therapy: A Training Handbook. 2nd edition*. Chichester: Wiley.

Dryden, W., & DiGiuseppe, R. (1990). *A Primer on Rational-Emotive Therapy*. Champaign, IL: Research Press.

Dryden, W., DiGiuseppe, R., & Neenan, M. (2003). *A Primer on Rational Emotive Behavior Therapy. 2nd edition*. Champaign, IL: Research Press.

Dryden, W., DiGiuseppe, R., & Neenan, M. (2010). *A Primer on Rational Emotive Behavior Therapy. 3rd edition.* Champaign, IL: Research Press.

Dryden, W., Ferguson, J., & Clark, A. (1989). Beliefs and inferences: A test of a rational-emotive hypothesis, 1: Performing in an academic seminar. *Journal of Rational-Emotive and Cognitive Behavior Therapy, 7,* 119–29.

Dryden, W., Ferguson, J., & McTeague, S. (1989). Beliefs and inferences: A test of a rational-emotive hypothesis. 2: On the prospect of seeing a spider. *Psychological Reports, 64,* 115–23.

Dryden, W., Ferguson, J., & Hylton, B. (1989). Beliefs and inferences: A test of a rational-emotive hypothesis. 3: On expectations about enjoying a party. *British Journal of Guidance & Counselling, 17,* 68–75.

Dryden, W., Horton, I., & Mearns, D. (1995). *Issues in Professional Counsellor Training.* London: Cassell.

Dryden, W., & Neenan, M. (2003). *The REBT Therapist's Pocket Companion.* New York: Albert Ellis Institute.

Dryden, W., & Neenan, M. (2011a). *Learning from Mistakes in Rational Emotive Behaviour Therapy.* Hove: Routledge.

Dryden, W., & Neenan, M. (2011b). *Working with Resistance in Rational Emotive Behaviour Therapy.* Hove: Routledge.

Dryden, W., & Neenan, M. (2015). *Rational Emotive Behaviour Therapy: 100 Key Points and Techniques. 2nd edition.* Hove, East Sussex: Routledge.

Dryden, W., & Neenan, M. (2021). *Rational Emotive Behaviour Therapy: 100 Key Points and Techniques. 3rd edition.* Abingdon, Oxon: Routledge.

Dryden, W., Neenan, M., & Yankura, J. (1999). *Counselling Individuals: A Rational Emotive Behavioural Handbook, 3rd Edition.* London: Whurr.

Dryden, W. & Vasco, A. (1991). *Dryden on Counselling Volume 2: A Dialogue.* London: Whurr.

Ellis, A. (1959). Requisite conditions for basic personality change. *Journal of Consulting Psychology, 23,* 538–40.

Ellis, A. (1962). *Reason and Emotion in Psychotherapy.* Secaucus, NJ: Lyle Stuart.

Ellis, A. (1972). *Psychotherapy and the Value of a Human Being.* New York: Albert Ellis Institute for REBT.

Ellis, A. (1980a). Rational-emotive therapy and cognitive behavior therapy: Similarities and differences. *Cognitive Therapy and Research, 4,* 325–40.

Ellis, A. (1980b). The value of efficiency in psychotherapy. *Psychotherapy: Theory, Research and Practice, 17,* 414–18.

Ellis, A. (1983). The philosophic implications and dangers of some popular behavior therapy techniques. In: M. Rosenbaum, C. M. Franks and Y. Jaffe (eds), *Perspectives in Behavior Therapy in the Eighties* (pp.138–51). New York: Springer.

Ellis, A. (1987). The use of rational humorous songs in psychotherapy. In W. Fry, Jr. & W.A. Salameh (eds), *Handbook of Humor in Psychotherapy: Advances in the Clinical Use of Humor.* Sarasota, FL: Professional Resource Exchange Inc.

Ellis, A. (1989). Ineffective consumerism in the cognitive-behavioural therapies and in general psychotherapy. In W. Dryden & P. Trower (eds), *Cognitive Psychotherapy: Stasis and Change.* London: Cassell.

Ellis, A. (1991). Achieving self-actualization. In A. Jones & R. Crandall (eds), *Handbook of Self-Actualization.* Corte Madera, CA: Select Press.

Ellis, A. (1994). *Reason and Emotion in Psychotherapy* (revised and expanded edition). New York: Birch Lane Press.

Ellis, A. (1995). Changing rational-emotive therapy (RET) to rational emotive behavior therapy (REBT). *Journal of Rational-Emotive and Cognitive-Behavior Therapy, 13,* 85–9.

Ellis, A., & Dryden, W. (1987). *The Practice of Rational-Emotive Therapy.* New York: Springer.

Ellis, A., & Dryden, W (1997). *The Practice of Rational Emotive Behaviour Therapy, 2nd edition.* New York: Springer.

Ellis, A. & Harper, R. A. (1975). *A New Guide to Rational Living.* Hollywood, CA: Wilshire.

Ellis, A., & Joffe Ellis, D. (2011). *Rational Emotive Behavior Therapy.* Washington, DC: American Psychological Association.

Ellis, A., Sichel, J. L., Yeager, R. J., DiMattia, D. J., & DiGiuseppe, R. (1989). *Rational-Emotive Couples Therapy.* Elmsford, NY: Pergamon Press.

Feltham, C. (1997). Challenging the core theoretical model. *Counselling: The Journal BAC, 8*(2), 121–5.

Firestone, R. (1997). *Suicide and the Inner Voice.* Thousand Oaks, CA: Sage.

Franks, C. M. (1995). RET, REBT, and Albert Ellis. *Journal of Rational-Emotive and Cognitive-Behavior Therapy, 13,* 91–5.

Garfield, S. L. (1984). Research on client variables in psychotherapy. In A. E. Bergin & S. L. Garfield (eds), *Handbook of Psychotherapy and Behaviour Change, 4th Edition.* New York: John Wiley.

Garvin, C. D. & Seabury, B. A. (1984). *Interpersonal Practice in Social Work: Processes and Procedures.* Engelwood Cliffs, NJ: Prentice Hall.

Gilbert, P. (2007). *Compassion Focused Therapy: Distinctive Features.* Hove, East Sussex: Routledge

Greenberger, D., & Padesky, C.A. (1995). *Mind over Mood: Change the Way You Feel by Changing the Way You Think.* New York: Guilford.

Grieger, R & Boyd, J. (1980). *Rational-Emotive Therapy: A Skills-Based Approach.* New York: Van Nostrand Reinhold.

Haaga, D. A. F. & Davison, G. C. (1991). Disappearing differences do not always reflect healthy integration: An analysis of cognitive therapy and rational-emotive therapy. *Journal of Psychotherapy Integration, 1*(4), 287–303.

Hauck, P. (1991). *Hold Your Head Up High.* London: Sheldon Press.

Hitchens, C (1995). *The Missionary Position: Mother Teresa in Theory and Practice.* London: Verso.

Horney, K (1942). *Self-Analysis.* New York: Norton.

Hoyt, M.F., & Talmon, M. (eds). (2014). *Capturing the Moment: Single Session Therapy and Walk-In Services.* Bethel, CT: Crown House Publishing Ltd.

Hoyt, M.F., Young, J., & Rycroft, P. (2020). Single session thinking 2020. *Australian & New Zealand Journal of Family Therapy, 41*(3), 218–30.

Hunt, P. A. (1985). *Clients' Responses to Marriage Counselling.* Rugby: NMGC.

Jourard, S. M. (1971). *The Transparent Self.* New York: Van Nostrand Reinhold.

Kelly, E. W. Jr. (1995). *Spirituality and Religion in Counselling and Psychotherapy: Diversity in Theory and Practice.* Lanham, MD: University Press of America.

Lazarus, A. A. (1981). *The Practice of Multimodal Therapy.* New York: McGraw-Hill.

Lazarus, A. A. (1989). *The Practice of Multimodal Therapy* (Update). Baltimore: Johns Hopkins University Press.

Lazarus, A. A. (1995). REBT: A sign of evolution or devolution? An historical perspective. *Journal of Rational-Emotive and Cognitive-Behavior Therapy, 13,* 97–100.

Magnusson, M (ed.) (1990). *Chambers Biographical Dictionary, 5th Edition.* Edinburgh: W & R Chambers Ltd.

Mahrer, A. R. (ed.) (1967). *The Goals of Psychotherapy.* New York: Appleton Century Crofts.

Maultsby, M. C. Jr. (1975). *Help Yourself to Happiness: Through Rational Self-counselling.* New York: Institute for Rational Living.

McCrae, R. R., & Costa, P. T (2002). *Personality in Adulthood: A Five-Factor Theory Perspective, 2nd Edition.* New York: Guilford Press.

Mearns, D., & Thorne, B. J. (1988). *Person-Centred Counselling in Action.* London: Sage.

Miller, D. J., & Thelen, M. H. (1986). Knowledge and beliefs about confidentiality in psychotherapy. *Professional Psychology: Research and Practice, 17,* 15–19.

Neenan, M. (1997). Reflections on two major REBT concepts. *The Rational Emotive Behaviour Therapist, 5*(1), 31–3.

Neenan, M. & Dryden, W. (1999). *Rational Emotive Behaviour Therapy: Advances in Theory and Practice.* London: Whurr.

Neenan, M. & Dryden, W. (2001). *Learning from Errors in Rational Emotive Behaviour Therapy.* London: Whurr.

Neff, K.D. (2003). Self-compassion: An alternative conceptualization of a healthy attitude toward oneself. *Self and Identity, 2,* 85–101.

Nelson-Jones, R. (1982). *The Theory and Practice of Counselling Psychology.* London: Cassell.

Nelson-Jones, R. (1984). *Personal Responsibility Counselling and Therapy: An Integrative Approach.* London: Harper & Row.

Nelson-Jones, R. C. & Coxhead, P. (1978). Whither BAC: a survey of members' views on policy and practices. *Counselling News, 21,* 2–5.

Norcross, J. C., Dryden, W., & DeMichele, J. T. (1992). British clinical psychologists, III: What's good for the goose? *Clinical Psychology Forum, 44,* 29–33.

Patterson, C. (1974). *Relationship Counselling and Psychotherapy.* New York: Harper & Row.

Persons, J. (1989). *Cognitive Therapy in Practice: A Case Formulation Approach.* New York: Norton.

Prochaska, J. O., & DiClemente, C. C. (1964). *The Transtheoretical Approach: Crossing the Traditional Boundaries of Therapy.* Homewood, IL: Dow Jones-Irwin.

Regan, A. M. & Hill, C. E. (1992). Investigation of what clients and counselors do not say in brief therapy. *Journal of Counselling Psychology, 39,* 168–74.

Robb, H., Backx, W. & Thomas, J. (1999). The use of cognitive, emotive and behavioral interventions in rational emotive behavior therapy when clients lack 'emotional' insight. *Journal of Rational-Emotive & Cognitive-Behavior Therapy, 17*(3), 201–9.

Rogers. C. R. (1951). *Client-Centered Therapy.* London: Constable

Rogers, C. R. (1957). The necessary and sufficient conditions for therapeutic personality change. *Journal of Consulting Psychology, 21,* 95–103.

Rogers, C. R. (1975). Empathic: An unappreciated way of being. *The Counseling Psychologist, 5*(2), 2–10.

Schofield, W. (1964). *Psychotherapy: The Purchase of Friendship.* Englewood Cliffs, NJ: Prentice-Hall.

Schulte, D., Kunzel, R., Pepping, G., & Schulte-Bahrenberg, T. (1992). Tailor-made versus standardised therapy of phobic patients. *Advances in Behaviour Research and Therapy, 14,* 67–92.

Strean, H. S. (1959). The use of the patient as consultant. *Psychoanalysis and Psychoanalytic Review, 46* (2), 36–44.

Talmon, M. (1990). *Single Session Therapy: Maximising the Effect of the First (and Often Only) Therapeutic Encounter.* San Francisco: Jossey-Bass.

Tjeltveit, A. C. (1986). The ethics of value conversion in psychotherapy: Appropriate and inappropriate therapist influence on client values. *Clinical Psychology Review, 6,* 515–37.

Truax, C. B. (1966). Reinforcement and non-reinforcement in Rogerian psychotherapy. *Journal of Abnormal Psychology, 71*, 1–9.

Walen, S. R., DiGiuseppe, R. & Dryden, W. (1992). *A Practitioner's Guide to Rational-Emotive Therapy, 2nd Edition.* New York: Oxford University Press.

Warren, R. & McLellarn, R. W. (1987). What do RET therapists think they are doing? *Journal of Rational-Emotive Therapy, 5*(2), 71–91.

Wessler, R. A. & Wessler, R. L. (1980). *The Principles and Practice of Rational-Emotive Therapy.* San Francisco: Jossey-Bass.

Woods, P. J. (1991). Orthodox RET taught effectively with graphics, feedback on rigid and extreme attitudes, a structured homework series, and models of disputation. In M. E. Bernard (ed.), *Using Rational-Emotive Effectively: A Practitioner's Guide.* New York: Plenum.

Yankura, J. & Dryden, W. (1990). *Doing RET: Albert Ellis in Action.* New York: Springer.

Index

voice
cadence 31
tone 31
voluntary-aided counselling agencies 45
vulnerability
vulnerability 283, 423
factors 78, 141
identify and use newly learned self-change methods
to deal with them productively 141

waiting lists 49
Walen, S. R. 500, 527
Walker, Jr. 254–6, 284
Walters, Matt 491
warmth, human 247, 276, 423, 484
Warren, R. 212, 527
Warwick University 228, 241, 244, 250,
468, 478, 482
Watchdog 260
Waterstone's bookshop 133
Watts, A. G. 501
weakness(es) 42, 43, 114, 116, 166, 167,
200, 246, 247, 357, 360, 361, 364,
366, 367, 369
weddings 191, 194
well-being 80, 139, 141, 159, 253, 256, 257
Wessler, R. A. 218, 220, 455, 527
Wessler, R. L. 218, 220, 527
'Windy Dryden Live!' 491
withdrawal 375, 389, 402
Woods, P. J. 527
Woolfe, R. 497, 503, 507, 510
work with one problematic theme at a time
26–7
working alliance 23, 70, 78, 125, 128, 129,
131, 153, 197, 213, 215, 228, 233, 467,
482–5, 489. 493
importance of in REBT 482–3
REBT's position on value of 70–1
working through 48, 484, 487
world view 29
worth tolerating component 300
writing mode 184
written handouts 18
wrongdoings 263, 405, 431, 436

Yankura, J. 62, 212, 498, 500–2, 504, 505,
523, 527
Yeager, R. J. 524